Cult
MOVIES

PHILIP FRENCH was a senior producer with BBC Radio for thirty years and since 1978 he has been the *Observer's* film critic. Among the books he has written and edited are *Age of Austerity 1945–51, The Movie Moguls, Westerns, The Faber Book of Movie Verse,* and *Malle on Malle.*

KARL FRENCH is TV previewer of the *Financial Times*. He co-wrote *The French Brothers' Film Quiz Book*, edited *The Marx Brothers' Screenplays*, and *Screen Violence*. French is author of *The A–Z of Apocalypse Now* and *The A–Z of This Is Spinal Tap.*

Cult
MOVIES

Karl French and Philip French

PAVILION

First published in Great Britain in 1999 by
PAVILION BOOKS LIMITED
London House, Great Eastern Wharf
Parkgate Road, London SW11 4NQ

Text © Karl and Philip French
Design and layout © Pavilion Books Ltd

Designed by Nigel Partridge

A CIP catalogue record for this book is available from the British Library.

ISBN 1 86205 172 0

Set in Futura
Printed in Singapore by Imago

2 4 6 8 10 9 7 5 3

This book can be ordered direct from the publisher. Please contact the Marketing
Department. But try your bookshop first.

CONTENTS

INTRODUCTION

Of the several dictionary definitions of a cult, the more informal ones relate to the subject of this book — i.e. 'an intense interest in and devotion to a person, idea or activity' and 'the person, idea etc. arousing such devotion'. The size of its following is not specified — the numbers can range from a handful to millions — and the object can take different forms. There is the implication, however, that a cult cannot be universal, official or orthodox. So while Christianity, for example, contains many cults, the Catholic Church and the Church of England are not cults.

The term 'cult movie' has been current for 20 years or more but the idea had been in the air since the first film was shown on the big screen to a paying audience. This was *La Sortie des Usines Lumière*, a 45-second shot of workers leaving the Lumière Brothers factory in Lyons, which was shown at the beginning of the selection of Lumière films at the Grand Café on the Boulevard des Capucines in Paris on 28th December 1895. It was followed by the more sensational *L'Arrivée d'un Train en Gare de la Ciotat*, which made nervous spectators duck for cover, and the first cinematic comedy, *L'Arroseur arrosé* (a little boy treading on a hose and causing it to spray water in a gardener's face), which made them laugh. For those Lyons labourers, the first people to see themselves up there on the screen, this film clip must have become an object of obsessive interest and they themselves would have constituted a cult drawn together by their fascination with it. Eight years later, Rudyard Kipling wrote his classic story 'Mrs Bathhurst', the first literary work of consequence about the cinema, turning upon a British soldier in South Africa who becomes obsessed with a newsreel that presented a glimpse of the eponymous New Zealand landlady. After 'The Arrival of a Train at La Ciotat', Lumière cameramen shot films of locomotive journeys around the world, and train films have been a major cult ever since. The National Film Theatre and similar cinémathèques can always fill their auditoriums with railway fans by showing programmes of vintage trains in action. Likewise *L'Arroseur arrosé*, which figured in posters all over Europe advertising the first Lumière show, became the iconic movie comedy and was re-created by François Truffaut in his feature debut, *Les Mistons*, as a homage to the Lumières and the birth of laughter on the screen.

From the 1920s to the 1960s, films played for a few weeks in the West End of London, passed on to the downtown cinemas of the big cities and then played for six days or a week in suburban cinemas (the neighbourhood movie houses that *Variety* calls 'nabes'). They might re-appear 'by public demand' but usually they went into backstreet fleapits until the prints were unshowable and then disappeared, often forever. Only a few movies were regularly reissued in new prints, and film companies didn't give a damn once a film had lost its commercial value. They did not systematically preserve their products: as late as the 1960s Warner Brothers allowed the negative of *My Fair Lady* to deteriorate, and Columbia did not keep the original negative of *Lawrence of Arabia*. Film archives were established around the world, but most of their curators saw their task as conserving films of distinction for posterity, rather than making them available for current viewing. Films of the past — a smallish canon of approved classics, mostly European — were available on 16mm from specialist distributors for film societies to show to their dedicated members who watched them from hard seats in draughty halls. At that time the passionate audience (as opposed to the casual filmgoers) was unevenly divided between serious, informed students of the cinema and dedicated, undiscriminating movie fans.

A major change came in the 1960s, brought about by the greater availability of movies through television and a radical shift in attitudes to popular culture. Commentators contrasted the older 'movie generation' of people who grew up with the cinema with the 'television generation' that was being reared in front of the small screen. But it was precisely that television generation that became steeped in, obsessed by, the movies. Seeing old movies at all times of the day and night at home, influenced by the criticism of the *Cahiers du Cinéma* critics who became fashionable directors (Truffaut, Chabrol, Godard *et al.*), they began to have a newly appreciative, less condescending attitude to Hollywood, and especially to those directors who worked in the traditionally despised or patronized genres – the Western, SF, the horror flick, and the thriller. New film magazines were started. Books on the cinema of the past and present began to appear, written in a different spirit from the few earnest volumes on film as art which had shaped the taste of cinéphiles. When the small handful of established film schools were forced to turn away thousands of prospective students, new film faculties sprang up across America, and departments of film were eventually created in conservative Britain. At the same time there occurred the so-called nostalgia boom, an American obsession with the art and artefacts of the recent past. This was partly caused, and certainly influenced, by the shock administered by the assassination of President Kennedy, an event that brought to an end his vision of a new Camelot and made the future seem less alluring. In Britain at the time there was the new hedonism that expressed itself in the phenomenon of 'Swinging London', which both embraced the new and glamorized the past, and the movies were its supreme expression.

It was in the mid-1960s that trivia quizzes became a passionate activity on US campuses, and at the Brattle Cinema in Cambridge, Mass., patronized by Harvard students, there began the cult of Bogart; which reached its apotheosis in 1969 with Woody Allen's Broadway hit *Play It Again Sam*. Walker Percy's subtle novel *The Movie-Goer*, winner of the National Book Award in 1962, assured its middle-class readers that films were not only as important as other forms of art, but as significant as life itself, and the book steadily took on classic status as the decade progressed. In 1964 Susan Sontag published her influential essay 'Notes on Camp', in which she wrote that 'movie criticism is probably the greatest popularizer of Camp taste today, because people still go to the movies in a high-

spirited and unpretentious way'. In the 1960s the old-fashioned, none-too-well-informed 'film fan' was replaced by a new figure, 'the movie buff', a picturegoer steeped in popular cinema, versed in the minutiae of movie history, possessing an encyclopaedic knowledge of films. Not to be confused with the discriminating cinéphile of old, the movie buff in his or her extreme form might have been defined by Oscar Wilde as a man who knows the credits of everything and the value of nothing. The term 'buff', in this sense, had until the mid-century signified an enthusiast for fires and firefighting, the name deriving from the buff uniform once worn by New York's volunteer fire brigades.

Movie buffs saw films, wrote about films, and made films. Following the example of the French New Wave directors, young American film-makers began putting in references to the movies of the past (former critic Peter Bogdanovich led the way with *Targets* and *The Last Picture Show*). In a Hollywood picture of the 1950s, a TV set in the background invariably showed a chase from an anonymous B-feature Western. From the late 1960s, whenever a TV set is on in the background it is showing a recognizable film that comments in some way on the movie we're watching. In the 1960s your favourite movies came to reveal the sort of person you were, and choosing a film for cult status became a way of creating a personal niche of taste and identity in an amorphous mass culture and a threatening mass society. A cult movie can be a link between friends as exemplified by the group of former radicals in John Sayles's film *Return of the Secaucus Seven* (1980), who in their student days during the 1960s adopted as 'their film' Herbert Biberman's *Salt of the Earth*, the left-wing movie made by black-listed artists and shown abroad but proscribed in the US. Or, less attractively, demonstrated by the French delinquents in Bertrand Tavernier's *The Bait* who can quote (in French) every line in Brian DePalma's *Scarface*. The New York chums in *City Slickers* have chosen Howard Hawks's *Red River* as their cult movie, and John Travolta's movie buff in *Get Shorty* belongs to the cults that revere Hawks's *Rio Bravo* and Welles's *Touch of Evil*.

Some movies become cults because of difficulty of access, and in fact an astonishing number of movies that are regularly shown on TV or are available on cassette do not exist in a print fit to be projected in cinemas. Does this mean that when they become accessible, as the once elusive *Citizen Kane* now is, they are no longer cult movies? Perhaps, but not necessarily. *Casablanca,* which helped create the whole concept, remains the cornerstone of cult cinema. *Casablanca,* of course, has several of the qualities that make a cult movie – it's a picture you want to see again and again; it has unforgettable lines; and it seems to have a personal meaning for you and your friends. It was never, however, banned by the censors nor butchered by the producers, ignored by the public nor panned by the critics, a fate suffered by many cult movies. It isn't offensive, perverse, obscure, absurd, deeply flawed, ludicrous, full of preposterous dialogue or made on a shoestring – all of which are, in different combinations, the characteristics of a fair number of cult films. A good many cult pictures have the prime constituent of sad orphans – that of being abandoned and rejected; the problem is, do they retain their status as waifs after being adopted by a large, welcoming family? When Danny Peary published his three large volumes of *Cult Movies* in the 1980s, many readers felt that he was doing to their personal favourite pictures what travel writers do when they write about an idyllic, little-visited Greek island as 'the Aegean's best-kept secret'.

There are cult movies, cult directors, cult actors, and even cult film composers – Ennio Morricone, for instance, and, until they were posthumously adopted by the music critics, Erich Wolfgang Korngold and Bernard Herrmann. There are also cult posters and cult stills. Some films are local cults, some only cults outside their country of origin. Ealing comedies have always been too popular, too acceptable to polite middle-class audiences to become the subject of a cult in Britain, but among anglophiles in the States they have a cult following. Some directors who have never attained a large following or were overlooked by critics during their working lives have had cult status imposed on their whole oeuvres – Jacques Tourneur, Joseph H. Lewis, Edgar G. Ulmer, for instance. Others have produced the odd cult work, and virtually every famous film-maker has one or two pictures, not necessarily their best, for

which their admirers have a special affection. Certain actors recur in cult movies without being themselves cult figures – Jeff Bridges, for example. Jack Nicholson, an actor who has got better and better over some 40 years, is only a cult figure for his early horror films, biker movies, Westerns and early seventies road movies directed by Roger Corman, Richard Rush, Monte Hellman and Bob Rafelson. The less well-known Dick Miller, however, an amiable performer of no great distinction, is a cult actor for his 1950s Corman films like *A Bucket of Blood* and *The Little Shop of Horrors,* and because of that cult status he has been given roles in movies produced or directed by, among others, Steven Spielberg, Quentin Tarantino and Joe Dante. Vincent Price, Peter Cushing and Christopher Lee became cult actors from their appearances in horror movies, as did Boris Karloff and Bela Lugosi, who in Ulmer's *The Black Cat* were credited simply as 'Karloff and Lugosi'. The cult status of Donald Pleasence and Patrick McGoohan, on the other hand, depends less on the sort of roles they played than on the outlandish style of their performances though McGoohan is a cult TV figure for *The Prisoners.*

We decided at the outset to have only one movie per director and as this led in most cases to some argument between us over the choice of films, it is unlikely that all, or indeed most, readers will agree with our particular choices. We did not decide, however, to limit actors to one appearance each, and a good number show up two, three or four times.

In writing this book we have greatly benefited from discussions with many people, but most especially Patrick French, Sean French and Kersti French, the last named having made a major contribution to the editing of the text and the clarification of the prose.

KARL FRENCH
PHILIP FRENCH
London, February 1999

PHILIP FRENCH'S TOP 20 CULT FILMS

Atlantic City
Bad Day at Black Rock
The Bride of Frankenstein
Bring Me the Head of Alfredo Garcia
The Company of Wolves
Dead of Night
Detour
Fat City
Five Easy Pieces
Gun Crazy

The Hustler
Man of the West
The Manchurian Candidate
Once Upon a Time in the West
Pimpernel Smith
Point Blank
Se7en
Sherlock Jr
Shock Corridor
Two-Lane Blacktop

KARL FRENCH'S TOP 20 CULT FILMS

Big Wednesday
Blade Runner
Casablanca
A Clockwork Orange
Duck Soup
Eraserhead
Freaks
Get Carter
La Jetée
The Night of the Hunter

Peeping Tom
Performance
Pink Flamingos
Plan 9 from Outer Space
Reservoir Dogs
The Rocky Horror Picture Show
Some Like It Hot
The Texas Chain Saw Massacre
This is Spinal Tap
Withnail and I

ABBREVIATIONS

ADD SC	ADDITIONAL SCENES
ANIM	ANIMATION
ART DIR	ART DIRECTOR
BW	BLACK AND WHITE
CO-PR	CO-PRODUCER
COL	COLOUR
COST	COSTUMES
D	DIRECTOR
DES	DESIGNER
ED	EDITOR
EXEC PR	EXECUTIVE PRODUCER
M	MUSIC
MD	MUSICAL DIRECTOR
M SUP	MUSICAL SUPERVISOR

NARR	NARRATION
PH	PHOTOGRAPHY (CINEMATOGRAPHY)
PIC ED	PICTURE EDITOR
PR	PRODUCER
PR DES	PRODUCTION DESIGN
PR SC	PRODUCTION AND SCREENPLAY
SC	SCREENPLAY
SD	SOUND
SD ED	SOUND EDITOR
SP EFF	SPECIAL EFFECTS
SP PH	SPECIAL EFFECTS PHOTOGRAPHY
ST	STORY
★	PICTURE IN COLOUR SECTION

AIRPLANE!

US, 1980, PARAMOUNT, 88 MINS

D JIM ABRAHAMS, DAVID ZUCKER, JERRY ZUCKER; **PR** JON DAVISON, HOWARD W. KOCH JR.; **SC** JIM ABRAHAMS, DAVID ZUCKER, JERRY ZUCKER; **PH** JOSEPH F. BIROC; **M** ELMER BERNSTEIN; **ED** PATRICK KENNEDY

CAST ROBERT HAYS (TED STRIKER), JULIE HAGERTY (ELAINE DICKINSON), LLOYD BRIDGES (McCROSKEY), LESLIE NIELSEN (DR RUMACK), PETER GRAVES (CAPTAIN OVEUR), ROBERT STACK (KRAMER), KAREEM ABDUL JABBAR (ROGER MURDOCK), LORNA PATTERSON (RANDY), STEPHEN STUCKER (JOHNNY)

THE STORY Ted Striker boards a transcontinental flight in the hope of patching up his relationship with ex-girlfriend Elaine. Things start to go wrong when the plane hits some rough weather, and get worse when the entire flight crew bar Elaine are struck down by food poisoning. Ted is the only man quali-fied to land the plane, but he is still traumatized by his experi-ences in Nam. At last, with the help of the sage Dr Rumack and an hysterical ground crew, Ted lands the plane safely and is reconciled with Elaine.

THE FILM From its opening shot in which a plane's wing-tip is slicing through the clouds accompanied by John Williams's haunting theme from *Jaws* (1976), *Airplane!* was a winner. It created an instant adoring following. It was not merely odd, anarchic and quotable, it set up the challenge for the viewer to remember their favourite scenes and lines. This quality in turn, just before the spread of the VCR, gave it an inbuilt marketing tool. It worked not merely by word of mouth, but by encourag-ing the same people to see it again to catch the jokes they had missed the first time round. It made its immediate precursors,

▼ *AIRPLANE! Robert Hays (Striker) and Julie Hagerty (Elaine) betray their anxiety while the autopilot is perfectly satisfied.*

Animal House (1978), the Abrahams/Zucker brothers' own *The Kentucky Fried Movie* (1977), and its other antecedents – *Hellzapoppin* (1941), The Marx Brothers and The Three Stooges – seem restrained in comparison. It would be physically difficult and part of an exercise beyond comedy, to achieve a film with more gags, both verbal and visual. Apart from the obvious references to *Airport* (1969) and more specifically its sequel *Airport '75* (1974), the film makes fun of *The Wizard of Oz* (1939), *Knut Rockne – All American* (1940), *Pinocchio* (1940), *Casablanca* (1942), *From Here to Eternity* (1953) and *Saturday Night Fever* (1977).

ODD/SALIENT FACTS The Abrahams/Zucker/Zucker team was formed in 1970 when the three of them made up the satirical multimedia show that they called Kentucky Fried Theater. They patented their approach to films in *Kentucky Fried Movie*, in which they lampooned famous films and added the essential ingredient of an occasional flash of naked breasts to complete the format that would prove irresistible to adolescents and undergraduates everywhere. While they have largely stuck to their winning formula, being variously responsible for *Top Secret* (1984), *The Naked Gun* (1988) and its sequels, *Naked Gun 2½* (1991) and *Naked Gun 33⅓* (1994), based on their TV show *Police Squad*, and *Hot Shots* (1991), Jerry Zucker has made a stab at legitimacy with *Ghost* (1990) and *My Life* (1993).

MEMORABLE MOMENTS The spoof of *Saturday Night Fever*, where Ted and Elaine dance in a dive not noticing a murder, and the two women whose fight lasts throughout the night.

The use of the very human automatic pilot, who collapses requiring manual inflation from Elaine, which leads to a broad smile and a shared post-coital smoke.

KEY LINES

Old Lady: 'Nervous?'
Ted: 'Yes.'
Old Lady: 'First time?'
Ted: 'No, I've been nervous lots of times.'

Roger Murdock: 'You have clearance, Clarence.'
Captain Oveur: 'Roger, Roger. What's our vector, Victor?'
Tower: 'Tower's radio clearance, over.'

> **TED: 'Surely you can't be serious'**
> **RUMACK: 'I am serious, and don't call me Shirley.'**

Oveur: 'That's Clarence Oveur. Over.'
Tower: 'Roger.'
Murdock: 'Huh?'
Tower: 'Roger, over.'
Murdock: 'Huh?'
Oveur: 'Huh?'

Oveur: 'You ever been in a cockpit before?'
Joey: 'No, sir, I've never been in a plane before.'

Oveur: 'You ever seen a grown man naked?'

Ted: 'My orders came through. My squadron ships out tomorrow. We're bombing the storage depots at Daiquiri at 1800 hours. We're coming in from the north, below their radar.'
Elaine: 'When will you be back?'
Ted: 'I can't tell you that. It's classified.'

Rumack: 'You'd better tell the Captain we've got to land as soon as we can. This woman has to be gotten to a hospital.'
Elaine: 'A hospital? What is it?'
Rumack: 'It's a big building with patients, but that's not important right now.'

Ted: 'Surely you can't be serious.'
Rumack: 'I am serious, and don't call me Shirley.'

ALL THAT HEAVEN ALLOWS

US, 1955, UNIVERSAL-INTERNATIONAL, 89 MINS
D DOUGLAS SIRK; **PR** ROSS HUNTER; **SC** PEG FENWICK (FROM A STORY BY EDNA AND HARRY LEE); **PH** (TECHNICOLOR) RUSSELL METTY; **ED** FRANK GROSS; **M** FRANK SKINNER
CAST JANE WYMAN (CARY SCOTT), ROCK HUDSON (RON KIRBY), AGNES MOORHEAD (SARA WARREN), CONRAD NAGEL (HARVEY), VIRGINIA GREY (ALIDA ANDERSON), GLORIA TALBOTT (KAY SCOTT), WILLIAM REYNOLDS (NED SCOTT), JACQUELINE DE WIT (MONA PLASH), CHARLES DRAKE (MICK ANDERSON), LEIGH SNOWDON (JO-ANN), MERRY ANDERS (MARY ANN), DONALD CURTIS (HOWARD HOFFER), ALEX GERRY (GEORGE WARREN), MANUEL (NESTA PAIVA)

▲ *ALL THAT HEAVEN ALLOWS* Rock Hudson and Jane Wyman *contemplate a sunny future together.*

THE STORY Cary Scott, a wealthy fortyish widow with two grown-up children, lives in an affluent New England dormitory town where the country club bears the sign 'For Members Exclusively'. The thirtyish Ron Kirby, an agricultural college graduate who's taken over his father's nursery business, has been tending her garden since before her husband's death, but Cary first notices him trimming her trees one day in autumn. Cary, who's being courted by a rich friend of her late husband, is impressed by Ron's indifference to social success, his love of nature and the simple life, and by his colourful rural friends.

When she falls in love with him, and he proposes marriage, her snobbish, conventional neighbours are shocked and they patronize and insult Ron at a party. Her son (a Princeton student) and daughter (a psychiatric social worker in New York) are outraged because of Ron's age and social status. In consequence, she breaks off their relationship. But at Christmas, the son and daughter announce they'll both be leaving for good and present her with a TV set to keep her company. After her doctor tells her that her recurrent headaches are psychosomatic and that she should return to Ron, she drives out to the converted mill where he lives, but he's out hunting. Trying to attract her attention as she drives away, Ron falls over a small cliff into a snow drift and suffers concussion. When he comes to in his living room, the doctor and Ron's friends have summoned Cary to his bedside, and she'll stay with him.

THE FILM In the 1950s *All That Heaven Allows* was considered a slick woman's picture, another in the glossy series directed by Douglas Sirk and produced by Ross Hunter, that turned Rock Hudson from a minor Universal contract actor into a major star. Its cult reputation stems from the 1960s when, after his retirement to Europe, its German-Danish director's reputation grew through the acclaim he received on the continent, especially in France. When Rock Hudson came out of the closet as he was dying of Aids in the late 1980s, this added to the cult status of the pictures he made at Universal, first the dramas with Sirk, then the comedies with Doris Day. Beneath its deceptively conventional surface, *All That Heaven Allows* offers a sharp critique of the suffocating conformity of the Eisenhower era. The contrast between the artificial life of Cary's middle-class circle and the honest naturalness of Ron's country friends may be none too subtle, but it is brilliantly realized through dress and decor. The film touches on issues of class, social hypocrisy, relations between parents and children, and on female sexuality, with considerable insight and without despising the conventions of its genre. And while it exposes the fissures beneath the complacency and false confidence of the 1950s, it does so in the name of Henry David Thoreau, the nineteenth-century New England dissident from whose book, *Walden*, Cary reads a famous passage. In many of his movies Sirk plays off a simple, consistent character against a complex, divided one – here the extrovert Hudson against the emotionally disturbed Wyman, though we now, of course, see in Hudson the guardian of his society's deeply buried secret.

13

ODD/SALIENT FACTS Henry David, Thoreau's *Walden* had been one of Sirk's favourite books in his early teenage years and helped shape his idea of what America stood for. Sirk's German disciple Rainer Werner Fassbinder used *All That Heaven Allows* as the model for one of his most popular films, *Fear Eats the Soul*, in which the mother is a white, lower middle-class widow and her young lover a North African *Gastarbeiter* in Berlin.

MEMORABLE MOMENTS Cary shocking her son by coming downstairs in a low-cut red dress ('Typical Oedipal reaction,' says daughter).

Cary in her empty house crying as she looks at carol singers in the snow.

Cary seeing her own reflection filling the television screen as the salesman says: 'All you have to do is turn that dial and you have all the company you want right there on the screen – drama, comedy, life's parade at your fingertips.'

KEY LINES

Alida, wife of Ron's best friend: 'I don't think Ron's ever read it [i.e. Thoreau's *Walden*], he just lives it.'

Ron: 'You're running away from something because you're afraid – of many things.'

Sara, Cary's best friend: 'A situation like this brings out the hateful side of human nature.'

Society matron: 'Have we ever met before?'
Ron: 'Probably in your garden. I've been pruning your trees for the last three years.'

L'ANNÉE DERNIÈRE À MARIENBAD (LAST YEAR AT MARIENBAD)

FRANCE/ITALY, 1961, TERRA FILMS ETC. (PARIS), CINERIZ (ROME), 94 MINS

D ALAIN RESNAIS; **PR** PIERRE COURAU, RAYMOND FROMENT; **SC** ALAIN ROBBE-GRILLET; **PH** (BW DYALISCOPE) SACHA VIERNY; **ED** HENRI COLPI, JASMINE CHASNEY; **M** FRANCIS SEYRIG

CAST DELPHINE SEYRIG (A), GIORGIO ALBERTAZZI (X), SACHA PITOËFF (M), FRANÇOISE BERTIN

▲ *LAST YEAR AT MARIENBAD* Delphine Seyrig and Giorgio Albertazzi wondering whether Marienbad is his place or hers.

THE STORY At a large, baroque hotel standing in extensive ornamental gardens, one of the handsome guests, X, who acts as the film's narrator, claims that the previous year at Marienbad he met another guest, the beautiful young woman, A. She alleges not to have met him, nor to have agreed to leave M, 'the man who may be her husband'. X persists and enters into a series of games played with matches with M, which he always loses. But eventually X persuades A and she leaves the hotel with him.

THE FILM *L'Année dernière à Marienbad* was the third collaboration in a row between Resnais and a practitioner of the French *nouveau roman*, following the Auschwitz documentary *Nuit et Brouillard* (1956), scripted by Jean Cayrol, and *Hiroshima Mon Amour* (1959), scripted by Marguerite Duras.

Like them it is about time and memory; unlike them it is an apolitical film and a chilly, formalistic work. Audiences loved or loathed it and it excited passionate discussion. With its sweeping camera movements around the elegant hotel, the carefully arranged grouping of actors inside the hotel and in the garden, it is a beautiful film to behold, and the music, combined with the flat, almost incantatory delivery of the dialogue and the narration and the hieratic style of acting add to the mesmeric effect. What is it about? Few films have left it so open to the audience – who in fact are the movie's 'reality'. Only in the published text are the three main characters identified as A, X and M. L'Année dernière may be a mystery story. Perhaps the hotel is an asylum where X and A are patients and the commanding, unsmiling M is the chief psychiatrist. On the other hand it could be X's dream, or a collective dream. Yet again, X, A and M might be one person, or the Id, Ego and Superego. These are just a few of the explanations that were advanced in the early 1960s when the Marienbad match game (which turns on the binomial theorem) was all the fashion. But they're all reductive interpretations of a work of rare purity in which form and content are indivisible. The antecedents of L'Année dernière are Renoir's La Règle du Jeu and Sartre's Huis Clos. It came out at the same time as Antonioni's L'Avventura and La Notte, and the two directors revolutionized the way time and space were used in the cinema. The film's influence on high and low culture was shallow but widespread – immediately on Joseph Losey (The Servant) and Ingmar Bergman (The Silence), later on Dick Lester and Nicolas Roeg, and pervasively on fashion photography, TV commercials, music videos. Unlike Casablanca, which grew from its cult following into a universally adored picture, L'Année dernière went from being one of the hottest pictures of its time, an avant-garde work that broke through into the popular conscience, back to small-time cult status.

ODD/SALIENT FACTS Much was made at the time by the film's detractors of the supposed fact that Resnais thought something had happened between the couple at Marienbad and Robbe-Grillet didn't. Actually both were deliberately ambivalent. In the film's most famous scene in which characters are arranged in

> M: 'I have another game to suggest instead: I know a game I always win.'
> X: 'If you can't lose it's not a game.'
> M: I can lose. But I always win.'

the gardens like statuary, the shadows they cast were painted on the ground. Though the film was a Franco-Italian co-production and the studio work done in Paris, the location shooting was in Bavaria at various Munich palaces. When Robbe-Grillet said that the couple couldn't have met in Marienbad because it didn't exist, he made a historical point. Marienbad was the German name of Mariánskí Lázne, adopted in 1808 when it became a spa town. Goethe, Chopin, Wagner, Ibsen, Edward VII and Kafka were among its patrons. After the Communist takeover of Czechoslovakia in 1948 the old name was readopted, and the hotels steadily decayed.

MEMORABLE MOMENTS The opening tracking shots around the deserted hotel and garden.

The male guests lined up indoors for pistol shooting.

The guests seen from the hotel standing like statues.

KEY LINES
M: 'I have another game to suggest instead: I know a game I always win.'
X: 'If you can't lose it's not a game.'
M: 'I can lose. But I always win.'

X: 'You never seemed to be waiting for me – but we kept meeting at every turn of the paths – behind every bush, at the foot of each statue, near every pond. It is as if it had been only you and I in all that garden'. 'It seemed, at first glance, impossible to get lost here … at first glance … down straight paths, between the statues with frozen gestures and the granite slabs, where you were already getting lost, forever, in the calm night, alone with me.'

Unidentified guests talking on soundtrack: "I think this game's silly.' 'There's a trick you have to know.' 'All you have to do is take an uneven number.' 'There must be rules.' 'It's the one who goes first who loses.' 'I remember how Frank used to play this last year … Yes, yes, he did, I'm sure of it.' 'What you have to do is take the complement of seven each time.' 'In which row?'

APOCALYPSE NOW★

US, 1979, OMNI ZOETROPE, 153 MINS AND C. 300 MINS

D FRANCIS COPPOLA; **PR** FRANCIS COPPOLA, FRED ROOS, GRAY FREDERICKSON, TOM STERNBERG; **SC** JOHN MILIUS, COPPOLA, AND MICHAEL HERR; **PH** VITTORIO STORARO; **DES** DEAN TAVOULARIS; **M** CARMINE COPPOLA AND FRANCIS COPPOLA; **ED** RICHARD MARKS

CAST MARTIN SHEEN (CAPT. WILLARD), MARLON BRANDO (COL. KURTZ), ROBERT DUVALL (LT. COL. KILGORE), FREDERIC FORREST (CHEF), ALBERT HALL (CHIEF), SAM BOTTOMS (LANCE), LARRY FISHBURNE (CLEAN), DENNIS HOPPER (PHOTOJOURNALIST), G. D. SPRADLIN (GENERAL), HARRISON FORD (COLONEL), JERRY ZIESMER (CIVILIAN), SCOTT GLENN (COLBY)

THE STORY At the height of the Vietnam War, Willard, a US Army captain, is given his new mission. He is to head up the Nung River and terminate the command of Kurtz, a Green Beret colonel who has gone native and mad. On the journey up-river, Willard and the crew encounter an Air Cavalry platoon and their crazed leader, Kilgore; then a tiger; witness a USO show featuring Playboy bunnies; and pass through the final outpost of American military at Do Long Bridge, before reaching Cambodia. There they carry out a mini My Lai massacre on the occupants of a sampan. Clean, the youngest member of the boat's crew, is killed in a firefight. The boat's captain, Chief Phillips, is killed by a spear before the boat finally pulls into Kurtz's compound in the middle of the jungle. There Willard and the two surviving crew members are met by Kurtz's crazy sidekick, a photojournalist. Chef is decapitated, Lance is absorbed by the Montagnards and Willard finally confronts Kurtz, who tries to explain the motivation behind his murderous activities and makes Willard promise to convey these explanations and his memoirs to his son. In parallel with a ritual tribal sacrifice of an ox, Willard kills Kurtz, retrieves Lance and together they leave the compound and head back down the river.

THE FILM Coppola came to this project on the back of the enormous critical and commercial success of the two *Godfather* films. The first draft was written in 1969 by John Milius, with a little help from George Lucas. The plan was for the film to be quickly and cheaply made, employing a documentary style and unknown actors. As it evolved, eventually with script input from Coppola himself, the film attained a level of moral ambiguity as the right-wing views of Milius were filtered through the more liberal vision of the director. The shoot began on 20 March 1976 and continued for 238 days, enduring the vagaries of both the Philippine weather and air force, the nearly fatal heart-attack and breakdown of Martin Sheen, and the problem of Marlon Brando, an overpaid, overweight and under-prepared cameo star. The film that emerged from this painful gestation succeeds for a number of reasons: the wonderful set designs by Dean Tavoularis; beautiful photography from Vittorio Storaro; an extraordinary extended editing process; great acting; a relatively honed and deceptively cohesive script; innovative sound design; and the inspired decision to commission a voiceover narration from Michael Herr, the author of the definitive Vietnam War document, *Dispatches*. It is a film that achieved widespread international success at the box office, but one that also retains an appeal in which the most fleeting reference or quotation instantly establishes a shared knowledge and obsession.

'Saigon. Shit.'

ODD/SALIENT FACTS The plot of the film is a loose transposition of Joseph Conrad's novella *Heart of Darkness* to the Vietnam War. Many incidents survive relatively unchanged in the process, and several of the characters have their source in Conrad, chiefly Kurtz, Marlow and the photojournalist. The project was conceived by Milius as a right-wing corrective to what he saw as the unfair treatment doled out to Col. Robert Rhéault, who was court-martialled for ordering the summary execution of a Vietnamese spy who he suspected – like Kurtz, and almost certainly with justification – was a double agent. Many of the more fantastical-seeming war sequences like those involving Kilgore, and the events around the Do Long Bridge, are in fact closely based on documented events of the war (with Michael Herr and the photographer Philip Jones Griffiths being particularly important source writers).

There is a cult within the cult, with some of the film's fans enthusing about the near-mythical five-hour cut of the film. This has been seen by several people in an illicit video version and includes extensions to certain scenes, such as the Air Cavalry's raid on the coastal village, a second appearance of the Playboy bunnies and an entire sequence at a French rubber plantation, including the military burial of Clean. Its ghostly existence in the minds of fans enhances the film's mythic appeal and points to its enduring cult status.

MEMORABLE MOMENTS The opening scene in which the plot is foretold and Willard's tortured state of mind is suggested.

The dawn raid which contains choreographed helicopters, planes and surfing.

The execution of Kurtz by Willard juxtaposed with the slaughter of the ox.

KEY LINES

Willard's opening line: 'Saigon. Shit.'

Kilgore's speech to Willard after the napalm drop: 'I love the smell of napalm in the morning. You know one time we had a hail bomb ... for twelve hours ... and when it was all over I walked up. We didn't find one body. Not one stinking dink body. But the smell, you know that gasoline smell ... the whole hill. It smelled like ... victory. Some day this war's gonna end.'

▲ *ASSAULT ON PRECINCT 13* Austin Stoker (Ethan Bishop), a modern day John Wayne, defends his precinct from a multi-cultural gang hell-bent on revenge.

ASSAULT ON PRECINCT 13
US, 1976, CKK, 91 MINS

D *JOHN CARPENTER;* **PR** *IRWIN YABLANS;* **SC** *JOHN CARPENTER;* **PH** *(COL, PANAVISION) DOUGLAS KNAPP;* **M** *JOHN CARPENTER;* **ED** *JOHN T. CHANCE*
CAST *AUSTIN STOKER (BISHOP), DARWIN JOSTIN (WILSON), LAURIE ZIMMER (LEIGH), MARTIN WEST (LAWSON), TONY BURTON (WELLS), CHARLES CYPHERS (STARKER), NANCY LOOMIS (JULIE), PETER BRUNI (ICE CREAM MAN), JOHN J. FOX (WARDEN), MARC ROSS (PATROLMAN TRAMER), ALAN KOSS (PATROLMAN BAXTER), HENRY BRANDON (CHANEY), KIM RICHARDS (KATHY), FRANK DOUBLEDAY (WHITE WARLORD), GILBERT DE LA PENA (CHICANO WARLORD), PETER FRANKLAND (CAUDELL), AL NAKAUCHI (ORIENTAL WARLORD), JAMES JOHNSON (BLACK WARLORD)*

THE STORY A police ambush in which several LA gang members get killed leads to a pact between various ethnic gangs sealed with a blood oath. A middle-aged man and his young daughter are lost driving through a rough part of the city. A bus drives through the city taking three prisoners (one of them very sick) to death row. A black police lieutenant receives his first commission, to look after a precinct on the last night before it is officially closed down. The young girl is shot and killed by the White Warlord who is in turn shot and killed by her father. Suddenly catatonic, he runs into the police station. Meanwhile the young prisoner on the bus becomes so ill that the prisoners and guards also have to seek refuge in the station. The mixed group is whittled down to just four survivors as the gang cut off all communications to the precinct and launch an attack with guns fitted with silencers, but they ultimately withstand the assault.

THE FILM The film is an object lesson in narrative economy. Carpenter has spent his career in the margins between cultism and mainstream commercial cinema and glories in his role as the last great director of B-movies. His debut was the deliberately off-beat *Dark Star* (1974), which had begun as a student piece. This, his follow-up, features a cast of unknowns and blends the tautness and wit of a Hawks film with the structure and horror of a zombie movie. As a supreme auteur, Carpenter not only writes, directs and edits, but also supplies the film's haunting synthesizer score borrowed by U2 who used it for the bass-line of their hit 'New Year's Day'. For *The Thing* – (1982), like this film a Hawks update featuring a scene in which a man is chained to a dangerously, scarily sick colleague – the score was composed by Ennio Morricone, who delivered a perfect pastiche of a Carpenter soundtrack. The most inspired idea in the film is the gang's use of silencers in their attack. This enhances the tension and adds an ironic comment on urban life (borrowed in *Die Hard*, 1988) that a full-on, sustained military-style attack can take place in the middle of a city without anyone on the outside noticing.

ODD/SALIENT FACTS The movie is in part an updated urban reworking of the Howard Hawks western *Rio Bravo* (1959). This is already suggested in the opening credits with the editing attributed to John T. Chance (in fact Carpenter himself), John Wayne's character in that film. *Rio Bravo* is further quoted from in the very brief set piece in which Bishop throws a shotgun to Wilson, who spins around, catches the gun and fires it in one movement which echoes the sequence in Hawks's film in which Nelson throws a gun to Wayne. The climax, where Bishop shoots at the flares attached to the top of the canister of explosive gas, is a version of Wayne, Nelson and Dean Martin firing at the sticks of dynamite thrown by Walter Brennan. The film also contains an unusual reference to another hero of Carpenter's, Alfred Hitchcock. Bishop is having a chat with Leigh (who herself later evokes Hawks's discovery, Lauren Bacall, in the way she lights her cigarette and extinguishes the match) about how he grew up just four blocks away. When he was about four or five his dad sent him to the police station with a note to hand to the detective. When he reads the note, the detective tells him: 'We lock up little boys who can't behave.' This is a story that Hitchcock would tell in interviews throughout his life, as an explanation of his fear of policemen which is such a feature of his films. Once he was asked what he wanted written on his tombstone and he said: 'This is what we do to bad little boys.'

> 'Son, there's something about you. You got something to do with death.'

MEMORABLE MOMENTS The emotionless shooting of the little girl at the ice cream van, itself including a sly reference to *The Manchurian Candidate*.

The gang's first attack on the precinct: the silenced gunshots with bullets smashing windows and the Venetian blinds and a piece of paper dancing above the desk as it is repeatedly struck.

KEY LINES

Wilson on the bus recalling what a preacher said to him as a kid: 'Son, there's something about you. You got something to do with death.' The line is a near quotation of the comment Cheyenne makes to Jill about Harmonica in *Once Upon a Time in the West*: 'People like that have something inside, something to do with death.'

While the depleted group are trying to evolve an escape strategy, Wells, the black convict says: 'In the meantime I've got a plan. It's called "Save ass".'

ATLANTIC CITY

France/Canada, 1980, Cine-Neighbour (Montreal)/Selta Films-Elie Kfouri (Paris), 105 mins

D Louis Malle; **PR** John Kemeny, Joseph Beaubien, Denis Heroux; **SC** John Guare; **PH** (col) Richard Ciupka; **ED** Suzanne Baron

CAST Burt Lancaster (Lou Paschall), Susan Sarandon (Sally), Kate Reid (Grace), Michel Piccoli (Joseph), Hollis McLaren (Chrissie), Robert Joy (Dave), Al Waxman (Alfie), Robert Goulet (Singer in hospital), Moses Znaimer (Félix, hitman), Angus MacInnes (Vinnie, hitman), Louis Del Grande (Mr Shapiro), Cec Linder (President of hospital), Wallace Shawn (Waiter), Joyce Parks (Queenie)

THE STORY Dave, a Canadian hippie, hi-jacks a consignment of Mafia cocaine and drives with his pregnant girlfriend, Chrissie, to visit Sally (his estranged wife and Chrissie's sister) in Atlantic City. Sally works at a seafood counter in a casino but wants to become a croupier. Lou Paschall, an ageing criminal, lives in the same dilapidated apartment block and is secretly in love with her. Lou is the kept man of Grace, a bedridden, hypochondriac widow, and fears his pathetic job as a runner for the numbers racket will be wiped out by legal gambling. Dave engages Lou to sell the cocaine. When Mafia hitmen kill Dave, Lou is left with the drugs. He becomes Sally's trusted friend through his handling of Dave's funeral, and they sleep together. Sally loses her job, and when two Mafia hitmen come for her, Lou kills both of them and drives south with Sally to Florida. At a motel, Sally steals some of Lou's drug money to start a new life as a croupier in Monte Carlo. Lou happily releases her and heads back to Atlantic City. Grace leaves her bed, helps Lou sell the remainder of the cocaine, and they promenade together along the Boardwalk.

THE FILM *Atlantic City*, Louis Malle's second US picture (the first was *Pretty Baby*), is one of the great movies about American

▼ *ATLANTIC CITY Ageing voyeur Burt Lancaster observes waitress Susan Sarandon's lemon therapy.*

life. It failed to reach a large public, but was a critical success. Malle's cinematic roots are in documentary, and the movie links private lives to public events as it tells a fictional story of everyday crime while documenting a city in transition. It prophesied the corruption of 1980s America, the decade in which Donald Trump, one of the creators of the new Atlantic City, would be a tarnished hero.

As Bob Rafelson had shown in *The King of Marvin Gardens* (1972), Atlantic City is a suggestive metaphor for America and the American Dream: a fashionable turn-of-the-century holiday resort; a favourite interwar playground for mobsters and adulterers; home of the Miss America pageant; the setting of the original Monopoly board; a town that, in 1980, was attempting to turn itself around as this film was being made. Burt Lancaster gives one of his very best performances, lending a comic twist to two very different kinds of roles he's played over the years: the tragic *film noir* loser of Siodmak's *The Killers*, and the detached, dignified dandy in Visconti's *The Leopard* and *Conversation Piece*.

ODD/SALIENT FACTS Malle's first choice for Lou was Robert Mitchum, but the Canadian producers thought that Lancaster would be bigger box office. Michel Legrand wrote a full score that was recorded but never used; the film has only source music. Nominated for five Oscars (best film, screenplay, director, actor and actress), the movie won nothing. When the representatives of Price, Waterhouse (the Academy's accountants) brought out the sealed envelopes, the Oscars host Johnny Carson quipped that 'They really know how to keep a secret – they also handled the distribution of *Atlantic City*'.

MEMORABLE MOMENTS Voyeur Paschall (Lancaster) looking across the ventilation shaft between his flat and Sally's (Sarandon) to watch her rubbing her breasts and arms with lemons.

Lancaster in a white slouch hat and new overcoat and Kate Reid in a veiled hat and fur coat nonchalantly walking along the Boardwalk (top property in Monopoly) at the end of the movie; in a single take they walk past the camera which pans up to a wrecker's ball smashing into an abandoned apartment block, again and again, as on the soundtrack we hear Tommy Dorsey's 'Song of India', 'Atlantic City, My Old Friend' (music and lyrics by Paul Anka), the 1945 number 'On the Boardwalk of Atlantic City', a few bars of twanging-guitar country music, and some cool jazz *à la Brubeck* played on piano with drum and bass accompaniment.

KEY LINES

Lou to Dave: 'Yes, it used to be beautiful, what with the rackets, whoring, guns. Sometimes things would happen and I'd have to kill a few people. I'd feel bad for a while. But I'd jump into the ocean and swim way out and come back feeling nice and clean and start all over again. The Atlantic Ocean was something then. Yes, you should have seen the Atlantic Ocean in those days.'

Paul Anka song, sung by Robert Goulet at the inauguration of the hospital's Sinatra Wing, while Sally arrives to identify ex-husband's body: 'I'm glad to see you born again, Atlantic City my old friend, you're back upon the map again, you sure came through.'

BAD DAY AT BLACK ROCK
USA, 1955, MGM, 81 MINS

D JOHN STURGES; *PR* DORE SCHARY; *SC* MILLARD KAUFMAN (FROM THE STORY BAD TIME AT HONDO BY HOWARD BRESLIN); *PH* (EASTMANCOLOR, CINEMASCOPE) WILLIAM C. MELLOR; *M* ANDRÉ PREVIN; *ED* NEWELL P. KIMLIN

CAST SPENCER TRACY (JOHN J. MACREEDY), ROBERT RYAN (RENO SMITH), ANNE FRANCIS (LIZ WIRTH), DEAN JAGGER (SHERIFF TIM HORN), WALTER BRENNAN (DOC VELIE), JOHN ERICSON (PETE WIRTH), ERNEST BORGNINE (COLEY TRIMBLE), LEE MARVIN (HECTOR DAVID), RUSSELL COLLINS (MR HASTINGS), WALTER SANDE (SAM)

THE STORY Late 1945, early morning, a few months after the end of the Second World War. The Super Chief locomotive stops at Black Rock, a tiny community huddled beneath the mountains of the south-western desert a couple of hundred miles east of Los Angeles. One man gets off – the one-armed John MacReedy. He becomes the subject of suspicion and hostility, especially as he wants to visit Adobe Flat, erstwhile home of a Japanese farmer called Komoko. Only Doc Velie gives MacReedy a welcome. The others in town – Hastings the telegraph clerk, Pete the hotel manager, his sister Liz who runs the local garage, Tim the drunken sheriff, Sam, owner of the town's diner, and the thuggish cowboys Hector and Coley – are all under the thumb of the racist rancher, Reno Smith. MacReedy

▲ *BAD DAY AT BLACK ROCK* One-armed stranger Spencer Tracy gets a cold Western welcome from Robert Ryan and Lee Marvin.

is told Komoko was relocated after Pearl Harbor, but at Adobe Flat he discovers a burnt-out ranch house, a well and signs of an unmarked grave. Smith, furious when Komoko discovered water on the worthless land he'd sold him, had got 'patriotic drunk' with Hector, Coley, Hastings, Sam and Pete after Pearl Harbor, and they had driven out to Komoko's ranch and killed him. MacReedy is in Black Rock to present Komoko with a medal posthumously awarded to his son after saving MacReedy's life in Italy. They intend to silence MacReedy, but

he uses his karate skills to lay out Coley, and he and Doc persuade Pete to redeem himself by helping MacReedy escape. Hector is knocked out by Doc, and Liz drives MacReedy out of town and into a trap set by Reno, whom she loves. Reno shoots her dead, and MacReedy makes a Molotov cocktail, turning Reno into a human torch. The conspirators are taken away by the state police, and Doc gets MacReedy to leave the medal to the town.

THE FILM One of the leanest thrillers ever made, *Black Rock* takes place over exactly 24 hours and was the first film to touch on a nasty American secret, i.e. the treatment of the Nisei, the American citizens of Japanese descent, robbed of their property and corralled in remote prison camps in the deserts of

21.

California and Nevada. The film also reflected the anxieties of the McCarthy era with MacReedy an embattled representative of probity in the manner of *High Noon's* Marshal Kane. But this picture is far more specific in its attack on the racism and xenophobia of those who purport to uphold the pioneer tradition of the West. *Black Rock* had a special appeal for embattled liberals who identified with MacReedy, the peaceful man, quite literally unarmed, who reasons until provoked beyond endurance, and wins by his superior intelligence and special skills. It's the definitive liberal revenge movie, justifying and ultimately revelling in retaliatory violence. Few movies have offered such a trio of venomous heavies as those played by Ryan, Borgnine and Marvin, and appropriately Tracy uses Eastern martial arts on the thug who calls him a 'yellow-bellied Jap lover'. The movie was among the first to use the widescreen for dramatic effect as in the anxious conference between the conspirators standing apart and straddling the railroad line, and the diner sequence where there are only three or four edits before the fight breaks out. The film made John Sturges a favourite among cinephiles, most of whom regard it as superior to more spectacular later films such as *The Magnificent Seven* and *The Great Escape*.

ODD/SALIENT FACTS *Bad Day* was the first Western shown in competition at Cannes and brought Tracy the best actor award. The film had the first important score by André Previn.

MEMORABLE MOMENTS MacReedy inspecting Adobe Flat.

Coley's provocation of MacReedy in the diner and the ensuing fight.

MacReedy, stalked by the gun-toting Reno, using guerilla tactics to make a Molotov cocktail.

KEY LINES

Train conductor: 'Man, they look woebegone and far away.'
MacReedy: 'I'll only be here 24 hours.'
Conductor: 'In a place like this that could be a lifetime.'

MacReedy to Reno: 'What did Komoko have to do with Corregidor?'

Reno to MacReedy: 'Someone is always looking for

Coley: 'You're a yellow-bellied Jap-lover, am I right or wrong?'

something in this part of the West. For the historian it's the Old West. For the bookwriter it's the Wild West. For the businessman it's the undeveloped West. They say we're all poor and backward and I guess we are. We don't even have enough water. But to us it's our West, and I wish they'd leave us alone.'

Coley: 'You're a yellow-bellied Jap-lover, am I right or wrong?'
MacReedy: 'You're not only wrong, you're wrong at the top of your voice.'

BADLANDS

US, 1973, Pressman/Williams/Badlands, 94 mins
D *TERRENCE MALICK;* **PR** *TERRENCE MALICK;* **SC** *TERRENCE MALICK;* **PH** *BRIAN PROBYN, TAK FUJIMOTO, STEVAN LARNER;* **M** *GEORGE TIPTON;* **ED** *ROBERT ESTRIN*
CAST *MARTIN SHEEN (KIT), SISSY SPACEK (HOLLY), WARREN OATES (FATHER), RAMON BIERI (CATO), ALAN VINT (DEPUTY), GARY LITTLEJOHN (SHERIFF), JOHN CARTER (RICH MAN), BRYAN MONTGOMERY (BOY), GAIL THRELKELD (GIRL), CHARLES FITZPATRICK (CLERK), HOWARD RAGSDALE (BOSS), JOHN WOMACK SR. (TROOPER), DONA BALDWIN (MAID), BEN BRAVO (GAS ATTENDANT)*

THE STORY Holly, a teenager who lives in a small South Dakota town with her widowed father, begins an affair with Kit, a mentally unstable garbage collector. When Holly's dad, who strongly disapproves of the liaison, tries to stop Kit taking her away, Kit shoots him dead. Kit and Holly live a wild life hiding out in the country until they are discovered and approached by three bounty hunters, all of whom Kit kills. The couple visit Cato, Kit's friend from the garbage round, but Kit shoots him too when he suspects that he is about to betray them. Kit leads a young couple, who come to call at Cato's remote house, into a storm shelter, locks them in and fires two shots, possibly killing them. A national manhunt is launched, and Kit and Holly briefly seek refuge in the house of a rich man. They take his car and drive into the Badlands, a barren region of South Dakota and Montana where Holly begins to tire of Kit. When they are pur-

22

▲ **BADLANDS** *Sissy Spacek (Holly) and Martin Sheen (Kit) get to know each other before embarking on their murderous spree.*

sued by a helicopter, she refuses to go along with him, and after a final pursuit, Kit gives himself up. He becomes an instant hero to the young rangers who surround him. As they fly off, Holly reveals in her voice-over narration that Kit will be electrocuted and she will marry the son of her defence attorney.

THE FILM Kit, one of two cold killers memorably played by Sheen in the 1970s, is a cruel, wilful but sentimental child trapped in an adult body. He casually challenges his buddy to eat a dead dog they find on their round. He kills because he has a gun and: 'I always wanted to be a criminal, just not this big a one.' He wants to leave a mark, is obsessed with establishing memorials to himself and encourages his own cult status. He commemorates his and Holly's first sexual encounter with a rock, which he instantly exchanges for a smaller one. Later he sends off a time capsule dedicated to their love in a red balloon. During the climactic chase he adjusts the rear-view mirror

so he can watch himself being pursued. He then marks the spot of his own arrest with a small pile of stones and dishes out his paltry personal possessions, convinced of his status as a lasting icon. Kit and Holly are rebels without a cause who abandon their lives and adopt the personae of two icons of their time, James Dean and Priscilla Presley. Terrence Malick has ensured that he has remained the enduring cult figure of the modern Hollywood era by being its least prolific genius. After this, his debut, he waited five years before directing his next film, the beautiful *Days of Heaven* (1978). There followed a gap of twenty years before his third directorial offering, *The Thin Red Line* (1999).

ODD/SALIENT FACTS The events of the film are based on the actions of the 1950s spree killer, Charles Starkweather. On 1 December 1957, the James Dean-fixated Starkweather, along with his petite red-headed girlfriend Caril Ann Fugate, killed the first of their victims, a petrol pump attendant. They murdered another ten, including Fugate's step-parents, as they travelled across America, before being arrested in Wyoming. Fugate received a life sentence, Starkweather went to the electric chair. Malick himself makes an odd cameo appearance as the man dressed in white who comes to visit the rich man being held captive by Holly and Kit. The credits offer thanks to Arthur Penn, director of one of the seminal 'lovers on the run' movies, *Bonnie and Clyde* (1967). George Tipton's soundtrack was borrowed in Tony Scott's *True Romance* (1993).

MEMORABLE MOMENTS The burning of the house as we cut between images of a piano, a doll, a doll's house, a bed and Holly's father being consumed by the blaze as Kit's fake-suicide recording plays on the record player outside.

The final farewell dance in the car's headlights on the eve of Kit's capture.

KEY LINES

Holly in her narration: 'Little did I realize that what began in the alleys and backways of this quiet town would end in the Badlands of Montana.'

Holly: 'He wanted to die with me and I dreamed of being lost forever in his arms.'

Kit, concluding his fake-suicide record: 'I can't deny we've had fun though. That's more than I can say for some.'

Holly, after Kit has killed her father and shot Cato and his two young friends: 'Suddenly I was thrown into a state of shock. Kit was the most trigger-happy person I'd ever met.'

BARBARELLA

FRANCE/ITALY, 1968, DINO DE LAURENTIIS SP. A MARIANNE PRODUCTIONS, 98 MINS

D ROGER VADIM; **PR** DINO DE LAURENTIIS; **SC** TERRY SOUTHERN, ROGER VADIM, CLAUDE BRULE, VITTORIO BONICELLI, CLEMENT BIDDLE WOOD, BRIAN DEGAS, TUDOR GATES, JEAN-CLAUDE FOREST, BASED ON A STORY BY JEAN-CLAUDE FOREST; **PH** (COL, PANAVISION) CLAUDE RENOIR; **PR DES** MARIO GARBUGLIA; **M** BOB CREWE, CHARLES FOX; **ED** VICTORIA MERCANTON

CAST JANE FONDA (BARBARELLA), JOHN PHILIP LAW (PYGAR), UGO TOGNAZZI (MARK HAND), DAVID HEMMINGS (DILDANO), MILO O'SHEA (DURAN DURAN), ANITA PALLENBERG (THE BLACK QUEEN), MARCEL MARCEAU (PROFESSOR PING), VÉRONIQUE VENDELL (CAPTAIN MOON), SERGE MARQUAND (CAPTAIN SUN)

▲ *BARBARELLA John Philip Law as the blind Pygar and Jane Fonda as the eponymous space adventurer strive once more to banish war from the Universe.*

> **'Weapon? Why would anyone want to invent a weapon?'**

THE STORY In the year 40,000, Barbarella, a space adventurer, receives her new mission: to discover the whereabouts of Duran Duran, the man who has invented the positronic ray gun, in a time when war has been abolished. She embarks on a series of erotic adventures in which she encounters diabolical dolls, blind angel Pygar, the rebel Dildano and the Black Queen, before saving the Universe from the megalomaniacal Duran Duran.

THE FILM You can never trust a film with eight writers credited. But even had the screenplay been coherent, there would still have been the matter of Roger Vadim's ineptitude as a filmmaker. What Vadim was competent at was spotting cult potential, as he proved when launching the Brigitte Bardot phenomenon with ... *et dieu créa la femme* (... And God Created Woman, 1956). It has a kitschy feel to it from the start and is rendered watchable by Fonda's performance and the lavish production design. David Hemmings and Milo O'Shea seem to have been given little cohesive direction, and the former delivers by some distance the worst performance of his career. The camp but expensive studio sets are undermined by the deliberately bad *Flash Gordon*-style special effects. *Barbarella*, based on Jean-Claude Forest's adult comic strip, was conceived as a cult film and has duly become one.

ODD/SALIENT FACTS The film might have worked had it stuck to just one writer and become the crazed sexual satire conceived by Terry Southern. Southern was one of the key cult figures of the 1950s and '60s, contributing to the screenplays of both *Dr Strangelove* (1964) and *Easy Rider* (1969) – a project initiated by, and starring, Jane Fonda's brother Peter – as well as co-writing *Candy* and writing alone *The Magic Christian* and *Blue Movie*. Fonda herself was reluctant to do the film, but

24

was eventually persuaded by her then husband, Vadim. In his autobiography, *Memoirs of the Devil*, he writes:

> She didn't enjoy shooting *Barbarella*. She accepted the part because I was enthusiastic about the project, but she disliked the central character for her lack of principle, her shameless exploitation of her sexuality, and her irrelevance to contemporary social and political realities. In fact Barbarella, for all its extravagant fantasy, contains a good deal of ruthless satire on the problems of our times. But humour is not one of Jane's strong points unless it is stated explicitly.

MEMORABLE MOMENTS What makes the film memorable and what surely has sealed its enduring reputation as a kitsch classic is the opening scene in which Fonda strips out of her space suit while the credits roll.

KEY LINES
The greeting: 'Love'. Then Barbarella's shock at learning that Duran Duran has devised the positronic ray: 'Weapon? Why would anyone want to invent a weapon?'

BARTON FINK

USA, 1991, CIRCLE FILMS, 116 MINS

D JOEL COEN; **PR** ETHAN COEN; **SC** ETHAN COEN, JOEL COEN; **PH** (DUART COLOR) ROGER DEAKINS; **ED** RODERICK JAMES; **M** CARTER BURWELL

CAST JOHN TURTURRO (BARTON FINK), JOHN GOODMAN (CHARLIE MEADOWS), JUDY DAVIS (AUDREY TAYLOR), MICHAEL LERNER (JACK LIPNICK), JOHN MAHONEY (W.P. MAYHEW), TONY SHALHOUB (BEN GEISLER), JON POLITO (LOU BREEZE), STEVE BUSCEMI (CHET), DAVID WARRILOW (GARLAND STANFORD), ISABELLE TOWNSEND (BATHING BEAUTY)

THE STORY Autumn 1941. Young New York Jewish playwright Barton Fink is brought to Hollywood by Jack Lipnick, head of Capitol Pictures, to write scripts. Barton's next-door neighbour at the seedy Hotel Earle is Charlie Meadows, an insurance man. Barton has writer's block and asks help from drunken novelist Bill Mayhew, whose lover eventually spends a night with

Barton and is found dead in his room next morning. Charlie offers to dispose of the body, then goes off leaving Barton with a big parcel. Two cops arrive saying Charlie is serial killer Mad Man Mundt. Barton begins to write very fast, finishing a screenplay. The cops return to hotel as does Charlie. A fire breaks out and Charlie shoots the cops and retires to his room. Next day Lipnick, wearing a post-Pearl Harbor beribboned uniform run up by the studio's costume department, tells Barton his screenplay is no good and he's the property of Capitol Pictures for the time being. Barton is last seen on the beach carrying Charlie's parcel and meeting a bathing beauty who's seemingly stepped out of a picture on his hotel-room wall.

THE FILM The Coen Brothers are cult film-makers *par excellence*. All their films live in a quirky world of their own. Only their most orthodox film, *Fargo*, did notably well at the box-office. *Barton Fink* is arguably their oddest, most disturbing film and the only one to deal directly with their Jewishness and the business of movie-making. It is a black comedy, a psychological thriller, one of the cruellest of Hollywood pictures, with a succession of striking performances. Lerner's Jewish tycoon is a mixture of Louis B. Mayer, Jack Warner and Harry Cohn. Turturro's Barton is sad and touching but also a self-righteous prig. His wiry, vertically combed hair and glasses make him

▼ *BARTON FINK* John Turturro's Fink from another world gazes across the Pacific as the credits roll.

25

look like George S. Kaufman, but his Broadway play is in the poetic proletarian manner of Clifford Odets, and the name Fink suggests a man who, like Odets, both sold out to Hollywood and betrayed his friends to the House Un-American Activities Committee. Barton never listens to anyone and goes on about wanting to highlight the problems of 'the common man', while the perfect subject is living next door in the form of Charlie Meadows. America's entry into the war has no impact on him.

The atmosphere of the film is increasingly nightmarish, but is it a dream or something going on in Barton's head? If a dream, does it begin when Barton leaves New York? A slow dissolve between a wave breaking on the Pacific shore and the lobby of the Earle makes the hotel appear to be under water. Or does the nightmare begin with the virtuoso tracking shot from Barton and Audrey in bed, into the bathroom, down the sink and through a pipe into oblivion. After Audrey's death Barton takes a Gideon Bible from the desk drawer, opens it at random and reads an Old Testament verse in which Nebuchadnezzar says 'I recall not my dream; if ye will not make known unto me my dream, and its interpretation, ye shall be cut in pieces and your tents shall be made a dunghill.' The vast, decaying Hotel Earle is reminiscent of the Overlook Hotel in Kubrick's *The Shining*, home of another blocked writer. It's an evil haunted place, the wind roaring through empty corridors, the wallpaper slimy and peeling. As in hell, the fire makes the guests uncomfortably hot but does not consume them.

Among the numerous references to other movies, one of the most significant is to *Deadline at Dawn* (1946), a *film noir* thriller adapted by Clifford Odets from a novel by pulp writer William Irish (aka Cornel Woolrich), where a drunk finds that the woman he spent the night with has been murdered, and is driven around town by a kindly philosophical taxi-driver who turns out to be the real murderer.

ODD/SALIENT FACTS At the 1991 Cannes Festival the jury awarded Barton Fink the Palme d'Or and named Joel Coen best director and John Turturro best actor. The editing is credited to a non-existent Englishman, Roderick James, to whom they later

> '*I guess I write about people like you. The average working stiff. The common man.*'

attributed a highly critical introduction to the published screenplays of *Barton Fink* and *Miller's Crossing*.

MEMORABLE MOMENTS Jack Lipnick getting on his knees to kiss Barton's feet.

Charlie Meadows charging down the blazing corridor shouting 'Look upon me! I'll show you the life of the mind.'

Barton on the beach with the parcel and the dream girl.

KEY LINES

Lipnick: 'The writer is king here at Capitol Pictures.'

Barton: 'I guess I write about people like you. The average working stiff. The common man.'

Barton: 'But Charlie, why me?'
Charlie: 'Because you DON'T LISTEN ... You're a tourist with a typewriter. I live here.'

THE BATTLESHIP POTEMKIN
USSR, 1925, FIRST GOSKINO PRODUCTION, MOSCOW, 1,740 METRES (APPROX. 72 MINS)

D SERGEI EISENSTEIN; **PR** JACOB BLIOKH; **SC** SERGEI EISENSTEIN (FROM A STORY BY NINA AGADJHANOVA AND SERGEI EISENSTEIN); **PH** (BW) EDOUARD TISSÉ; **ED** EISENSTEIN; **M** (FOR ORIGINAL SILENT PRODUCTION) EDMUND MEISEL
CAST A. ANTONOV (VAKULINCHUK), VLADIMIR BARSKY (COMMANDER GOLIKOV), GRIGORY ALEXANDROV (SENIOR OFFICER GILYAROVSKY), M. GOMOROV (SAILOR MATYUSHENKO), ANONYMOUS WORKMAN (SHIP'S SURGEON SMIRNOV), ANONYMOUS GARDENER FROM SEVASTOPOL (PRIEST), LEVCHENKO (BOSUN), REPNIKOVA (WOMAN ON THE STEPS), MARUSOV (OFFICER), SAILORS OF THE RED NAVY, CITIZENS OF ODESSA, MEMBERS OF THE PROLETCULT THEATRE (VARIOUS PARTS)

THE STORY Set during the short-lived Russian revolution of 1905, the film unfolds in five parts, which Eisenstein saw as corresponding to the five-act structure of tragedy.

1. MEN AND MAGGOTS The revolutionary seamen Vakulinchuk and Matyushenko, serving on the Imperial Navy's *Battleship Potemkin* in the Black Sea, discuss the need to join the revolutionary workers on the mainland. Mutiny looms when sailors reject their maggot-ridden food.

▲ *THE BATTLESHIP POTEMKIN* *The grieving mother confronts the relentless military executioners as they descend the Odessa Steps.*

2. DRAMA ON THE QUARTER-DECK The marines are called on deck to execute some scapegoats. They refuse to fire, the sailors rebel, and the officers are killed or thrown overboard, but not before the sadistic Commander Golikov has shot Vakulinchuk.

3. AN APPEAL FROM THE DEAD (aka *The Dead Man Cries Out For Vengeance*) Vakulinchuk's body is taken ashore and laid out as a revolutionary martyr on the dock at Odessa. The citizens of the town pay their respects and express solidarity with the sailors of the *Potemkin*. The Red Flag is raised on the battleship.

4. THE ODESSA STEPS The people of Odessa rejoice and fraternize with the sailors. Suddenly the army descend on the town, a row of soldiers in white tunics advance steadily down the wide Odessa Steps in the centre of town, methodically shooting unarmed civilians, while at the bottom of the steps a troupe of Cossack cavalry attack the crowd with sabres. The battleship retaliates by turning its guns on the Odessa Theatre, headquarters of the military commanders.

5. MEETING THE SQUADRON The *Potemkin* puts to sea, expecting to do battle with the other ships of the Black Sea fleet. But their fellow sailors refuse to fire on them and the *Potemkin* sails by, its crew cheering.

THE FILM The work of the most powerful mind ever to be actively engaged in film-making, *The Battleship Potemkin* is in every sense a revolutionary movie – a picture that employs innovatory techiques to excite its audience to rebel. Using 1,400 separate shots in seventy minutes, the film keeps up an extraordinary pace and is a great piece of graphic story-telling. Banned as inflammatory in many countries for years, it has lost little of its power and is an angry picture, demonizing the officer class while making a collective hero of the ship's crew, whose muscular bodies are admiringly observed and lovingly photographed in the below-deck scenes, given a homoerotic quality by the gay Sergei Eisenstein. The citizens of Odessa have a formidable unity taking in all classes; an anti-semite who shouts 'Down with the Jews' is turned upon and beaten. But they are also characterized so that when the massacre takes

> **'Comrades, the time has come to act. What are we waiting for?'**

place identifiable individuals are being killed. Oddly the movie has never been widely popular in the USSR or elsewhere, and has been most keenly appreciated by art-house audiences, film-makers and students of cinema. Probably no sequence in the history of the movies has had such a hold over people as the Odessa Steps massacre, influencing artists as different as Francis Bacon, Sam Peckinpah and Brian De Palma. The use of a non-professional cast helped inspire the neo-realist movement.

ODD/SALIENT FACTS The film was intended as part of a larger work on the 1905 Revolution and was completed just in time for the twentieth anniversary celebrations. The final reel was being edited while the first one was being shown at the Bolshoi Theatre in Moscow on 21 December 1925. There was a mutiny on the *Potemkin*, the navy's largest battleship, in 1905, and the mutineers put in to Odessa, but the massacre is the invention of Eisenstein and his co-writer. Although it wasn't given a certificate for public exhibition in Britain until the 1960s, it slipped past the censor's net during the Second World War when, under the title *Seeds of Freedom*, it was presented as an inspirational story told by an ageing *Potemkin* mutineer to encourage flagging Soviet soldiers to go back into battle against the Nazis. (The additional material was filmed in New York in English.)

MEMORABLE MOMENTS A sailor working in the officers' mess angrily smashing a plate bearing the words 'Give us this day our daily bread.'

The ten *Potemkin* sailors covered in a tarpaulin on the quarterdeck waiting to be executed by a firing squad.

Commander Golikov's apoplectic expression when the marines refuse to fire.

Vakulinchuk's dead body cradled by ropes hanging beside the ship.

The Odessa Steps sequence.

KEY LINES

Lenin, the film's epigraph: 'Revolution is the only lawful, equal, effectual war. It was in Russia that this war was declared and won.'

Vakulinchuk: 'Comrades, the time has come to act. What are we waiting for? All Russia is rising. Are we to be the last?'

The Potemkin's *priest:* 'Lord, reveal Thyself to the unruly.'

Matyushenko: 'Ring up the signal – don't fight us, join us.'

A BETTER TOMORROW

HONG KONG, 1986, CINEMA CITY/FILM WORKSHOP, 95 MINS
D/SC JOHN WOO; **CO-PR** TSUI HARK; **PH** WONG WING HUNG; **M** JOSEPH KOO
CAST CHOW YUN FAT (MARK), TI LUNG (HO), LESLIE CHEUNG (KIT), EMILY CHU (JACKIE), LE CHE HUNG (SHING)

THE STORY Mark and Ho, close friends and gangsters, execute assignments for the Hong Kong syndicate around the Pacific Rim. Ho's younger brother Kit, unaware of his brother's profession, has joined the Hong Kong police and developed an attachment to Jackie, the classical musician who cares for their sick father. Accompanied by the ambitious Shing, Ho delivers a case of counterfeit money in Taiwan but is double-crossed and a bloody shoot-out ensues. Trapped by the police he lets Shing escape and serves three years in jail. Meanwhile in Hong Kong Ho's father is killed by a Taiwanese gangster sent to kidnap him, and Mark is shot in the leg while seeking revenge on those said to have betrayed Ho. Returning from jail, Ho decides to go straight, becoming a taxi driver for a firm that employs ex-convicts. But his brother holds him responsible for their father's death and his own failure to secure promotion. The crippled Mark works as an odd-job man for Shing, now deputy

▲ *A Better Tomorrow* *Chow Yun Fat, both guns blazing in a show of selfless bravery, a typical Woo combination of piety and pyrotechnics.*

head of the syndicate, and is ritually humiliated. Eventually Mark and Ho are reunited against Shing, who is attempting to frame Ho and take over the whole organization. In a final gunfight on the docks, Mark gives his life to save his friend and Ho convinces his brother that he is going straight. In the final shot Ho puts the handcuffs around his own wrist and allows Kit to take him in.

THE FILM In the 1980s, Chinese and Taiwanese films stormed into European and American art-house cinemas while for less fastidious audiences Hong Kong provided cult action films, first Kung Fu pictures then gangster flicks. John Woo became the Crown Colony's hottest director through his kinetic crime pictures that filtered the lyrical violence of Sergio Leone, Sam Peckinpah and Walter Hill through an Asian sensibility and re-exported it to the States where Quentin Tarantino became a major admirer. Woo's trademarks are the stand-off, where two

or more gunmen hold each other at bay, and the ferocious gunfight in which dozens of people are killed and restaurants blown apart as the hero pirouettes and somersaults while blasting away with two automatic pistols to throbbing, synthesized Western music. *A Better Tomorrow* is a characteristic fable of male friendship, stoicism, courage, and men living by a personal code, in which women are marginalized. It made an overnight star of Chow Yun Fat, who appeared in most of Woo's pictures. The handsome, reserved, athletic Chow is the epitome of Hong Kong movie cool, a moral man in an amoral world, his character much the same whatever side of the law he is on. The movie also introduced Leslie Cheung, who was to become an iconic figure in mainland Chinese movies.

ODD/SALIENT FACTS Woo made his Hollywood debut in 1993 with *Hard Target* and went on to direct John Travolta in *Broken Arrow* and *Face/Off*. Chow Yun Fat's first American film was *Replacement Assassin* (1997), in which he played a hitman who develops a conscience. *A Better Tomorrow* is one of the favourite movies of the video-store hero of *True Romance* (1993), scripted by Tarantino.

MEMORABLE MOMENTS A gangster lighting a cigar with a counterfeit $100 bill.

Mark concealing spare pistols in a row of plant pots on his way to a shootout in a private dining room.

Mark putting his artificial leg on a restaurant table and pouring whisky over it as a gesture of contempt.

An Andy Warhol print of Greta Garbo on the wall of Kit's flat.

KEY LINES

Mark to Kit: 'If you don't stop pointing that gun you'll have to use it.'

Kit: 'I never realized Hong Kong was so beautiful at night. It will vanish one day, that's for sure.'

Ho: 'Do you believe there's a God?'
Kit: 'Yes. I'm one, you're one. A god is someone who controls his destiny.'

> 'If you don't stop pointing that gun you'll have to use it.'

BIG WEDNESDAY ★
US, 1978, WARNER/A-TEAM, 119 MINS

D JOHN MILIUS; **PR** BUZZ FEITSHANS; **SC** JOHN MILIUS, DENNIS AABERG; **PH** (COL, PANAVISION) BRUCE SURTEES; **M** BASIL POLEDOURIS; **ED** ROBERT L. WOLFE

CAST JAN MICHAEL VINCENT (MATT JOHNSON), WILLIAM KATT (JACK BARLOW), GARY BUSEY (LEROY SMITH), PATTI D'ARBANVILLE (SALLY JOHNSON), LEE PURCELL (PEGGY GORDON), WAXER (DARRELL FETTY), (JIM KING), SAM MELVILLE ('THE BEAR'), GERRY LOPEZ (HIMSELF), HANK WARDEN ('SHOPPING CART'), JOE SPINELL (PSYCHOLOGIST), BARBARA HALE (MRS BARLOW), ROBERT ENGLUND (FLY), STEVE KANALY (SALLY'S HUSBAND), CHARLENE TILTON (GIRL ON BEACH)

THE STORY THE SOUTH SWELL, SUMMER 1962. The narrator, an unnamed young surfer, talks of three young surfers, Jack, Matt and Leroy, and their friends on a beach in Southern California. They surf and party and fight, travel to Mexico and confront adulthood and the swell with the help of their mentor and board-maker, the Bear.

THE WEST SWELL, FALL 1965. The young men receive their draft papers for Vietnam. At the draft board, the friends adopt a variety of ruses to avoid being accepted. All succeed apart from Waxer, and Jack who did not try to avoid it.

THE NORTH SWELL, WINTER 1968. Waxer has been killed in action in Vietnam. Jack returns and finds that his teenage sweetheart has got married. Matt is depressed at getting older and Bear is ruined, while Leroy travels around as a prominent surfer.

THE GREAT SWELL, SPRING 1974. The three friends gather to do combat with the big wave, Big Wednesday. They approach the sea, feeling no need to exchange words. They surf, and Matt barely survives. He gives his board to a young surfer, and the three friends go their separate ways once more.

THE FILM *Big Wednesday* should have been the project that put John Milius on a par with his friends and contemporaries, Coppola, Spielberg, De Palma and Scorsese. But it failed at the box office, though it instantly becoming a cult film among the surfers of Southern California and its reputation spread, and select fans around the world were soon stoked by its radical tubularity. Milius himself had been a surfer on the same beaches as in the film and the opening credits conclude with a photograph of the young writer/director as surfer dude. He has said: 'Surfing was a big part of my life for a long time. Surfing is a mystical thing, but is also this useless Californian thing – it doesn't achieve anything. But at the same time it is kind of grand.' Milius had wanted to serve in Nam but was rejected by the Marines because of his chronic asthma. The film bears the Milius signature with its mix of machismo, mysticism and mythology. Bear is a figure consumed with the myths and traditions of surfing. His character is a fusion of Arthurian and Germanic – legend, with the surfboard he creates the equivalent of a legendary sword that can be wielded only by a hero.

ODD/SALIENT FACTS Milius has an enduring attachment to John Ford's *The Searchers* (1956). Several of the films with which he has been involved have been twists on its plot to retrieve a young relative from enemy hands, among them *Hardcore* (1978) and *Uncommon Valor* (1983). In *Big Wednesday* 'Shopping Cart' is played by Hank Warden, who played the eccentric, rocking-chair-fixated Mose in the earlier film. Matt Johnson, like Lance Johnson (Sam Bottoms) in

Apocalypse Now, is based on Lance Carson, a legendary surfer who rode the waves on the beaches south of Los Angeles, and a good friend of Milius's. Fly, one of Jack's surfer buddies, seen saying goodbye to him as he is about to go off to Vietnam, is played by Robert Englund, who was later to play Freddie Kreuger in Wes Craven's *Nightmare on Elm Street* films.

MEMORABLE MOMENTS The draft board scene. This begins with the boys, accompanied by a drum beating out a military rhythm, preparing for their ploys to avoid acceptance into the army with military precision. Leroy, dressed as a bum, applies fish, wine and gasoline and convinces everyone, including his friends, that he is insane. Matt pretends to be lame, while another of the crowd poses as a Nazi. Waxer's attempt to feign homosexuality fails to save him and Jack makes no attempt to avoid service.

The three friends get drunk and visit Waxer's grave. Matt delivers a eulogy: 'He was a good surfer, and a really great guy. He had a nice cutback, rode the nose really well.'

The film's climax, beginning with Matt, Jack and Leroy meeting up once again and marching to their destiny among the waves like legendary heroes.

KEY LINES

The narrator: 'Bear made our boards and told us stories. He knew where the waves came from and why. Like the surfers who came before us, we saw everything in the Bear.'

Bear, on his mystical surfboard: 'It'll be a swell so big and strong it'll wipe clean everything that went before it. That's when this board'll be ridden.'

The narrator: 'Who knows where the wind comes from? Is it the breath of God? Who knows what really makes the clouds? Where do the great swells come from? And for what? Only that now was time and we had waited so long.'

> **'It'll be a swell so big and strong it'll wipe clean everything that went before it. That's when this board'll be ridden.'**

BILL & TED'S EXCELLENT ADVENTURE

US, 1989, CASTLE PREMIER/INTERSCOPE COMMUNICATIONS/SOISSON-MURPHEY PRODUCTIONS/DE LAURENTIS FILM PARTNERS, 89 MINS

D STEPHEN HEREK; **PR** SCOTT KROOPF, MICHAEL S. MURPHEY, JOE SOISSON; **SC** CHRIS MATHESON, ED SOLOMON; **PH** TIMOTHY SUHRSTEDT; **M** DAVID NEWMAN; **ED** LARRY BOCK, PATRICIA RAND

CAST KEANU REEVES (TED 'THEODORE' LOGAN), ALEX WINTER (BILL S. PRESTON), GEORGE CARLIN (RUFUS), TONY CAMILIERI (NAPOLEON), DAN SHOR (BILLY THE KID), TED STEEDMAN (SOCRATES), ROD LOOMIS (FREUD), AL LEONG (GENGHIS KHAN), JANE WIEDLIN (JOAN OF ARC), ROBERT V. BARRON (ABRAHAM LINCOLN), CLIFFORD DAVID (BEETHOVEN), HAL LANDON JR. (CAPTAIN LOGAN), BERNIE CASEY (MR RYAN), AMY STOCK-POYNTON (MISSY/MOM), J. PATRICK MCNAMARA (MR PRESTON), FRAZIER BAIN (DEACON), DIANE FRANKLIN (PRINCESS JOANNA), KIMBERLEY LA BELLE (PRINCESS ELIZABETH)

AND

BILL & TED'S BOGUS JOURNEY

US, 1991, COLUMBIA TRISTAR/ORION/NELSON ENTERTAINMENT, 93 MINS

D PETER HEWITT; **PR** SCOTT KROOPF; **SC** CHRIS MATHESON, ED SOLOMON; **PH** OLIVER WOOD; **M** DAVID NEWMAN; **ED** DAVID FINFER

CAST KEANU REEVES (TED 'THEODORE' LOGAN), ALEX WINTER (BILL S. PRESTON), WILLIAM SADLER (GRIM REAPER), JOSS ACKLAND (DE HOMOLUS), PAM GRIER (MS WARDROE), GEORGE CARLIN (RUFUS), AMY STOCK-POYNTON (MISSY), HAL LANDON JR. (CAPTAIN LOGAN), ANNETTE AZCUY (ELIZABETH), SARAH TRIGGER (JOANNA), CHEECHIE ROSS (COL. OATES), TAJ MAHAL (GATEKEEPER), J. PATRICK MCNAMARA (MR PRESTON)

THE STORIES Bill and Ted (alias rock band Wyld Stallyns) are supremely dim buddies about to flunk out of high school for failing history. Not only would this mean that Ted would be sent to military school but this separation of the two would change the course of history. So Rufus, a representative from the future that is shaped by the boys and their music, is sent back to San

31

Dimas, California, in 1988 to give them the time machine with which they can gather famous figures from the past so as to score an A+ in the following day's history presentation. This they do, collecting Napoleon, Socrates (pronounced So-crates throughout), Sigmund Freud (pronounced Frood), Beethoven, Joan of Arc and Genghis Khan. After some time-travel conundrums, a sequence in which the historical figures experience mall life and Napoleon goes to a waterworld, the greatest-ever oral history presentation is given and the future of the world ensured.

In the sequel, the future is once again threatened, this time by De Homolus who, resentful of the insidious influence of Bill and Ted, sends robot versions of them back in time to kill and discredit them. The androids take the time-travelling telephone box back to San Dimas, kill Bill and Ted, wreck their apartment, and threaten to kill their girlfriends, the medieval princesses, at the battle of the bands at which they will destroy the potential musical heritage of the Wyld Stallyns. Meanwhile the dead Bill and Ted are met by Death. They are

▲ BILL & TED'S BOGUS JOURNEY *The good, dead Bill and Ted briefly find they have a lot in common with their alter egos. Excellent.*

shown a glimpse of their own private hells, but get another shot at life after defeating the Grim Reaper in a series of contests. Returning to the present, with the help of Death, a couple of Martians and good robot versions of themselves, Bill and Ted defeat the bad robots, rescue the princesses and send their music around the world in a global broadcast.

'Party on, dude.'

THE FILMS Bill & Ted emerged at roughly the same time as Wayne & Garth and cover almost identical territory, being dorky teenage friends whose world views do not extend much beyond babes, cheesy TV and, most important of all, heavy rock. They share similar, sometimes identical jargon ('Excellent', 'Party on' , 'No way', 'Yes way' etc.) but what makes Bill & Ted cults and Wayne & Garth mainstream? Both Wayne's World films were more financially successful for a start, and this points at the smoother, more conventional approach of these projects. The Bill & Ted films are arguably funnier and more intelligent, certainly more complex and with a sharper satirical content. They are characters who think that Joan of Arc is Noah's wife and that her surname is 'Of Ark' in the same way that they address Billy the Kid as 'Mr The Kid'. They inhabit a world in which the meaning of life is to be found within the lyrics of a soft rock anthem. Somewhere not too deep below the surface is the suggestion that although the two are likeable and sympathetic, they represent the shallowness of modern American media, which is in danger of becoming the planet's lasting, dominant cultural legacy. Above all, the films succeed because they are funny in a quirky way, and they are well acted. Alex Winter simply looks very odd, but more important is the presence of Keanu Reeves. Reeves is a little like his generation's equivalent of John Travolta, who makes a succession of peculiar career choices, suggesting that he is unsure whether or not he wants to be mainstream. As a person, like Travolta, he projects an odd mixture of intuitive smartness and an ingenuousness that borders on the stupid. Not much is known of Alex Winter except that he has gone on to direct some pop videos (for heavy rock bands we hope) but you suspect, and even hope a little, that Keanu who has his own, reputedly lousy, rock band is in real life rather like Ted.

MEMORABLE MOMENTS
Excellent Adventure: The scenes in the mall in which Billy the Kid and Socrates try to chat up a couple of babes.
Bogus Journey: Death informs the recently deceased duo that they can return to life if they defeat him in a contest, so they challenge and beat him in games of Battleships, Cluedo, table football and Twister. This is a variation on Woody Allen's own variation on the Knight's game of chess against death in *The Seventh Seal* (1957). In Allen's short story *Death Knocks*, the protagonist challenges Death to a game of gin rummy and, as here, the Grim Reaper turns out to be a very bad loser.

KEY LINES
Excellent Adventure. The farewell of the future inspired by Bill & Ted's own brief awkward visit is: 'Be excellent to each other.' To which the response is: 'Party on, dude.'

Bill, reading Socrates: 'The only wisdom consists in knowing that you know nothing.'
Ted: 'That's us, dude.'

Bogus Journey:
Bad robot Ted on seeing a photograph of the princesses:
 'I've got a full-on robot chubby.'

▬

BLADE RUNNER – THE DIRECTOR'S CUT
US, 1982, THE LADD COMPANY, 112 MINS (ORIG, 117 MINS)
D *RIDLEY SCOTT;* **PR** *MICHAEL DEELEY;* **SC** *HAMPTON FANCHER, DAVID PEOPLES, BASED ON THE NOVEL* DO ANDROIDS DREAM OF ELECTRIC SHEEP? *BY PHILIP K. DICK;* **PH** *(COL, PANAVISION) JORDAN CRONENWETH;* **M** *VANGELIS;* **ART DIR** *DAVID SNYDER;* **ED** *TERRY RAWLINGS*

CAST *HARRISON FORD (DECKARD), RUTGER HAUER (BATTY), SEAN YOUNG (RACHAEL), EDWARD JAMES OLMOS (GAFF), M. EMMET WALSH (BRYANT), DARYL HANNAH (PRIS), WILLIAM SANDERSON (SEBASTIAN), BRION JAMES (LEON), JOE TURKEL (TYRELL), JOANNA CASSIDY (ZHORA), JAMES HONG (CHEW), MORGAN PAULL (HOLDEN), KEVIN THOMPSON (BEAR), JOHN EDWARD ALLEN (KAISER), HY PYKE (TAFFEY LEWIS)*

THE STORY Los Angeles, 2019. Deckard, a blade runner, is brought into the police department and forced out of retirement to kill four escaped androids, advanced Nexus 6 replicants: Leon, Roy Batty (their leader), Zhora and Pris. At the Tyrell corporation (where they were made), Deckard discovers that Tyrell's assistant, Rachael, is herself an android. Deckard finds some photographs and a single scale from a snakeskin in Leon's flat. Leon and Batty visit Chew, the designer of their eyes, who advises them to visit their maker, Tyrell, via the genetic designer, J. S. Sebastian. Pris befriends Sebastian. Deckard, sitting at his piano, dreams of a unicorn. By studying Leon's photographs and the scale, Deckard tracks down Zhora. He kills her, and his life is saved when Rachael kills Leon, who was about to kill him. Sebastian takes Batty to see Tyrell who tells him he can't extend his four-year life-span. Batty kills him. Deckard tracks Pris down to Sebastian's apartment and kills her. Batty returns and fights with Deckard. Climbing around the tops of the city's buildings, Batty saves Deckard's life before suddenly dying. Deckard returns to his apartment to escape with Rachael. On the way out he finds an origami figure, a unicorn, and, suddenly disturbed, leaves.

▲ *BLADE RUNNER Harrison Ford (Deckard) travels down LA's futuristic mean streets aiming to retire a bunch of replicants.*

THE FILM This was Ridley Scott's follow-up to the remarkable, and commercially successful *Alien* (1979). It was a box-office failure, but its brilliant creation of a dystopian future LA in which an old-fashioned, arcane, psychologically and philosophically complex *film noir* thriller is played out, made it an instant cult film. The *noir* style of the film was enhanced in the release version by the addition, against the wishes of Scott and Harrison Ford, of a hard-boiled and explicatory voice-over. This device was insisted on by a studio who feared that an audience would become lost in the opaque plot. In fact the story line is rather simple. Bounty hunter comes out of retirement to track down and kill four outlaws. This is overlaid by the love interest being unmasked herself as an android and so being added to the hit-list. There is also the understated suggestion that Deckard himself may be an android. Having accomplished his task, Deckard leaves with Rachael and, picking up Gaff's origami figure, he hears once again Gaff's parting words: 'It's too bad she won't live, but then again who does?' As he and Rachael escape (incidentally the scenery that they fly over is made up of out-takes from the opening sequence of Stanley Kubrick's *The Shining*, 1980), his voice-over explains that Gaff had been there but let

Rachael live. Deckard reassures the audience that Rachael, unlike the other androids, has no inbuilt death date, so he does-n't know how much time they have together, 'but who does?'

In *The Director's Cut*, the film is shorter than the original, and the narration has been removed. What has been restored is Deckard's dream of a unicorn which is crucial to the real end of the film. As Deckard picks up Gaff's origami unicorn and recalls his words, he is horrified because it confirms his suspicions. Gaff was there thinking of a unicorn, a recurring dream of Deckard's. The dream may even be borrowed from Gaff's own mind. After this bleak punchline there is no need for any further coda.

ODD/SALIENT FACTS The end of the chess game in which Sebastian, with help from Batty, defeats Tyrell, is inspired by the endgame of 'The Immortal Game' in which Adolf Andersson beat Lionel Kieseritzky in London in 1851. *Blade Runner* is based on a novel by Philip K. Dick, *Do Androids Dream of Electric Sheep?* The story is much altered although many of the names and characters remain (Roy Baty becomes Roy Batty) as do certain key details such as hover cars, videophones and androids being detected by empathy tests and the specific example of asking a question about boiled dog. Dick was a much married science-fiction visionary who, having consumed large quantities of LSD, believed that he was, for an extended period of time, in regular direct contact with God. He died in March 1982 shortly before the release of *Blade Runner*.

MEMORABLE MOMENTS Deckard's brief dream of the unicorn. The view of LA night life. Hover cars fly through the air, adverts are on massive electronic billboards and floating space craft, people mill around in the drizzle clutching umbrellas with luminous handles. The camera zooms in on a man sitting outside a garishly lit window reading a newspaper, and we catch a first glimpse of Deckard.

KEY LINES

Tyrell: 'What seems to be the problem?'
Batty: 'Death.'
Tyrell: 'Death, well, I'm afraid that's a little out of my league.'
Batty: 'I want more life, fucker!'

Batty: 'I've seen things you people wouldn't believe. Attack ships on fire off the shoulder of Orion. I watched C-beams glitter in the dark near the Tannhauser Gate. All those moments will be lost in time like tears in rain. Time to die.'

THE BLOB

US, 1958, PARAMOUNT/TONYLYN, 86 MINS

D IRVIN S. YEAWORTH; **PR** JACK H. HARRIS; **SC** THEODORE SIMONSON, KATE PHILLIPS, FROM AN ORIGINAL IDEA BY IRVINE H. HILLGATE; **PH** (COL) THOMAS SPALDING; **M** RALPH CARMICHAEL; **ED** ALFRED HILLMAN

CAST STEVEN MCQUEEN (STEVE ANDREWS), ANETA CORSEAUT (JANE MARTIN), EARL ROWE (LT. DAVE), OLIN HOWLIN (OLD MAN), STEVEN CHASE (DR T. HALLEN), JOHN BENSON (SGT. JIM BEST), GEORGE KARAS (OFFICER RITCHIE), ELBERT SMITH (HENRY MARTIN), VINCENT BARBI (GEORGE, THE CAFÉ OWNER), AUDREY METCALF (ELIZABETH MARTIN)

THE STORY It is night-time on the outskirts of a small town. Steve and Jane are necking in his car, watching the shooting stars, when they see one come really close. The meteorite lands and the red goo it contains attacks an old man. Steve and Jane nearly collide with him and take him to Dr Hallen for some tests. The doctor asks the two kids to drive up to the old man's place to see what they can find out. While Steve and Jane are away, the Blob consumes the old man, then a nurse and finally the doctor. When Steve returns he catches a glimpse of the doctor being attacked. He goes to the police, who don't believe him but are convinced that it is a juvenile prank. Meanwhile the Blob, on the loose, eats a car mechanic. Steve and Jane, out to find proof, notice that Steve's dad's shop is open in the middle of the night. They are menaced by the Blob, and when they take refuge in the store's deep-freeze room notice that the Blob retreats. Finally Steve and his buddies use the air-raid siren to alert the town's citizens. The Blob attacks a movie projectionist and finally engulfs the diner in which are Steve, Jane, Jane's brother, the café owner and his wife. As the monster slithers towards them in the basement, Steve attacks it with a carbon-dioxide extinguisher and once more it retreats. Just in time, the Blob is frozen and air-lifted to the Arctic.

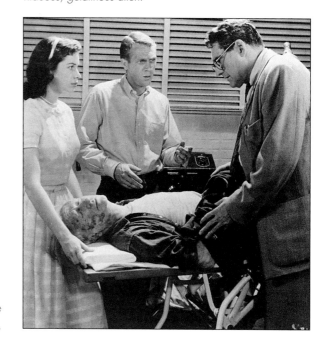

▼ **THE BLOB** *Steve McQueen, the oldest teenager in town, his girl and the local doctor examine the first victim of the hideous, gelatinous alien.*

THE FILM Several major stars and directors began their film careers in the mass of sci-fi and horror B-movies churned out in the 1950s and early '60s. Clint Eastwood featured as a lab technician in *Revenge of the Creature* (1955) and as one of the pilots zapping the vast spider with napalm in *Tarantula* (1955). Jack Nicholson's early credits include *The Little Shop of Horrors* (1961), *The Raven* (1962) and *The Terror* (1962). Early appearances of cinematic icons are always fascinating, but *The Blob* – whose opening was one of the key influences on *Alien* (1979) – not only features Steve McQueen's third screen role, and second as a star, but remains one of the great cheap horror films. The smallness of the budget is betrayed by the few special-effects sequences and their basicness when they do come, featuring an amorphous mass of red jelly. It is a horror film of enduring charm, and one which almost entirely neglects to be horrifying. McQueen's own, quiet, slow-burn persona is already formed here, but he is also clearly mimicking the screen techniques of his late contemporary, James Dean.

> 'It's the most horrible thing I've ever seen in my life.'

ODD/SALIENT FACTS The cult, camp status of the film is confirmed by its appearance in *Grease* (1978). The kitschy, unscary title song is an early Burt Bacharach composition, co-written with Mack David. Steve McQueen was offered profit points in the film in lieu of his $3,000 fee. He turned it down, and it went on to return $4,000,000 on a budget of $150,000. He was already on the way to stardom and later that year he made his first appearances on TV in *Wanted: Dead or Alive*. The film also sees the last time he was billed as Steven.

MEMORABLE MOMENTS *The Blob* marks an early use of the device, later used in *Targets* (1968) and *Scream 2* (1998) – with perhaps the earliest being Hitchcock's *Saboteur* (1942), of having a horror scene in a cinema showing a horror film. Here a late-night bill of cheap horror movies is interrupted when the Blob oozes through the vent in the projection box and absorbs the projectionist. The monster then seeps through the windows and vents into the auditorium. The effect of this is undermined by the bizarrely tame scenes of the terrified audience fleeing the cinema, with the extras either laughing or looking very obviously bored.

KEY LINES

The nurse, having thrown some acid over the Blob, to no avail: 'Doctor, nothing will stop it.'

Dave, on his superior officer's unfair dislike for Steve: 'Just because some kid smashes into his wife on the turnpike doesn't make it a crime to be 17.' (McQueen at 28, making an unconvincing 17-year-old.)

Dave: 'It's the most horrible thing I've ever seen in my life.'

Dave, on the radio to an Air Force officer: 'I think you should send us the biggest transport plane you have, and take this thing to the Arctic or somewhere and drop it where it'll never thaw out.'

… and with a prescient, ecologically minded final thought:
Dave: 'At least we've got it stopped.'
Steve: 'Yeah, as long as the Arctic stays cold.'

BLOW OUT

US, 1981, FILMWAYS/CINEMA 77/GERIA, 108 MINS
D BRIAN DE PALMA; **PR** PAUL DYLBERT; **SC** BRIAN DE PALMA;
PH (COL PANAVISION) VILMOS ZSIGMOND; **M** PINO DONAGGIO;
ED PAUL HIRSCH
CAST JOHN TRAVOLTA (JACK), NANCY ALLEN (SALLY), JOHN LITHGOW (BURKE), DENNIS FRANZ (MANNY KARP), PETER BOWDEN (SAM), CURT MAY (DONAHUE), JOHN AQUINO (DETECTIVE MACKEY), JOHN MCMARTIN (LAWRENCE HENRY), DEBORAH EVERTON (HOOKER)

THE STORY Jack Terry is a movie sound man who is out one night gathering new effects for his library. As he is recording, a passing car suffers a blow-out and plunges into the river running alongside the road. Jack rescues Sally from the back of the car, but the driver, senator MacRyan, is killed. Convinced that the tyre was shot out, Jack studies the tape he made which confirms this, and further backs this up by matching it up with film made from the photographs of the accident taken by Manny Karp. Karp and Sally had been planning to blackmail the senator. Meanwhile, Burke who fired the shot, wanting to kill Sally to tie up the loose ends of the plot, accidentally kills the wrong

▲ *BLOW OUT* *John Travolta as sound man Jack, searching for the perfect scream and the truth behind a mysterious crash.*

woman and disguises this mistake by making it the first in a killing spree themed around Philadelphia's imminent Liberty Day celebrations. Burke poses as a TV reporter in order to get hold of the incriminating tape and kill Sally. Wired by Jack, Sally walks into the trap. Jack, who is trailing her, catches up too late to save her but does kill Burke. Jack dubs Sally's bloodcurdling death scream into the latest slasher movie he is working on.

THE FILM This flashy thriller managed to be a flop despite starring Travolta near the peak of his first period of stardom. De Palma, who started out as a satirical political film-maker before making a detour into the slasher genre, tosses everything into the mix. Inspired by Chappaquiddick and the Zapruder film as well as borrowing from several other

'It's a good scream.'

films, most obviously Antonioni's *Blow-Up* (1966), and Coppola's *The Conversation* (1974), De Palma steals from not one but two of his old movie buddies. The sudden appearance of the senator's head in the submerged car is a clear homage to the great shock moment in *Jaws* (1975). But De Palma's hero has always been Hitchcock, and he is barely able to make any film without quoting from the shower sequence in *Psycho* (1960), which he does here in the opening scene. Hitchcock always considered it a big mistake that the suspense sequence in *Sabotage* (1936) should end with the bomb going off, killing the boy. He understood that with this decision the film lost the audience's sympathy. De Palma rejoices in playing with unwritten narrative rules. He invented the shock second ending in *Carrie* (1976), repeated *Psycho*'s surprise killing off of the leading lady in *Dressed to Kill* and continually confounds audience's expectations. What effectively marginalizes *Blow*

Out is the decision to have a lengthy climactic pursuit end in the violent death of the film's co-star, all to provide a little punch-line. Despite some narrative laxity, it is a dazzling and dark film that, in its mixture of stunning camera work and nastiness, offers an effective look at the haphazardness of a nascent conspiracy.

ODD/SALIENT FACTS During the editing process two reels of footage from the Liberty Parade sequence were stolen and were never to be seen again. This meant that the scenes had to be reshot at a cost of $750,000. Vilmos Zsigmond was no longer available so for these reshoots he was replaced by his compatriot Laszlo Kovacs, who was the cinematographer on *Easy Rider* (1969) and *Five Easy Pieces* (1970). Like Hitchcock, De Palma bases his most famous cinematic predilection, in his case voyeurism, on a specific childhood incident. When he was a child his parents split up, his mother accusing his father of infidelity. The young De Palma spent several days stalking his dad with recording equipment, hoping to find evidence to confirm his mother's suspicions.

In the partly improvised restaurant sequence where Jack and Sally get to know one another, she asks him how he became a soundman. Jack explains: 'It all started in school. I was the kind of kid who fixed radios, made my own stereos, won all the science fairs. You know the type.' In 1998, responding to Mark Cousins's question about his early cinematic inspiration, De Palma recalls: 'I was more of a kind of computer nerd at high school, built computers, won science fairs.'

MEMORABLE MOMENTS Jack tells Sally about a traumatic incident from the time when he was investigating police corruption. There is a flashback to when he rigged up a wire on his colleague to trap a crooked police captain. He taped the device to the man's chest and waist and followed him in a car. In time there is strong static coming across the line. It transpires that the man is so nervous, he is sweating profusely and this is shorting the circuit and burning the man's stomach. Realizing the danger, Jack follows him into a garage toilet only to find him already dead, having been found out and hanged with remarkable alacrity.

KEY LINES

Jack's final assessment of Sally's audio legacy: 'It's a good scream.'

BLOW-UP
UK, 1966, MGM, 111 MINS

D MICHELANGELO ANTONIONI; **PR** CARLO PONTI; **SC** MICHELANGELO ANTONIONI, TONINO GUERRA, FROM A SHORT STORY BY JULIO CORTAZAR (ENGLISH DIALOGUE BY EDWARD BOND); **PH** (METROCOLOR) CARLO DI PALMA; **ED** FRANK CLARKE; **M** HERBIE HANCOCK

CAST DAVID HEMMINGS (THOMAS), VANESSA REDGRAVE (THE WOMAN IN THE PARK), RONAN O'RAHILLY (MAN IN THE PARK), PETER BOWLES (RON), SARAH MILES (PATRICIA), JOHN CASTLE (BILL, THE PAINTER), JANE BIRKIN AND GILLIAN HILLS (TEENAGE GIRLS AT STUDIO), VERUSHKA (FIRST MODEL), HARRY HUTCHINSON (MAN AT ANTIQUES SHOP)

THE STORY Early on a Saturday morning Thomas, a baby-faced fashion photographer, leaves a London doss-house where he has been posing as a tramp to gather pictures for a book. Returning to his studio in his Rolls-Royce convertible, he conducts a fashion shoot, visits the abstract painter who works next door, and drives to a suburban antiques shop he's thinking of buying. Killing time before the owner returns, he walks into a park and takes some photographs of a young woman he sees embracing a middle-aged man. The woman demands that he gives her the negatives, but he refuses and, meeting his manager Ron for lunch, he decides that the peaceful park pictures would be the perfect closing images for his gritty book. The woman tracks him to his studio and after she's attempted to seduce him, he gives her a false roll of film. Developing the pictures and blowing up certain features, Thomas comes to believe that, far from an idyllic scene, he has recorded a killing. He goes back to the park after dark and discovers the man's corpse, but returning home he finds the blow-ups and negatives have been stolen. Thomas seeks help from Ron, who's stoned at a party and unable to assist. Next morning he visits the park again but the body is no longer there. Some students wearing clowns' make-up, first seen at the opening of the film, turn up and two of them begin to mime a game on the park's tennis court. When the

> 'I've gone off London this week. It doesn't do anything for me.'

▲ *BLOW-UP David Hemmings (Thomas) finds there is more in the park than meets the eye when he snaps Vanessa Redgrave at play.*

non-existent ball is struck out of the court Thomas throws it back and walks away.

THE FILM A mystery without a solution, a paranoid thriller made in Britain by Italians and based on a story set in Paris by an Argentinian, *Blow-Up* is one of the great movies about the illusory nature of reality, alienation and existential dread. This characteristic Antonioni movie, his first full-length work in English, has always divided audiences into those who think it pretentious tosh and those who love even its most portentous moments. Antonioni's combination of fastidious Marxist contempt for contemporary society and a fascination with fashion, eroticism and the high life found a happy focus in the shallow world of Swinging London, which for a few years in the mid-1960s was a centre of international attention. One of the dominant social heroes of the time was the classless photographer – Armstrong Jones, Bailey, Duffy et al. – the cool observer whose camera is

the extension of his eye, played here by an iconic figure of the period, David Hemmings. Two other icons of the time, Vanessa Redgrave and Sarah Miles, the one upper-class, the other lower, are on hand. What makes *Blow-Up* survive where most of the other Swinging London films (e.g. *A Hard Day's Night*, *Darling*, *Morgan*) seem extremely dated, is the stylized quality (including the painting red of whole suburban streets) and the discreet use of Herbie Hancock's jazz score.

ODD/SALIENT FACTS Despite the customary spelling of the title as *Blow-Up*, the print itself at the beginning and end bears the title BLOWUP. The enormous neon sign that provides the light source for the night scene in the park was created by designer Assheton Gorton and has no meaning, though if it reads TOA (rather than FOA) it might come from Antonioni's name. The street number of Thomas's studio – 39 – clearly alludes to Hitchcock and the MacGuffin of the traditional thriller.

MEMORABLE MOMENTS Thomas's first sight of the couple in the park.

The developing, printing and enlargement of the roll of pictures from the park.

His frolic in the studio with the two provocative teenage 'dolly birds'.

The return to the park at night.

The mimed tennis match.

KEY LINES

Bill (on his paintings): 'They don't mean anything when I do them – just a mess. Afterwards I find something to hang on to – like that leg. Then it sorts itself out and adds up. It's like finding a clue in a detective story.'

Thomas (about his book): 'I've got something fab for the end – in a park. I just took them this morning. It's very beautiful, very still, the rest of the book will be pretty violent, so it's best to end like that.'

Thomas: 'I've gone off London this week. It doesn't do anything for me.'

THE BLUES BROTHERS★

US, 1980, UNIVERSAL, 133 MINS

D JOHN LANDIS; **PR** ROBERT K. WEISS; **SC** JOHN LANDIS; **PH** (COL) STEPHEN M. KATZ; **M** IRA NEWBORN, PLUS VARIOUS; **ED** GEORGE FOLSEY JR.

CAST JOHN BELUSHI (JOLIET JAKE), DAN AYKROYD (ELWOOD), KATHLEEN FREEMAN (SISTER MARY STIGMATA), CAB CALLOWAY (CURTIS), JAMES BROWN (REVEREND CLEOPHUS JAMES), CHAKA KHAN (CHOIR SOLOIST), CARRIE FISHER (MYSTERY WOMAN), HENRY GIBSON (HEAD NAZI), JOHN LEE HOOKER (STREET SLIM), ARETHA FRANKLIN (SOUL-FOOD CAFÉ OWNER), RAY CHARLES (RAY), STEVE CROPPER, DONALD 'DUCK' DUNN, MURPHY DUNNE, WILLIE HALL, TOM MALONE, LOU MARINI, MATT MURPHY (THE BAND)

THE STORY Elwood and his jailbird brother Jake vow to come up with the $5,000 in back taxes to save the orphanage where they were both raised. They reform the Blues Brothers Band, rounding up former members from a show band, a posh restaurant and a soul-food café. Elwood and Jake improvise a number of practice gigs, before the lucrative climactic reunion concert. All the time they are relentlessly pursued by an ever-expanding fleet of police cars, a vengeful ex-girlfriend and a group of neo-

Nazis. The payment is made in the nick of time but the trail of destruction leads Jake to be re-incarcerated, this time with the whole band in tow.

THE FILM *The Blues Brothers* is perhaps the ultimate 1980s film. It has the presence of that decade's most notoriously decadent Hollywood figure, John Belushi, who only enjoyed its first two years before his seedy, premature death. It is simultaneously an enormous vanity project for its director and two stars, and a film with a precise mission. It shares the sense of purpose that the brothers in the film adhere to with religious zeal – that is to restore the full gamut of black music to its deserved place at the centre of American cultural achievement. Even if it had not turned out to be fun in its own right – and it is hugely enjoyable – the film is genuinely worthwhile in this endeavour. In between scenes of exploding buildings, destroyed malls, insane car pile-ups, we are entertained with performances by several of the greatest singers in popular music. The brothers' childhood mentor, Curtis, is played by Cab Calloway who, after a brief early appearance, pops up again at the final concert to act as MC and perform his classic 'Minnie the Moocher'. When Jake has his epiphany, the inspirational reverend is James Brown. John Lee Hooker is a street singer, Ray Charles a music-shop owner, Aretha Franklin a café owner. Each gets to sing a knockout number, occasionally accompanied by some over-the-top choreography.

ODD/SALIENT FACTS John Landis has some strange habits as a director. In every one of his films he somehow sneaks in the line "See you next Wednesday" as a kind of lucky charm. Here we get to see it as an upcoming film advertised on a roadside billboard. He also has an unaccountable fondness for including other film directors in cameo roles. In *Spies Like Us*, a tent in the middle of the desert is occupied by several directors including Terry Gilliam and Costa-Gavras. In this film Frank Oz and Steven Spielberg have small roles. Any illusions that the band was just for fun and the singers were aware of their amateur status were dispelled by the commercial success that they achieved with their three albums, and the pompous, serious stance taken by Aykroyd in interviews. He has said of their musical philosophy: 'We were always a Chicago electrified urban blues band with the Memphis Stax movement.' The on-screen effects were not achieved without careful planning. The mall sequence came about only after a location scout had discovered a derelict mall. The effect of the endlessly falling car, carrying the two Nazis to their death, but not before a final declaration of love, was achieved by dropping it from a helicopter hovering over an empty building site in the middle of Chicago. It was only allowed to go ahead after the film-makers had verified the car's unairworthiness, i.e. that it would not suddenly take flight and land over an inhabited area. By the time *The Blues Brothers 2000* (1997) came to be made, nearly twenty years later, like many modern sequels it didn't add to, so much as rework, the original. It still has good musical numbers and many of the same performers. But it falls flat not because it lacks John Belushi, Cab Calloway and John Candy (all of whom had the good sense to die in the interim) but because the idea had already been fully realised in the first film. So the dismal failure of the sequel is in a sense a further tribute to the original.

MEMORABLE MOMENTS/ICONIC SCENES

All the star turns, chiefly perhaps Aretha Franklin's 'Think'.

The climactic chase which encapsulates the wilful extravagance of the venture with pile-ups involving an absurd number of police cars, ending with the brothers pursued by hundreds of extras.

KEY LINES

Elwood: 'We're on a mission from God.'

Just before embarking on the final leg of their mission.
Elwood: 'It's 106 miles to Chicago, we've got a full tank of gas, half a pack of cigarettes, it's dark and we're wearing sunglasses.'
Jake: 'Hit it.'

BRAZIL

UK, 1985, EMBASSY, 142 MINS

D *TERRY GILLIAM;* **PR** *ARNON MILCHAN;* **SC** *TERRY GILLIAM, TOM STOPPARD, CHARLES MCKEOWN;* **PH** *ROGER PRATT;* **M** *MICHAEL KAMEN;* **ED** *JULIAN DOYLE*

CAST *JONATHAN PRYCE (SAM LOWRY), ROBERT DE NIRO (HARRY TUTTLE), KATHERINE HELMOND (MRS IDA LOWRY), IAN HOLM (MR KURTZMANN), BOB HOSKINS (SPOOR), MICHAEL PALIN (JACK LINT), IAN RICHARDSON (MR WARREN), PETER VAUGHAN (MR HELPMANN), KIM GREIST (JILL LAYTON), JIM BROADBENT (DR JOFFE), BARBARA HICKS (MRS TERRAIN), CHARLES MCKEOWN (LIME), DERRICK O'CONNOR (DOWSER), KATHRYN POGSON (SHIRLEY), BRYAN PRINGLE (SPIRO), SHEILA REID (MRS BUTTLE)*

THE STORY It is Christmas, 8:49 p.m., some time in the twentieth century. The world is gripped by the fear of terrorism, and in an anonymous office a dead fly falls into a printer causing a printout to read Buttle instead of Tuttle. This leads to the arrest and death of an innocent man. Sam Lowry, a middle-management bureaucrat working in Records, finds out about this error and visits the man's widow. He has recurring dreams of flying and meeting a mysterious woman. The woman of his dreams, Jill, turns out to live in the apartment above the widow's. Involved in some suspicious, possibly terrorist activity, she escapes and Sam can't track her down. His wealthy mother wants to set Sam up with a dull girl and get him promoted to the Department of Information Retrieval. He eventually accepts the job when he discovers that it will enable him to trace his dream girl. Meanwhile his own flat is becoming the battle-ground for official heating engineers and the renegade Tuttle, and all the while the boundaries between reality and Sam's fantasies of battling various supernatural foes (a gigantic Samurai warrior, a brick monster) are becoming blurred. He finally meets Jill, but is soon arrested and strapped in a chair in the middle of an enormous domed building, awaiting torture from an old colleague. Rescued in the nick of time by a posse led by Tuttle, he flees and, about to realize his fantasy with Jill, finds himself back in the torture chair.

THE FILM *Brazil*, with its self-contained world of bureaucracy, grotesque plastic surgery, organic heating systems and shifting realities, was an expensive commercial flop. Depending on your point of view the film is either a breathtaking accomplishment, a fully realized masterpiece of visual imagination, with almost every shot interesting and extraordinary, or it is a madly indulgent folly, difficult to follow and lacking any story-line. The involvement of Tom Stoppard and the opening scene of a tiny event leading to grave consequences suggests that we are going to get a biting political satire on the dangers of state control and faceless, intransigent bureaucracy. This we partly do get but Gilliam is a director so obsessed with visuals and so indifferent to narrative that the film becomes a work of deliberate entropy.

The action occurs in a startlingly designed lo-tech dystopia, which looks like an idea of a possible future world projected from the England of the 1940s. The film's title comes from the popular forties song of that name and suggests both an idyllic and idealized escape that Sam and Jill so nearly achieve, and

also that the song itself may be an important trigger that inspires Sam's mind and so the events in the film. People watch Marx Brothers films (Sam's introduction into the story echoes that of Groucho's Rufus T. Firefly in *Duck Soup*) and B-Westerns on their televisions. As we get further into the story it becomes less and less linear. In the film's great moment when we and Sam finally find ourselves back in the torture dome, it is unclear whether it is merely the last twenty minutes that have taken place inside Sam's schizophrenic mind, or the entire film.

ODD/SALIENT FACTS With the structure of this film and Gilliam's direction of *The Twelve Monkeys*, his assertion that he has never even seen *La Jetée* seems incredible. The fatuousness of Hollywood studios is seen at its starkest in Universal's treatment of *Brazil*. What did they think they would achieve by shaving 17 minutes of the film's running time for its American release, other than an extra near-empty showing per day? This

▲ *BRAZIL Jonathan Pryce (Sam Lowry) escapes from the nightmare of reality through his dreams of flying.*

piece has come closer than any other on *Brazil* to end without once using the word Kafkaesque.

MEMORABLE MOMENTS The early scene of the raid on Tuttle's house is a device that Gilliam has used repeatedly – the notion of one world suddenly and without warning being invaded by another as in *Time Bandits*. It was one of the stock tricks of Monty Python to have the post-modern interruption of a sketch by a previous one and features in *Monty Python's The Meaning of Life* (1983) when the accompanying short bursts into the main feature.

With Sam's mind accelerating out of control following his escape, Tuttle, finally unmasked, is consumed by litter and then vanishes without a trace.

KEY LINES

Jack (explaining why Records is a dead-end job): 'It's impossible to get noticed.'

Sam: 'I know, wonderful, marvellous, perfect.'

Jack: 'See you, Jack.'

Sam: 'Give my regards to Alison and the twins.'

Jack: 'Triplets.'

Sam: 'Triplets? Gosh, how time flies.'

BREATHLESS (À BOUT DE SOUFFLE)

FRANCE, 1960, IMPÉRIA FILMS, SOCIÉTÉ NOUVELLE DE CINÉMA, 89 MINS

D JEAN-LUC GODARD; **PR** GEORGES DE BEAUREGARD; **SC** JEAN-LUC GODARD, FROM AN ORIGINAL TREATMENT BY FRANÇOIS TRUFFAUT; **PH** RAOUL COUTARD; **M** MARTIAL SOLAL FROM MOZART'S CLARINET CONCERTO; **ED** CÉCILE DECUGIS WITH LILA HERMAN

CAST JEAN SEBERG (PATRICIA FRANCHINI), JEAN-PAUL BELMONDO (MICHEL POICCARD, ALIAS LASZLO KOVACS), DANIEL BOULANGER (INSPECTOR VITAL), HENRI-JACQUES HUET (ANTONIO BERRUTTI), ROGER HANIN (CARL ZOMBACH), VAN DOUDE (VAN DOUDE), LILIANE ROBIN (LILIANE), MICHEL FAVRE (PLAIN-CLOTHES POLICEMAN), JEAN-PIERRE MELVILLE (PARVULESCO), JEAN-LUC GODARD (INFORMER)

THE STORY Michel, a small-time wheeler-dealer, is driving along in a stolen car, planning to pick up some money he is owed and head off to Italy, when he finds himself pursued by a policeman. He kills the cop and flees to Paris where he steals a little money from an old girlfriend. He meets up with a woman with whom he has had a brief fling, Patricia, who sells the New York Herald Tribune and dreams of becoming a journalist. He steals some money to buy her lunch and they go back to her apartment. There they make love and talk. All the time he is trying to get hold of the man who owes him money. The following day Patricia interviews a novelist and is approached by a policeman looking for Michel, who is trying to sell a stolen car. They meet up again and finally get hold of Michel's debtor. The following morning Patricia betrays him. Down on the street, as the police arrive, a friend throws Michel a gun, which he picks up from the floor. A policeman shoots him in the back. Michel runs along the street, collapses at a junction, and shortly after the police and Patricia reach him, he dies.

THE FILM This, Jean-Luc Godard's first feature film, after a series of experimental shorts, was one of the markers of the beginning of the French *nouvelle vague* and a minor revolution in film-making. Three of the figureheads of the movement were involved in the project: Godard, François Truffaut (who devised the story), and Claude Chabrol (who served as an artistic and technical advisor). The directors had variously edited and contributed to *Cahiers du Cinéma*, in which they championed great Hollywood directors such as Hawks and Hitchcock as auteurs. *À Bout de Souffle* is equally a homage to the Hollywood gangster film and a rejection of traditional narrative cinema. Michel, besotted with Humphrey Bogart, is an amoral figure, stealing money and cars on impulse. The style of the film is disjointed, with jump-cuts representing either the continuous passage of time or a sudden shift forward. It is a work that contains some of the cool elements that would later inspire Tarantino, acknowledging the cult status of the American *film noir* and the iconic status of Bogie. Godard is already playing with the relationship between cinema and reality. It is a film that announces its own artifice with its jarring time-shifts and the sudden appearance of the director at a crucial stage of the action. Godard appears in what is a Hitchcockian cameo, but also as a *deus ex machina*, the director as informant, stepping into the action to hasten the film's end.

'Two things are important in life. For men, women. For women, money.'

ODD/SALIENT FACTS The film marks one of the three highpoints in the career of Jean Seberg. She made her debut as a seventeen-year-old in the title role of Otto Preminger's *Saint Joan* (1957). Shifting between France and the US she scored another personal triumph in *Lilith* (1964), directed by Robert Rossen. She continued to find work but never matched these performances, became involved with the Black Panthers and suffered problems with her mental health. She died in 1979 of a drugs overdose, probably suicide, and her life became the subject of an ill-fated musical in the 1980s. The novelist Parvulesco is played by Jean-Pierre Melville, the director of *Les Enfants* terribles (1950) and *Bob le fambeur* (1955), and one of the heroes of the *nouvelle vague*.

MEMORABLE MOMENTS The almost perfunctory shooting of the policeman: he is seen approaching on his motorbike, then there is a close-up of Michel's gun; a gunshot; the policeman falls off the side of the road; then a long shot of Michel running across a field; then cut to the city.

The two-minute take, shortly before Michel is killed, as he and Patricia walk in circles around the apartment, occasionally talking over one another, pondering love and betrayal.

▼ *BREATHLESS Jean-Paul Belmondo and Jean Seberg enjoy some peace before their brief affair ends in betrayal and death.*

KEY LINES

Michel to Patricia: 'It's silly, but I love you. I wanted to see you, to see if I'd want to see you.'

Patricia: 'I don't know if I'm unhappy because I'm not free, or if I'm not free because I'm unhappy.'

Patricia: 'Are you afraid of getting old? I am.'

Parvulesco: 'Two things are important in life. For men, women. For women, money.'

Michel: 'I'm tired. I'm going to die.'

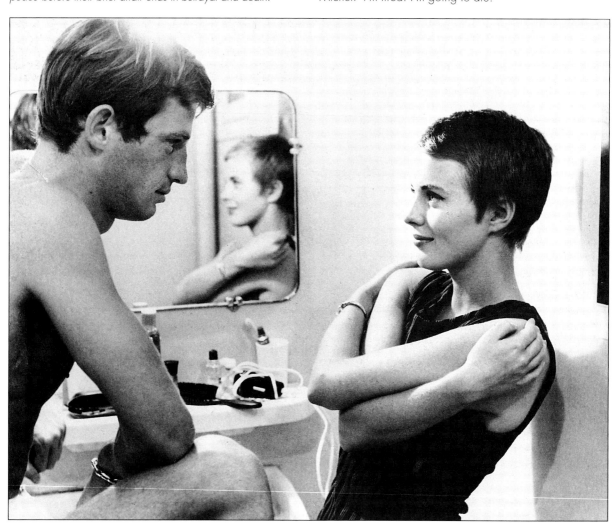

Parvulesco, asked what his ambition is: 'To become immortal, and then die.'

Michel's dying words: 'It's a bitch.' (The policeman tells her he said: 'You're a bitch.')

THE BRIBE

USA, 1949, MGM, 98 MINS

D *ROBERT Z. LEONARD;* **SC** *MARGUERITE ROBERTS (FROM A STORY BY FREDERICK NEBEL);* **PH** *(BW) JOSEPH RUTTENBERG;* **M** *MIKLOS ROZSA;* **ED** *GENE RUGGIERO*

CAST *ROBERT TAYLOR (RIGBY), AVA GARDNER (ELIZABETH HINTTEN), JOHN HODIAK (TUGWELL HINTTEN), CHARLES LAUGHTON (J. J. BEALER), VINCENT PRICE (CARWOOD)*

THE STORY Federal agent Rigby is dispatched to Carlota, main town of a small island off the coast of Latin America, to investigate a gang dealing in contraband war-surplus aero-engines. He falls in love with Elizabeth Hintten, wife of Tug Hintten, a drunken ex-US Air Force pilot with a bad heart who works for the gang. The racketeers' ringleader Carwood arranges for his obese henchman Bealer to offer Rigby a bribe and then attempts to murder him during a fishing expedition. Carwood has Bealer blackmail Elizabeth into drugging Rigby so the gang can escape, and subsequently kills the dying Hintten. But Rigby recovers in time to inform the mainland police and to kill Carwood, and while Carlota celebrates a fiesta, he's re-united with Elizabeth.

THE FILM In classic *noir* style, the chain-smoking Rigby (he has no Christian name) tells most of the story in flashbacks that begin as visions he sees on the rain-lashed window of his hotel room. His voiceover narration continues throughout as he battles with his conscience and tries to retain his honour in a world reeking of corruption. Laughton and Price are splendidly hammy villains and Gardner's nightclub singer is an innocent *femme fatale* in the manner of Rita Hayworth's Gilda.

ODD/SALIENT FACTS Robert Z. Leonard, prolific MGM contract director, is best known for musicals and the 1939 *Pride and Prejudice*. The carefully choreographed final gunfight illuminated by fireworks was shot several weeks after the production wrapped and was directed by Vincente Minnelli. Marguerite Roberts, one of MGM's leading scriptwriters, was

▲ *THE BRIBE Procine conspirator Charles Laughton sets up Robert Taylor, as femme fatale Ava Gardner looks on.*

blacklisted two years after *The Bribe*, and MGM removed her name from *Ivanhoe* (1952), another Robert Taylor film. She didn't work again until the 1960s when her credits, mostly on Westerns, included *True Grit*. Carl Reiner's *Dead Men Don't Wear Plaid* draws heavily on *The Bribe* and heads towards a climax on Carlota.

MEMORABLE MOMENTS Carwood accelerates the fishing-boat engine so that Rigby, strapped to his fishing rod, is pulled overboard by a hefty marlin and the young lad rescuing him is killed by a shark.

A passionate scene of Rigby and Elizabeth kissing on the beach after a moonlight swim (reminiscent of *The Postman Always Rings Twice* and *From Here to Eternity*).

The drugged Rigby deliberately trapping his hand in a door to wake himself up.

The climactic shoot-out between Carwood and Rigby staged in the middle of a spectacular firework display.

KEY LINES

Bealer: 'Who are you protecting? A bunch of taxpayers who'll get it in the neck anyway. Everyone's grafting nowadays, that's how people operate.'

Rigby: 'I never knew a crooked road could look so straight.'

Elizabeth: 'Your hand?'
Rigby: 'Yeah, it got caught in a broken promise.'

THE BRIDE OF FRANKENSTEIN

USA, 1935, UNIVERSAL STUDIOS, 75 MINS

D JAMES WHALE; **PR** CARL LAEMMLE JR; **SC** WILLIAM HURLBUT (ADAPTED BY HURLBUT AND JOHN L. BALDERSTON FROM THE NOVEL FRANKENSTEIN BY MARY SHELLEY; **PH** (BW) JOHN J. MESCALL; **M** FRANZ WAXMAN; **ED** TED KENT; **SP EFF** JOHN P. FULTON; MAKE-UP JACK PIERCE

CAST BORIS KARLOFF (THE MONSTER), COLIN CLIVE (BARON HENRY FRANKENSTEIN), VALERIE HOBSON (ELIZABETH), ERNEST THESIGER (DR PRETORIUS), ELSA LANCHESTER (MARY SHELLEY/THE BRIDE), GAVIN GORDON (LORD BYRON), DOUGLAS WALTON (P. B. SHELLEY), UNA O'CONNOR (MINNIE), E. E. CLIVE (BURGOMASTER), LUCIEN PRIVAL (ALBERT), O. P. HEGGIE (BLIND HERMIT), DWIGHT FRYE (KARL)

THE STORY One night as a storm lashes a castle in Switzerland, around the year 1816, Lord Byron, supported by his friend P. B. Shelley, urges Mary Shelley to spin out a sequel to *Frankenstein*. Her story, set nearly a century hence, sees Baron Frankenstein's evil mentor, Dr Pretorius, draw him back into the business of challenging God and creating life. The Monster, having survived the fire in the windmill (the conclusion of the 1931 *Frankenstein*), kills a married couple, is captured by villagers, escapes after killing some townspeople and learns to speak while living with a Blind Hermit. The Monster seeks a 'friend' and Pretorius uses him to blackmail Frankenstein. The Baron's wife, Elizabeth, is kidnapped, and Frankenstein agrees to create a bride for his Monster in exchange for her return. But when the Bride rejects her groom with shrieks of repulsion, the Monster turns on his creators. Bidding Frankenstein and his wife to flee from the laboratory, the Monster destroys the tower, taking his Bride and Pretorius with him.

▶ *THE BRIDE OF FRANKENSTEIN* Elsa Lanchester, the monster's bride, bridles at the sight of her mate.

THE FILM Along with *Godfather II*, this is the only sequel that is decisively superior to its predecessor. *Frankenstein* (1931) created the iconic version of Mary Shelley's monster as embodied by Boris Karloff. It is a seminal movie in which the plot creaks along with the doors of the baronial halls. But *The Bride* is a masterpiece that artfully combines high camp with gothic melodrama, pathos with low comedy, fastidiousness with casual violence, and it subversively challenges ideas about what is natural. Frankenstein's self-searching in the first movie has become full-blown neuroticism in the sequel; the humane values reside with the persecuted, misunderstood Monster and the

audience's sympathies go out to him. He is even identified with Christ when the villages lash him to a pole and raise him up as if to be crucified. Yet this Monster kills a dozen or more people in the course of the film, including an innocent husband and wife in the first two minutes, and the film was subjected to censorship everywhere and banned outright in several countries, including Sweden, Nazi Germany and Australia. Despite the excellent critical reception it was the last of Universal Studios, expensive, prestigious horror films, and for some years thereafter horror flicks were made on small budgets and the genre fell into disrepute.

The gothic castle with its sloping wall and vaulted ceilings is a place of fantasy and the vaguely Central-European setting has a timeless quality, the Baron and his wife dressing in 1930s clothes in a world lit by candles and oil-lamps and where transport is by horse-drawn carriages. The only specific date is on the tomb of the young woman whose corpse furnishes the Bride's body – 1899. The film's working title was *The Return of Frankenstein*, but despite the fact that Frankenstein's bride is really Elizabeth, Whale thought *The Bride of Frankstein* a more attractive title.

ODD/SALIENT FACTS James Whale was gay, as more obviously was Ernest Thesiger, and the picture has long been thought of as an allegory about outsiders, the weirdness of creation, and what we think of as natural. Both Colin Clive and cinematographer John J. Mescall were alcoholics and had to be constantly monitored during filming. This was one of nine films that the seventeen-year-old Valerie Hobson made during a two-year sojourn in Hollywood. Boris Karloff (who only played the monster three times) was credited simply as 'Karloff' in Universal pictures where he had star billing; his full name was used only when he was a supporting actor.

MEMORABLE MOMENTS The first shot of the Monster, up to his chest in water, emerging from the shadows under the burnt-out windmill.

Pretorius showing Frankenstein the mannikins of the king, queen, bishop, devil, ballerina and mermaid he has created in bottles.

The Monster being attracted by the Blind Hermit's violin playing.

The Bride beneath her shock of hair twitching and realizing she is alive.

KEY LINES

Maidservant announcing Dr Pretorius: 'He's a very queer-looking gentleman.'

Pretorius toasting partnership with Frankenstein: 'To a new world of gods and monsters.'

The Monster: 'I love dead, hate living.'

The Monster: 'She hates me, like others.'

BRING ME THE HEAD OF ALFREDO GARCIA

USA–MEXICO, 1974, UNITED ARTISTS/OPTIMUS PRODUCTIONS (HOLLYWOOD), ESTUDIOS CHURUBUSCO (MEXICO CITY), 112 MINS

D SAM PECKINPAH; **PR** MARTIN BAUM; **SC** GORDON DAWSON, SAM PECKINPAH (FROM A STORY BY PECKINPAH, FRANK KOWALSKI); **PH** (DE LUXE COL) ALEX PHILLIPS JR.; **ED** GARTH CRAVEN; **M** JERRY FIELDING

CAST WARREN OATES (BENNIE), ISELA VEGA (ELITA), GIG YOUNG (QUILL), ROBERT WEBBER (SAPPENSLY), HELMUT DANTINE (MAX), EMILIO FERNANDEZ (EL JEFE), DON LEVY (FRANK), JANINE MALDONADO (THERESA), KRIS KRISTOFFERSON (PACO), DONNY FRITTS (JOHN), JORGE RUSSEK (CUETO)

THE STORY Discovering that his daughter Theresa is pregnant, El Jefe, the rich, ruthless head of a feudal Mexican family, tortures her into confessing that the father is the womanizing Alfredo Garcia, then offers a million dollars to the person who brings him the miscreant's head. Max, head of an American business cartel, sets two gangsters, Quill and Sappensly, on Garcia's trail. They question Bennie, a penniless American pianist, who learns from his prostitute lover Elita that Garcia has been killed in a road accident and buried in his native village. Bennie sets off with a disgusted Elita to retrieve Garcia's head. He kills two bikers who attempt to rape Elita, but at the graveyard she is murdered and Bennie almost buried alive by two Mexicans who make off with the head. Bennie pursues and kills them, recovers the head, and has a shoot-out with Garcia's kinfolk, in which they and the double-crossing Quill and Sappensly end up dead. Bennie kills Max and his bodyguards, discovers El Jefe's identity and arrives at his hacienda as Theresa's son is being christened. He takes the reward, but doesn't hand over the head, kills El Jefe's lieutenants, and at Theresa's command shoots her father. Fleeing with Alfredo's head, Bennie is shot to pieces by the guards at the gate.

THE FILM Alfredo Garcia is Peckinpah's most complex, personal and controversial picture, a savage fable that never found a public following and divided critics into a large majority that hated it, and a small minority that loved it. It is located in the Mexico of Malcolm Lowry, Graham Greene and B. Traven (to

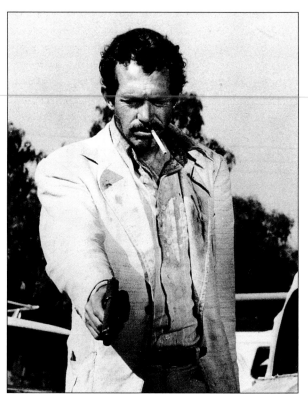

▲ BRING ME THE HEAD OF ALFREDO GARCIA Gun in hand, cigarette in mouth, Warren Oates (Bennie) dispenses some rough justice South of the Rio Grande.

whose Treasure of the Sierra Madre it alludes). It's an eclectic combination of existential quest, gothic tale, a political critique of US involvement in Latin America (the smooth capitalist reads Time with a Watergate cover story) and a love story about two losers challenging destiny. The ultimate terror resides in the central image of a low-life character transporting a decomposing head across Mexico for a reward. It's all drawn together by Peckinpah's grand vision of a doomed, dangerous world spiralling towards destruction, and two dozen or more killings are presented with Peckinpah's customary slow-motion lyricism. Warren Oates, a great character actor and member of the Peckinpah rep company, had top starring roles in only three movies – Two Lane Blacktop, Dillinger and Alfredo Garcia, all cult masterworks – and they will ensure him immortality.

> **'Nobody loses all the time.'**

ODD/SALIENT FACTS *Alfredo Garcia* was Peckinpah's challenge to Hollywood and Nixon's America: 'I'm an American resident. When Nixon was elected president, I said "I'm getting the fuck out, this cocksucker is going to ruin this country."' Pauline Kael said: 'I think Warren was imitating Sam in the picture because that was his idea of how to become a star.' Emilio Fernandez (1904–86), who plays El Jefe (and also appeared in Peckinpah's *Wild Bunch* and *Pat Garrett*) is the greatest figure in Mexican cinema as actor/writer/producer, and his bizarre career clearly appealed to Peckinpah. He was sentenced to twenty years in 1923 for revolutionary activities, jailed in the 1950s for shooting a film critic, and served time in 1976 for killing a troublesome farm labourer while on location. Helmut Dantine, the film's executive producer and chief American heavy, came to Hollywood in the late 1930s as an Austrian refugee, making memorable appearances in *Mrs Miniver* and *Casablanca*.

MEMORABLE MOMENTS Bennie in opaque shades at his bar piano.

Bennie, after a night with Elita, plucking crabs from his pubic hair and pouring tequila over his groin.

Bennie knocked out over Garcia's grave and waking to find himself buried beside his dead lover.

Bennie's intimate conversations with Alfredo Garcia's head in its burlap bag.

Bennie turning on El Jefe and his household.

KEY LINES

Bennie (to the head in the sack): 'Come on Al, we're going home.'

Bennie (to Elita): 'You pack the lunch – because we're going on a picnic, we're going to find the golden fleece, baby.'

Bennie: 'Listen, the church cuts off the feet, fingers and any other thing from a dead saint. What the hell. Alfredo's our saint, he's the saint of our money and I'm going to borrow a piece of him.'

Bennie (standing gun in hand, about to kill the man who murdered his lover): 'Why? Because it feels so goddam good.'

Bennie: 'Nobody loses all the time.'

Bennie (giving locket containing Garcia's photograph to Theresa): 'Listen, take this, you take care of the boy, I'll take care of the father.'

BRINGING UP BABY
US, 1938, RKO PICTURES, 102 MINS

D HOWARD HAWKS; **PR** CLIFF REID; **SC** DUDLEY NICHOLS, HAGAR WILDE, FROM A STORY BY HAGAR WILDE; **PH** (BW) RUSSELL METTY; **M** ROY WEBB; **ED** GEORGE HIVELY
CAST CARY GRANT (DAVID HUXLEY), KATHARINE HEPBURN (SUSAN VANCE), MAY ROBSON (AUNT ELIZABETH), CHARLES RUGGLES (MAJOR APPLEGATE), FRITZ FIELD (DR LEHMANN), GEORGE IRVING (ALEXANDER PEABODY), VIRGINIA WALKER (ALICE SWALLOW), BARRY FITZGERALD (ALOYSIUS GOGARTY), WALTER CATLETT (CONSTABLE SLOCUM), LEONA ROBERTS (HANNAH GOGARTY), TALA BIRRELL (MRS LEHMANN)

THE STORY David Huxley is a starchy paleontologist who is eagerly awaiting three significant events in his life: the arrival of the recently unearthed fossil of a brontosaurus's intercostal clavicle, the final bone in the enormous skeleton he is assembling in the Stuyvesant Museum of Natural History; the confirmation of a grant of $1 million for the museum; and his marriage the following day to his co-worker, the equally stiff Alice. While on the golf course trying to seal the grant from the donor's attorney, Mr Peabody, David has a fateful encounter with the eccentric Susan Vance. Their frantic adventures over the next several days result in a stolen golf ball, two stolen cars, a flattened top hat, ripped tails, a torn dress, the arrival of a tame leopard called Baby, the knocking unconscious of Mr Peabody, the eating of two swans valued at $150, the loss of the crucial bone, the arrival on the scene of a second wild and dangerous leopard, the incarceration of David, Susan, the inebriate gardener Gogarty, Susan's aunt Elizabeth and her aunt's big-game hunter gentleman friend, Major Applegate, before everything ends happily with the collapse of the brontosaurus skeleton.

THE FILM Howard Hawks, the man who made *Rio Bravo* (1957), which John Carpenter loosely reworked as *Assault on Precinct 13*, was arguably the most versatile director in the

49

history of Hollywood, achieving noted successes in every genre he essayed: war, musical, western, gangster, historical, comedy. The second of four films co-starring Grant and Hepburn – *Sylvia Scarlett* (1936), *Holiday* (1938) and *The Philadelphia Story* (1941) – this is one of the best of the screwball comedies. A variation on 'the comedy of remarriage' a sub-genre with which Grant had several successes, this is, like *Holiday*, a comedy of premarriage. Remarkably the film was a box-office flop. This financial underperformance further damaged Hepburn's reputation which had been seriously dented by her topping the Independent Theatre Owners Association list of performers judged 'box-office poison'. It is unaccountable as

▲ *Bringing up Baby* Cary Grant (in glasses), Katharine Hepburn (in the hat), and the crucial intercostal clavicle (in the box).

> '*Your golf ball! Your car! Is there anything in the world that doesn't belong to you.*'

Hepburn and Grant make an hilarious couple, each playing rather against type. Grant is a stuffy, intellectual nerd, equally repelled by and attracted to Hepburn's Susan, with her hare-brained schemes pursued with unshakeable upper-class confidence, throughout the action teetering on the brink of hysteria.

ODD/SALIENT FACTS Everyone involved in the project was petrified at the sight of Nissa, the leopard who played Baby, except Katharine Hepburn who claims to have found her playful. Olga Celeste, the animal's trainer told a reporter: 'If Miss Hepburn should ever decide to leave the screen, she could make a very good animal trainer.'

Peter Bogdanovich, the critic-briefly-turned-boy wonder director chose to remake and update *Bringing Up Baby* as his third feature film *What's Up Doc* (1971) in which the Hepburn and Grant roles were taken by Barbra Streisand and Ryan O'Neill. This was, along with the Coen Brothers' *The Hudsucker Proxy* (1994), the most successful of the modern attempts to recreate the screwball comedy.

Cary Grant was a bisexual icon of the golden age of Hollywood, whose affair with Randolph Scott endured as a friendship until Grant's death in 1986. In 1935 Grant, Hepburn and Howard Hughes all met one another for the first times and so began an odd troilistic relationship in which Grant and Hepburn became friends while both had on-off affairs with Hughes (see *Key lines* below).

MEMORABLE MOMENTS The meeting between Susan and David on the golf course predicts the way their relationship will progress. She is the eccentric, possibly insane predatory woman who falls almost instantly in love with David who is desperately clinging on to his dignity and eager to gain the grant to further his scientific work. The scene ends with Susan getting into David's car by mistake and crashing it in the parking lot (see *Key lines* below).

Grant and Hepburn performing a cross between a 'goose-step' and a pre-war lambada as David walks tightly behind Susan after her evening dress rips off, to conceal her underwear and protect her reputation.

KEY LINES

When David protests about Susan's crashing his car, she cries out: 'Your golf ball! Your car! Is there anything in the world that doesn't belong to you?'

Forced by circumstances and Susan's crazed plotting to wear a woman's flimsy fur-trimmed dressing gown, an extremely agitated David is confronted by a bewildered Aunt Elizabeth. She asks why he is dressed in this way. He responds: 'Because I just went gay all of a sudden.' The word 'gay' is applied here in the sense of giddy, but this possibly marks the first known use of it with its modern meaning.

THE BROOD

CANADA, 1979, LES PRODUCTIONS MUTUELLES/ELGIN INTERNATIONAL, 91 MINS

D DAVID CRONENBERG; **PR** CLAUDE HÉROUX; **SC** DAVID CRONENBERG; **PH** (COL) MARK IRWIN; **M** HOWARD SHORE; **ED** ALLAN COLLINS

CAST OLIVER REED (DR HAL RAGLAN), SAMANTHA EGGAR (NOLA CARVETH), ART HINDLE (FRANK CARVETH), CINDY HINDS (CANDICE CARVETH), HENRY BECKMAN (BARTON KELLY), NUALA FITZGERALD (JULIANA KELLY), SUSAN HOGAN (RUTH MAYER), MICHAEL MAGEE (INSPECTOR MRAZEK), JOSEPH SHAW (DR DESBOROUGH) GARY MCKEEHAN (MIKE TRELLAN)

THE STORY Dr Raglan runs the Somafree clinic in which he works on his theory of psychoplasmics, his study of the physical manifestations of mental illness. One of his patients is Nola Carveth who was abused as a child by her mother Juliana and has in turn abused her own daughter, Candice. When Candice returns from a visit to the clinic with a bruised back her father, Nola's estranged husband Frank becomes worried. Juliana, while looking after Candice, is attacked and killed in her kitchen by a bizarre-looking dwarf. Juliana's estranged husband Barton comes to town and is himself killed by one of these dwarfs. Candice's teacher, on whom Frank is keen, is killed by two of the dwarfs who abduct Candice. At Somafree Frank learns from

▼ *THE BROOD Candice Carveth (Cindy Hinds) is menaced by the brood – mutant dwarfs born of her mother's rage.*

Dr Raglan that the dwarves are the children of Nola's rage and take violent revenge against those who have angered her. Raglan goes to rescue Candice from the brood while Frank confronts Nola, who is in the process of giving birth to another of these creatures. The brood turn on Raglan and kill him and are attacking Candice when Frank strangles and kills Nola. Frank and Candice drive off to apparent safety when we see a close-up of two mysterious scars on Candice's arm.

THE FILM Gerald Scarfe has talked of people writing letters of sympathy for him, saying how awful it must be to have the thoughts in his head that he expresses in his art. But it functions partly as therapy for artist and viewer/audience. Similarly David Cronenberg channels into his work all his darkest thoughts on bodily mutations and the uncomfortable symbiosis of humans and technology. As he explains in *Cronenberg on Cronenberg* (Faber & Faber, 1992): 'It's saying, if you give the devil his due, and you admit to the possibilities of the most horrific things, then maybe they won't happen. It's what I do when I make movies. You're hoping it's going to stay on the screen and not come into your own life. That's little understood by critics. It's as though they think you want those things to happen.'

This is only partly true of *The Brood* because as Cronenberg admits, it is an autobiographical film based on the then-recent breakdown of his own marriage, his wife's attempts to gain custody of their daughter and his successful kidnapping of her, which led to his gaining sole custody. The film has all the characteristic Cronenberg touches. The acting is strange and muted with even Oliver Reed relatively underplaying. The action deals with mutation, the duality of mind and body, and takes place in strange modern institutions in aseptic, anonymous buildings. It concerns sinister experiments and theories that involve decay and death. It is in the genre that Cronenberg invented, 'body horror'. It combines fascinating and repulsive ideas, is cleanly photographed and is simultaneously compelling and disgusting.

ODD/SALIENT FACTS Cronenberg saw the project as a corrective to the saccharine picture of divorce presented by *Kramer vs. Kramer*. *The Brood* is one of Cronenberg's least funny films, but at least he was amusing if sincere when he said of it: 'I'm not being facetious when I say I think it's more realistic, even more authentic, than *Kramer*. I felt that bad. It was that horrible,

> **'Thirty seconds after you're born you have a past and sixty seconds after that you begin to lie about it.'**

that damaging.' Dr Raglan's theory of psychoplasmics is detailed in his book *The Shape of Rage* of which Cronenberg says: 'I'd love to write *The Shape of Rage*. I'm sure it would be a big bestseller.' This is one of many books within films such as *Beyond the Fragile Geometry of Space* in *Don't Look Now* (1973), *Baby Steps* in *What About Bob* (1991) and *The Poems of John Lillith* in *The Man With Two Brains* (1983).

MEMORABLE MOMENTS The murder of Candice's teacher by the two dwarfs using toy wooden hammers. Frank rushes in and, finding her body in a pool of dark, viscous blood, covers it with the first thing that comes to hand, a child's drawing.

Later when Frank has the final confrontation with Nola, she opens up her gown and Frank recoils in horror. She is producing another mutant child. She removes the body from its birth sack and licks the bloody mucus from its body, saying: 'No! I disgust you.' Cronenberg uses virtually the same line in a similar if more blatantly humorous context in *The Fly* (1986). There Seth (Jeff Goldblum) is in mid-mutation into a fly, and when he is visited by Veronica (Geena Davis) he vomits predigestive fluid on to the doughnut he is about to eat, before apologizing: 'I'm sorry. That was disgusting.'

KEY LINES

Juliana to Frank: 'Thirty seconds after you're born you have a past and sixty seconds after that you begin to lie about it.'

CALIFORNIA SPLIT
USA, 1974, COLUMBIA, 109 MINS
D ROBERT ALTMAN; **PR** AARON SPELLING, LEONARD GOLDBERG; **SC** JOSEPH WALSH; **PH** (METROCOLOR/PANAVISION) PAUL LOHMANN; **ED** LOU LOMBARDO
CAST ELLIOTT GOULD (CHARLIE WATERS), GEORGE SEGAL (BILL DENNY), ANN PRENTISS (BARBARA MILLER), GWEN WELLES (SUSAN PETERS), EDWARD WALSH (LEW), JOSEPH WALSH (SPARKIE), BERT REMSEN ('HELEN BROWN'), BARBARA LONDON (WOMAN ON BUS), BARBARA RUICK (RENO BARMAID), JAY FLETCHER (ROBBER), JEFF GOLDBLUM (LLOYD HARRIS), SIERRA BANDIT (WOMAN AT BAR), JOHN CONSIDINE (MAN AT BAR)

▲ CALIFORNIA SPLIT *Breezy bartender Barbara Ruich pours drinks for George Segal and Elliott Gould as they assess a Reno poker school.*

THE STORY Compulsive gamblers Charlie Waters and Billy Denny meet at a down-market Los Angeles poker casino where a disgruntled redneck loser, Lew, accuses them of cheating and fells Bill with a hefty punch. Later that night, after they have been drinking together in a bar, Bill and Charlie are attacked in a car park by Lew and two thugs, robbed of their winnings and badly beaten. (Later in the film Charlie spots Lew at a racetrack, follows him to the lavatory and after a retaliatory beating takes his money back.) The pair are arrested for being drunk and disorderly, and become inseparable friends. Charlie, a professional gambler, shares a house with two kookie prostitutes, the forceful Barbara and the slow, soulful Susan. Bill, an editor for a publisher of glossy magazines, is separated from his wife and owes several thousand dollars to Sparkie, his bookie. The two go to the races and prize fights together, sometimes taking Susan and Barbara. Faced with an ultimatum from

Sparkie, Bill sells most of his possessions (including his car) and sets out to clear his debts by making a killing in Reno. Charlie goes with him, becoming an equal partner, and as Charlie drinks, Bill remains determinedly sober, winning steadily at poker, blackjack, roulette and craps. He splits the $82,000 he's made with Charlie, but declares that this winning streak has robbed him of the desire to gamble and goes home.

THE FILM Everyone has a favourite Robert Altman movie, but hard-core cult fans usually end up voting this seemingly inconsequential buddy movie their favourite. It has the improvisional quality of the great modern jazz Altman heard in the Kansas City of his childhood, with wonderful verbal and visual rhythms. The tortured internalized Segal complements and challenges the confident, extrovert Gould. They play together like Parker and Gillespie and have never been better. In Poker you have to watch everywhere, and Altman uses the widescreen and eight-track stereo in a way that keeps you wondering what you should be watching, who you should be listening to. Two marvellous scenes that should focus on the dejected Bill (Segal) place him in the background while the foreground is occupied respectively by a whining bottomless waitress, her buttocks on a table dominating the left half of the screen, and a row between a foul-mouthed hooker and a client. One of the great gambling movies, the film is a meditation on the psychology of winning, losing, and playing games. Apart from being very funny, it comments laconically on the casual acceptance of violence in everyday American life and shows its painful aftermath.

ODD/SALIENT FACTS Jeff Goldblum (who made his screen debut as an uncredited mugger in Michael Winner's *Death Wish* (1974), got his first movie credit delivering a single line as George Segal's boss. *California Split* is dedicated 'For Barbara 1933–1973'. She's Barbara Ruick, the bubbly 1950s actress (she was Carrie in the 1956 film of *Carousel*), who died before the film was released.

MEMORABLE MOMENTS Bill staggering out of the poker casino on his knees after one terrible punch.

Bill and Charlie's first bet – naming the Seven Dwarfs.

Charlie amusing Bill with his one-armed piccolo-player routine.

Charlie with a mugger's gun at his head only agreeing to give him half of the $1460 he and Bill have won that day.

Charlie sticking toilet paper up his bleeding nostrils as he straddles Lew's recumbent body retrieving cash from his wallet.

Charlie going round the Reno poker table characterizing the players for Bill based on their appearance and body language – and winning the approval of the barmaid in a white stetson.

KEY LINES

Promotional film behind credits: 'Acquiring the skills for a game like poker is a social asset … Sit erect, maintain a quiet bearing, avoid nervous habits. During the game avoid conversation on matters not related to poker.'

Charlie: 'I feel like a winner, but I know I look like a loser.'

Bill: 'You get out of here. You're gonna kill the streak.'

Charlie: 'Do you always take a big win this hard?'
Bill: 'Charlie there was no special feeling.'

Bill: 'I have to go home.'
Charlie: 'Where do you think that is?'

CARRY ON CLEO

UK, 1965, ANGLO AMALGAMATED/INSIGNIA, 92 MINS
D GERALD THOMAS; **PR** PETER ROGERS; **SC** TALBOT ROTHWELL, FROM AN ORIGINAL IDEA BY WILLIAM SHAKESPEARE; **PH** (COL) ALAN HUME; **M** ERIC ROGERS; **ED** ARCHIE LUDSKI
CAST KENNETH WILLIAMS (JULIUS CAESAR), SID JAMES (MARK ANTHONY), KENNETH CONNOR (HENGIST POD), CHARLES HAWTREY (SENECA), JOAN SIMS (CALPURNIA), JIM DALE (HORSA), AMANDA BARRIE (CLEOPATRA), JULIE STEPHENS (GLORIA), SHEILA HANCOCK (SENNA POD), VICTOR MADDERN (SERGEANT MAJOR), JON PERTWEE (SOOTHSAYER), FRANCIS DE WOLFF (AGRIPPA), MICHAEL WARD (ARCHIMEDES), BRIAN OULTON (BRUTUS), TOM CLEGG (SOSAGES), TANYA BINNING (VIRGINIA), DAVID DAVENPORT (BILIUS), PETER GILMORE (GALLEY MASTER), WARREN MITCHELL (SPENCIUS), GERTAN KLAUBER (MARCUS), WANDA VENTHAM (PRETTY BIDDER), E. V. H. EMMETT (NARRATOR)

THE STORY Hengist Pod, the British inventor of the square wheel, and his neighbour Horsa are captured by the invading Roman army. Sold into slavery, the two escape by disguising themselves as Vestal Virgins and, with Hengist unconscious, Horsa foils a plot to assassinate Julius Caesar. Horsa flees and Hengist takes the credit, and a post as Caesar's bodyguard. Anthony travels to Egypt where he falls in love with Cleopatra and the two conspire against Caesar. Anthony returns to Rome and extends Cleopatra's invitation to visit her in Egypt. On the boat journey a second assassination attempt is foiled by Horsa, now an escaped galley slave, and again Hengist takes the credit. In Egypt Hengist and Horsa save Caesar's life one more time, but Caesar is finally killed in the senate. Hengist and Horsa return to Britain and Anthony and Cleopatra end up in a bath of ass's milk together.

THE FILM For over a quarter of a century, the *Carry On* films appeared at the rate of at least one a year and brought the humour of Donald McGill cartoons to celluloid life. It is a world where men are effete or lecherous, women either fat battleaxes or scrubbers. The productions were notorious for their cheapness, but *Carry On Cleo* is the one film that can be called relatively sumptuous because of its access to the Pinewood sets used for the lavish flop *Cleopatra* (1963). The film opens in characteristic *Carry On* form with credits rolling over simple Egyptian style cartoons including a phallic Cleopatra's Needle and two very breastlike pyramids, before the opening caption: 'Whilst the characters and events in this story are based on actual characters and events, certain liberties have been taken with Cleopatra.' The punch line is emphasized with a 'whooop' whistling sound effect lest the joke be missed. One of the series' better scripts with references to Churchill and Macmillan is of course stuffed with childish humour and the essential *doubles entendres*. Kenneth Williams was outspoken in his contempt for the intellectual depths of the films but nevertheless agreed to speak his first line, while suffering from a British cold: 'Ooh, I do feel queer.' Again it is hard to

▼ *CARRY ON CLEO Sid James (Mark Antony) seems disappointed when at last he gets a glimpse of Cleopatra's famous asp.*

see beyond the *single entendre* of the exchange between Williams (Caesar) and Hawtrey (Seneca): 'Beware the Ides of March.' Caesar: 'Oh, shut up, you silly old faggot.' The screenplay is a pretty basic mix of schoolboy jokes on Latin and history (an exhausted Sid James emerging from Cleopatra's bedchamber, sighing: 'Puer, o puer, o puer!') together with the more risqué material of sexual jokes (Caesar, about to meet Cleopatra: 'Tony, I am undone. My end is in sight.' Anthony: 'Well, you better do yourself up again quick. You can't meet her like that.') and lavatorial character names (Senna Pod). In spite or because of this parochial, typically English humour that marks the series, like that of the other icon of bawdy English humour, Benny Hill, the films have gained a cult status on American TV.

55

ODD/SALIENT FACTS Beneath the surface misanthropy of the series lay undercurrents of gloom, depression and misery. Williams and James disliked one another. James, a boozer and womaniser, would die on stage in 1976. Hawtrey was a depressive alcoholic who drank himself to death, but was at least relatively comfortable with his homosexuality. Williams was a deeply confused man, never at ease in his own skin, wanting to be recognized as an erudite man, a classical actor famous for and trapped by his awkward persona that was tailor-made for the *Carry On* films. He was himself obsessed with lavatorial humour and one of his japes was what he called 'the vag trick' in which he would flash people with his genitals tucked between his closed legs. His favourite joke on the set of *Carry On Cleo* was just a touch more conventional in that he liked to lift up his toga and expose himself to the cast and crew. The film's narration was recorded by E. V. H. Emmett, whose voice was instantly familiar to the film's original audience as that of Gaumont-British and Universal news.

> '**Of all the gin joints in all the towns in all the world, she walks into mine.**'

MEMORABLE MOMENTS Horsa and Hengist flee the slave market and seek refuge in the Palace of Vesta where only Vestal Virgins and eunuchs are allowed to enter. Seeing no option but to enter, Hengist says: 'Oh yeah, what have we got to lose?'

KEY LINES

The most famous line from all the Carry Ons *comes when Caesar's life is threatened by Bilius and the other guards. He also seeks refuge in the Palace of Vesta, where he exclaims:* 'Infamy! Infamy! They've all got it in for me.'

CASABLANCA

USA, 1943, Warner Brothers, 102 mins
D MICHAEL CURTIZ; **PR** HAL B. WALLIS; **SC** JULIUS J. EPSTEIN, PHILIP G. EPSTEIN, HOWARD KOCH (BASED ON THE UNPERFORMED PLAY EVERYONE COMES TO RICK'S BY MURRAY BURNETT AND JOAN ALLISON); **PH** ARTHUR EDESON; **M** MAX STEINER; **ED** OWEN MARKS
CAST HUMPHREY BOGART (RICK), INGRID BERGMAN (ILSA), PAUL HENREID (VICTOR LASZLO), CLAUDE RAINS (CAPTAIN LOUIS RENAULT), CONRAD VEIDT (MAJOR STRASSER), SYDNEY GREENSTREET (SEÑOR FERRARI), PETER LORRE (UGARTE), S. Z. SAKALL (CARL), MADELEINE LEBEAU (YVONNE), DOOLEY WILSON (SAM), MARCEL DALIO (CROUPIER), CURT BOIS (PICKPOCKET), HELMUT DANTINE (JAN BRANDEL)

THE STORY In 1941, after the German occupation of France and before the United States have entered the Second World War, Rick, an American adventurer, is running a nightclub in Casablanca, where European refugees get exit visas to take them via Lisbon to America. Rick has run guns in Abyssinia and fought in the Spanish Civil War, but professes neutrality when the German Major Strasser comes seeking the killer of two German couriers bearing letters of transit. Working with Strasser is Captain Renault, the cynical French prefect of police who represents Pétain's Vichy government. In fact Rick got the letters from the thief Ugarte before police shot him. Into this nest of intrigue comes charismatic resistance leader, Victor Laszlo, and his Norwegian wife Ilsa, who need exit visas for the States. Rick and Ilsa had an affair in Paris when she believed Victor had been killed by the Nazis. Discovering Victor was alive, she abandoned Rick, and black pianist Sam, without any explanation. Rick and Ilsa are still in love, and Ilsa is prepared to do anything to get Victor a permit. So Rick takes charge, ditches Ilsa gently for the greater cause and gets the Laszlos on the plane to Lisbon so that Victor can get to America and continue his resistance activities. Strasser tries to stop the plane, so Rick kills him. Renault and Rick walk off to join the Free French army in West Africa.

THE FILM Popular from the start, never out of distribution, *Casablanca* helped create the idea of the cult movie. Of all propaganda films made during the Second World War, this is the one that captures what the war was about – a conflict between democracy and totalitarianism – and expresses it through attractive characters whose style embodies their politics and morality. Rick and Ilsa sacrifice themselves to the general good, putting duty before love, which results in the immediate death of the rigid Nazi Strasser and the pricking of Renault's conscience. In a fascinating sexual transference, Ilsa and the cool, smug Victor Laszlo heading off across the Atlantic are replaced on screen, and in the audience's hearts, by the jocu-

▲ *CASABLANCA In one of the world's great gin joints, Rick, Louis, Victor and Ilsa prepare to ascend a hill of beans.*

lar, homo-erotic buddy relationship between Rick and Louis.

Casablanca turned Bogart into a major romantic star and confirmed the status of Ingrid Bergman. It was the perfect expression of the cosmopolitan, polyglot culture of Hollywood in its heyday with an expatriate cast drawn from all over Europe, no fake accents and great actors like Marcel Dalio, Peter Lorre and Curt Bois in walk-on roles. For the first time a black actor, Dooley Wilson, played the hero's sidekick without any explicit reference to the colour of his skin. The movie is an object lesson in perfection arising from confusion with endless discussion over the casting, the script being constantly rewritten and the actors not knowing how the film would end. The screenwriters made different contributions – the wit and irony came from the Epstein brothers, the radical politics from Howard Koch, and the sophisticated romance from the uncredited Casey Robinson.

ODD/SALIENT FACTS The release of the movie coincided with Operation Torch, the January 1943 allied invasion of Morocco and Tunisia and the secret meeting at Casablanca between Franklin Roosevelt and Winston Churchill. Producer Hal Wallis wrote and directed the final scene between Bogart and Rains, and when, on Oscar night in 1943, he began his stately walk to pick up the Award for Best Picture, the head of the studio, Jack Warner, darted ahead of him and grabbed the statuette. A few months later Wallis left Warner to set up his own unit at Paramount.

MEMORABLE MOMENTS Ilsa's entry into Rick's Café Américain.

Rick nodding to the band leader, permitting him to play 'La Marseillaise' (a homage to Jean Renoir's *La Grande Illusion*).

Ilsa asking Sam to play 'As Time Goes By'.

Rick's speech of abnegation at the airport.

Rick and Louis striding down the tarmac en route to political commitment.

KEY LINES

Rick: 'You'll excuse me gentlemen, your business is politics, mine is running a saloon.'

Rick: 'Of all the gin joints in all the towns in all the world, she walks into mine.'

Rick: 'Here's looking at you kid.'

Ilsa: 'Play it Sam, play "As Time Goes By".'

Rick: 'We'll always have Paris.'

Rick: 'The Germans wore grey, you wore blue.'

Rick: 'Ilsa, I'm no good at being noble but it doesn't take much to see that the problems of three little people don't amount to a hill of beans in this crazy world. Someday you'll understand that.'

Louis: 'Round up the usual suspects.'

Rick: 'Louis, I think this is the beginning of a beautiful friendship.'

As someone once said of *Hamlet*, it's just full of quotations.

▼ *UN CHIEN ANDALOU* The squirm-in-your-seat eye-opening, razor-edged shot that launched one of the most controversial films ever made.

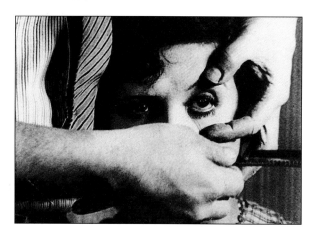

UN CHIEN ANDALOU ('THE ANDALUSIAN DOG')
FRANCE, 1929, 17 MINS

D LUIS BUÑUEL; **PR** LUIS BUÑUEL; **SC** LUIS BUÑUEL, SALVADOR DALÍ; **PH** (BW) ALBERT DUVERGER; **ED** LUIS BUÑUEL
CAST SIMONE MAREUIL (THE YOUNG WOMAN), PIERRE BATCHEFF (THE YOUNG MAN), JAIME MITRATVILLES, SALVADOR DALÍ, LUIS BUÑUEL

AND

L'AGE D'OR ('THE GOLDEN AGE')
FRANCE, 1930, 63 MINS

D LUIS BUÑUEL; **PR** LE VICOMTE DE NOAILLES; **SC** LUIS BUÑUEL, SALVADOR DALÍ; **PH** (BW) ALBERT DUVERGER; **ED** LUIS BUÑUEL; **M** SELECTIONS BY BUÑUEL FROM MENDELSSOHN, MOZART, BEETHOVEN, DEBUSSY, WAGNER, GEORGE VAN PARYS
CAST GASTON MODOT (THE MAN), LYA LYS (THE WOMAN), GERMAINE NOIZET (THE WOMAN'S MOTHER, THE MARQUESS OF X), BONAVENTURA IBAÑEZ (THE WOMAN'S FATHER, THE MARQUIS OF X), LIONEL SALEM (THE DUC DE BLANGIS), MAX ERNST (THE BANDIT LEADER)

THE STORIES Although they have narratives these films can be described shot by shot, but are beyond summary or synopsis. In the silent *Un Chien Andalou* a woman sees a man on a bicycle wearing a Dutch maid's headdress fall from his bike and apparently die. The man subsequently appears in her apartment and attempts to make love to her, before he is attacked by, and kills, his doppelgänger. The woman runs out and appears on a rocky beach to greet another man. There are no dialogue titles and in the brief final scenes, announced as 'In the Spring', the woman and the man from the beach are buried up to their waists, apparently blind and deaf.

After its prologue, a lecture on scorpions, *L'Age d'Or* shows some bandits on a seashore, apparently standing up against an invasion force of civic dignitaries, officers and church leaders. A young man and a beautiful woman make love in the mud and are separated by guards. He is appointed representative of the Assembly of Goodwill and is reunited with his lover at a party given by her aristocrat parents at their mansion outside Rome. There's a row with the Marquess, the Man and Woman make love in the garden, and the Man gets a phone call from the President of the Assembly of Goodwill, who commits suicide after accusing the Man of causing riots and massacres. The Man throws a burning tree, a bishop, plough and wooden giraffe through the window. The film ends with an allusion to the Marquis de Sade's *20 Days in Sodom*, with the Duke of Blangis, dressed as the biblical Christ, accompanied by three debauched aristocrats, and a wooden cross embellished by hanks of hair blowing in the breeze.

THE FILMS These movies belong together as the most abiding achievement of the cinematic avant-garde of the late 1920s, as collaborations between Buñuel and Dalí, and as the debut of one of the greatest of cult directors. The films were the first to be accepted by the leaders of the Surrealism movement as truly surreal and they have lost none of their power to shock, mystify, infuriate and offend. They are intended to be waking dreams that dip into the subconscious, and are not intended to make rational sense. Critics and historians invariably arrive at differing interpretations of individual scenes. In the opening sequence of *Un Chien Andalou*, one of the most disturbing in the cinema, a man (Buñuel himself) slices a woman's eye in half with a cut-throat razor. Buñuel himself said: To produce in the spectator a state which could permit the free association of ideas, it was necessary to produce a near-traumatic shock at the very beginning of the film; hence we began it with a shot of an eye being very efficiently cut open. The spectator enters into the cathartic state necessary to accept the subsequent events of the film.

ODD/SALIENT FACTS The small budget for *Un Chien Andalou* was provided by Buñuel's Spanish mother; the more expensive *L'Age d'Or* was financed by the French aristocrat Le Vicomte de Noailles and his wife. Right-wing groups wrecked the Paris cinema where *L'Age d'Or* was showing, and the police intervened preventing further screenings. Both films were subject to bans in most countries and were only seen at clubs or privately. When Dalí was reconciled to General Franco and the Catholic church in the 1940s, he dissociated himself from *L'Age d'Or*, claiming Buñuel had betrayed his ideas. The eye cut in the opening of *Un Chien Andalou* is that of a dead donkey. The film's title comes from Buñuel's first collection of poems and was his nickname for a group of aesthetic Spanish poets he disliked.

MEMORABLE MOMENTS Almost every scene, but especially: In *Un Chien Andalou*: the sliced eye; the hands coming through holes in the door holding a cocktail shaker; the books turning into pistols.

In *L'Age d'Or*: the civic dignatories raising their hats to the skeletons dressed in bishops' clothes; a maid emerging in flames from the kitchen and being ignored by the Count and Countess's guest; the Woman sucking the toe of the statue; the body of the suicide lying on the ceiling after he's shot himself.

▬

A CLOCKWORK ORANGE ★
UK, 1971, WARNER BROS, 136 MINS

D STANLEY KUBRICK; **PR** STANLEY KUBRICK; **SC** STANLEY KUBRICK, BASED ON THE NOVEL BY ANTHONY BURGESS; **PH** (COL) JOHN ALCOTT; **M** WALTER CARLOS PLUS VARIOUS; **ED** BILL BUTLER

CAST MALCOLM MCDOWELL (ALEX), PATRICK MAGEE (MR ALEXANDER), MICHAEL BATES (CHIEF GUARD), WARREN CLARKE (DIM), JOHN-CLIVE (STAGE ACTOR), ADRIENNE CORRI (MRS ALEXANDER), CARL DUERING (DR BRODSKY), PAUL FARRELL (TRAMP), CLIVE FRANCIS (LODGER), MICHAEL GOVER (PRISON GOVERNOR), MIRIAM KARLIN (CATLADY), JAMES MARCUS (GEORGIE), AUBREY MORRIS (DELTOID), GODFREY QUIGLEY (PRISON CHAPLAIN), SHEILA RAYNOR (MUM), MADGE RYAN (DR BRANOM), JOHN SAVIDENT (CONSPIRATOR), ANTHONY SHARP (MINISTER), PHILIP STONE (DAD), PAULINE TAYLOR (PSYCHIATRIST), MARGARET TYZACK (CONSPIRATOR), STEVEN BERKOFF (TOM), DAVID PROWSE (JULIAN)

THE STORY Alex and his droogs relish their violent sprees of raping and fighting. After a violent assault on a Catlady, Alex is betrayed by his droogs and arrested. In prison, he is selected for revolutionary, fast-acting corrective treatment. Over two weeks of aversion therapy, he is drugged to induce extreme sensations of nausea and is forced to watch scenes of violence in films, while listening to his beloved Beethoven. On release he is rejected by his parents, beaten up by a tramp he previously attacked, and then picked up by Dim and George, his droogs, now policemen, who beat him up. He arrives by chance at the home of Mr Alexander, whose wife died after the rape committed by Alex and his gang. When Alexander recognizes him, he and his friends, opponents of the government who sanctioned Alex's treatment, drug him, lock him in a garret room and pump Beethoven's music through the floor. Driven to despair Alex jumps out of the window. Recovering in hospital, he is treated to counter the effects of the aversion therapy, reconciled with his parents and set up with a soft job by the panicking government, while Alexander is condemned and imprisoned.

THE FILM Kubrick's obsessive approach to his work means that his films became not merely a major cinematic event, but a kind of cult film before even released. *A Clockwork Orange* explores the nature of humanity and argues that it is better to have the choice and choose badly than to do good with no option to do otherwise. In Britain after the film's release, there were cases of gangs dressing as the droogs and singing 'Singin' in the Rain' as they went about their business. The film was blamed by the judiciary and media, and in 1972, a year after its release, Kubrick withdrew it from distribution in Britain. It remains unknown whether he took this decision believing it the film to be dangerous to the public, or to himself – it was rumoured that he received threats of violence against his family if the film was not withdrawn. An already dark ambiguous fable has thus been lent the added frisson of forbidden fruit.

> *'Oh, bliss ... bliss and heaven. Oh, it was gorgeousness and gorgeosity made flesh.'*

ODD/SALIENT FACTS The idea for the book was partly inspired by Burgess and his wife's witnessing a riot between mods and rockers in Brighton, the same phenomenon that produced *Quadrophenia* (1979). Phil Daniels, the star of that film, later played the role of Alex in the London stage musical version of the story at the Barbican Theatre. The title is said to have come from a remark on a bus overheard by Burgess: 'Oh, he's as queer as a clockwork orange.' The Eighties group Heaven 17 took their name from one of the bands mentioned by Marty, the woman Alex chats up in the record shop: 'Who you getten, bratty? Goggly Gogol? Johnny Zhivago? The Heaven Seventeen?'

MEMORABLE MOMENTS Alex and his droogs in the opulent, futuristic house of the Alexanders, wearing masks with comical noses. Alex sings 'Singin' in the Rain' while performing a rhythmic assault on Mr Alexander and disrobing and raping his wife.

The sequence in which Alex and the two women have sex in his room. To the strains of the 'William Tell Overture' (it was originally to have been Mozart's 'Eine Kleine Nachtmusik') the three of them have a slapstick, high-speed orgy. They were filmed at two frames per second, so a sequence that took eight minutes to film takes up forty seconds of screen time.

The two images of Alex's face – in the opening frames in close-up with long fake lashes adorning his right eye, and when he is strapped in the chair at the Brodsky Institute, electrodes plugged into his brain and his eyes held open, forcing him to watch the violent images.

KEY LINES

Alex's opening voice-over: 'There was me, that is Alex, and my three droogs, that is Pete, Georgie, and Dim and we sat in the Korova milkbar trying to make up our rassoodocks what to do with the evening. The Korova milkbar sold milk-plus, milk plus vellocet or synthemesc or drencrom, which is what we were drinking. This would sharpen you up and make you ready for a bit of the old ultra-violence.'

Alex on Beethoven: 'Oh, bliss ... bliss and heaven. Oh, it was gorgeousness and gorgeosity made flesh. It was like a bird of rarest spun heaven metal, or like silvery wine flowing in a space ship, gravity all nonsense now. As I slooshied I knew such lovely pictures.'

Inspector: 'Violence makes violence.'

THE COMPANY OF WOLVES

UK, 1984, PALACE, 95 MINS

D NEIL JORDAN; **PR** CHRIS BROWN, STEVE WOOLLEY; **SC** ANGELA CARTER, NEIL JORDAN (FROM A STORY BY ANGELA CARTER); **PH** BRYAN LOFTUS; **M** GEORGE FENTON; **ED** RODNEY HOLLAND; **PR DES** ANTON FURST

CAST ANGELA LANSBURY (GRANNY), DAVID WARNER (FATHER), TUSSE SILBERG (MOTHER), SARAH PATTERSON (ROSALEEN), GEORGIA SLOW (ALICE), KATHRYN POGSON (BRIDE), STEPHEN REA (GROOM), MICHA BERGESE (HUNTSMAN), BRIAN GLOVER (AMOROUS BOY'S FATHER), TERENCE STAMP (PRINCE OF DARKNESS)

THE STORY Rosaleen, a pubescent girl, is asleep in a locked bedroom of a handsome country house when her mother and father return home and ask her elder sister to wake her. The family Alsatian scratches at the bedroom door and the sister knocks on it, but Rosaleen, wearing her sister's lipstick, dreams on, her dolls and toys entering into her dream. First she sees her elder

▲ *THE COMPANY OF WOLVES Lupine metamorphosis is the central motif of Angela Carter's feminist re-reading of* Little Red Riding Hood.

sister running through a fairy-tale forest pursued to her death by wolves. After attending her sister's funeral Rosaleen goes to stay with her bespectacled granny, who warns her about consorting with wolves, acquaints her with the folklore of werewolves, and tells her a story of a woman marrying a man who turns out to be a wolf. When Rosaleen goes into the woods, a wolf appears; her father and other villagers set a trap, and the wolf they kill turns into a man. Rosaleen tells her mother a story of a pregnant peasant girl who breaks in on her aristocratic lover's wedding feast and transforms the guests into wolves. Wearing her red shawl, Rosaleen encounters a handsome huntsman in the winter woods on the way to her Granny's house, and he bets her that with his compass he can get there before her. The huntsman, a werewolf, kills the grandmother, and is himself shot and tamed by Rosaleen, who tells him a story of a wounded she-wolf who became a human and after being treated with kindness by a priest, returned to the underworld. When her parents arrive at the grandmother's, Rosaleen herself appears to have become a wolf. As she stirs from sleep in her real bedroom, wolves appear to be leaping into the house.

'The worst kind of wolf is hairy on the inside.'

THE FILM The Irish short-story writer Neil Jordan, made his striking directorial debut with the Boorman-produced *Angel* (1982), the best movie up to then about the Ulster Troubles. Nothing he has since done has failed to astonish (even when being flatly conventional like the 1989 re-make of *We're No Angels* with a David Mamet script, and Robert DeNiro and

Demi Moore). *The Company of Wolves* is one of the great second films (to rank beside *The Magnificent Ambersons*, *Jaws* and *The Driver*). It has an uncompromising boldness in its approach to screen fantasy and has come as near as the screen ever did to capturing the violence, surrealism and moral force of Hans Christian Andersen and the Brothers Grimm. This is an English *Wizard of Oz* without the songs, the projection of a pubescent girl's anxieties about her sexuality and impending womanhood, and the sexual conduct of her parents, into the form of a dream. The film constructs and deconstructs traditional fairy stories, particularly 'Little Red Riding Hood', showing how such tales embody both truths and old wives' tales, and act as conduits of knowledge and counsel, and sources of experience. As the film progresses, Rosaleen grows and matures from a child who secretly wishes to kill her older sister to someone with an understanding of love and desire, who in her subconscious has come to recognize the beast in man, and that the handsome huntsman and the predatory wolf are the same person.

In addition to a fine cast, Jordan is especially endebted to two key collaborators. One is the novelist Angela Carter, a feminist with a leaning towards magic realism. The other is the production designer, Anton Furst, who conjured up the fairy-tale world of menace and wonder. He went on to work with Kubrick on *Full Metal Jacket* and with Tim Burton on *Batman*, for which he won an Oscar. Carter died of cancer in 1992 at the age of 52; Furst committed suicide in 1991 at the age of 47.

Odd/salient facts This was the second of Stephen Rea's six appearances in Jordan films.

Memorable moments/iconic scenes

The wolves surrounding the heroine's sister in the forest.

The Travelling Man coming back to his wife, turning into a wolf and being decapitated by her second husband.

Rosaleen climbing a tree to find a bird's nest with eggs that open to reveal small ceramic dolls.

Key lines

Granny: 'Never stray from the path, never eat a windfall apple, and never trust a man whose eyebrows meet.'

Granny: 'The worst kind of wolf is hairy on the inside.'

Rosaleen: 'I'm sorry, I never knew a wolf could cry. I'll tell you a story of a wounded wolf.'

THE COOK, THE THIEF, HIS WIFE, HER LOVER

UK/France, 1989, Palace/Allarts Cook/Erato Films, 124 mins

D Peter Greenaway; **PR** Kees Kasander; **SC** Peter Greenaway; **PH** (col) Sacha Vierny; **PR DES** Ben Van Os, Jan Roelfs; **COST** Jean Paul Gaultier; **M** Michael Nyman; **ED** John Wilson

CAST Richard Bohringer (Richard), Michael Gambon (Albert), Helen Mirren (Georgina), Alan Howard (Michael), Tim Roth (Mitchell), Liz Smith (Grace), Ciaran Hinds (Cory), Gary Olsen (Spangler), Ewan Stewart (Harris), Roger Ashton Griffith (Turpin), Ron Cook (Mews), Emer Gillespie (Patricia), Janet Henfrey (Alice), Annie Breeveley (Eden), Tony Alleff (Troy), Paul Russell (Pup), Alex Kingston (Adele), Ian Sears (Philippe), Willie Ross (Roy), Ian Dury (Fitch), Diane Langton (May Fitch), Prudence Oliver (Corette Fitch), Roger Lloyd Pack (Geoff), Bob Goodie (Starkie), Peter Rush (Melter)

The story Within the restaurant he owns, over several days, Albert holds court around the table with his wife Georgina, various cronies and rival gangsters, discussing food and sex. Georgina starts an affair with Michael, a regular of the restaurant. Albert finds out about the affair and goes berserk. Helped to escape by Richard, the cook, Michael and Georgina spend a brief idyll out in a book depository. Albert and his gang discover the hiding place and kill Michael, by force-feeding him with a book. Georgina begs Richard to cook Michael and serve him up to Albert. So, a procession of people who have been injured and humiliated by Albert brings in the cooked body of Michael. Georgina forces Albert at gunpoint to eat. He takes a mouthful, then she shoots him dead.

The film This film is a distillation of all Greenaway's obsessions and all the recurrent themes in his work, chiefly art, decay and death. Albert is a violent philistine, unable to pronounce the names of the dishes served in his own restaurant. Treating the place like his personal salon, he beats, bullies and humiliates all around him, and expounds crudely on a variety of subjects. A deeply vulgar man, he is also the alter ego of the director, as he shares his thoughts on the vital connections between sex, food and excrement. The film is a mournful look at the fleeting nature of romantic love. Greenaway is obsessed with structure in his work. Here the story unfolds as a number of menus, over nine evenings from a Thursday to the following Friday. Perhaps Greenaway's central concern is his presentation of man as aspiring to order, beauty and understanding through the constructs of art, books, costume and architecture, while being frustrated and disgusted by the constraints and ugliness of the body and its functions. Tim Roth has spoken of how the only direction he received on the film was to move fractionally to one side or the other to enhance the symmetrical composition of the shot. This essay on food and sex, decay and death and art takes place on dazzling sound-stages. The gangsters are dressed in clothes designed by Jean Paul Gaultier in an echo of Frans Hals's painting of Dutch burghers, an enlarged

▼ THE COOK, THE THIEF, HIS WIFE, HER LOVER *(Foreground l-r) The lover (Alan Howard), the cook (Richard Bohringer), the wife (Helen Mirren), the thief (Michael Gambon) and his henchman (Tim Roth).*

reproduction of which hangs on the wall of the restaurant. It presents the notion that merely to patronize, and consume great art does not rid one of crassness and vulgarity. The arenas in which the action takes place are colour-coded: dark exteriors, green kitchen and storage area, red restaurant and white lavatories. In the impressive, fake pans between these rooms, Georgina's costumes change colour to fit the surroundings.

ODD/SALIENT FACTS The four central characters are named after the actors that Greenaway originally had in mind to play them: Albert Finney; Georgina Hale; he had initially wanted Michael Gambon to play the sensitive bibliophile; Richard Bohringer was Greenaway's first choice for the cook. Sacha Vierny, Greenaway's regular cinematographer since *A Zed and Two Noughts* (1985), has worked with Chris Marker and Alan Resnais, notably on *Last Year at Marienbad* (1961), Greenaway's favourite film.

MEMORABLE MOMENTS The final sequence. It is Friday, and Georgina heads a procession bringing the veiled, cooked body

of Michael into the restaurant. When the glazed, steaming cadaver on a bed of vegetables is revealed, Albert is stunned. At gunpoint, he takes a forkful and vomits. Georgina encourages him, he eats. She says: 'Bon appetit. It's French.' She shoots him and concludes, 'Cannibal.' The curtains close.

KEY LINES

Albert: 'What you've gotta realize is that a clever cook puts unlikely things together, like duck and orange, like pineapple and ham. It's called artistry. You know, I'm an artist in the way I combine my business and my pleasure. Money's my business, eating's my pleasure, and Georgie's my pleasure too. Though in a more private kind of way than stuffing the face and feeding the sewers. Though the pleasures are related, because the naughty bits and the dirty bits are so close together that it just goes to show how eating and sex are related.'

Georgina: 'If you don't read does that make you safe?'
Michael: 'Only from bad books.'

Albert: 'How do I care what he ate? It all comes out as shit in the end.'

Richard: 'Eating black food is like eating death.'

> ' How do I care what he ate? It all comes out as shit in the end.'

CUL-DE-SAC

UK, 1966, COMPTON-TEKLI, 111 MINS

D *ROMAN POLANSKI;* **PR** *GENE GUTOWSKI;* **SC** *POLANSKI AND GÉRARD BRACH;* **PH** *(BW) GILBERT TAYLOR;* **M** *KRZYSZTOF KOMEDA;* **ED** *ALASTAIR MCINTYRE*

CAST *DONALD PLEASENCE (GEORGE), FRANÇOISE DORLÉAC (TERESA), LIONEL STANDER (RICHARD), JACK MACGOWRAN (ALBERT), WILLIAM FRANKLYN (CECIL YORK), ROBERT DORNING (PHILIP FAIRWEATHER), MARIE KEANE (MARION FAIRWEATHER), IAIN QUARRIER (CHRISTOPHER), GEOFFREY SUMNER (CHRISTOPHER'S FATHER), RENEE HOUSTON (CHRISTOPHER'S MOTHER), JACQUELINE BISSET (JACKIE), TREVOR DELANEY (HORACE)*

THE STORY Two wounded, fugitive criminals are stranded on the causeway leading to a small island off the Northumberland Coast when their stolen car runs out of petrol. Richard, a boorish American, leaves his dying Irish comrade, Albert, in the car, and goes to the island's eleventh-century castle to call his boss, Mr Katelbach, for assistance, and takes prisoner its only occupants – the middle-aged retired businessman, George, made-up and dressed in a nightie by Teresa, his young wife. Richard has them push the stalled car up the flooded causeway to the house. When Albert dies they are made to dig a grave. George's oldest friend Philip drops in, meeting Teresa for the first time. He's accompanied by his wife and Horace, their obnoxious little boy, and a local couple, Cecil and his trendy girlfriend. Teresa pretends that Richard is a servant and gets him to serve lunch, and she flirts with Cecil. To drive away the guests George insults them and they leave after Horace has used Cecil's shotgun to smash a medieval stained-glass window in the room where Scott is said to have written Rob Roy. Teresa plays a vicious practical joke on the sleeping Richard inserting a lighted match between his toes and when he hits her she tells George he tried to kiss her. Giving George Cecil's gun, she provokes him into shooting Richard, who as he dies fires a Tommy gun, setting George's white Jaguar alight. Cecil returns to retrieve his shot-gun, Teresa drives off with him, and the bereft George sits on a rock in the sea, shouting the name of Agnes, his first wife.

THE FILM *Cul-de-Sac* was Polanski's third feature film, and like the Polish psychological drama, *Knife in the Water* (1962), and the British psychiatric horror story, *Repulsion* (1965), the characters play deadly games with a cruelty ranging from the mischievous to the calculatedly sadistic. As black comedy, or comedy of menace, the film has affinities with Beckett, Albee and Pinter; Richard and Albert descend on the disturbed, fugitive George like Goldberg and McCann pursuing Stanley in *The Birthday Party*. Pleasence, before he became a cult movie actor, was a celebrated stage exponent of Pinter, while MacGowran was one of Samuel Beckett's favourite actors. *Cul-de-sac* is a wonderfully perverse picture – it is Richard's persecution and humiliation of his reluctant host that releases George from his inhibitions, enabling him to insult his so-called friends, and killing Richard empowers him to triumph over his

A CLOCKWORK ORANGE

Alex (Malcolm McDowell) in the Korova Milkbar, viddies the audience and enjoys a quick glass of milk plus vellocet in preparation for setting out with his droogs for a bit of the old ultra-violence.

Big Wednesday

Above: Tubular beaux Leroy (Gary Busey), Jack (William Katt) and Matt (Jan Michael-Vincent) head off to face the awe-inspiring wave of the title.

Apocalypse Now

Left: Willard's predecessor Colby (Scott Glenn) and his band have gone native and stand in front of a plinth bearing their motto and the film's title.

THE BLUES BROTHERS

*Joliet Jake (John Belushi) and Elwood (Dan Aykroyd) are on a
mission from God to re-form their band, save an orphanage
and restore the reputation of black American music.*

GET CARTER

LEFT: London gangster Jack Carter (Michael Caine) brings hot coals to Newcastle when he returns to avenge his brother's death at the hands of local thugs.

EASY RIDER

BELOW: Billy (Dennis Hopper), Wyatt (Peter Fonda) and alcoholic lawyer George Hanson (Jack Nicholson) are yet to discover that they blew it.

JAWS

Hooper (Richard Dreyfuss), Brody (Roy Scheider) and Quint
(Robert Shaw) finally hook Bruce and discover that they
really do need a bigger boat.

MAD MAX II

ABOVE: Max the 'Road Warrior' (Mel Gibson) finds himself at the sharp end of the protracted fuel war in George Miller's designer-dystopian future.

THE KING OF COMEDY

RIGHT: Sociopathic stand-up Rupert Pupkin (Robert De Niro) accepts the adulation of the crowd as he is crowned the new 'King of Comedy'.

MONTY PYTHON'S LIFE OF BRIAN

A lisping Pontius Pilate (Michael Palin) introduces Biggus Dickus (Graham Chapman) to the Jerusalem mob as 'the highest wanking Woman'.

▲ *CUL-DE-SAC The shaven-headed Pleasence, alone and at the end of his tether, as day breaks on his remote Northumberland retreat.*

treacherous wife. The film has its roots in both Polanski's, and his co-author Gérard Brach's, wishing to exact dramatic revenge on the women who had recently deserted them when they wrote the first draft in 1963.

ODD/SALIENT FACTS Polanski and Brach wrote the exploitation horror flick *Repulsion* in 17 days, hoping that if it succeeded, the producers, Compton-Tekli, would finance *Cul-de-sac*, which they'd been trying to set up in France for two years. *Repulsion* won the Silver Bear in Berlin and was a big box-office success; *Cul-de-Sac* won the Golden Bear the following year but was liked by only a small number of critics and puzzled most audiences. For *Repulsion*, Polanski, Brach and the producer, Gene Gutowski, split $5,000. The superbly atmospheric monochrome photography is by the British cinematographer Gilbert Taylor, who had just lit

> **'Here we are, in the shit.'**

Dr Strangelove, A Hard Day's Night and *Repulsion*, and went on to light Hitchcock's *Frenzy* and *Star Wars*. Originally intended to be made in Britanny (as *If Katelbach Comes*), the picture was shot entirely on location at Holy Island (aka Lindisfarne) three miles off the Northumbrian coast. Two hundred actresses were tested for the role of Teresa before Catherine Deneuve, the star of *Repulsion*, recommended her sister, Françoise Dorléac, for the part. Dorléac was killed the

following year in a car crash. The gravel-voiced Lionel Stander, an established Hollywood character actor, was blacklisted after appearing before the House Un-American Activities Committee in the early 1950s and didn't work again in Hollywood for nearly twenty years.

MEMORABLE MOMENTS Françoise Dorléac first seen frolicking half-naked in the sand dunes with the teenage son of her husband's friends.

The dying Albert looking through his pebble-spectacles at the sea water rising around his car.

The virtuoso eight-minute take on the beach as Richard and

George talk, Teresa goes down to bathe and returns, a plane flies over and Richard fires off his gun.

KEY LINES

Albert: 'Here we are, in the shit.'

Richard: 'You've got to be out of your skull to live in a place like this.'

George, to his guests: 'Take your bloody filthy insinuations and get out of my fortress.'

CUTTER'S WAY

US, 1981, UNITED ARTISTS/GURIAN ENTERTAINMENT, 109 MINS

D IVAN PASSER; **PR** PAUL R. GURIAN; **SC** JEFFREY ALAN FISKIN (FROM THE NOVEL CUTTER AND BONE BY NEWTON THORNBURG); **PH** (TECHNICOLOR) JORDAN CRONENWETH; **M** JACK NITZSCHE; **ED** CAROLINE FERRIOL

CAST JEFF BRIDGES (RICHARD BONE), JOHN HEARD (ALEX CUTTER), LISA EICHHORN (MAUREEN 'MO' CUTTER), ANN DUSENBERRY (VALERIE DURAN), STEPHEN ELLIOTT (J. J. CORD), PATRICIA DONAHUE (MRS CORD), ARTHUR ROSENBERG (GEORGE SWANSON), NINA VAN PALLANDT (WOMAN IN HOTEL), JON TERRY (POLICE CAPTAIN)

THE STORY Upper-class beach bum, boat salesman and part-time gigolo Richard Bone is sitting in his car in a deserted side street in Santa Barbara, when the driver of a limousine deposits something in a trash can and speeds off. Next morning garbage collectors discover the mutilated body of a seventeen-year-old girl. Bone cannot identify the man in the alleyway and is arrested as a suspect. The following day he's at the Fiesta parade with his friend Alex Cutter, a one-eyed, one-legged, one-armed Vietnam veteran, and Cutter's alcoholic wife, Mo. As a middle-aged man rides by on a white stallion, Bone recognizes him as the man by the trash can. This man is J. J. Cord, an oil tycoon and member of a prominent family. The embittered, aggressive, hard-drinking Cutter becomes obsessed with building up a case against Cord. It gives a purpose to his life, and he draws the victim's sister Valerie into his scheme, as well as a reluctant Bone, though his wife Mo opposes it. Bone goes to bed with the vulnerable, rejected Mo, but then slips

away and spends the rest of the night on a boat. Next morning the Cutters' house is found burnt down with Mo inside. Cutter believes it was Cord's doing and that the intended victim was Bone, and he persuades Bone to join him in gatecrashing a party at Cord's mansion. Security men drag Bone into Cord's study, Cutter mounts a white stallion in the stables, and is fatally wounded by guards as he rides towards the house. Crashing through the window he says 'It was him,' and dies. 'It was you,' Bone says. 'What if it were?' says Cord, as he puts his dark glasses on. Raising the gun, still clutched in Cutter's hand, Bone fires at Cord as the screen fades to black.

THE FILM *Cutter's Way* is one of the most powerful works from a cycle of post-Vietnam pictures where the moral poison of the war is seen working itself into the body politic through the failure of America to assimilate returning veterans. The film is also a fine example of the paranoid political thriller of a kind made by Frankenheimer and Pakula. The cinematographer Jordan Cornenweth gives the picture a sickly hue; the characters seem afflicted by some malaise; little is explained about their backgrounds; the plot remains unresolved.

Ivan Passer made his name in the 1960s with the Czech New Wave, writing screenplays for Milos Forman and like Forman he went into American exile after the Russian invasion

▼ *CUTTER'S WAY* Crippled one-eyed Vietnam veteran John Heard pursues his paranoid campaign against corporate turpitude.

of 1968, but never enjoyed anything like Forman's success. Of his eight American films, only *Cutter's Way* is of real interest, but it is enough to ensure a cult reputation. The unusual music by Jack Nitzsche, who composed the scores for *Performance* and *One Flew Over the Cuckoo's Next*, is performed on a zither, glass harmonica and electric strings.

ODD/SALIENT FACTS United Artists initially released the film in the States as *Cutter and Bone*, but after unfavourable reviews it was withdrawn and put out as *Cutter's Way* by United Artists Classics and had a considerable success at festivals and on the art-house circuit.

MEMORABLE MOMENTS Cutter deliberately insulting blacks in a bar to bring about a confrontation.

Bone relaxing at sea with the murdered girl's sister, an emblematic oil-rig in the background.

Bone, a small, nervous presence in the imposing entrance hall of Cord Consolidated Oil.

Cutter pulling out a pistol to blast the target at a shooting gallery, and then smashing up the doll he's won and blasting it apart.

KEY LINES

Cutter: 'Richard Bone, doing what he does best – walking away.'

Cutter: 'When you were getting laid in the Ivy League, I was getting my ass shot off.'

Cutter: 'I watched the war on TV just like everybody else. Oh, I thought the same damn things, you know. What you thought when you saw a picture of a young woman with a baby lying face down in a ditch. Two gooks. You had three reactions, Rich. The same as anyone else. First one, real easy. I hate the United States of America. Yeah. You see the same thing next day and you move up a notch. There *is* no God. But you know what you finally say, what everybody finally says, no matter what? I'm hungry. He's responsible, because it's never their ass on the line, never theirs.'

Cutter: 'The routine grind drives me to drink. Tragedy I take straight.'

DEAD OF NIGHT

UK, 1945, EALING STUDIOS, 104 MINS

D ALBERTO CAVALCANTI, CHARLES CRICHTON, BASIL DEARDEN, ROBERT HAMER; **PR** MICHAEL BALCON; **SC** JOHN V. BAINES, ANGUS MACPHAIL (BASED ON STORIES BY BAINES, MACPHAIL, E. F. BENSON, H. G. WELLS), ADDITIONAL DIALOGUE T. E. B. CLARKE; **ED** CHARLES HASSE; **PH** (BW) STAN PAVEY, DOUGLAS SLOCOMBE; **M** GEORGES AURIC

CAST MERVYN JOHNS (WALTER CRAIG), ROLAND CULVER (ELIOT FOLEY), MARY MERRALL (MRS FOLEY), GOOGIE WITHERS (JOAN CORTLAND), FREDERICK VALK (DR VAN STRAATEN), ANTONY BAIRD (HUGH GRAINGER), SALLY ANN HOWES (SALLY O'HARA), RICHARD WYNDHAM (DR ALBURY), JUDY KELLY (JOYCE GRAINGER), MILES MALLESON (HEARSE DRIVER), MICHAEL ALLAN (JIMMY WATSON), BARBARA LEAKE (MRS O'HARA), RALPH MICHAEL (PETER CORTLAND), ESMÉ PERCY (MR RUTHERFORD, THE ANTIQUE DEALER), BASIL RADFORD (GEORGE PARRATT), NAUNTON WAYNE (LARRY POTTER), PEGGY BRYAN (MARY LEE), PETER JONES (GOLF CLUB BARMAN), ALLAN JEAYES (MAURICE OLCOTT), MICHAEL REDGRAVE (MAXWELL FRERE), ELIZABETH WELCH (BEULAH), HARTLEY POWER (SYLVESTER REE), MAGDA KUHN (MITZI)

67

THE STORY Architect Walter Craig arrives at Eliot Foley's country house. Meeting the other guests he recognizes them from a dream and predicts certain events, which do occur. The psychiatrist Van Straaten provides rational explanations but the others reveal they have had similar experiences, and five main guests tell their tales.

1. Hugh, the racing driver, dreamt he heard the driver of an old-fashioned hearse say to him 'Just room for one more, sir.' Those words spoken by a bus conductor stopped him from boarding the bus that plunged over an embankment.

2. Sally recalls a children's Christmas party at a country house, a game of hide-and-seek and her comforting a little boy who turned out to be the ghost of a child killed 80 years before by a jealous older sister.

3. Joan describes how she gave her fiancé Peter a Victorian triple mirror, in which he sees the reflection of a room where a jealous husband strangles his wife. The mirror comes to dominate Peter, and Joan narrowly escapes being murdered by smashing the glass.

4. Eliot breaks the tension with a comic tale. Two obsessive golfers in love with the same woman, decide to settle the dis-

▲ *DEAD OF NIGHT* Schizophrenic ventriloquist Michael
Redgrave in jail with Hugo, his manipulative dummy.

pute through an 18-hole match. George wins by cheating, and
Larry's ghost returns to torment him.

5. The ventriloquist Maxwell Frere has been charged with the
attempted murder of an American ventriloquist he believed tried
to steal his dummy, Hugo. Dr Van Straaten as expert witness,
concludes the ventriloquist is a schizophrenic whose mind has
been possessed by his creation.

After this story the mood darkens. Craig attempts to strangle
Van Straaten, and experiences a surreal nightmare in which he
meets the characters of the various stories, and awakes as Hugo
the dummy is strangling him in a police cell. A phone call from
Eliot Foley brings him back to where the film began.

THE FILM Not the first of horror/supernatural portmanteau
movies, but arguably the best. People telling ghost stories
around a fire is as cosy and traditional as Christmas, but the
movie is taking place in the mind of Craig, an ordinary man in
whose subconscious the images and incidents from all the films
he sees coalesce into one great nightmare.

Dead of Night stands alongside the classic Ealing comedies
that followed on, as a peak in the Ealing Studios postwar
achievement. It went into production before the war ended, yet
it never refers to it, and its social ambience is clearly the 1930s.

The shaggy-dog golfing story reunited the British cinema's
greatest cult duo, Basil Radford and Naunton Wayne, who
first appeared as the insouciant Charters and Caldicott,
upper-middle-class cricket fans in Alfred Hitchcock's *The Lady
Vanishes* (1938).

The co-author of the screenplay, Angus Macphail, was one
of Hitchcock's influential friends, providing him with the anec-
dote about (and concept of) the MacGuffin, and it is
inconceivable that *Psycho* wasn't influenced by the ventriloquist
sequence in *Dead of Night*. Anthony Perkins's gestures
and body movements reflect those of his fellow bi-sexual
Michael Redgrave.

ODD/SALIENT FACTS For *Dead of Night* the great French
composer Georges Auric wrote his first postwar score. Charles
Barr, author of *Ealing Studios* (1977), has suggested that the
film is an image of Ealing at work with the Czech actor
Frederick Valk as the rational shrink standing in for the Studio's
common-sensical Jewish boss, Michael Balcon.

MEMORABLE MOMENTS Joan Cortland dispelling the evil images
in the mirror by the act of will of clutching her fiancé's hand.

Maxwell slapping his dummy's face.

Craig waking from his nightmare and driving out in his little
sports car to re-start his dream.

KEY LINES

Craig: 'Everyone in this room is part of my dream.'

Eliot: 'So we're all powerless in the grip of Craig's
    dreams. That's a solemn thought.'

Peter: 'The trouble's not in the mirror, it's in my mind.'

Craig: 'Hamlet was right doctor, there are more things in
    heaven and earth than are dreamed of in your
    philosophy.'

Maxwell: 'Hugo is the only one who can help me. You
    see, he's more to blame than I am.'

DETOUR

USA, 1945, PRC, 68 MINS

D EDGAR G. ULMER; **PR** LEON FROMKESS; **SC** MARTIN GOLDSMITH (FROM HIS OWN NOVEL); **PH** BENJAMIN H. KLINE; **M** LEON ERDODY; **ED** GEORGE MCGUIRE

CAST TOM NEAL (AL ROBERTS), ANN SAVAGE (VERA), CLAUDIA DRAKE (SUE HARVEY), EDMUND MACDONALD (CHARLES HASKELL JR.) TIM RYAN (GUS, DINER MANAGER), ROGER CLARK (DILLON)

THE STORY The unshaven, self-pitying Al Roberts is hitchhiking to Los Angeles to join his girlfriend Sue, a singer in the third-rate New York nightclub where he played piano in the band. Sue wants a career in Hollywood. In Arizona he is picked up by Charles Haskell, a smooth gambler with a bad heart who has

▼ *DETOUR Doomed anti-hero Tom Neal discovers he's dialled M for murder by accidentally strangling sad pick-up Vera with a telephone cord.*

scratches on his hand from a woman he gave a lift to. While Al drives, Haskell falls into a deep sleep and when Al opens the car door Haskell falls out, hitting a rock. Fearing that he'll be suspected of murder, Al leaves the corpse in the desert, takes the car and Haskell's identity paper, and the following day picks up Vera, a female hitchhiker who proves to be the woman Haskell had assaulted. The vicious, consumptive Vera blackmails Al, first into taking her to LA to sell the car, then into impersonating Haskell to inherit the fortune of Haskell's dying father from whom he was estranged. One night at their rented apartment, Vera gets drunk and threatens to call the police, and Al tugs at the cord running under her locked bedroom door and she's strangled. Al goes on the run, expecting to be picked up at any time for two murders.

THE FILM *Detour* is the ultimate in cult movies, an ultra-low budget *film noir* by the strange Viennese intellectual, Edgar G. Ulmer (1904–72). Having been assistant to the great Max Reinhardt and designer for F. W. Murnau, Ulmer co-directed

Menschen am Sonntag (People on Sunday, 1929), the seminal German precursor of neo-realism, before devoting his life to endless low-budget pictures in Europe and America, mostly genre films, but also comedies and musicals in Yiddish and Ukrainian or aimed at American black audiences. These modest projects offered him considerable creative freedom, and his usually bleak pictures are an astonishing mixture of artistic sophistication and slapdash execution. His two finest achievements are The Black Cat (1934), a demented Karloff-Lugosi horror flick set in a disturbed postwar Europe, and Detour, set in a tawdry America of diners, cheap hotels, seedy nightclubs and desert roads. The self-despising, deeply unsympathetic Al is an all-American fall guy, accidentally killing a worthless, dying conman, and a ferocious, blackmailing harpie. The film's overwrought script, with its almost non-stop voice-over narration, is in a hard-boiled, epigrammatic pulp vein.

ODD/SALIENT FACTS The film was shot in six days on a budget of under $20,000 for the PRC (Producers Releasing Corporation), a small company on Poverty Row specializing in double-bills for back-street cinemas. Ulmer is the principal model for Max Castle, the mysterious director whose career obsesses the hero of Theodore Roszak's Flickers (1991), one of the best novels about movie-making. Actor Tom Neal's life is even sadder than Al Roberts's. The son of a wealthy banker, Neal (1914–72) graduated from Harvard Law School before being signed by Hollywood where virtually all his pictures were second features. After injuring Franchot Tone during a brawl over actress Barbara Payton, Neal was shunned by the industry. He married Payton, started a gardening business and went bankrupt. In 1965 he was charged with murdering his third wife and spent six years in jail for involuntary manslaughter, dying of a heart attack eight months after his release.

MEMORABLE MOMENTS Al and Sue walking through the fog of New York discussing their bleak future.

The depressed Al playing a crazed boogie-woogie version of Brahms in the New York nightclub.

Al's erotic vision of Sue while he's on the road – she's singing 'I Can't Believe That You're in Love With Me' with the shadows of a clarinettist, a saxophonist and a trumpeter on the wall beside her.

> 'That's life – whatever way you turn fate sticks out a foot to trip you up.'

The final scene of the abject Al imagining himself being arrested by highway patrolmen.

KEY LINES

Al: 'Don't you know that a million people go out there [Hollywood] every year and end up polishing cuspidors?'

Al: 'I was tussling with the most dangerous animal in the world – a woman.'

Al: 'That's life – whatever way you turn fate sticks out a foot to trip you up.'

Al: 'Life's like a ball game, you've got to take a swing at whatever comes along before you wake up and find it's the ninth inning.'

Al: 'I know that someday a car will pick me up that I never thumbed. Yes, fate or some mysterious force can put the finger on you or me for no good reason at all.'

THE DEVILS
UK, 1970, WARNER BROTHERS, 111 MINS

D KEN RUSSELL; **PR** RUSSELL AND ROBERT SOLO; **SC** RUSSELL, BASED ON THE PLAY BY JOHN WHITING AND THE DEVILS OF LOUDUN BY ALDOUS HUXLEY; **PH** (COL, PANAVISION) DAVID WATKIN; **M** PETER MAXWELL DAVIES; **ED** MICHAEL BRADSELL **CAST** VANESSA REDGRAVE (JEANNE, MOTHER SUPERIOR), OLIVER REED (GRANDIER), DUDLEY SUTTON (BARON DE LAUBARDEMONT), MAX ADRIAN (SURGEON), GEMMA JONES (MADELEINE), MURRAY MELVIN (MIGNON), MICHAEL GOTHARD (BARRÉ)

THE STORY 1634 in the fortified city of Loudun, 150 miles south-west of Paris. The handsome, well-born, Jesuit-educated Father Grandier has created many enemies through his libertine life (a love-child, a secret marriage to a young woman), his liberal views and his support of the Huguenots. Cardinal Richelieu's people and local landowners vow the destruction of Grandier, taking advantage of the terror of the plague and Jeanne's warped love for Grandier. Jeanne, the hunchbacked Mother Superior of an Ursuline convent, and other hysterical

▲ *THE DEVILS* Director Ken Russell (left) looks on encouragingly as Oliver Reed's libidinous Father Grandier examines a possessed Vanessa Redgrave.

nuns are encouraged by the witchhunter Father Barré to testify that they have been possessed by devils working for Grandier, and he is put on trial for obscenity, blasphemy and sacrilege. After being tortured, Grandier is burnt at the stake and the walls of Loudun are torn down.

THE FILM The artistic credentials of *The Devils* are impeccable. Commissioned by the Royal Shakespeare Company in 1961 from a highly regarded playwright with a coterie reputation, it was based on a celebrated study of a real-life case of mass hysteria by one of the century's most respected literary intellectuals. The stage presentation with Richard Johnson as Grandier and Virginia McKenna as Jeanne was a restrained, if harrowing affair, as was the 1961.Polish film on the same subject, Jerzy Kawalerowicz's *Mother Joan of the Angels*, which

was an allegory about the false accusations and show trials in Eastern Europe. The film is something else again with Ken Russell, the *enfant terrible* of British film-making, upping the ante after his wild Tchaikovsky flick, *The Music Lovers*, to make a truly demented picture, a weird mixture of sado-masochistic melodrama and camp comedy, reflecting the hysteria of the nuns. Anti-clerical movies centring on the sexual shenanigans between nuns and priests had been a staple of continental movies for decades (frequently in hard and soft-core melodrama). In *The Devils*, Ken Russell (himself raised as a Catholic) brought this European tradition into a mainstream Anglo-American cinema where nuns were usually genteel creatures played by the likes of Ingrid Bergman, Deborah Kerr and Audrey Hepburn. Devoid of spirituality or thoughtfulness, the film sets out to shock and offend with scenes of a priest bedding his confessees; a Mother Superior fantasizing herself as the lover of Christ; orgies involving dozens of incensed nuns frolicking in the nude; torture; exorcism with hideous instruments;

72

the King shooting Huguenots for sport; and a final execution in which you can almost smell the burning flesh. As the obsessed Mother Superior, Vanessa Redgrave goes over the top, quite literally chewing her rosary, but Oliver Reed and Gemma Jones as his 'wife', providing a still centre of rationality, seem oblivious to the madness around them. The film is given a curious appearance by the gleaming black-and-white sets, theatrical and unconvincingly pristine. The jarring, atonal score is by the British avant-garde composer Peter Maxwell Davies. Brutal cross-cutting emphasizes thematic points, and dramatic elisions result in scenes that begin near their climax – as when Barré gathers the nuns in the woods and gives them the choice of being shot or accusing Grandier. This all contributes to the frenzied atmosphere and the calculated bad taste that Russell, for all his efforts, hasn't subsequently matched.

> *Sin can be caught as easily as the plague.'*

ODD/SALIENT FACTS The making of the picture was attended by stories of extras (especially those playing nuns) complaining of being assaulted and walking off the set, though these were very likely the concoctions of publicists. The censorship problems the film raised (exacerbated by a scandal-mongering tabloid press and not helped by hostile critics) prepared the way for attacks some months later on two other cult British productions, that dealt with sex and violence: Peckinpah's *Straw Dogs* and Kubrick's *A Clockwork Orange*. The sets for *The Devils* were designed by Derek Jarman who was to become one of the cult directors of the 1970s and '80s.

MEMORABLE MOMENTS/ICONIC SCENES The Mother Superior reaching out through a grill to attack Grandier's lover.

The Mother Superior engaged in self-flagellation.

The gleeful Surgeon and Chemist going about their business of purging with gigantic syringes.

The Duc presenting the Mother Superior with a charred bone as a souvenir.

KEY LINES

Peasant woman of Grandier: 'Now there's a man worth going to hell for.'

Louis XIV after shooting down a Huguenot who has run the gauntlet dressed in a blackbird costume: 'Bye bye blackbird.'

Grandier: 'Secluded women have given themselves to God, but something within them cries out to be given to man.'

Barré: 'Sin can be caught as easily as the plague.'

Grandier: 'You have turned the house of the Lord into a circus and its people into clowns.'

DIAL M FOR MURDER

USA, 1954, WARNER, 105 MINS

D ALFRED HITCHCOCK; **SC** HITCHCOCK (FROM THE PLAY BY FREDERICK KNOTT); **PH** (3-D) ROBERT BURKS; **M** DIMITRI TIOMKIN; **ED** RUDI FEHR

CAST RAY MILLAND (TONY WENDICE), GRACE KELLY (MARGOT WENDICE), ROBERT CUMMINGS (MARK HALLIDAY), JOHN WILLIAMS (CHIEF INSPECTOR HUBBARD), ANTHONY DAWSON (CAPTAIN LESGATE)

THE STORY Tony Wendice, a former tennis star now in his forties, has an indifferently paid job selling sports equipment and lives in central London with his wife Margot, whom he has married for her money. Suspecting her of an affair with Mark Halliday, an American writer of crime novels and television scripts, he blackmails a shady conman, Captain Lesgate, into agreeing to murder her at the Wendices' flat while Tony is attending a dinner, but during the ensuing struggle Margot kills Lesgate with a pair of scissors. Tony then frames her for murder, planting evidence on Lesgate to prove that he was blackmailing Margot over the affair with Mark. Chief Inspector Hubbard's investigations lead to Margot's being sentenced to death for murder. But on the eve of her execution, Hubbard the cop and Mark the crime writer, working on the case from different angles, put Tony on the spot, the crucial piece of evidence being the key stolen from Margot's purse that enabled Lesgate to enter the flat.

THE FILM *Dial M for Murder,* based on a successful, conventional stage thriller, is the only film made by a director of the first rank during the Hollywood majors' brief flirtation with stereo-scopic cinema in 1953 following the surprise success of the low-budget *Bwana Devil* the previous year. But it was shown in 3-D in only a few American cinemas and Europe had to wait for thirty years to see it as originally conceived. This virtuoso film takes its place alongside another filmed play, *Rope*, in Hitchcock's canon. Whereas other 3-D films used the process for shock effects (e.g. an arrow flying off the screen past the spectator's ear in *Hondo*), there is no aggression in *Dial M for Murder*. Hitchcock appreciated that, far from contributing to the illusion of cinematic realism, 3-D increased the artificiality. People and objects are equalized through the flatness in depth, an effect suited to a play dealing in human cyphers and phys-ical clues. The film rarely moves out of the spacious living room of the Wendices' flat and the screen is often used like a prosce-nium arch so that the audience seems to be watching from the front stalls or occasionally from the circle. The theatricality of performance, dialogue, decor and lighting is emphasized, and when Margot kills Lesgate she reaches out for the scissors which appear to be a few inches from the spectators' eyes and we find ourselves willing her to seize them, though in the two-dimensional prints of the film we can hardly see the scissors until she picks them up. There are no close-ups or subjective shots of the stabbing.

ODD/SALIENT FACTS Hitchcock shot the film in 36 days and had a pit built so that the camera could be used at floor level to simulate the view from the orchestra stalls. For the disturbing close-up of Tony phoning Margot (to lure her from the bedroom to be killed by Lesgate), a giant telephone was built with a King Kong-size finger to work the dial. *Dial M for Murder* (which was originally written for TV) has been remade as *A Perfect Murder* (Andrew Davis, 1998).

MEMORABLE MOMENTS Tony manipulating the crooked Lesgate.

Margot reaching out for the scissors.

The use of theatrical space to focus our attention on the door at the rear of the stage, the opening of which provides the final climax.

Hitchcock's signature appearance on a college reunion pho-tograph which identifies him as an old friend of the two crooks Lesgate and Tony Wendice.

KEY LINES

Inspector Hubbard: 'They talk about flat-footed policemen, may the saints protect us from the gifted amateur.'

Hubbard to a policeman carrying Margot's handbag: 'You can't walk down the streets like that or you'll be arrested.'

▼ *DIAL M FOR MURDER Grace Kelly answers the phone before plunging the scissors into would-be assassin Anthony Dawson.*

DIVA

FRANCE, 1981, LES FILMS GALAXIE/GREENWICH FILM PRODUCTIONS , 123 MINS
D JEAN-JACQUES BEINEIX; **PR** IRENE SILBERMAN; **SC** JEAN-JACQUES BEINEIX, JEAN VAN HAMME, DIALOGUE BY JEAN-JACQUES BEINEIX, BASED ON THE BOOK BY DELACORTA; **PH** (COL) PHILIPPE ROUSSELOT; **M** VLADIMIR COSMA; **ED** MARIE-JOSEPHE YOYOTTE, MONIQUE PRIM

CAST FRÉDÉRIC ANDRÉÏ (JULES), ROLAND BERTIN (SIMON WEINSTADT), RICHARD BOHRINGER (GORODISH), GÉRARD DARMON (SPIC), CHANTAL DERUAZ (NADIA KALONSKY), JACQUES FABBRI (INSPECTOR JEAN SAPORTA), PATRICK FLOERSHEIM (MORTIER), THUY AN LUU (ALBA), JEAN-JACQUES MOREAU (KRANTZ), DOMINIQUE PINON (LE CURÉ), ANNY ROMAND (PAULA), WILHELMENIA WIGGINS FERNANDEZ (CYNTHIA HAWKINS, THE DIVA)

THE STORY Jules, a mobilette courier, makes a bootleg recording of a Cynthia Hawkins recital. After the concert he goes backstage to meet the Diva, and as he leaves her dressing room, steals one of her dresses. The following day outside a Parisian station, a woman, Nadia, pursued by men posing as policemen, secretes a tape cassette in Jules's panier. Jules leaves not knowing that the woman is about to be killed by Le Curé, one of the men. Jules meets up with Alba, a young oriental model, and visits the flat she shares with Gorodish, a mystic/wheeler-dealer. It turns out that the tape contains Nadia's revelations of the prostitution and drugs ring with which she was involved. Jules spends a night with a prostitute and gets her to wear the Diva's dress. He is being pursued by two men who

▼ *DIVA* Deaf psycho Spic (Gérard Darmon) and his sidekick Le Curé (Dominique Pinon) in hot pursuit of Jules and the incriminating tape.

are working for the corrupt Inspector Saporta. Jules returns the dress to Cynthia and they begin an affair. Meanwhile Cynthia, who has never released a recording, is being held to ransom by Taiwanese gangsters over the bootleg tape, which is worth a fortune. Jean takes refuge in the prostitute's flat where he listens to the beginning of Nadia's tape. It instantly reveals that Saporta is a crook and then that the prostitute is probably working for Saporta. He rushes out of the flat and is pursued through Paris by Spic and Le Curé. Having been shot, and about to be killed, Jules is rescued by Gorodish. In a fiendishly clever plot by Gorodish, blackmail money is extorted from Saporta. Then the Taiwanese, Le Curé, Spic and finally Saporta are killed. Jules returns the tape to Cynthia who hears herself sing for the first time.

THE FILM *Diva* marked the debut as feature director of the unprolific Jean-Jacques Beineix. He and his co-writer Jean Van Hamme adapted a cultish crime novel by Delacorta, the pen name of Swiss poet and novelist Daniel Odier. The source novel has the basic elements of the film but the adaptors improved on it, stripped it down and enhanced it brilliantly. There is one neat touch in the book that they don't use, in that Gorodish knew Saporta, having started out as his chauffeur, but otherwise the film is slicker and smarter, with Saporta becoming a bent copper rather than just a criminal, and the addition of the comically sinister double act in pursuit of Jules. Their most striking amendment is in the conclusion where the decent Zen-crook Gorodish effortlessly comes up with a succession of ingenious set-pieces to outwit the criminals. The film set the tone for cool cult crime films, with Beineix creating a clean, ridiculously flashy surface for a devious plot. With its operatic soundtrack, slick camerawork and studied hipness, it influenced a generation of commercial directors. *Diva* is a Hitchcockian thriller stripped of all psychological depth. It is a film about sound, where the characters struggle to control and own other people's voices and the psycho-killer is instantly recognizable by his hearing aid.

ODD/SALIENT FACTS Beineix followed the cult success of *Diva* with the ludicrous *The Moon in the Gutter* (1983) before rediscovering his touch with *Betty Blue* (1986), which became an instant cult hit and launched the career of Béatrice Dalle. Beineix seemed to have shifted into retirement after *Roselyne and the Lions* (1989), but was reinvigorated by his experiences producing a short documentary film on Jean-Dominique Bauby. Bauby, a French journalist who suffered a stroke and subsequent paralysis, termed 'locked-in syndrome', wrote his account of these experiences in *The Diving Bell and the Butterfly*, which he dictated via blinks. The author died shortly after the publication of this memoir and Beineix has suggested he may be tempted to direct the film of the book.

MEMORABLE MOMENTS The ingenious climax which begins with Saporta getting into the assigned car and playing the tape, on which Gorodish says: 'You're on board an 11 horsepower Citroën, a bit of history. This model was once favoured by the police but also by gangsters. It seemed very appropriate for you.'

KEY LINES

Gorodish to Jules, on the philosophy of the baguette:
   'Some people get high on airplane glue, detergents, all sorts of fancy gimmicks. Me, my satori is this – the Zen of buttering bread.'

> 'Some people get high on airplane glue, detergents, all sorts of fancy gimmicks. Me, my satori is this – the Zen of buttering bread.'

LA DOLCE VITA

ITALY/FRANCE, 1960, RIAMA FILM/GRAY FILMS/PATHÉ CINÉMA, 178 MINS

D FEDERICO FELLINI; **PR** GIUSEPPI AMATO; **SC** FEDERICO FELLINI, ENNIO FLAIANO, TULLIO PINELLI, BRUNELLO RONDI; **PH** (BW, SCOPE) OTELLO MARTELLI; **ED** LEO CATTOZZO; **M** NINO ROTA

CAST MARCELLO MASTROIANNI (MARCELLO RUBINI), ANOUK AIMÉE (MADDALENA), ANITA EKBERG (SYLVIA), YVONNE FURNEAUX (EMMA), ALAIN CUNY (STEINER), LEX BARKER (ROBERT), ANNIBALE NICHI (MARCELLO'S FATHER), MAGALI NOËL (FANNY), NADIA GRAY (NADIA), WALTER SANTESSO (PAPARAZZO)

THE STORY Marcello, a gossip columnist from a middle-class provincial family, works for what his mentor, the illustrious author Steiner, calls 'the semi-fascist press', reporting on the scandalous activities of Rome's fashionable café society along the Via Veneto, accompanied by the photographer Paparazzo. Callously ignoring his neurotic mistress Emma, he has an affair with the rich heiress Maddalena, becomes obsessed with the Swedish movie star Sylvia, and reports on sensational events like the two children who claim to have seen the Madonna. Marcello's father (by implication a fascist supporter before the war) comes to Rome and collapses while attempting to have sex with Fanny, a French dancer to whom Marcello has introduced him. Steiner, the despairing intellectual, kills his two children and commits suicide. Before and after Steiner's death, Marcello attends extended parties at aristocratic homes. Soon he has not only given up the possibility of being a serious writer, but also become a drunken publicity agent and a self-despising leader of the revels at an orgy. At dawn when the partygoers come to inspect a strange fish stranded on the beach, he sees in the distance an innocent young woman he has previously encountered at a seaside café, only now he cannot hear what she is saying.

THE FILM *La Dolce Vita* ended postwar Italian cinema, bringing down the curtain on neo-realism, the movement that Fellini helped create, and opening up a new phase of expansive movie-making. The film identified and criticized a new world of media-created celebrity, a corrupt international culture where journalists, plutocrats, aristocrats, show-biz folk, film-makers and politicians meet and merge. It is a world that has banished or been deserted by God, a place where all values have been abandoned, all personal relations severed, and the goal of life reduced to the fulfilment of desire. As several references to Dante confirm, it is a form of hell, and it consumes Marcello, its observer and participant. A good deal of the film's appeal, as with all late Fellini, is the way it relishes that which it condemns. Fellini found in the minor Italian movie star Mastroianni his cinematic alter ego who was to feature thus in a succession of films (most notable *8½*), and would become one of European cinema's most prolific stars. When Fellini re-created the neon-lit, traffic-choked Via Veneto at Cinecittà, he brought the movies back from the streets and into the studio, challenging the polarization of reality and artifice. His film has a vibrancy and sadness that keeps it alive.

ODD/SALIENT FACTS Producer Dino de Laurentiis left the project when Fellini refused to cast Paul Newman as the gossip columnist. In the final sequence Marcello is attacked for publicizing a client in a fan magazine as an actor with 'a Greek profile and modern acting style that equates him with Paul Newman'.

> ### 'You are the first woman on the first day of creation. You are mother, sister, lover, friend, angel, devil, earth, home.'

The film contributed to the language its ironic title 'La Dolce Vita', and the collective term 'paparazzi' (from Marcello's photographer friend) for the hordes of celebrity-chasing photographers. Paparazzo's name was borrowed from a hotelier in *By the Ionian Sea* (1901), a travel book by George Gissing. Alain Cuny, the French actor who played the unctuous Steiner, was the European cinema's all-purpose intellectual, and in 1974 he played a suave philosopher of sex in *Emmanuelle*.

MEMORABLE MOMENTS The helicopter carrying a statue of Christ with outstretched arms away from Rome across the Vatican.

Anita Ekberg dressed as a Catholic priest in St Peter's and later wading through the Trevi Fountain at night with the besotted Marcello.

The climactic encounter with the weird beached creature reminiscent of the mysterious female body washed ashore in the early 1950s, which launched the Montesi Scandal that was to shake Italy.

KEY LINES

Sylvia (masquerading as a priest in the Vatican): 'I must remember to tell Marilyn.'

Marcello (to Sylvia): 'You are the first woman on the first day of creation. You are mother, sister, lover, friend, angel, devil, earth, home.'

Steiner (to Marcello): 'Don't be like me. Salvation doesn't lie within four walls. I'm too serious to be a dilettante and too much a dabbler to be a professional. Even the most miserable life is better than a sheltered existence in an organized society where everything is calculated and perfected.'

Transvestite (at the final party): 'By 1965 there'll be total depravity. How squalid everything will be.'

DUCK SOUP
US, 1933, PARAMOUNT PICTURES, 72 MINS

D LEO MCCAREY; **PR SC** STORY, MUSIC AND LYRICS BY BERT KALMAR AND HARRY RUBY, ADDITIONAL DIALOGUE BY ARTHUR SHEEKMAN AND NAT PERRIN; **MD** ARTHUR JOHNSTON; **PH** HENRY SHARP; **ED** LEROY STONE

CAST GROUCHO MARX (RUFUS T. FIREFLY), HARPO MARX (PINKY), CHICO MARX (CHICOLINI), ZEPPO MARX (BOB ROLAND), MARGARET DUMONT (MRS TEASDALE), RAQUEL TORRES (VERA MARCAL), LOUIS CALHERN (TRENTINO), EDMUND BREESE (ZANDER), LEONID KINSKY (AGITATOR), CHARLES B. MIDDLETON (PROSECUTOR), EDGAR KENNEDY (STREET VENDOR)

THE STORY The land of Freedonia is on the verge of war with neighbouring Sylvania. Rufus T. Firefly is appointed leader with the support of the country's chief benefactor, Mrs Teasdale. In his embassy, Sylvanian ambassador Trentino learns that revolution in Freedonia has been averted by Firefly's popularity. His spies Pinky and Chicolini gain positions in Firefly's government. With war seemingly inevitable, Trentino sends Pinky and Chicolini to steal Freedonia's battle plans from Mrs Teasdale's. Chicolini is arrested and charged with treason. His show trial is interrupted by the news that the Sylvanian troops are advancing. When a last-minute attempt to secure peace fails, war is declared. In the conflict Firefly, his secretary Bob Roland, Chicolini, Pinky and Mrs Teasdale are holed up in a small house near the front. Eventually Trentino is captured and victory is Freedonia's.

THE FILM *Duck Soup* is the last film the Marx Brothers made for Paramount and the last featuring Zeppo. When they came to negotiate a new contract with MGM, it was initially suggested that they should be paid less since there were now fewer of them. Groucho is said to have remarked: 'Without Zeppo we're worth twice as much.' Following the success of *Horse Feathers* in 1932, this film was initially to have been directed by Ernst Lubitsch. The script went through various titles (*Oo La La, Cracked Ice* and *Grasshoppers*) before settling on its final form. It was ultimately assigned to director Leo McCarey, who had experience working with Laurel & Hardy (whose trademark style is noticeable in the peanut-stand sequence with Edgar Kennedy) and Eddie Cantor, and would go on to work with W. C. Fields

▶ *LA DOLCE VITA* Sex symbol Anita Ekberg lights up the Roman night as she treads on all those coins in the Trevi Fountain.

and Harold Lloyd among others. Although less successful than its predecessor and the first two MGM films that followed it, it was far from a financial disaster. The film was technically – in terms of production design, direction and writing – the most accomplished the brothers had appeared in up to that point and was improved by the absence of harp and piano sequences. It is in every respect the Marx Brothers' finest hour and ten minutes and remains among the greatest comedy films ever made.

ODD/SALIENT FACTS When Mickey Sacks, the Woody Allen character, is at his lowest point in *Hannah and Her Sisters* (1986), he wanders the streets of New York City for hours before stumbling into a cinema in which *Duck Soup* is showing. The scene on the screen is the elaborate *Freedonia's Going to War* musical number, and Mickey feels instantly better, saying: 'And I started to feel how can you even think of killing yourself? I mean, isn't it so stupid? I mean, I – look at the people up there on the screen. You know, they're real funny, and, and what if the worst is true? What if there's no God …?'

MEMORABLE MOMENTS The film's enduring great sequence comes when Chicolini and Pinky have broken into Mrs Teasdale's house to steal the battle plans. Chicolini is upstairs

▲ *DUCK SOUP Enemy spies Pinky (Harpo) and Chicolini (Chico) find gainful employment in the office of Freedonia's new leader Rufus T. Firefly (Groucho).*

while Pinky is downstairs trying to unlock the safe. Both are disguised as Firefly. When the safe turns out to be a radio, which blares uncontrollably, Firefly comes down to see what is going on. Panicked, Pinky runs into a mirror which smashes, so when Firefly approaches him he pretends to be Firefly's mirror image in a ludicrously protracted sequence. The fake mirror routine was a stock sketch in music hall revues and had been used on screen by Charlie Chaplin and Max Linder.

KEY LINES

Firefly to Mrs Teasdale: 'Can't you see what I'm trying to tell you. I love you.'
Mrs Teasdale, bashfully: 'Oh, Your Excellency!'
Firefly: 'You're not so bad, yourself.'

Vera Marcal, to Firefly: 'Perhaps we get a chance to dance together.'

Firefly: 'I could dance with you till the cows come home.'
Vera: 'Yes?'
Firefly: 'On second thoughts I'd rather dance with the cows
   till you come home.'

*Chicolini, reporting his and Pinky's espionage activities to
   Trentino:* 'All right, I tell you. Monday we watch Firefly's
   house, but he no come out. He wasn't home. Tuesday,
   we go to the ball game, but he fool us. He no show up.
   Wednesday he go to the ball game, but we fool him.
   We no show up. Thursday was a double header.
   Nobody show up. Friday it rained all day. There was
   no ball game so we stayed home and we listened to it
   on the radio.'
Trentino: 'Then you didn't shadow Firefly?'
Chicolini: 'Sure we shadow Firefly. We shadow him all
   day.'
Trentino: 'What day was that?'
Chicolini: 'Shadderday.'

EASY RIDER★

US, 1969, RAYBERT/PANDO, 94 MINS

D DENNIS HOPPER; **PR** PETER FONDA, BERT SCHNEIDER, WILLIAM
L. HAYWARD; **SC** PETER FONDA, DENNIS HOPPER, TERRY
SOUTHERN; **PH** (COL) LASZLO KOVACS; **ED** DONN CAMBERN
CAST PETER FONDA (WYATT), DENNIS HOPPER (BILLY),
ANTONIO MENDOZA (JESUS), PHIL SPECTOR (CONNECTION),
MAC MASHOURIAN (BODYGUARD), WARREN FINNERTY
(RANCHER), TITA COLORADO (RANCHER'S WIFE), LUKE ASKEW
(STRANGER ON HIGHWAY), LUANA ANDERS (LISA), SABRINA
SCHARF (SARAH), SANDY WYETH (JOANNE), ROBERT WALKER JR.
(JACK), ROBERT BALL, CARMEN PHILLIPS, ELLIE WALKER AND
MICHAEL PATAKI (MIMES), JACK NICHOLSON (GEORGE
HANSON), GEORGE FOWLER JR. (GUARD), KEITH GREEN
(SHERIFF), HAYWARD ROBILLARD (CAT MAN), ARNOLD HESS JR.
(DEPUTY), BUDDY CAUSEY JR., DUFFY LAMONT, BLASE
M.DAWSON AND PAUL GUEDRY (CUSTOMERS IN CAFE), TONI
BASIL (MARY), KAREN BLACK (KAREN), LEA MARMER (MADAME),
CATHI COZZI (DANCING GIRL), THEA SALERNO, ANNE
MCCLAIN, BEATRIZ MONTELLI AND MARCIA BOWMAN
(HOOKERS), DAVID C. BILLODEAU AND JOHNNY DAVID (MEN IN
PICKUP TRUCK)

THE STORY Wyatt and Billy pull off a coke deal, hide the
money in the petrol tank of Wyatt's bike and drive across country. Having spent some time in a hippie commune, they are
arrested and jailed for a minor offence in a small town. In jail
they meet drunken lawyer George Hanson, who pays for their
release and joins them on their journey. The three of them sit
around a camp-fire getting
stoned. The following night
having been threatened by a
group of local rednecks, they
are violently attacked in their
sleep and Hanson is killed.
Wyatt and Billy head off to
New Orleans and the
whorehouse recommended
by Hanson. Together with
Mary and Karen, they wan-
der around the Mardi Gras
and drop acid. They ride out of New Orleans and are shot
dead by two rednecks in a pick-up truck.

> 'They're not scared
> of you, they're
> scared of what you
> represent ... What
> you represent to
> them is freedom.'

THE FILM Wyatt and Billy are modern cowboys who ride their
bikes across the Monument Valley of John Ford Westerns, and
in a sequence of heavy-handed symbolism, tend to a flat tyre
as old-timers nearby shoe a horse. In the entry on Dennis
Hopper in his *Biographical Dictionary of Cinema*, David
Thomson writes: 'Then came *Easy Rider*, a disaster in the history
of film to set beside the early loss of Technicolor, the invention
of gross participation, the early death of Murnau, and the
longevity of Richard Attenborough.' The film is continually re-
examined and discussed to discover why such an obviously if
inarticulately cultish, anti-establishment film should not merely
make all those involved in its creation rich, but also help to
change the make-up of Hollywood. There is in fact very little to
the film and it is easy to see how the project could have been
pitched in a couple of sentences and all the details be ironed
out in one short session on Peter Fonda's tennis court. This
oblique if loud statement of intent from the new generation is
presented in a film conceived, written, produced, acted and
eventually seen by stoned people. Editorial consultant Henry
Jaglom recalls being present at an early screening when the film
ran for around four hours. He was the only person not to appreciate the lengthy sequences in which the two bikers travelled
through endless beautiful landscapes to the backing of endless

hippie songs. As he says: 'I wasn't high. I was in real time.' The film retains some power, making its impact from just a few key ingredients, such as its attitude of defiance, the notion that some-how the heroes blew it, and the still shockingly sudden and pessimistic end.

ODD/SALIENT FACTS The authorship of the film is still dis-puted. What is acknowledged is that Terry Southern was an enthusiast for the project and was keen to help in any way he could. This eagerness led an already successful novelist and screenwriter of the counter-culture to perform the mundane task of rendering the work-in-progress of Hopper and Fonda into the recognizable shape of a movie script. With his name attached to the project it helped to raise the meagre $360,000 budget. His primary achievement, beyond fleshing out the character of Hanson, was to supply the film's title. In production Hopper became predictably crazed, but with the help of the dedicated cast and crew managed to deliver usable footage which was ultimately worked into the relatively coherent finished form. At the height of the production chaos, Hopper complained that everyone was conspiring to ruin his movie. As Fonda recalls still annoyed: 'His movie? I thought it was supposed to be ours.'

MEMORABLE MOMENTS The scenes which most symbolize the tension between old and new are those in which they are treated to what Hanson characterizes as 'country witticisms' in the café and the final sequence in which they are blown away by the forces unable to understand or accept the new frontier spirit of the modern rebels.

KEY LINES

As they are about to leave the hippie commune, Wyatt turns to Billy and says approvingly: 'They're gonna make it. Dig, man, they're gonna make it.'

Around the camp-fire Hanson remarks: 'You know, this used to be a hell of a country… They're not scared of you, they're scared of what you represent… What you represent to them is freedom.'

Wyatt: 'You know, Billy, we blew it.'
Billy: 'You go for the big money, you're free, dig.'
Wyatt: 'We blew it.'

ENTER THE DRAGON
US/HONG KONG, 1973, WARNER/CONCORD, 99 MINS
D ROBERT CLOUSE; **PR** FRED WEINTRAUB, PAUL HELLER, RAYMOND CHOW; **SC** MICHAEL ALLIN; **PH** (COL, PANAVISION) GILBERT HUBBS; FIGHT SEQUENCES STAGED BY BRUCE LEE; **ED** KURT KIRSCHLER, GEORGE WATTERS

CAST BRUCE LEE (LEE), JOHN SAXON (ROPER), JIM KELLY (WILLIAMS), AHNA CAPRI (TANIA), SHIEH KIEN (HAN), BOB WALL (OHARRA), ANGELA MAO YING (SU LIN), BETTY CHUNG (MEI LING), GEOFFREY WEEKS (BRAITHWAITE), YAN SZE BOLO (PETER ARCHER)

THE STORY Lee, Roper and Williams are invited to attend a martial arts competition on the private island of Han. Lee has been asked by the British secret service to investigate Han's drugs and prostitution racket. As they approach the island the story of each of the three leading characters is fleshed out in flashbacks. Lee is out to avenge the murder of his sister by Han's sidekick Oharra. Roper is facing a massive personal debt. Williams, a black man, has encountered violent harassment from the American police. On the island each man fights suc-cessfully in the early bouts, Lee killing Oharra. Williams and Roper enjoy the women supplied by Han. Lee makes a noctur-nal excursion to investigate the dark secrets of Han's island complex, an outing for which Williams is erroneously blamed and savagely beaten by Han. Roper is taken around Han's underground opium factory and asked to become an American representative. He seems tempted before he sees the beaten body of his Vietnam vet buddy Williams. With Lee releasing the peasants held captive by Han, there is a great climactic fight in which Han is killed and his men defeated.

THE FILM *Enter the Dragon* is a crudely plotted and poorly edited film. It is a lame pastiche of the James Bond movies com-plete with snarling villain with pussy cat and fake claw, underground complex, torture museum and vat whose sole pur-pose seems to be for lowering rivals into. It is enlivened and made intermittently extraordinary by the presence of Lee. Pauline Kael has described him as the Fred Astaire of martial arts movies and his talents are what made this film, Hollywood's first mainstream chop-socky movie, a success. He has an odd, geek-ish hairstyle and is given to making peculiar howling noises but his graceful movements and sheer, taut physical presence are captivating. A philosophy graduate born in San Francisco, Lee

▲ ENTER THE DRAGON *Bruce Lee (Lee) sporting designer scars is lost in a hall of mirrors in the climactic mortal combat.*

combat. Lee was always painfully aware of this limitation in the genre's appeal and the writers make a perfunctory stab at dismissing this narrative niggle. When Lee is first approached by Braithwaite with the commission, he suggests, naturally: 'Guns. Now why doesn't somebody pull a 45 and settle it?' Braithwaite explains that Han has a great fear of guns, guns are an offence, guns are not allowed. The basic objection is: 'Any bloody fool can pull a trigger.'

ODD/SALIENT FACTS Lee died, supposedly as the result of a brain oedema just weeks before the release of *Enter the Dragon*. He was 32 years old. The rumours that always circulate around the early deaths of the beautiful and famous began almost at once. They suggested that he was murdered by Triads or tongs or perhaps died of a drug overdose. In a grim irony, his son Brandon, also apparently on the verge of becoming a Hollywood action star, died in unusual circumstances, killed by the residual powder in a blank cartridge fired at him at close range on the set of the film *The Crow* (1994). The film, like his father's *The Game of Death* (1979), was completed with added footage and a stand-in and released posthumously.

MEMORABLE MOMENTS The final confrontation between Lee and Han is staged as a knowing updated, kung fu version of the climactic duel in *Swashbucklers*, as the two fight one another in the midst of the general maul before moving to more private quarters. Han gets to use two special serrated fake hands from his Swiss-army-knife arsenal and inflicts a few photogenic slashes on Lee's torso. The finale of this scene is a borrowing from the end of *The Lady from Shanghai* (1948) as the two fight it out in a bewildering hall of mirrors, before Han is finally impaled on his own spear sticking through a mirrored door.

KEY LINES

Lee doles out some gnomic advice to his protégé: 'Don't think, feel. It is like a finger pointing away to the moon. Don't concentrate on the finger or you will miss all that heavenly glory.'

Han: 'It is defeat that you must learn to prepare for.'
Williams: 'Man, I don't waste my time. When it comes, I won't even notice it.'
Han: 'Oh? And how is that so?'
Williams: 'I'll be too busy looking good.'

had been a minor TV actor appearing in *Batman* and *The Green Hornet* before moving to Hong Kong to become an instant cult star. It is possible, given the success of this film, that Lee and the genre in which he became a success would have moved into the mainstream, at least briefly. As it is he will remain fixed in the minds of his followers as a charismatic cult icon.

In *Raiders of the Lost Ark* (1981), in a famous joke, Indie is confronted by a baddie in the market chase, who dazzles the hero with a display of threatening sword play. An unmoved Jones simply pulls his gun and shoots the man dead. The crucial problem in all martial arts films is the credibility of unarmed

ERASERHEAD

US, 1976, 89 MINS

D DAVID LYNCH; **PR** DAVID LYNCH; **SC** DAVID LYNCH; **PH** (BW)
FREDERICK ELMES; **SD** ALAN R. SPLET AND DAVID LYNCH; **PIC ED**
DAVID LYNCH; **SD ED** ALAN R. SPLET

CAST JACK NANCE (HENRY SPENCER), CHARLOTTE STEWART
(MARY X), ALLEN JOSEPH (MR X), JEANNE BATES (MRS X), JUDITH
ANN ROBERTS (BEAUTIFUL GIRL ACROSS THE HALL), LAUREL NEAR
(LADY IN THE RADIATOR), JACK FISK (MAN IN THE PLANET),
DARWIN JASTON (PAUL), NEIL MORAN (THE BOSS), HAL LANDON
JR. (PENCIL MACHINE OPERATOR), JENNIFER LYNCH (LITTLE GIRL),
PEGGY LYNCH AND DODDIE KEELER (PEOPLE DIGGING IN THE
ALLEY), V. PHIPPS WILSON ('MR ROUNDHEELS', LANDLADY)

THE STORY Henry is a man with strange dreams of a celestial
body, a tiny foetal creature and a man with a scarred face
operating levers in a shadowy room. He has dinner with the
unusual parents of his friend Mary. Mary gives birth to a mutant
baby and moves into Henry's apartment. The constant whim-
pering of the baby drives Mary out of the flat. A woman with
lumpy jowls walks on to the stage behind Henry's radiator, and
treads on stringy foetuses thrown onstage. Mary returns and as
she sleeps, Henry retrieves stringy foetuses that she is exuding
and tosses them against the wall. Henry meets the woman from
across the hall. They embrace and descend into a milky liquid.
The woman on the stage sings a song. Henry imagines his
head being detached and made into pencil-top rubbers. Back
in the apartment Henry removes the bandages which had covered the baby below the neck, and plunges a pair of scissors
into its neck. Thick effluent pours from the wound and the baby's
neck stretches out. A hole is blown in the planet, the man in the
shadowy room pulls on his levers and Henry hugs the jowly
woman behind the radiator.

THE FILM David Lynch is a cult director. He is a true auteur with
a cinematic vision inspired by the workings of his own bleakly
fecund imagination. His films are characterized by a prevailing
mood of moral confusion and darkness, urban alienation and
disconcerting noises. Lynch created his darkest and most fully
realized film with *Eraserhead*. Like all his best work it has a
strongly autobiographical basis with Lynch coming up with the
notion of the hideous mutant baby from his own experience of
his daughter Jennifer, who suffered from club feet as a child.
The film is in part an extended and deeply unsettling essay on

▲ *ERASERHEAD Jack Nance (Henry) trapped in Lynch's nightmarish fable of fatherhood amid a bleak industrial landscape.*

the nightmare of fatherhood, or at least a specific experience
of fatherhood, and a revulsion at the anatomy of sex and procreation. Henry is so disturbed and displaced by the bleating
mutant that in his nightmare the baby grows out from his trunk,
supplanting his own head, his whole identity. Lynch would continue to explore ideas of isolation, freakishness and tortured,
grim sexuality in his other two masterpieces *The Elephant Man*
(1980) and *Blue Velvet* (1986). He still directs films occas-
sionally, and has ventured into the TV world with the typically
cultish *Twin Peaks* series.

ODD/SALIENT FACTS The film was partly financed by Sissy
Spacek. Hal Landon Jr., who plays the Pencil Machine
Operator, later played Ted's father Captain Logan in both *Bill
and Ted* films. Lynch is obsessively secretive about all aspects

of the elongated shoot, especially the mechanics of the mutant baby. When asked about the genesis of the child, Lynch has at different times responded: 'It was born nearby' and 'Maybe it was found.' The film, shot entirely at night, was five years in the making, which should have created an impossible strain in the relationship between director and star. Luckily in Jack Nance, Lynch found someone he described as 'a zero-motivated actor'. Nance's requirements for entertainment for the hours, days and weeks between takes were nothing beyond a room and a chair. One of the defining qualities of David Lynch's work is his use of sound. *Eraserhead* is never silent, filled with the amplified noises of shrieks and moans, sinister laughing, even eye rubbing. At its quietest, the industrial vibration recedes to a background hum. In John Alexander's *The Films of David Lynch*, the director says:

> There's not one particular kind of sound that I like but if I had to pick a category it would be factory sounds. I like the power of them and it makes a picture in my mind … I like the idea of factories and factory life probably because I don't know that much about them. I can just imagine a world and it leads to a bigger place where many strange and beautiful things can happen.

MEMORABLE MOMENTS The scene in which Henry visits Mary and her parents. The salad is tossed by immobile grandma, by mother placing the bowl in her lap, the spoons in her hands, and then manipulating her hands to mix the salad. Mary's father, Mr X has bought miniature man-made chickens, the 'strangest darn things'. He advises Henry to: 'Just cut 'em up like regular chickens.' When he does they begin to ooze blood and vibrate. Mary's mother in turn starts to squeal, gets up from the table and leaves the room.

KEY LINES

Henry is accosted by Mrs X who asks him if he has had sexual intercourse with her daughter.
Mrs X: 'There's a baby at the hospital…'
Mary: 'Mom.'
Mrs X: '… and you're the father.'
Mary: 'Mother, they're still not sure it is a baby.'

THE EXORCIST
US, 1973, WARNER/HOYA, 122 MINS

D *WILLIAM FRIEDKIN;* **PR** *NOEL MARSHALL;* **SC** *WILLIAM PETER BLATTY (FROM HIS NOVEL);* **PH** *(METROCOLOR) OWEN ROIZMAN;* **M** *KRZYSZTOF PENDERECKI, HANS WERNER HENZE, GEORGE CRUMB, ANTON WEBERN, MIKE OLDFIELD, JACK NITZSCHE;* **ED** *JORDAN LEONDOPOULOS*

CAST *ELLEN BURSTYN (CHRIS MACNEILL), MAX VON SYDOW (FATHER MERRIN), LEE J. COBB (LT. WILLIAM KINDERMAN), KITTY WINN (SHARON SPENCER), JACK MACGOWRAN (BURKE DENNINGS), JASON MILLER (FATHER DAMIEN KARRAS), LINDA BLAIR (REGAN MACNEILL), WILLIAM O'MALLEY (FATHER DYER), MERCEDES MCCAMBRIDGE (VOICE OF THE DEVIL)*

THE STORY In a prologue, Jesuit archaeologist Father Damien on a dig in Northern Iraq discovers a medallion depicting Mary and the baby Jesus near a figurine of a demon. The setting swiftly cuts to Georgetown, Washington DC, where movie star Chris MacNeill lives with her twelve-year-old daughter Regan while making a film called *Crash Course* on the campus of the Catholic Georgetown University, directed by an alcoholic Englishman, Burke Dennings. Chris is soon disturbed by odd noises in the attic and Regan reveals she and an imaginary friend have played with an Ouija board. Regan's conduct deteriorates, objects fly around her room, and she utters gross obscenities in a strange voice. Doctors operate on her, but she deteriorates further. When Burke Dennings, the film director, dies on the steps outside the MacNeill home, homicide cop Lt. Kinderman enters the scene.

Meanwhile Father Karras SJ, counsellor at Georgetown, is losing his faith and is guilty about his mother dying in a paupers' hospital. Baffled doctors suggest exorcism in Regan's case, and Chris is put in touch with Karras, who is joined by Father Merrin. During nocturnal exorcism, Merrin and Karras are subjected to physical and verbal abuse and Merrin has a fatal heart attack. When the furious Karras attacks Regan, the evil spirit leaves her body for his and he leaps to his death. Regan recovers, remembers nothing, and leaves town with her mother, who presents Karras's superior with the silver medallion Father Merrin found in Iraq.

I'm telling you that that person up there isn't my daughter.'

84

THE FILM Five of the six national newspaper critics gave *The Exorcist* a black spot – 'indicates antipathy' – in *Monthly Film Bulletin,* but the public embraced it and made it a box-office success. But it was no feel-good movie. Stories appeared in the papers of people becoming obsessed with the film and others rushing from the cinema as if possessed. It had been preceded by numerous pictures involving transactions with the devil (most famously Polanski's *Rosemary's Baby,* 1958) and many others followed, among them *The Omen* trilogy. But none had, or has had, the visceral appeal of *The Exorcist.* Friedkin's picture is both obscure and up-front, its background unexplained and dramatic ellipses accompanied by gross-out scenes of Regan

▲ *THE EXORCIST The ironic surreal image of Father Merrin confronting the ultimate evil in suburban Washington DC.*

splattering her interrogators with streams of green goo and obscene abuse that would set the special effects agenda for the next two decades.

The low-key lighting makes Washington DC look sinister and menacing. This is an insecure world, between the American withdrawal from Vietnam and the fall of Saigon, and Nixon wrestling with his personal devils. Chris MacNeill is out of a bad marriage but her daughter is attached to her Rome-based, uninvolved father. Chris despises the film she's appearing in and whose director is an alcoholic. The guilt-ridden Father Karras is losing his faith while his Jesuit colleagues have made too easy an accommodation with secular society.

Crude as it often is, *The Exorcist* touched a nerve at Watergate time. It gets below our rational guard, asking us how evil might insinuate itself within the complacencies of our society. In *Eichmann in Jerusalem* (1963), Hannah Arendt coined the phrase 'the banality of evil'; *The Exorcist*, as melodramatic metaphor, suggests that in our daily lives evil may customarily propose itself in apparently banal terms.

ODD/SALIENT FACTS Blatty, hitherto author of comic works, was inspired by a newspaper item he read while at Georgetown University, about a 14-year-old boy disturbed after using a Ouija board. Max von Sydow's performance was based on the Jesuit theologian Pierre Teilhard de Chardin (1881–1955). During the filming nine people associated with the film died, among them Jack MacGowran and von Sydow's brother, and a request was made to exorcise the set. People at early screenings vomited and went into convulsions, and though the film was briefly available on video in Britain it was subsequently banned by British censors to prevent adolescent girls from seeing it alone in bed.

MEMORABLE MOMENTS Father Merrin confronting the demonic statue in the Iraqi sunset.

Regan's head twisting through 360 degrees.

The arrival of Father Merrin in Washington, silhouetted against the MacNeill's house at night, a shot influenced by a Magritte painting.

Father Karras throwing himself through Regan's bedroom window.

KEY LINES

Regan, stabbing herself in the crotch with a crucifix: 'Let Jesus fuck you.'

Chris MacNeill: 'I'm telling you that that person up there isn't my daughter.'

Father Merrin: 'The demon is a liar. He would like to confuse us, but he will also mix lies with the truth to attack us. The attack is psychological and powerful, so don't listen. Remember that, do not listen.'

FANTASIA
USA, 1940, DISNEY/RKO, 120 MINS

D (STORY) JOE GRANT, DICK HUEMER, (INDIVIDUAL MUSIC NUMBERS) SAMUEL ARMSTRONG, JAMES ALGAR, BILL ROBERTS, PAUL SATTERFIELD, HAMILTON LUSKE, JIM HANDLEY, FORD BEEBE, T. HEE, NORM FERGUSON, WILFRED JACKSON; **MD** EDWARD H. PLUMB **D** BEN SHARPSTEEN

CAST DEEMS TAYLOR, LEOPOLD STOKOWSKI AND THE PHILADELPHIA SYMPHONY ORCHESTRA

SYNOPSIS Deems Taylor, musicologist and resident presenter of the New York Symphony Orchestra's network radio broadcasts, introduces the film as the musicians take their place and tune up. Stokowski mounts the podium and lifts his baton for:

1. 'Toccata and Fugue in D Minor' by J. S. Bach accompanied by abstract images influenced by Kandinsky and avant-garde cinema.

2. 'The Dance of the Sugar Plum Fairy' from Tchaikovsky's *Nutcracker Suite*, illustrated by fairies, mushrooms, flowers, fish and cutie snowflakes dancing.

3. Paul Dukas's 'The Sorcerer's Apprentice' featuring Mickey Mouse as the magician's hubristic assistant who draws on his master's powers to launch an unstoppable batallion of brooms fetching buckets of water, threatening to drown the Sorcerer's home. The Sorcerer awakes to banish the intruders and chastise Mickey. At the end of the piece Mickey climbs up to the podium and shakes hands with Stokowski.

4. Part 1 of the suite of Igor Stravinsky's ballet *The Rite of Spring*, the film's only work by a living composer. This has little to do with the sensational 1913 presentation in Paris by the Russian Ballet, when the combination of peasant fertility ceremonies and a dissonant, arhythmic score produced a near-riot. The Disney version (at the risk of offending fundamentalists) traced the geological creation of our planet, the development of life, the battles and extinction of the dinosaurs, and the resurgence of the world.

5. Beethoven's Sixth Symphony (the Pastoral) rendered as a campus picnic on Mount Olympus attended by bra-busting nymphs, preening sports-squad centaurs and a jocular Bacchus.

6. Ponchielli's 'Dance of the Hours' from the opera *Gioconda*, a ballet performed with comic grace and restrained ferocity by hippos, alligators, elephants and ostriches, animals not noted for their dexterity.

7. Moussorgsky's 'A Night on Bald Mountain', [sic] a gothic *Walpurgisnacht* in which spirits rise from the grave to make obeisance to the Black God, Tchernobog, gives way to Schubert's 'Ave Maria' as dawn breaks. Evil draws back into its lair, and trails of candles bear light out into the countryside.

THE FILM Animated films are probably the most labour-intensive activity since the Pyramids were built, and Walt Disney is one of the greatest, most complex artists of this century. *Fantasia* was its most ambitious picture. Four years in production, it was not only made for adult audiences but in a stereo-sound system for which no cinemas were equipped. *Fantasia* runs the gamut from the kitsch of the Beethoven, which Stokowski loathed, to the magnificent handling of *The Rite of Spring*, which was praised by the astronomer Edwin P. Hubble and the biologist Julian Huxley. Stravinsky held his tongue at the time but later called Stokowski's conducting 'execrable' and said of the animation: 'I will say nothing about the visual complement as I do not wish to criticize an unresisting imbecility.' The movie is, of course, locked in the visual ideas and social attitudes of its time

and has a reverential attitude towards high art. It is also sentimental and cute, especially in the traditional Disney preoccupation with maternal love. But in a disturbing and stimulating fashion the film expresses Disney's vision of a world torn between stability and chaos, the former being symbolized by home, the latter by metamorphosis. His feeling, or fear, that anything can readily become anything else varies from the playful to the terrifying. In *The Nutcracker* thistles become cossack dancers, toadstools turn into mandarins; in 'A Night on Bald Mountain' [sic] men are transformed into demons, giving this penultimate sequence a nightmare quality that the pallid 'Ave Maria' cannot obliterate.

Patronized by many critics and disappointing popular audiences that had rigid expectations of a Disney product, the film initially failed. Along with *Citizen Kane*, which opened a few months later, it was one of Hollywood's great 'flops d'estime' of

▼ *FANTASIA* The young rodent apprentice, in thrall to the Disney work ethic, tries to out-sorcer his master.

the early 1940s. Like Welles's masterpiece it became a cult movie, and it has never quite lost that status. For the drug generation of the late 1960s and '70s it was a trip film to get high on, like Kubrick's *2001*.

ODD/SALIENT FACTS Disney drifted accidentally into *Fantasia*, while planning a comic short based on Dukas's 'Sorcerer's Apprentice' to revive the flagging fortunes of Mickey Mouse. An encounter with Stokowski launched the movie. Stokowski was devoted to bringing classical music to a mass public and saw a collaboration with Disney as a great opportunity. According to one ex-employee Walt couldn't even pronounce the names of Bach ('Batch') and Beethoven ('Beath-uven'). Made at great expense with Stokowski conducting a pick-up Los Angeles band, the 'Sorcerer's Apprentice' film was too long and too expensive to be put out on its own. When the movie took off as a two-hour feature, the Philadelphia Orchestra, which he had conducted from 1912 to 1938, was brought in. The film was cut from 116 to 81 minutes in the States and released in a double-bill with a Western. In wartime Britain it fared better, though it couldn't be shown in stereo.

KEY LINES

A dialogue following *The Sorcerer's Apprentice*:
Mickey Mouse: 'Mr Stokowski. Mr Stokowski. [Whistling to attract attention] My congratulations, sir.'
Leopold Stokowski: 'Congratulations to you, Mickey.'
M.M.: 'Gee thanks. Well so long. I'll be seeing you.'
L.S.: 'Bye.'

FAREWELL MY LOVELY (AKA MURDER, MY SWEET)

US, 1944, RKO, 95 MINS

D *EDWARD DMYTRYK;* **PR** *ADRIAN SCOTT;* **SC** *JOHN PAXTON (FROM RAYMOND CHANDLER'S NOVEL FAREWELL, MY LOVELY;* **PH** *(BW) HARRY J. WILD;* **ED** *JOSEPH NORIEGA;* **M** *ROY WEBB* **CAST** *DICK POWELL (PHILIP MARLOWE), MIKE MAZURKI (MOOSE MALLOY), CLAIRE TREVOR (VELMA VALENTO/HELEN GRAYLE), ANNE SHIRLEY (ANN GRAYLE), MILES MANDER (MR GRAYLE), DOUGLAS WALTON (LINDSAY MARRIOTT), OTTO KRUGER (JULES AMTHOR), DON DOUGLAS (LT. RANDALL), PAUL PHILLIPS (DET. NULTY), RALF HAROLDE (DR SONDERBORG), ESTHER HOWARD (MRS FLORIAN)*

THE STORY Los Angeles private detective Philip Marlowe, his eyes bandaged, is being interrogated by Lt. Randall and others about a series of murders. In an extended flashback he explains how a recently released convict, the dim-witted giant Moose Malloy, hired him to find Velma Valento, his lover, whom he hasn't seen since he went to jail eight years back. Marlowe tracks down Jessie Florian, the alcoholic widow of the man who employed Velma as a singer. He is next hired by the prissy artist Lindsay Marriott, who's involved in the return of a stolen necklace and needs a bodyguard. Marlowe is knocked out, Marriott is murdered, and Marlowe is brought in for questioning. Ann Grayle, a millionaire's daughter, shows interest in his investigations. Visiting the Grayle mansion in Brentwood he meets Grayle and his much younger wife, Helen. He is dragged to quack psychologist Amthor's apartment, knocked out again and taken to a private hospital to be given truth drugs. Amthor is involved in blackmail and sets up rich women as targets for Marriott, a gigolo and thief. Helen Grayle is Moose's long-lost Velma, wanting to protect her new identity. In a final showdown at the Grayles' beach house, Helen is killed by her husband, who in turn kills and is killed by Moose Malloy, who's already murdered Amthor. Ann Grayle, a witness to the killings, clears Marlowe of all charges. She accompanies him home, and they kiss in the back of a taxi.

> **'She was as cute as lace panties, a redhead.'**

THE FILM *Farewell My Lovely* is double-distilled *film noir* set in a decadent Los Angeles of phoneys and criminals, old money protecting family skeletons. Linking high and low is Velma/Mrs Grayle, ex-mistress of a criminal, present wife of a patrician and, as played by Claire Trevor, one of the screen's greatest *femmes fatales*. Hardboiled, wise-cracking, incorruptible Philip Marlowe is played by lightweight musical comedy star Dick Powell. The role changed the direction of Powell's career, and he became one of the screen's new tough guys. 'It ended my ten-year effort to escape musical', he said. 'Offers for hardboiled roles poured in after the picture was released and a new career was opened for me.' The film also provided Edward Dmytryk with his first major opportunity as director.

The movie rights to *Farewell My Lovely* had been acquired by RKO for $2,000 and turned into the B-movie *The Falcon*

Takes Over (1942), featuring George Sanders. The success of Warner Brothers' *The Maltese Falcon* (1941) and the word that Chandler was working at Paramount on an adaptation of James M. Cain's *Double Indemnity* persuaded RKO that an A-picture of *Farewell My Lovely* might be profitable, and so Dick Powell became the screen's first Philip Marlowe. Many still think him the best, though Chandler's ideal actor for the role was Cary Grant and Humphrey Bogart was his favourite among those who played him in his lifetime.

ODD/SALIENT FACTS The film was premiered in the States as *Farewell My Lovely*, but fearing audiences would think it a Powell musical, RKO at the last minute decided to release it as *Murder My Sweet*. Chandler's reputation was much greater in Britain where it was shown under the original title. Edward Dmytryk and the film's producer, Adrian Scott, were both members of the Communist Party and as two of the 'Hollywood Ten' they went to jail in the late 1940s for refusing to answer questions before Un-American Activities Committee. In 1975 there was another first-rate version of *Farewell My Lovely*, directed by Dick Richards, starring Robert Mitchum as Marlowe, Charlotte Rampling as Velma, and pulp novelist Jim Thompson as Mr Grayle. Dr Sonderberg and Jules Amthor were conflated into the lesbian brothel owner Frances Amthor.

▼ *FAREWELL MY LOVELY* Dick Powell, the screen's first Marlowe, ignites femme fatale Claire Trevor.

MEMORABLE MOMENTS The blindfolded Marlowe being interrogated by the cops in a room illuminated by neon lights from across the street.

Dick Powell evoking his days as a hoofer with a little hop-scotch dance on the chequered hall floor of the Grayle mansion.

Marlowe's expressionist nightmare in which he's pursued through a succession of identical doors by a man with a hypodermic syringe.

KEY LINES

Moose on Velma: 'She was as cute as lace panties, a redhead.'

Marlowe: 'I caught the blackjack behind my ear. A black pool opened up at my feet. It had no bottom.'

Ann: 'I don't think you know which side you're on.'
Marlowe: 'I don't know which side anyone's on, I don't even know who's playing today.'

Mrs Grayle: 'This will be the first time I ever killed someone I knew so little and liked so well.'

FAT CITY

US, 1972, RASTAR/COLUMBIA, 96 MINS

D JOHN HUSTON; **PR** RAY STARK; **SC** LEONARD GARDNER (FROM HIS OWN NOVEL); **PH** (EASTMANCOLOR) CONRAD HALL; **ED** MARGARET BOOTH; **M SUP** MARVIN HAMLISCH **CAST** STACY KEACH (BILLY TULLY), JEFF BRIDGES (ERNIE MUNGER), SUSAN TYRRELL (OMA), CANDY CLARK (FAYE), NICHOLAS COLOSANTO (RUBEN), ART ARAGON (BABE), CURTIS COKES (EARL), SIXTO RODRIGUEZ (LUCERO), BILLY WALKER (WES), WAYNE MAHAN (BUFFORD), RUBEN NAVARRO (FUENTES)

THE STORY Stockton, an inland town in Central California. The drunken, 29-year-old ex-boxer Billy Tully sees 18-year-old Ernie Munger punching a bag in the YMCA, spars with him and tells him to see his former manager, Ruben. Believing he might have a white heavyweight contender on his hands, Ruben arranges several amateur fights for Ernie. But Ernie marries Faye, his teenage girlfriend, and gives up boxing. Meanwhile Billy

▲ *FAT CITY* Ex-champ John Huston shows Stacey Keach how to throw a straight left.

moves in with Oma, a helpless alcoholic whose black husband is doing time, and who works as a casual agricultural labourer. Ernie and Billy meet up again labouring in the fields and both decide to return to the ring. Ruben takes them both on and persuades Billy to leave Oma. Ernie wins his first professional fight in the same bill in which, as the chief attraction, Billy narrowly defeats an ailing Mexican by technical knockout. But Billy's eye is badly damaged, his cut of the purse is a mere $100, and in disgust he takes to drink and stops fighting. Some while later, a drunken bum, Billy meets Ernie who's now a father and has several minor wins to his credit. They have a cup of coffee together, sitting in silence at the counter.

THE FILM After years largely devoted to empty big-budget movies with major stars, John Huston made this small-scale, superbly acted minor masterpiece. A critical success that the general public rejected as too downbeat, *Fat City* replaced

Beat the Devil as the cult Huston movie. It's his only picture dealing with one of his great passions, prizefighting, and it examines the theme running through his best work – the pursuit of illusory dreams and the way we always finish up as losers. The film's title is a slang term for a low-life dreamer's golden paradise or the idea of having made it. Unlike most boxing pictures, *Fat City* isn't an indictment of the brutality, degradation and corruption of the fight game (though these issues are touched on); it springs from a love of boxing and a respect for its practitioners. Moreover the hopeless dreamers – Ruben the manager and Billy the fighter – are small men living in an undistinguished town with no real prospects of getting into the big time. By the end Ernie seems to have set aside his illusions to settle for points decisions in unimportant bouts. The movie has a documentary feeling in its treatment of the agri-business and of gymnasium life, and it makes great play of the contrast between the dark interiors of Stockton's seedy bars and the bright, piercing sunlight of the world outside. The film makes big, unsignalled leaps in time from sequence to sequence, and after their initial meeting at the YMCA Billy's and Ernie's paths don't cross again until the movie has been running for an hour. The film's initial mood is established by Kris Kristofferson singing his poignant 'Help Me Make It Through the Night' over the opening credits as Billy gets up in a dismal flophouse, and the tune is subsequently played on the soundtrack by a mariachi band.

ODD/SALIENT FACTS The first choice for the role of Billy was Marlon Brando, who couldn't make up his mind if he wanted the part. John Huston left school at 14 to train as a boxer and became amateur lightweight champion of California. Nicholas Colosanto, who plays Ruben, achieved his greatest success as another sporting figure, 'Coach', bartender in the first series of the TV sitcom *Cheers*.

MEMORABLE MOMENTS Billy meeting the drunken Oma and her black lover in a bar.

The labourers waiting in the pre-dawn to be hired for fruit picking.

Ruben tossing Ernie's boxing trunks to the next fighter saying 'Don't worry – it's not your blood.'

The Mexican fighter Lucero urinating blood before the fight.

Billy and Ernie's final meeting in the diner.

KEY LINES

Ernie: 'I saw you fight once.'
Billy: 'Did I win?'
Ernie: 'No.'

Ruben: 'When I got my jaw broken and I had to suck everything through a straw, I began asking if it was all worthwhile.'

Billy justifying a day spent gathering walnuts: 'I tell you it's almost as good as roadwork for getting you back into shape.'

Ruben after Billy's fluke win: 'I defy you to say this guy isn't great, we got a real winner here, the most colourful attraction in northern California.'

Billy: 'A lousy hundred bucks – is that all my blood and sweat is worth?'

FITZCARRALDO
WEST GERMANY, 1982, WERNER HERZOG
FILMPRODUKTION/PRO-JECT FILMPRODUKTION, 158 MINS
D WERNER HERZOG; **PR** WERNER HERZOG, LUCKI STIPETIC;
SC WERNER HERZOG; **PH** (COL) THOMAS MAUCH; **ED** BEATE MAINKA-JELLINGHAUS; **M** POPOL VUH
CAST KLAUS KINSKI (BRIAN SWEENEY FITZGERALD, CALLED 'FITZCARRALDO'), CLAUDIA CARDINALE (MOLLY), JOSÉ LEWGOY (DON AQUILINO), MIGUEL ANGEL FUENTES (CHOLO), PAUL HITTSCHLER (PAUL, SHIP'S CAPTAIN), HUEREQUEQUE ENRIQUE BOHORQUEZ (HUEREQUEQUE)

THE STORY The setting is early twentieth-century Peru. The Irish adventurer Brian Sweeney Fitzgerald, whose name has been transformed by Spanish speakers into Fitzcarraldo, is obsessed with opera. He makes a 1,200-mile journey down the Amazon with his lover, brothel-owner Molly, using a paddle when the motor gives out, just to see Caruso and Sarah Bernhardt perform at the Manaus opera house in Brazil. He's determined to build an opera house in the Peruvian river port of Iquitos, but is penniless following the failure of his schemes to establish a Trans-Andean Railway and an ice factory. Mocked by the rubber-barons who run the town, Fitzcarraldo decides to finance his opera house by laying claim to a remote area of rubber trees that remain untouched because of the ferocious Jivaro tribe and the impassable Pongo rapids. Financed by Molly, he buys a steamboat, hires a barbaric crew, and plans to take the boat, christened *Molly Aida*, across a steep isthmus between two rivers. When all but three of his crew desert, the Jivaro Indians assist the portage of the boat, believing it to be the realization of an ancient prophecy of liberation. After the engineering feat that takes the Molly Aida to the other river, the Jivaro cut the mooring ropes and it floats down to the Amazon whence it came, battered but miraculously surviving the rapids. Don Aquilino buys the boat back, but before delivering it, Fitzcarraldo brings an opera company from Manaus to perform Bellini's *I puritani* on deck as it steams past Iquitos.

THE FILM Werner Herzog's pictures centre on loners in flight from rational society; they embrace the sophistication of the primitive world and reject the barbarism of developed civilization. Colonialism, the means by which the supposedly developed impose their values on the supposedly undeveloped, is the ultimate evil whether practised in Latin America or Australia. Herzog is a mystical, obsessive questor, the kind of person cults grow around. He makes pictures in which the whole cast is made up of dwarfs (*Even Dwarfs Started Small*), or all the actors are hypnotized (*Heart of Glass*), or the central role is played by a mentally retarded lavatory attendant (Bruno S. in *Kaspar Hauser*). In five Herzog pictures the hero was the ubiquitous Klaus Kinski (1926–91), who forever hovered on the edge of madness, and their most lunatic collaboration was on *Fitzcarraldo*. Like many Herzog pictures it was shot in English (the dialogue in this case written by playwright Sam Shepard), then dubbed into German to keep laughter at bay. Despite the frequent crudeness, the film has an epic grandeur in its modern re-enactment of the punishment of

> ### 'Why are they slaving for us?'

Sisyphus, and there is much beauty in its images. The outcast Fitzcarraldo, the decent old sea-dog Paul he hires to captain the *Molly Aida*, and the up-river journey inevitably evoke Joseph Conrad's *Heart of Darkness*.

ODD/SALIENT FACTS *Fitzcarraldo* was made under difficult conditions in the Peruvian jungle, initially as a film starring Jack Nicholson that never got underway, then as a film co-starring Jason Robards and Mick Jagger that was abandoned after a few weeks' shooting, and finally as the picture starring Kinski. Shooting it in the Amazonian jungle was a horrendous experience that matched Fitzcarraldo's own travails, and Les Blanc's detached *cinéma-vérité* account of the production, *Burden of Dreams*, is more important than the completed film, being the art work of which the movie called *Fitzcarraldo* is the evidence.

MEMORABLE MOMENTS Fitz and Molly demanding entry to the gala performance in Manaus.

Fitz ringing the bell on the Iquitos tower to demand attention.

The Jivaro Indians lined up on Fitz's boat, their fingers gently touching the rails to capture its magic.

The epic transportation of the *Molly Aida* from river to river.

KEY LINES

The Manager of the Manaus Opera: 'The better-off citizens of Manaus send their laundry to Lisbon because they consider the Amazon impure.'

Fitzcarraldo (to a rubber-baron who insults him at a banquet): 'I swear I will bring opera to Iquitos. I will eclipse you. I will out-million you. I will out-perform you. I will re-discover rubber. I'll really put rubber on the map, sir. The reality of your world is just a crude caricature of the make-believe of grand opera.'

Missionary (speaking of old Indians): 'They seem to have the idea which we cannot dispel that everyday life is an illusion behind which lies the reality of dreams.'

Fitzcarraldo (of Jivaro Indians working to transport his steamship): 'Why are they slaving for us?'

▼ *FITZCARRALDO Indians go about their lives as Fitzcarraldo's boat is hauled across an Amazonian isthmus.*

FIVE EASY PIECES

US, 1970, BBS PRODUCTIONS, 98 MINS

D BOB RAFELSON; **PR** BERT SCHNEIDER; **SC** ADRIEN JOYCE (FROM A STORY BY RAFELSON AND JOYCE); **PH** (COL) LASZLO KOVACS; **ED** CHRISTOPHER HOLMES, GERALD SHEPPARD; **M** PIANO WORKS BY CHOPIN, MOZART AND BACH PLAYED BY PEARL KAUFMAN, COUNTRY AND WESTERN SONGS SUNG BY TAMMY WYNETTE

CAST JACK NICHOLSON (ROBERT EROICA DUPEA), LOIS SMITH (PARTITA DUPEA), RALPH WAITE (CARL FIDELIO DUPEA), WILLIAM CHALLEE (NICHOLAS DUPEA, THEIR FATHER), KAREN BLACK (RAYETTE DIPESTO), SUSAN ANSPACH (CATHERINE VAN OST), BILLY 'GREEN' BUSH (ELTON), FANNIE FLAGG (STONEY), HELENA KALLIANIÒTES (PALM APODACA), TONI BASIL (TERRY GROUSE), SALLY ANNE STRUTHERS (BETTY), MARLENE MACGUIRE (TWINKY), JOHN RYAN (SPICER), LORNA THAYER (WAITRESS)

THE STORY Bobby Dupea works as an oilrigger in Southern California and lives in a dilapidated frame house with Rayette, a good-hearted, dim-witted waitress. He spends most of his time drinking and bowling with his workmate Elton and Elton's wife Stoney. Bobby is a professional pianist in flight from his cultured family, and crisis comes when Rayette becomes pregnant, Elton is arrested for jumping bail, and Bobby learns his father has suffered two strokes and is dying. He decides to visit the family home on an island in Puget Sound in the Pacific North West and reluctantly takes Rayette with him. They give a lift to an aggressive lesbian couple heading for Alaska to escape civilization. Bobby leaves Rayette at a motel and joins his family – sister Partita, a neurotic pianist, his speechless father attended by a male nurse, his supercilious violinist brother Carl, and Carl's pianist fiancée, Catherine. While Carl is away Catherine urges Bobby to play Chopin for her, and they finish up in bed. Rayette turns up and is out of place. There is a row when some pretentious visitors annoy Catherine, patronize Rayette, and drive Bobby into a furious denunciation. The following day

▼ *FIVE EASY PIECES Impromptu concert performance by déraciné Jack Nicholson caught in a Californian tail-back.*

Bobby attempts to talk to his father about his problems, before driving off. At a filling station, Bobby slips away, leaving his car and wallet for Rayette as he hitches a lift from a truck-driver heading north into the wilds of Canada.

THE FILM *Five Easy Pieces* is the best of the six Rafelson-directed pictures Nicholson has appeared in, and his performance confirmed his star status, Bobby laying the basis for the roles of his maturity. Bobby exemplifies the rebellious mood of the Vietnam War era, but *Five Easy Pieces* transcends its times to present a superb portrait of an American malcontent. The oppressively overcultured world of the Dupea family is sharply contrasted by art director Tobe Rafelson with the garish blue-collar culture of trailer parks, bowling alleys and diners. On the soundtrack there is nothing between Bach, Chopin and Mozart on the one hand, and Tammy Wynette's declamatory C&W songs on the other. There is in fact an imbalance in the film, as in cinematic terms the world of oil rigs and trailer parks is more attractive than the claustrophobic Dupea household, and the brash, sensual Karen Black is more inviting than the repressed Susan Anspach. The classical piano pieces can't compete with the driving up-front appeal of Wynette singing about standing by your man and D-I-V-O-R-C-E. To middle-class audiences in 1970 she was a liberating force, an introduction to the hard-hat blues of Nashville. Bobby flees from the emotionally chilly family to the sentimental trailer-park ambience of Rayette and Elton, and ends up rejecting both. The ending is one of the toughest, most uncompromising in American cinema.

ODD/SALIENT FACTS The roadside diner 'No substitutions' scene was inspired by screenwriter Joyce's seeing an aggressive, young actor doing a similar routine in a Sunset Strip restaurant. She later came to know him as Jack Nicholson.

MEMORABLE MOMENTS Bobby getting mad in an early morning traffic jam, leaving his car, jumping on to a removal truck and playing Chopin on an upright piano.

Bobby's reunion with his sister in a Los Angeles recording studio.

The conversations with the two women heading for Alaska. Bobby trying to order in the roadside diner.

The tracking shot taking in the cultural family environment during his performance of Chopin.

> **'You play that thing one more time and I'm going to melt it down into hairspray.'**

Bobby's conciliatory speech to his unresponding father on a frosty promontory.

The final long take as Bobby heads off, leaving Rayette with his wallet and the clapped-out car.

KEY LINES
Bobby to Rayette about 'Stand By Your Man': 'You play that thing one more time and I'm going to melt it down into hairspray.'

Waitress: 'I don't make the rules.'
Bobby: 'OK I'll make it as easy for you as I can. I'd like an omelette plain and a chicken salad sandwich on wheat toast. No mayonnaise, no butter, no lettuce, and a cup of coffee.'
Waitress: 'Number Two. Chicken sal san, hold the butter, the lettuce and the mayonnaise. And a cup of coffee. Anything else?'
Bobby: 'Yeah. Now all you have to do is hold the chicken, bring me the toast, and give me the check for the chicken salad sandwich, and you haven't broken any rules.'
Waitress: 'You want me to hold the chicken, huh?'
Bobby: 'I want you to hold it between your knees.'
Waitress: 'You see that sign sir? I guess you'll have to leave. I'm not going to stand any more of your smartness and sarcasm.'
Bobby: 'You see this sign?' (sweeping everything off the table)

FORBIDDEN PLANET
US, 1956, MGM, 98 MINS

D FRED MCLEOD WILCOX; *PR* NICHOLAS NAYFACK; *SC* CYRIL HUME (BASED ON A STORY BY IRVING BLOCK AND ALLEN ADLER); *PH* (TECHNICOLOR, CINEMASCOPE) GEORGE J. FOLSEY; *ED* FERRIS WEBSTER; *M* ('ELECTRONIC TONALITIES') LOUIS AND BEBE BARON

CAST WALTER PIDGEON (DOCTOR MOBIUS), ANNE FRANCIS (ALTAIRA), LESLIE NIELSEN (COMMANDER ADAMS), WARREN STEVENS (LT. 'DOC' OSTROW, JACK KELLY (LT. FAIRMAN), RICHARD ANDERSON (CHIEF QUINN), EARL HOLLIMAN (COOK)

▲ **FORBIDDEN PLANET** *Anne Francis, a young Leslie Nielsen and Walter Pidgeon attend to Robbie the Robot.*

THE STORY 2200 AD. The US Planet Cruiser C5 7D under Commander Adams approaches the Planet Altair and lands against the protest of Doctor Mobius, who lives there with his daughter, Altaira. His spaceship, *Bellerophon*, crashed on the planet twenty years before and subsequently his wife and crew were killed. Adams and his men are met by Mobius's servant, Robbie the Robot, a multilingual genius, and they're entertained at his palatial home. They're all attracted to Mobius's beautiful daughter who has never before met any earthlings. It transpires that Altair was once occupied by the Krel, a superior race who were mysteriously wiped out, and one by one Adams's crew are killed by a strange force. It appears that this destructive enemy is a projection of the Id, first that of the Krel, now of Mobius. Only by an act of will can he confront it, killing himself, and releasing Adams to escape with Altaira from the forbidden planet before it explodes into atomic dust.

THE FILM Freud meets Shakespeare in this cunning, highly sophisticated outer-space version of *The Tempest*, in which Mobius is Prospero, Altaira a sexy 1950s Miranda, and the crucial aspects of Ariel and Caliban are divided between the loveable Robbie and the threatening Evil Force out there. Nothing dates so much as a society's idea of the future, and

Shakespeare's fable of a 'brave new world' here becomes frozen in a touchingly naive 1950s notion of the next millennium, and the special-effects designers draw on ideas of gracious living from *Better Homes and Gardens* and flying saucers from the covers of *Amazing Science Fiction*. But the explosion of the Id it predicted came about in the revolution of the 1960s. *Forbidden Planet* was the first time a major Hollywood studio made a movie set in outer space and it attracted an immediate cult following, paving the way for *Star Trek* and *2001*.

ODD/SALIENT FACTS Director Fred Wilcox spent his whole life working for MGM and is best-known for his first picture, *Lassie Come Home* (1943). Leslie Nielsen, the spaceship's commander, became a straight-faced figure in disaster movies (e.g. as Captain of the *USS Poseidon*) and then as star of genre send-ups (e.g. *Airplane*, *The Naked Gun*). Robbie the Robot reappeared in MGM's *Invisible Boy*. The film has one of the screen's first electronic scores, and includes one of the first scenes in which characters are 'beamed up' to their spaceship.

MEMORABLE MOMENTS Robbie's first appearance to escort the earthlings.

The cook conniving with Robbie to obtain alcohol in a similar playful way to that of the drunken butler Stephano in *The Tempest* when he goes on a spree with Caliban.

Mobius's final confrontation with the fiery Id.

KEY LINES

Mobius: 'I didn't come by him [Robbie], I created him during my first months here.'

Altaira: 'What's a bathing suit?'

Mobius: 'In times long past, this planet was the home of a mighty, noble race of beings who called themselves the Krel. Ethically and technologically they were a million years ahead of humankind. For in unlocking the meaning of nature they had conquered even their baser selves, and when in the course of eons they had abolished sickness and insanity, crime and all injustice, they turned, still in high benevolence, upwards towards space. Then having reached the heights, this all but divine race disappeared in a single night, and nothing was preserved above ground.'

Mobius: 'My evil self is at that door, and I have no power to stop it.'

Mobius, rejecting the force: 'I deny you, I give you up!'

FORCE OF EVIL

US, 1948, MGM/ENTERPRISE PRODUCTIONS, 78 MINS
D ABRAHAM POLONSKY; **PR** BOB ROBERTS; **SC** ABRAHAM POLONSKY, IRA WOLFERT (FROM WOLFERT'S NOVEL TUCKER'S PEOPLE); **PH** (BW) GEORGE BARNES; **M** DAVID RAKSIN; **ED** ART SEID
CAST JOHN GARFIELD (JOE MORSE), THOMAS GOMEZ (LEO MORSE), BEATRICE PEARSON (DORIS LOWRY), ROY ROBERTS (BEN TUCKER), MARIE WINDSOR (EDNA TUCKER), HOWLAND CHAMBERLAIN (FRED BAUER), JACK OVERMAN (JUICE), PAUL FIX (FICCO), GEORGIA BACCHUS (SYLVIA MORSE), SID TOMACK (TAYLOR), STANLEY PRAGER (WALLY)

THE STORY Ambitious young lawyer Joe Morse has risen from the New York slums to become partner in a Wall Street firm and legal adviser to gangster Ben Tucker. Morse and Tucker are planning a gambling fix forcing small-time bookies into bankruptcy so they can take over the numbers racket and turn it into a legal lottery. But Morse's elder brother Leo, who put Joe through college and runs a small illegal betting office, refuses to join. The public prosecutor is conducting a campaign to drive out the numbers racketeers, and Tucker's strong-arm partner Ficco wants a piece of the action. Joe gets Leo to work for Tucker, but then falls in love with Leo's secretary, Doris, who wants him to abandon the rackets. Joe's phone is tapped by the investigators and his partner is working against him. When Ficco's men kill Leo, Joe confronts Tucker and Ficco, kills them both, and he and Doris decide to collaborate with the crime busters.

THE FILM This quasi-biblical, quasi-Marxist movie, written in a heightened poetic manner with an anguished voice-over, was

▼ *FORCE OF EVIL* Guilt-ridden John Garfield goes 'down to the bottom of the world' to find his brother's body beneath the George Washington Bridge.

one of the first to present crime as a branch of, and metaphor for, the capitalist system. Tucker is more a ruthless tycoon than a gangster. Leo sees himself as a regular businessman and runs his set-up as if it were a family. He knows he's a crook but feels it is impossible to be honest under the present American system. Every relationship is corrupted and the film carries a terrible weight of doom. The movie gets progressively darker, David Raksin's music becomes increasingly dissonant, until the final dawn when Joe, seen from a distance, descends a great stone staircase to find his dead brother and start a new life.

Polonsky, a screenwriter and first-time director, and Garfield, a politically committed actor, both of them left-wing and Jewish, put themselves on the line with *Force of Evil*, one of the most genuinely radical pictures to come out of Hollywood. It became a cult movie after Polonsky was blacklisted for refusing to testify before HUAC in 1950 (he didn't get his name on a film again until 1968 when he scripted Don Siegel's *Madigan* and 1969 when he directed the Robert Redford Western *Tell Them Willie Boy is Here*): and Garfield, the film's moving force, died of a heart attack aged 39, his health undermined as a result of his persecution by HUAC.

ODD/SALIENT FACTS The existing copies of the film are ten minutes shorter than the director's cut to fit into a double bill. George Barnes (who won an Oscar for Hitchcock's *Rebecca*) shot the movie; to get the right look, Polonsky gave him a book of Edward Hopper's Third Avenue paintings. The film's composer David Raksin, who did the music for Chaplin's *Modern Times* and Preminger's *Laura*, requested Polonsky's permission to name him as a fellow communist before appearing as a friendly witness at a 1953 HUAC hearing. The assistant director was Robert Aldrich, one of the outstanding cult directors of the 1950s, '60s and '70s.

MEMORABLE MOMENTS Joe Morse testing his secret line to Tucker after being told it is tapped.

Morse and Doris discussing the ethics of capitalism in the back of a taxi (anticipating the taxi sequence in *On the Waterfront*).

Leo's book-keeper Bauer murdered in a café after acting as his employer's Judas.

Joe on a deserted Wall Street at twilight, walking away with a gun in his belt from a world he's renouncing.

'What do you mean, "gangsters" – it's business.'

Joe descending the steps to find his brother's body on the rock.

KEY LINES

Joe's opening statement over a high angle shot of skyscrapers dwarfing St Andrew's Church, Wall Street: 'This is Wall Street and today was important because tomorrow's July Fourth. I intended to make my first million dollars, an exciting day in any man's life. Temporarily the enterprise was slightly illegal. You see I was the lawyer to the numbers racket.'

Joe to his Harvard-educated WASP colleague who's lost everything in the Wall Street crash: 'Tucker's making me rich now, and I'm the partner that's making you rich. I wear his old school tie and you wear mine. You can buy one for yourself at lunchtime off any pushcart.'

Leo to Joe: 'All that Cain did to Abel was kill him.'

Wally, Ficco's hitman: 'What do you mean, "gangsters" – it's business.'

FREAKS
US, 1932, MGM, 90 MINS

D TOD BROWNING; **PR** IRVING THALBERG, HARRY SHAROCK; **SC** WILLIS GOLDBECK, LEON GORDON, AL BOASBERG, EDGAR ALLEN WOOLF; **PH** MERRITT B. GERSTAD; **M** GAVIN BARNS; **ED** BASIL WRANGELL

CAST OLGA BACLANOVA (CLEOPATRA), HENRY VICTOR (HERCULES), WALLACE FORD (PHROSO), HARRY EARLES (HANS), LEILA HYAMS (VENUS), ROSCOE ATES (ROSCOE), ROSE DIONE (MME TETRALINI), DAISY AND VIOLET HILTON (SIAMESE TWINS), SCHLITZE (HERSELF), PETER ROBINSON (HUMAN SKELETON), ELISABETH GREEN (BIRD WOMAN), RANDION (LARVA MAN OR LIVING TORSO), JOSEPH-JOSEPHINE (ANDROGYNE), JOHNNY ECK (TRUNK MAN), FRANCES O'CONNOR AND MARTHA MORRIS (WOMEN WITHOUT ARMS), OLGA RODERICH (BEARDED WOMAN), KOO-KOO (HERSELF), EDWARD BROPHY AND MAT-MAC HUCH (THE ROLLO BROTHERS), ANGELO ROSSITTO (ANGELENO), DAISY EARLES (FRIEDA), ZIP AND FLIP (PINHEADS)

▲ *FREAKS Director Todd Browning, the ambivalent patriarch, standing in the midst of his family of freaks.*

THE STORY The film opens as a barker tells his customers the story of his star exhibit, once a beautiful woman, known as 'the peacock of the air' . We cut to Cleopatra, a trapeze artist working in the circus of Madame Tetralini. Cleopatra is having an affair with Hercules, the strong man, but is admired by Hans, one of the dwarves, much to the annoyance of his fiancée, Frieda. When Cleo finds out that Hans has inherited a fortune she decides to seduce, marry and poison him, thus gaining possession of the money. At the wedding, the fellow freaks all sing a song and pass around a loving-cup to welcome Cleopatra to their brotherhood. A drunken Cleo is disgusted, rejects the drink and with the help of Hercules humiliates Hans. Hans falls ill, but his friends discover what is happening and decide to

save Hans and take revenge. On a stormy night as the circus caravans are on the road, the freaks pursue and kill Hercules, and then chase after Cleopatra. Cut back to the barker introducing Cleopatra, who has been transformed into a stunted human chicken.

THE FILM A lengthy prologue informs the viewer of the attitude of the film we are about to see. It talks of the historical ill-treatment of people born with physical abnormalities and makes it clear that the film wishes to avoid demonising them. This sensibility is partly a true reflection of the film's approach. We see a crude estate manager bringing the land owner along to see a group of dancing pinheads in the hope that he will share his revulsion and eject the freaks. But Madame Tetralini is there to plead their case, and the noble aristocrat is happy for them to stay on his land. The film understands that the viewer will be shocked and fascinated by the physical deformities, and shows us the human torso light and smoke a cigarette, and Johnny Eck running around on his arms. The idea is that after the shock of the difference, we get used to the humanity of the characters, the obvious sweetness of the pinheads, the romantic entanglements of the (fake) Siamese twins. We never see the characters at work in the circus, only in their normal lives. The film features some stilted performances and is slow, and crudely moralistic until the wedding feast. Here Cleopatra is given a sinister welcome into the freaks' brotherhood that clearly foreshadows the film's climax. This and the film's horrific/comic finale reverse the thrust of the film. The characters are remarginalized, given sinister powers that suggest that they live on the outside because they belong there. This dark horror that exploits the freakishness of the freaks made the film uncomfortable for audiences. It received only a limited release in the US and none at all in Britain until 1963. This delay made it seem all the more dangerous, ensuring its continuing cult status.

ODD/SALIENT FACTS In the early cuts of the film, the sequence in which Hercules is chased by the freaks ends with the clear implication that they castrate him before killing him. Browning had achieved his greatest success with *Dracula* (1931) which was filmed scene-by-scene in a Spanish-language version on the same sets and with Bela Lugosi still in the lead

▼ *FRITZ THE CAT Fritz stepping far out in one of his drug-fuelled fantasies from Ralph Bakshi's adult cartoon.*

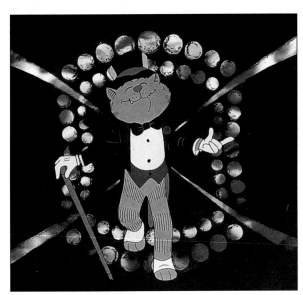

role. Browning went on to make just three more films before retiring in 1939. He had hoped to adapt the recently published *They Shoot Horses, Don't They?*, but was frustrated. The project didn't reach the screen until Sidney Pollack's version in 1969.

MEMORABLE MOMENTS The film's two standout scenes are the menacing wedding party and the final chase in which the menace is realized. The former begins when the dwarf Angeleno stands on the table, pours a loving-cup and starts the creepy, magic song, 'Gooble-Gobble, Gooble-Gobble, We'll make her one of us.' Cleopatra reacts badly to the threat: 'You filth, make me one of you, will you?' before carrying off her diminutive husband on her shoulders while her lover joins in the fun playing a tune on the trumpet.

KEY LINES

When the circus people visit the newborn baby of the bearded woman, Phroso the clown says: 'Ain't it cute. What is it?'

With Cleopatra revealed as the mutant chicken woman, the barker concludes: 'How she got that way will never be known. Some say a jealous lover, others that it was the code of the freaks, others the storm. Believe it or not, there she is.'

FRITZ THE CAT
US, 1971, FRITZ PRODUCTIONS/AURICA, 78 MINS
D RALPH BAKSHI; **PR** STEVE KRANTZ; **SC** RALPH BAKSHI, BASED ON CHARACTERS CREATED BY ROBERT CRUMB; **PH** (COL) GENA BORGHI; **ANIM** VIRGIL ROSS, MANUEL PEREZ, JOHN SPAREY; **M** ED BOGAS, RAY SHANKLIN; **ED** RENN REYNOLDS
VOICES SKIP HINNANT, ROSETTA LE NOIRE, JOHN MCCURRY, JUDY ENGLES, PHIL SEULING

THE STORY It is the 1960s and Fritz is a horny, hippie New York City cat who plays guitar in the park with his buddies. Chatting up three women he invites them round to his apartment for an orgy. There various other friends join in a feast of sex and drugs which is interrupted by two pig cops. Fritz is chased through a synagogue before hanging out in Harlem with some black crows. He gets very stoned, has some more sex and preaches revolution before his friend gets killed in a street riot. Fritz flees with his girlfriend Winston for a journey west, but the two fall out on the road and Fritz hooks up with some revolutionary, sexually abusive types. They encourage Fritz to blow up a refinery and set him up to be killed. Finally, fully recovered in hospital he enjoys some more group sex with his girlfriends.

THE FILM Robert Crumb is a cartoonist with a bizarre talent and himself the subject of a cult documentary *Crumb* (1995). In the 1960s his already-warped visual style was forever changed by his experiments with LSD. He became the cult cartoonist of the Haight-Ashbury set with his stoner satire and strange sexual obsessions. One of his creations Fritz the Cat was taken and put into this full-length picaresque satire of the counterculture. There is the strong suspicion that those responsible for this semi-coherent if visually impressive film were taking as many drugs as the characters in the film. The satire gets rather muddled, and the humour tends to be broad at best, perhaps proving the fundamental rule that dope and humour are a bad mix. This is a period piece, something specifically of its time targeted at a very narrow audience – i.e. it barely makes any sense without drugs. It may well ultimately serve as a useful gauge. If you find the satire relevant then you know you are living in some sad hippie past and if you find it funny you are clearly far too stoned and should go straight to bed. Once a must-see for rebellious teenagers, the film now has some nostalgic appeal but is recommended for heavy-duty Cheech and Chong fans only.

ODD/SALIENT FACTS This film marked the first directorial feature for Ralph Bakshi, who had honed his skills in Terrytoons and running the New York Division of Paramount cartoons. He went on to direct the bizarre experiment in cartoon film-making, *The Lord of the Rings* (1978), in which live action was painted over for a cartoon effect, and the similar noble failure, the animation/live action fusion *Cool World* (1992).

MEMORABLE MOMENTS The opening sequence in which a passing hippie is pissed upon from a great height by a workman.

KEY LINES

One of the women patronizing the black crow on yet another instance of racist attitudes towards black people: 'Why does a great actor like James Earl Jones always have to play black men?'

GET CARTER★
UK, 1971, MGM, 112 MINS

D *MIKE HODGES;* **PR** *MICHAEL KLINGER;* **SC** *MIKE HODGES, BASED ON THE NOVEL* JACK'S COMING HOME *BY TED LEWIS;* **PH** *(COL) WOLFGANG SUSCHITZKY;* **M** *ROY BUDD;* **ED** *JOHN TRUMPER*

CAST *MICHAEL CAINE (JACK CARTER), IAN HENDRY (ERIC PAICE), BRITT EKLAND (ANNA), JOHN OSBORNE (CYRIL KINNEAR), TONY BECKLEY (PETER), GEORGE SEWELL (CON MCARTY), GERALDINE MOFFATT (GLENDA), DOROTHY WHITE (MARGARET), ROSEMARIE DUNHAM (EDNA), PETRA MARKHAM (DOREAN), ALUN ARMSTRONG (KEITH), BRYAN MOSLEY (BRUMBY), GLYNN EDWARDS (ALBERT SWIFT), BERNARD HEPTON (THORPE), TERENCE RIGBY (GERALD FLETCHER), JOHN BINDON (SID FLETCHER), GODFREY QUIGLEY (EDDIE), KEVIN BRENNAN (HARRY)*

THE STORY Jack Carter travels back to his native Newcastle to investigate the murder of his brother. He reimmerses himself in the city's sleazy underworld, and learns that his brother

'You're a big man, but you're in bad shape.'

was involved in a vice and drugs ring that was run by Kinnear and included Eric Paice, Con McArty, Brumby and Albert Swift. The sudden realization that Dorean, his niece who is also possibly his daughter, was coerced into appearing in a cheap porn film with Albert pushes Jack over the edge. He murders Albert and Brumby, watches impassively as Kinnear's girlfriend, with whom he has just slept, is drowned, sets up Kinnear to be raided by giving his brother's girlfriend a fatal overdose, and kills Paice, his brother's killer, before being shot himself by an anonymous sniper.

THE FILM This is about as bleak as the British thriller, a generally bleak genre, gets. It specifically evokes the world of Chandler, with Carter reading *Farewell My Lovely* on the train up north, but this is a parochial film. It stands alongside *Performance* as a movie that examines the brutality and darkness of the English criminal underworld and how the working and upper classes intersect. It contains the finest performance of Michael Caine's career – although you are left to wonder how a Geordie native ends up sounding like a Londoner – and shows what a powerful performer he is when he drops all attempts to show any sympathetic side to his character. He is gentle only briefly to Dorean, advising her with his parting words: 'Be good and don't talk to boys.' Otherwise he kills with no sign of enjoyment or repulsion. The murder of Albert is surprisingly perfunctory and unrealistic but its drabness, ugliness and understatement fit perfectly with the general mood of the film. Carter is a 1970s man, who encourages his lover to masturbate while he talks in an early example of phone sex, and mentally undresses Kinnear's flaky girlfriend in a classically cheesy car/sex boy's fantasy montage. He is utterly ruthless in a world, and a film, that offer no escape and no hope.

ODD/SALIENT FACTS Mike Hodges has said of his film: 'The real villains come out from the cinema and say it's one of the best pictures they've ever seen. In point of fact they're proud to be portrayed accurately instead of looking like idiots.' Without *Get Carter* there would probably have been no *Long Good Friday* but even more obviously no *The Sweeney*. The two central characters of this gritty 1970s TV drama, George Carter and Jack Regan, were presumably named consciously or otherwise after Jack Carter. The film contains an odd double, with the murders of Albert and Brumby, in the violent dispatching of two men who would later emerge as TV favourites in *Minder* and *Coronation Street* respectively. In William Hall's biography, *Raising Caine,* the star discusses the importance of the film's air of authenticity: 'I modelled him on an actual hard case I once knew. I watched everything the man did. I even saw him once put someone in hospital for eighteen months. Those guys are very polite, but they act right out of the blue. They're not conversationalists about violence, they're professionals.' Michael Caine says succinctly: 'Carter was real.'

MEMORABLE MOMENTS Jack and the landlady Edna are surprised in bed by the sudden arrival of Con and Peter who have been dispatched by Gerald to bring Jack back to London. As they talk to him, Jack rolls off the bed and feels around underneath by the chamber pot and emerges with the shotgun he had hidden there. As Jack directs them out of the door, Con says with a laugh: 'Come on, Jack, put it away, you know you won't use it.' Peter adds: 'That's the gun, he means.' As they descend the stairs Con and Peter are framed by Jack's legs. The still naked Jack marches his assailants out on to the suburban street, shocking an elderly neighbour into dropping her milk bottle and provides a small distraction for a young majorette in the band practising on the street.

KEY LINES

When Jack barges into his house late at night, Brumby gets angry, but Jack puts him in his place: 'You're a big man, but you're in bad shape. With me it's a full-time job. Now behave yourself.'

THE GOLD RUSH
US, 1925, CHARLES CHAPLIN STUDIO, 74 MINS

D CHARLES CHAPLIN; *PR* CHARLES CHAPLIN; *SC* CHARLES CHAPLIN; *PH* R. H. TOTHEROE, JACK WILSON
CAST CHARLES CHAPLIN (THE LONE PROSPECTOR), MACK SWAIN (BIG JIM MCKAY), TOM MURRAY (BLACK LARSEN), GEORGIA HALE (THE GIRL), BETTY MORRISSEY (CHUM OF THE GIRL), MALCOLM WHITE (JACK CAMERON), HENRY BERGMAN (HANK CURTIS)

THE STORY It is the 1898 Klondike Gold Rush. The Lone Prospector and Big Jim McKay, a man who has discovered a fortune in gold, seek refuge in the hut occupied by Black Larsen, a violent wanted man. After drawing lots, Larsen heads off to find provisions. He stumbles upon and kills two law officers who were looking for him. Back in the hut Jim and the Prospector are reduced to eating the latter's boot. Eventually the two fight but are interrupted by the arrival of a bear which Charlie shoots, thus providing food. They go their separate ways. Jim comes across Black Larsen who has stolen his gold. The two fight, Jim is knocked out, and Larsen escapes with the gold, but falls to his death over a cliff. The Prospector arrives in the town and falls for a dance-hall girl. He invites her and her friends for New Year's Eve dinner at the shack he is looking after. He prepares an elaborate party but she forgets about him. Meanwhile a dazed Jim comes to town and recruits the Prospector to help him locate the hut and therefore the claim. This they do, narrowly avoiding death as the hut is blown to the edge of a cliff. The now rich men travel south in luxury aboard a ship on which the girl is a passenger in steerage. The Prospector poses as a tramp to be photographed for a rags-to-riches story. The girl sees him, takes him for a stowaway and protects him from the ship's officers. But the truth is revealed and all ends happily.

▶ *THE GOLD RUSH Charlie Chaplin in his iconic costume and exuding characteristic pathos as the Lone Prospector in the Klondike Gold Rush.*

THE FILM Charlie Chaplin was for a while the biggest film star and probably the most famous person in the world, yet now enjoys only minority appeal – cult status. *The Gold Rush*, his personal favourite movie, is a gem of film-making. It contains the self-pity, and sentimental, patronizing, almost masochistic attitude towards the down-trodden little man of whom he regarded himself the spokesman, that has led to him becoming a less fashionable, more marginal artist. But the simple narrative and inspired comic invention still hold an audience. With a working title of *Lucky Strike*, and then 'The Northern Story' the film entered production in early 1924 and was released in June of the following year and achieved international success.

ODD/SALIENT FACTS For the chicken sequence the special effects of Charlie becoming a chicken in Jim's eyes had to be achieved on set in the camera, using fades and Chaplin himself in the chicken costume. The original female star of the film was the 15-year-old Lita Grey. Several sequences were shot with her but soon she became pregnant by Chaplin – who reluctantly agreed to marry her – and was replaced by the little-known Georgia Hale. The film was reissued in 1942 with commentary from Chaplin. He changed the end, replacing the original climactic embrace with a fade-out as Charlie and Georgia mount the ship's stairs together.

MEMORABLE MOMENTS The Thanksgiving supper of Charlie's boot. He tends the simmering pot until he judges it perfectly cooked. He carves it, Jim getting the upper, Charlie the sole. The water is poured over the dish as gravy, the lace eaten like spaghetti and a nail offered to Jim as a wishbone.

Charlie falls instantly in love with Georgia at the saloon. She dances with him to provoke Jack. As they dance around the floor his trousers are falling down. He continually hoicks them up and then hooks them with his cane. As the two pause briefly by a table while Georgia talks to a friend, Charlie finds a piece of string which he hurriedly ties around his waist as a makeshift belt. When they recommence their dance the string turns out to be the lead of a dog, which they drag around the floor. Not realizing that they are attached to one another, Charlie repeatedly tries to kick the dog away, until a cat appears, causing the dog to chase it and pull Charlie to the floor.

As he waits pathetically for his guests to arrive on New Year's Eve, Charlie nods off and dreams of the perfect party. Instead of making a speech, he performs a little turn in which bread rolls speared with forks are used in a comical dance. At its première in Berlin, the Dance of the Rolls sequence earned the unusual accolade of a cinematic encore, with the film being rewound and replayed to rapturous applause.

KEY LINES

The hut has been blown to the edge of a precipice, and the two men inside gradually come to appreciate their perilous situation. The house is precariously balanced and the two of them are at the dangerous end when Jim says, in a line that would be adopted in the very similar scene in *The Italian Job* forty years later: 'Now listen, I've got a very good idea.'

GROUNDHOG DAY

US, 1993, COLUMBIA-TRISTAR, 101 MINS

D HAROLD RAMIS; *PR* TREVOR ALBERT, HAROLD RAMIS; *SC* DANNY RUBIN AND HAROLD RAMIS, FROM A STORY BY HAROLD RUBIN; *PH* (COL) JOHN BAILEY; *M* GEORGE FENTON; *ED* PEMBROKE J. HERRING

CAST BILL MURRAY (PHIL CONNORS), ANDIE MACDOWELL (RITA), CHRIS ELLIOTT (LARRY), STEPHEN TOBOLOWSKY (NED RYERSON), BRIAN DOYLE-MURRAY (BUSTER), MARITA GERAGHTY (NANCY), ANGELA PATON (MRS LANCASTER), RICK DUNCUMMUN (GUS), RICK OVERTON (RALPH), ROBIN DUKE (DORIS THE WAITRESS), CAROL BIVINS (ANCHORWOMAN), WILLIE GARSON (PHIL'S ASSISTANT KENNY), KEN HUDSON CAMPBELL (MAN IN HALLWAY), LES PODEWELL (OLD MAN), HAROLD RAMIS (NEUROLOGIST)

THE STORY Phil Connors, a cynical Pittsburgh weatherman, travels with his producer Rita and cameraman Larry to Punxsatawney for the annual Groundhog Day festival. There he finds himself reliving the same day, 2 February, again and again. Every day he is woken in his guesthouse room by the radio alarm playing Sonny and Cher's *I Got You Babe*. He encounters several friendly locals, including a high-school classmate, on the way to do his report from the town square. Trying to get out of town he is thwarted by a storm he failed to predict and, turning down a dinner invitation from Rita and Larry, goes to bed. He is by turns annoyed, exhilarated, bored and suicidal at the endless repetition. Then he sees the opportunity for self-improvement: he starts to help others and learns the piano as well as French and Italian and ice-sculpting. He finally lives the perfect day in which he saves at least three lives, changes

▲ *GROUNDHOG DAY The two Phils (Punxsatawney and Connors) contemplate desperate measures to avoid the nightmare of an endlessly repeated day.*

a car tyre for three old ladies, plays great jazz piano at the Groundhog Day party, becomes the most popular man in town, sleeps with Rita and wakes up redeemed on 3 February.

THE FILM Bill Murray comes from the same *Saturday Night Live* generation as Dan Aykroyd, John Belushi and Chevy Chase. Ramis, who starred alongside him in the *Ghostbusters* films, came up with the perfect vehicle for Murray's finely tuned cynical persona. It is a priceless example of a film that takes a basic premise, one idea of an endlessly repeated day, explores all its possibilities of humour and despair, and presents them in a way that is simultaneously profound and mainstream. In a sense it is a remake, or an updating of *It's a Wonderful Life* (1946) with the claustrophobia of small-town life turned into a comical nightmare. At one stage when Phil is beginning to sample the freedom and restrictions of his new life, he says to his drinking partners: 'What would you do if you were stuck in one place, and every day was exactly the same and nothing you did mattered?' One of his companions says: 'That about sums

it up for me.' Like *The Truman Show* (1998), itself a near remake of the film with spatial instead of temporal restriction, part of the idea is to suggest this plot, this extreme experience as a metaphor for everyone's life. Like those two films it is simultaneously a celebration of the simplicity and decency of small-town American life and an excoriation of its inherent claustrophobia. As in *It's a Wonderful Life* and *The Wizard of Oz* (1939) the action teeters on the edge of. and then dives straight into, the realms of nightmare only for the story to be resolved by the redemption of the cynic, the revelation that happiness is all around us and the key to finding it is mutual reliance. It is the most accomplished Hollywood comedy of the 1990s.

ODD/SALIENT FACTS *Groundhog Day* is the sixth collaboration between Murray and Ramis. Ramis attempted but failed to repeat the success of a film based on the notion of repetition with *Multiplicity* (1996), in which Michael Keaton appeared opposite Andie MacDowell and three successive clones of himself, all slightly different.

MEMORABLE MOMENTS/KEY LINES

Phil and Rita are chatting in a bar.

Rita: 'Believe it or not I studied nineteenth-century French poetry.'

Phil laughing: 'What a waste of time. (He regains his composure and improvises unsuccessfully.) I mean for someone else that would be an incredible waste of time. It's so bold of you to choose that. It's incredible, you must be a very, very strong person.'

Cut to the same scene.

Phil: 'I think people place too much emphasis on their careers. Gosh I wish we could all live in the mountains at high altitudes. That's where I see myself in five years. How about you?'

Rita: 'Oh I agree. I just like to go with the flow, see what happens.'

Phil: 'Well it's gotten you here.'

Rita: 'Uh huh. Of course it's a million miles from where I started out at college.'

Phil: 'Oh yeah? You m ean you weren't in broadcasting or journalism or anything like that.'

Rita: 'Believe it or not I studied nineteenth-century French poetry.'

Phil: 'La fille qui j'aimerai / Sera comme bon vin Qui se bonifiera / Un peu chaque matin.'

103

GUN CRAZY

US, 1949, UNITED ARTISTS-KING BROTHERS, 87 MINS

D JOSEPH H. LEWIS; **PR** MAURICE KING, FRANK KING; **SC** MACKINLAY KANTOR, MILLARD KAUFMAN (FROM A SATURDAY EVENING POST STORY BY MCKINLAY KANTOR; **PH** (BW) RUSSELL HARLAN; **ED** HARRY GERSTAD; **M** VICTOR YOUNG

CAST PEGGY CUMMINS (ANNIE LAURIE STARR), JOHN DALL (BART TARE), BERRY KROEGER (PACKET), MORRIS CARNOVSKY (JUDGE WILLOUGHBY), ANABEL SHAW (RUBY TARE), HARRY LEWIS (CLYDE BOSTON), NEDRICK YOUNG (DAVE ALLISTER), RUSS TAMBLYN (BART TARE, AGED 14); DON BEDDOE (HI-JACKED CAR DRIVER), ROBERT OSTERLOH (COP OUTSIDE HAMPTON BANK), RAY TEAL (CALIFORNIA BORDER COP)

THE STORY Bart Tare, a working-class boy raised by his elder sister, has been obsessed with guns since childhood and at age fourteen is sent to reform school for stealing a revolver. Returning to his small town after four years in the school and a stretch in the army, he goes with old schoolmates to a visiting carnival where he is captivated by Annie Laurie Starr, an English sharp-shooter working for sleazy showman Packy. After he's stepped up from the audience to outshoot her, Bart joins the act, but soon Packy becomes jealous and fires them both. They marry and rapidly lose their small savings in Vegas. The ruthless, ambitious Laurie persuades the reluctant Bart, who cannot bear shooting to kill, to turn to armed robbery and they drive around America robbing banks, hotels and filling stations, becoming notorious when Packy identifies them. When the guilt-ridden Bart threatens to quit, Laurie proposes a final big job, the payroll from a meat-packing plant. They get away, but not before Laurie has killed two people. The FBI trace them to Los Angeles through marked notes and they go on the run, leaving the loot at a hotel. They hide out at his sister's home, where Bart's old friends, one a reporter, the other a sheriff, urge them to surrender. Instead they drive away, pursued by the police and are finally cornered in the local mountains. When Laurie is about to shoot the approaching friends, Bart kills her and is himself shot dead.

THE FILM One of a number of pictures inspired by the antics of Bonnie Parker and Clyde Barrow, *Gun Crazy* is one of the finest films of cult B-movie maverick Joseph H. Lewis. Though made on a low budget this classic *film noir* is superbly shot and edited, and in its melodramatic fashion is both blatant and subtle, involving the audience in the characters' erotic fascination with guns. This is *amour fou* American style, the sad, soft guy who expresses his manhood by carrying a gun, being dragged down a one-way road beyond the social pale by a hard-bitten *femme fatale*, old beyond her years. The 30-year-old Dall and 23-year-old Cummins were already on the way down after their early experience of stardom and this gives a sadness and desperation to their performances, which were the best either gave. The movie features a virtuoso long take from the back of the hi-jacked Cadillac, which follows in a single unbroken shot the drive up to the bank, Laurie holding a cop's attention while Bart is inside, and the getaway.

ODD/SALIENT FACTS The film was first shown in the States as *Deadlier Than the Male*, but was withdrawn a few months later and re-released as *Gun Crazy*. The script was almost entirely the work of Dalton Trumbo, one of the Hollywood Ten,

▼ *GUN CRAZY* John Dahl restrains a gun-toting Peggy Cummins after a bank hold-up.

who was cited for contempt of Congress by the House Un-American Activities in 1947 and jailed for a year. This was one of his first scripts written during his thirteen years on the blacklist, and Millard Kaufman acted as a front. In 1956, working for the same producers, Trumbo won as Oscar under the pseudonym Richard Rich.

MEMORABLE MOMENTS The fourteen-year-old Bart stealing the pearl-handled revolver from a hardware story window on a dark, rainy night and falling down in a puddle before a policeman.

Laurie and Bart shooting at matches stuck in a crown worn on their heads during their sideshow contest.

The one-shot robbery of the Hampton bank.

KEY LINES

Ruby, Bart's sister: 'It's something else about guns that gets him, it's not killing.'

Laurie: 'I told you I was no good. I didn't kid you did I? Now you know. I've been kicked about all my life. Now I'm going to kick back.'

Laurie: 'I want a guy with spirit and guts, a guy who can kick over the traces and win the world for me.'

Bart: 'We go together Laurie. I don't know why. Maybe like guns and ammunition go together.'

HARD TIMES
(UK TITLE: THE STREETFIGHTER)

US, 1975, COLUMBIA, 93 MINS

D *WALTER HILL;* **PR** *LAWRENCE GORDON;* **SC** *WALTER HILL, BRYAN GINDORF, BRUCE HENTSELL (FROM A STORY BY GINDORFF AND HENTSELL);* **PH** *(PANAVISION, METROCOLOR) PHILIP LATHROP;* **ED** *ROGER SPOTTISWOODE;* **M** *BARRY DE VORZON*

CAST *CHARLES BRONSON (CHANEY), JAMES COBURN (SPENCER WEED AKA 'SPEED'), JILL IRELAND (LUCY SIMPSON), STROTHER MARTIN (POE), MAGGIE BLYE (GAYLEEN SCHOONOVER), MICHAEL MCGUIRE (CHICK GANDELL), ROBERT TESSIER (JIM HENRY), NICK DIMITRI (STREET), FELICE ORLANDI (LEBEAU), FRANK MCRAE (HAMMERMARN), BRUCE GLOVER (DOTY), EDWARD WALSH (PETTIBON)*

THE STORY During the 1930s Depression, Chaney, an unemployed man in his forties, rides a boxcar into the Deep South intending to make some money as a 'hitter' in the illegal sport of bare-knuckle boxing. He meets a charming gambler and fight promoter nicknamed Speed, who's in need of a new fighter, and they go down to New Orleans. There they meet Speed's 'permanent fiancée', Gayleen, and the middle-aged, alcoholic, Poe, a medical school dropout who's engaged to work as Chaney's second. The city's top hitter, Jim Henry, works for the wealthy businessman, Chick Gandell, who refuses a contest until Speed can put up a bet of $3,000. Speed raises the purse by borrowing at exorbitant rates from the gangster LeBeau and pitting Chaney against a Cajun champion. Meanwhile Chaney meets Lucy, whose husband is in

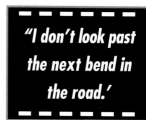

"I don't look past the next bend in the road."

jail, and they drift into an affair. After Chaney beats Jim Henry, Speed loses most of his money in a crap game and Gandell gets a hold over him by paying the interest on his loan. Poe tells Chaney he can save Speed's life by agreeing to fight Street, the new hitter Gandell has brought from out of town. Chaney intially refuses, but at the last minute he turns up and wins a brutal contest. He gives a generous share of his winnings to Poe and Speed, and heads north on a freight train.

THE FILM *Hard Times* was the debut of writer-director Walter Hill and the first of his cult fables (others include *The Warriors, The Driver* and *Streets of Fire*) centring on existential heroes with no disclosed past, living by unspoken personal codes in urban (often criminal) sub-cultures. His characters reveal themselves by what they do, not what they say. Like Robert Rossen's *The Hustler* and Norman Jewison's *Cincinatti Kid, Hard Times* creates a private world within the interstices of American life, where hard men engage in contests and where character is as important as skill or brawn. Like Newman in *The Hustler* and McQueen is *Cincinatti Kid* (for both of whom Hill had written screenplays), Bronson has one of his best roles: a drifting loner defined through the sport he practises and refusing to make long-term commitments. As always in Hill's movies, the tough, violent ambience is presented with considerable elegance and many of the interiors are lit to resemble paintings by Edward Hopper.

ODD/SALIENT FACTS Walter Hill's last picture as screenwriter before turning director was Sam Peckinpah's *The Getaway*, and *Hard Times* is edited by future director Roger Spottiswoode, who worked on three of Peckinpah's pictures. The film stars Peckinpah regulars Strother Martin and James Coburn. Hill's original and preferred title for the film, *The Streetfighter*, was used in Britain.

MEMORABLE MOMENTS The fights staged in deserted warehouses, empty factories and on docksides.

The lakeside Cajun party in the Bayou where Speed arranges Chaney's second fight.

Chaney breaking up a party in a pool hall as he attempts to claim the money withheld by the Cajun fighter's dishonest manager.

Chaney stretched out on his bed beneath a ceiling fan in his green-painted, ill-furnished room.

KEY LINES

Speed: 'I suppose you've been down the long hard road.'
Chaney: 'Who hasn't?'

▲ *HARD TIMES* James Coburn swallows an oyster as Charles Bronson puts his money where his fists are.

Chaney: 'I don't look past the next bend in the road.'
Speed: 'Well, you know Chick, like old momma said, next best thing to playing and winning is playing and losing.'

Chaney's exit line when asked where he's going: 'North.'

HEAT
US, 1971, SCORE/SARX, 103 MINS
D PAUL MORRISSEY; **PR** ANDY WARHOL; **SC** PAUL MORRISSEY, BASED ON AN IDEA BY JOHN HALLOWELL; **PH** (COL) PAUL MORRISSEY; **M** JOHN CALE; **ED** IAN JOKEL, JED JOHNSON **CAST** JOE DALLESANDRO (JOE), SYLVIA MILES (SALLY), ANDREA FELDMAN (JESSIE), PAT AST (MOTEL OWNER), RAY VESTAL (PRODUCER), LESTER PERSKY (SIDNEY), ERIC EMERSON (GARY), HAROLD CHILDE, JOHN HALLOWELL, GARY KOZNOCHA, PAT PARLEMAN, BONNIE WALDER

THE STORY Joe, a former child TV star, arrives at a Hollywood hotel. There he meets the other residents – Jessie a neurotic young woman who lives with her baby and girlfriend, two brothers who have sex with each other in their stage act – and sleeps with the motel owner to save on rent. Joe begins an affair with Jessie's mother, Sally, with whom he acted on TV. Soon Jessie, who is always demanding money from her mother, moves into Sally's mansion where Joe is already staying. Joe, who is hoping his liaison with Sally will help him professionally, begins a casual affair with Jessie. A producer friend of Sally's says he can use Joe only in the Western roles from which he is trying to break free. Joe, finding that he can't get the record deal that he was promised, is propositioned by the boyfriend of Sally's father. Declaring himself a star, Joe walks out on Sally. She follows him back to the motel, where she takes out a gun and goes to shoot him. The gun won't fire and she tosses it into the swimming pool.

THE FILM Andy Warhol's film career followed a similar, if less spectacular trajectory to his painting. He established himself as a creator of works that explored repetition and boredom as well as sexuality in the modern world, and having established a template, was able to pass the actual work on to collaborators or minions. Paul Morrissey had worked as a production assistant and camera operator on several Warhol films before working as director on *Trash* (1969). *Heat* is a camp spin on *Sunset Boulevard* (1950), complete with fading, ageing star and swimming-pool motif. The Warhol/Morrissey style as always makes it a film that is uncomfortable to watch, like a porn movie with curtailed sex scenes, or the out-takes from a substandard Cassavetes film. The camera work and lighting are equally abysmal, the editing amateurish, but somehow, something to do with the Warhol imprimatur, some genuinely off-beat humour, and the strange unreal realism make it compelling.

ODD/SALIENT FACTS Andy Warhol famously said of Sylvia Miles: 'She would attend the opening of an envelope.' The painfully stilted performance of Andrea Feldman reeks of authentic flakiness. Feldman, who also appeared in *Trash*, had been fixated on Warhol for some time and had taken to calling herself Andrea Warhola (Warhol's real surname) in the hope that he would marry her. The sequence in which she shows her cigarette burn scars to Joe is based on fact. In his definitive biography *Warhol*, Victor Bockris, the distinguished and prolific chronicler of the underground artistic elite, writes:

On one occasion she had come to the Factory, hysterical, her face covered with scabs and small round festering sores. According to one account, someone said to Warhol, 'She's very sick. Andrea should go to hospital. Did you see her face?' Warhol matter-of-factly replied, 'Well, she's putting cigarettes out on her face. She always does that.' In what had become an almost clichéd way of seeing things, Andy said she was going through a 'phase' and would get over it.

In September 1972, three weeks before the film's premiere in New York, Feldman killed herself by jumping out of a top-floor window, holding two Warhol-style icons, a rosary and a can of Coke.

▼ *HEAT Joe Dallesandro and Sylvia Miles cuddle up in this version of* Sunset Boulevard *updated and reprocessed by the Warhol factory.*

MEMORABLE MOMENTS The first sex scene between Joe and Sally in which she is continually making herself up and checking with Joe that she looks good. He is merely concerned that she will be able to help him with his career.

KEY LINES

Sally, about Bonnie: 'Do you sleep in the same room with her?'
Jessie: 'Sure, how else can I be a lesbian?'

Jessie: 'I heard you went to bed with your brother. Is that true?'
Gary: 'Yeah, but only on stage.'
Jessie: 'What do you do together?'
Gary: 'We just fool around.'
Jessie: 'Is it fun?'
Gary: 'I dunno. I guess so.'
Jessie: 'You must like it a lot, huh?'
Gary: 'Well, it's a living.'

Sally talking about Jessica: 'She can't even make a good dyke.'

Sidney, to Sally: 'You were an ageing, minor, practically unknown star … You were fantastic in every way [to Joe] but she couldn't act.'

HEAVEN'S GATE

US, 1980, UNITED ARTISTS/PARTISAN PRODUCTIONS, 219 MINS
D MICHAEL CIMINO; **PR** JOANN CARELLI; **SC** MICHAEL CIMINO; **PH** (PANAVISION/TECHNICOLOR) VILMOS ZSIGMOND; **ED** TOM ROLF; **M** DAVID MANSFIELD
CAST KRIS KRISTOFFERSON (JIM AVERILL), JOHN HURT (WILLIAM C. IRVINE), CHRISTOPHER WALKEN (NATE CHAMPION), SAM WATERSTON (FRANK CANTON), ISABELLE HUPPERT (ELLA WATSON), JOSEPH COTTEN (REVEREND DOCTOR), JEFF BRIDGES (JOHN H. BRIDGES), BRAD DOURIF (MR EGGLESTON), GEOFFREY LEWIS (WOLF TRAPPER), MICKEY ROURKE (NICK RAY), RICHARD MASUR (TULLY), TERRY O'NEILL (CAPTAIN MINARDI, US ARMY)

> **'There is only one crime in this country – to be caught.'**

THE STORY In 1870 Jim Averill and Billy Irvine, sons of prominent upper-class New England families, graduate from Harvard. Twenty years later in Wyoming, Billy is a sardonic alcoholic, a member of the Stock Growers' Association that represents Eastern business interests, and Jim is US marshal of Johnson County, Wyoming, who sides with the oppressed. Infuriated by the Eastern European immigrants settling in the state and rustling their cattle with impunity, the Association, under its leader Frank Canton, draws up a death list of 125 names and hires a mercenary army of 'enforcers' to invade Johnson County. One of the people on the list is Jim's lover, the brothel owner Ella Watson, who accepts cattle in exchange for her girls' favours. Ella is also loved by Nate Champion, himself an immigrant, and one of the Association's leading hitmen. When the mercenary army arrives, Nate changes sides and is killed, Ella is raped by enforcers, and the settlers, rallied by Jim, surround the attackers. Only the arrival of the US Cavalry saves the Association's hired guns from being massacred. A little later, as they are about to marry, Jim and Ella are ambushed by gunslingers led by Canton, and Ella is killed. In an epilogue set in Newport, Rhode Island, Averill has returned to his own class and is on a luxury yacht with his upper-class wife.

THE FILM Cimino's attempt to do for the Western what his earlier populist epic, *The Deer Hunter*, had done for the war movie, went wildly over budget and is reputed to have brought down United Artists, who withdrew the 219-minute version after hostile reviews, and released it at 149 minutes to empty cinemas. It is also said to have brought an end to a period in which Hollywood auteurs prevailed over producers, and to have killed off the Western (when Costner's *Dances With Wolves* went over budget in 1990 it was dubbed 'Kevin's Gate'). The film is in fact, for all its vagueness of characterization, one of the great radical Westerns, dealing in a complex manner with the contradictions of American life and taking the conflicts in the East Coast industrial cities out into the West. Visually rich, it is a carefully patterned movie, most especially in the way it handles the so-called class traitors Averill and Champion, and like Visconti's *The Leopard*, Coppola's *The Godfather*, Leone's *Once Upon a Time in the West* and Cimino's own *The Deer Hunter*, it eschews carefully paced

▲ *HEAVEN'S GATE Brothel keeper Isabelle Huppert tries out the carriage brought to her from St Louis by Kris Kristofferson.*

narrative in favour of powerfully animated, operatic set-pieces that are often extended beyond what puritanical northern temperaments think proper.

ODD/SALIENT FACTS The film is true in spirit to the issues involved, but the actual Johnson County War of 1892 resulted in less than half a dozen deaths, one of them that of Nate Champion. John Averill, who was a rustler, and his lover Ella Watson (known as 'Cattle Kate'), were both killed by Association assassins, but in 1888. Frank Canton, was a killer turned lawman, and he lived until 1927.

In 1983, two years after the truncated *Heaven's Gate* was released, a 207-minute version appeared in cinemas, and then a 220-minute version on TV, each containing material not found in the other two.

MEMORABLE MOMENTS Averill's arrival in the bustling, smokey frontier town of Caspar, Wyoming, having delivered a convicted woman to a federal hangman in St Louis.

Canton recruiting enforcers at night from miners at a pithead.

Champion executing an immigrant rustler.

The recent immigrants enjoying themselves at the Heaven's Gate roller-skating rink in Sweetwater, Wyoming.

KEY LINES

The Reverend Doctor (addressing the Harvard class of '70): 'It is the contact of the cultivated with the uncultivated. It doubly behoves us to look well to the influence we may exert of a high ideal – the education of a nation.'

Canton: 'This is no longer a poor man's country. These emigrants only pretend to be farmers. We know they are thieves, anarchists and outlaws.'

Averill: 'You're not my class, Canton, and you never will be. You'd have to die first and be born again.'

John Bridges (storekeeper/hotel owner): 'It's getting dangerous to be poor in this country.'

Capt. Minardi: 'Do you know what I really dislike about you, Jim? You're a rich man with a good name. You only pretend to be poor.'

Ella (to Jim): 'I never cheated on you. I always made Nate pay.'

A settler: 'There is only one crime in this country – to be caught'.

THE HUSTLER
US, 1961, TCF, 135 MINS

D *ROBERT ROSSEN;* **PR** *ROBERT ROSSEN;* **SC** *ROBERT ROSSEN, SIDNEY CARROLL, BASED ON THE NOVEL BY WALTER TEVIS;* **PH** *(CINEMASCOPE BW) EUGENE SCHUFTAN;* **M** *KENYON HOPKINS;* **ED** *DEDE ALLEN*

CAST *PAUL NEWMAN (EDDIE FELSON), JACKIE GLEASON (MINNESOTA FATS), PIPER LAURIE (SARAH PACKARD), GEORGE C. SCOTT (BERT GORDON), MYRON MCCORMICK (CHARLIE BURNS), MURRAY HAMILTON (FINDLAY), MICHAEL CONSTANTINE (BIG JOHN), STEPHAN GIERASCH (PREACHER), VINCENT GARDENIA (BARTENDER), CLIFFORD A. PELLOW (TURK), GORDON B. CLARKE (CASHIER), ALEXANDER ROSE (SCOREKEEPER), CAROLYN COATES (WAITRESS), CARL YORK (YOUNG HUSTLER), JAKE LA MOTTA (BARTENDER)*

THE STORY Fast Eddie and Charlie arrive at a bar posing as a couple of travelling salesmen. They stay a while, practise a well-worked routine while playing pool and hustle the owner and the patrons. Arriving at Ames, Eddie waits for the chance to play Minnesota Fats. Fats arrives at 6 o'clock sharp, and he and Eddie play. In an epic, fluctuating 25-hour match Fats, bankrolled by Bert Gordon, triumphs. Eddie walks out on Charlie and starts a relationship with Sarah, a lame, alcoholic, part-time student. Eddie meets up with Bert Gordon who offers to become his manager but Eddie won't accept his ungenerous terms. One night the regulars in a bar break Eddie's thumbs after he has flashily hustled a young pool player. Having been nursed to recovery by Sarah, Eddie takes Bert up on his offer and the three of them go on the road. In Louisville they attend a party at the house of the wealthy Findlay where Eddie plays carom billiards and Sarah gets drunk, reacting violently to something Bert whispers in her ear. Eddie loses the money that Bert supplies and then his own, which he retrieves from Sarah's purse. When Eddie rejects Sarah, Bert bankrolls him once more and Eddie cleans up. Eddie walks back to the hotel. Sarah sleeps

▲ *THE HUSTLER Paul Newman as Fast Eddie Felson lines up a shot and gets the feeling that he just can't miss.*

with Bert and then kills herself. Eddie returns to Ames' pool hall, plays and beats Fats. He refuses to give Bert his share and walks out of the club knowing that he will no longer be able to play the game.

THE FILM This bleak fable of talent, compromise, doomed love, death and redemption is a profoundly autobiographical work by the director. Rossen, who had contributed to the screenplays of *The Roaring Twenties* (1939) and *The Treasure of the Sierra Madre* (1948), was badly affected by his dealings with the House Un-American Activities Committee. He had been involved with the communist party in the 1930s and at his first HUAC appearance refused to name names, but ultimately changed his mind and spilled the beans on friends and colleagues. *The Hustler* is about a man who has the talent and the passion but sells his soul and betrays the one person who really knows and loves him in a Faustian pact to gain character. Bert Gordon is specifically likened to the devil by Findlay. Eddie emerges chastened and redeemed. Some of the dialogue is a touch portentous, especially in the love scenes, but it is a wonderfully exhilarating and depressing film that blends elements of period jazzy existentialism, moody religious parable, the quality of a simply great sports movie and terrific performances from all four leads.

ODD/SALIENT FACTS Newman has been dismissive of his own performance in the film saying: 'I was just working too hard, showing too much.' Newman was nominated for an Academy Award along with Schuftan and Rossen for direction, film and screenplay (and with Carroll), Gleason, Scott and Laurie. He finally won the Oscar for best actor for his performance as Felson in Martin Scorsese's belated sequel *The Color of Money* (1986). The part of the barman in the bar where Eddie and Sarah meet for the second time is played by Jake La Motta.

MEMORABLE MOMENTS The opening sequence in which Newman plays a character playing drunk in his successful hustle of the barflies.

The scene where the reckless and unchaperoned Eddie hustles the young hustler and enrages the gang in the bar. They drag him into the adjoining room where, with Eddie's face pressed against a frosted glass window, they break his thumbs.

KEY LINES

Charlie, on entering Ames' pool hall: 'Quiet.'
Eddie: 'Yeah, like a church. The church of the good hustler.'
Charlie: 'Looks more like a morgue to me. Those tables are the slabs they lay the stiffs on.'
Eddie: 'I'll be alive when I get out, Charlie.'

Charlie, before the first game with Fats: 'How do you feel?'
Eddie: 'Fast and loose.'
Charlie: 'In the gut, I mean.'
Eddie: 'Tight, but good.'

Eddie, playing Fats: 'You know, I got a hunch, fat man. I got a hunch that it's me from here on in. "1" ball corner pocket. I mean, that ever happen to you? You know, all of a sudden you feel like you just can't miss. 'Cos I dreamed about this game, fat man. I dreamed about

this every night on the road. Five ball. You know, this is my table, man. I own it.'

Bert to Fats: 'Stick with this kid, he's a loser.'

Eddie: 'Fat man, you shoot a great game of pool.'
Fats: 'So do you, Fast Eddie.'

IF . . . .

UK, 1968, PARAMOUNT/MEMORIAL PRODUCTIONS, 111 MINS
D LINDSAY ANDERSON; **PR** MICHAEL MEDWIN AND ANDERSON; **SC** DAVID SHERWIN (FROM THE STORY CRUSADERS BY SHERWIN AND JOHN HOWLETT); **PH** (EASTMANCOLOR) MIROSLAV ONDRICEK; **M** MARC WILKINSON; **ED** DAVID GLADWELL
CAST MALCOLM MCDOWELL (MICK TRAVIS), DAVID WOOD (JOHNNY KNIGHTLEY), RICHARD WARWICK (WALLACE), RUPERT WEBSTER (BOBBY PHILLIPS), ROBERT SWANN (ROWNTREE), CHRISTINE NOONAN (THE GIRL), PETER JEFFREY (HEADMASTER), ARTHUR LOWE (MR KEMP), GRAHAM CROWDEN (HISTORY MASTER), BEN ARIS (JOHN THOMAS), GEOFFREY CHATER (CHAPLAIN), MONA WASHBOURNE (MATRON)

THE STORY Set in an unnamed English public school.
1. COLLEGE HOUSE – RETURN The school assembles; prefects, 'whips', establish super-iority over new boys, 'scum'; three seniors – Travis, Knightley and Wallace – assert their uneasy independence.
2. COLLEGE: ONCE AGAIN ASSEMBLE The boys attend chapel and first lessons; the headmaster lectures sixth-formers on the role of the public school.
3. TERM TIME Travis, Wallace and Knightley discuss revolution; whip orders them to take cold baths for insolence and drinking.
4. RITUAL AND ROMANCE Phillips, a junior boy, is entranced by Wallace's gymnastic performance. Travis and Knightley go into town, steal a motorbike, pick up a girl at a café.
5. DISCIPLINE The whips administer a sadistic flogging to Travis, Wallace and Knightley.

> 'We are your new family ... help the house and you'll be helped by those in the house.'

6. RESISTANCE Travis makes a blood oath with Knightley and Wallace.

7. FORTH TO WAR The army cadet corps on manoeuvres. Travis and friends carry real ammunition and shoot the chaplain. The headmaster produces the chaplain from a drawer in his study to shake hands with the boys. The trio are assigned to clearing out the school's attics and find a cache of weapons.

8. CRUSADERS The Union Jack flies from the roof, the Establishment (a general, a bishop, a royal personage) assemble for Founder's Day ceremony in the Hall. Smoke from the floorboards creates panic, the audience flees into the quadrangle to engage in open warfare with Travis, his girlfriend, Knightley, Wallace and Phillips who target them from the roof with machine guns and grenades. The film concludes not with 'The End' but with 'If ....'

▼ *IF .... Rebels Malcolm McDowell and Christine Noonan take to the school roof on Founders Day.*

THE FILM Like Eisenstein's *Battleship Potemkin, If ....* is a film with powerful homoerotic undertones, aiming to involve a popular audience in the visceral excitement of being a violent revolutionary. Movies like *Goodbye Mr Chips* tend to take a sentimental view of the English public school. Anderson uses it as a metaphor for a society that perpetuates snobbery, sadism and empty tradition, and functions by making people exploit each other. Although some early scenes have an almost documentary realism (Anderson made his reputation as a documentarist), the film is influenced by the surrealists and the alienation effect of Bertolt Brecht, from whom it borrows the device of the chapter headings. The switches between colour and monochrome are both Brechtian and surreal, making us aware we are watching a film, disrupting our sense of reality. Travis and company are idealistic anarchists. No mainstream film of its time took such a revolutionary position, and the film proved a rallying point for sixties rebels. It is radical rather than left-wing, directed against authority. Anderson was gay, and the film attacks the whips for their sexual exploitation of the younger boys but romanticizes the platonic relationship between Wallace and Phillips.

ODD/SALIENT FACTS The title comes from Kipling's poem, but the movie is closer to *Stalky & Co,* his novel about three rebels at an English public school. Anderson's father, like the visiting speaker in the final scene, was a general in the British army, and the movie was made at Anderson's old school, Cheltenham College. *If ....* was the first film in his trilogy about the state of Britain, and McDowell and many of the other actors appear in the two subsequent pictures, *O Lucky Man* and *Britannia Hospital.* The final scene on the roof is a homage to Jean Vigo's *Zéro de Conduite* (1933). In his 1971 film *Horizon,* Pal Gabor pays tribute to Anderson when his rebellious young hero sees *If ....* in a Budapest cinema. The 1968 Cannes Festival was abandoned out of solidarity with the protesting students in Paris. The jury of the 1969 Festival awarded the Palme d'Or to *If ....,* the film that most embodied the spirit of *les Événements* of 1968.

MEMORABLE MOMENTS Travis' first appearance, wearing a slouch hat and a scarf to conceal his new moustache.

Phillips watching Wallace perform on the parallel bars.

The sadistic punishment of Travis.

Travis firing a machine gun from the roof, echoing a magazine photograph of a black revolutionary on his wall.

KEY LINES

Housemaster: 'We are your new family ... help the house and you'll be helped by those in the house.'

Headmaster: 'Work, play, but don't mix the two.'

Headmaster: 'College is a symbol of many things. Scholarship and integrity in public office; high standards in the television and entertainment worlds. Huge sacrifice in Britain's wars. Of course some of our customs are silly; you could say that we were middle-class. But a large part of the population is in the process of becoming middle-class, and many of the middle-class's moral values are values that the country cannot do without. So we must not expect to be thanked. Education in Britain is a nubile Cinderella, sparsely clad and much interfered with.'

THE IMMORAL MR TEAS

US, 1959, PAD PRODUCTIONS, 65 MINS

D *RUSS MEYER;* **PH** *RUSS MEYER;* **PR** *PETER A. DeCENZIE;*
NARR *EDWARD J. LAKSO*

CAST *BILL TEAS, ANN PETERS, MARILYN WESLEY, MISCHELE ROBERTS*

THE STORY An unnamed Californian, around forty with a greying goatee, identified by the narrator as the typical citizen of our stressful times, emerges from his house wearing a suit and straw boater and carrying a briefcase. He passes a little girl twirling a hula-hoop who throws a stone at him. At another house he changes into orange-coloured overalls and rides around on a bicycle making deliveries. He meets a dental nurse, a secretary and a waitress in a diner, all big-breasted and apparently not wearing brassières. He visits the beach and surreptitiously photographs a photographer taking pictures of a topless model. He fantasizes about seeing the girls in the nude, and spies upon them when they frolic naked by the sea. Paying a second visit to a psychiatrist, he imagines her sitting beside the couch, pen in hand, clutching her notebook, naked except for her horn-rimmed spectacles.

THE FILM Russ Meyer (b Oakland, California 1923) began making movies as a schoolboy, was a combat cameraman

▲ *THE IMMORAL MR TEAS* Bill Teas snaps well-considered trifles on the beach to feed his fantasies.

with the US Signals Corps in Europe during the Second World War and is the ultimate cult film-maker . As a nudie photographer he was one of *Playboy's* first contributors (he actually married a Playmate), and for forty years he has been making self-mocking, soft-core movies about sex and violence and women with large breasts. The popularity and immense financial success of his early movies led to Hollywood invitations. But after making *Beyond the Valley of the Dolls* (1970) and *The Seven Minutes* (1971) for Twentieth Century-Fox, he retreated into idiosyncratic independent productions. The low-budget *The Immoral Mr Teas* put Meyer on the map. It has none of the violence of later Meyer pictures like *Faster Pussycat! Kill! Kill!* (1965) and it's difficult to tell whether the apparent artlessness is the product of great sophistication or of naiveté. At the time most observers thought the former, seeing the picture as a parody of Jacques Tati's Hulot films and such avant-garde American pictures as James Broughton's *Loony*

Tom. The film has no spoken dialogue, just an arch commentary about the pressures of modern society, accompanied by a tinkling jazz score.

Teas, the sad, lonely voyeur, is a hopeless innocent, anything but immoral, looking at buxom, unattainable women and feeling guilty about his obsession. At the end the film relieves him of his guilt. *The Immoral Mr Teas* is an essential link between Hollywood's post-war fetishization of the female breast and the hard-core pornography of the 1970s. In the post-war decade Jane Russell, Marilyn Monroe, Jayne Mansfield, Mamie Van Doren et al. were shown in figure-hugging clothes. Meyer removed the sweaters in 1959, leading the way to the presentation of explicit sex a dozen years later in *Deep Throat* (1972) and *The Devil in Miss Jones* (1973), hardcore pictures that became socially acceptable. His own films, by comparison, remained curiously innocuous.

ODD/SALIENT FACTS *The Immoral Mr Teas* cost under $25,000 to make and took well over a million at the box office in a year when Hitchcock's *Psycho* did well with a gross of $4m. It was the thin end of a wedge that showed there was a respectable niche audience outside the cinematic mainstream for erotic pictures with a certain wit and style. Meyer salutes the European cinema that was penetrating America without being subjected to censorship by the rigid Hays Office Code by ending his movie not with 'The End' but with a jocular 'FIN'.

MEMORABLE MOMENTS The use of the spiral device from the credits of Hitchcock's *Vertigo* to introduce Teas's fantasies.

Teas peeling a phallic banana then anxiously holding two melons to his chest as he confronts a large pair of breasts briefly exposed from a window.

Teas on a fishing expedition accidentally hooking a brassière left on the branch of a tree by one of the objects of his desire.

KEY LINES

There is no dialogue in *The Immoral Mr Teas*. The key line in the commentary comes when Teas, his voyeuristic gaze apparently liberated, observes the naked psychoanalyst in the final scene: 'on the other hand some men just enjoy being sick'.

THE INCREDIBLE SHRINKING MAN
US, 1957, U-I, 81 MINS

D JACK ARNOLD; **PR** ALBERT ZUGSMITH; **SC** RICHARD MATHESON, FROM HIS OWN NOVEL; **PH** ELLIS W. CARTER; **SP PH** CLIFFORD STINE; **M SUP** JOSEPH GERSHENSON; **ED** AL JOSEPH

CAST GRANT WILLIAMS (ROBERT SCOTT CAREY), RANDY STUART (LOUISE CAREY), APRIL KENT (CLARICE), PAUL LANGTON (CHARLIE CAREY), RAYMOND BAILEY (DR THOMAS SILVER), WILLIAM SCHALLERT (DR ROBERT BRAMSON), FRANK SCANNELL (BARKER), HELENE MARSHALL (NURSE), DIANA DARRIN (NURSE), BILLY CURTIS (MIDGET)

THE STORY Scott and Louise Carey are on a boating holiday when a cloud of dust passes over them and coats Scott's skin in its shiny residue. Some time later, Scott begins to shrink. A battery of tests reveals that his body is gradually losing its stores of nitrogen, calcium and phosphorous, apparently due to his exposure to an insecticide spray as well as the radioactive cloud. He loses his job and is forced to sell his story to a newspaper. Now only 36 inches tall he finds brief solace in a friendship with Clarice, a circus midget, and the process of shrinking is arrested. When he begins to shrink again he is forced to live in a doll's house in his own living room. One day he is attacked by his cat and seeks refuge in the cellar. In this vast landscape he must secure food from a mousetrap, battle a spider and his own existential angst before arriving at a new mystical understanding of his place within the universe.

> 'Easy enough to talk of soul and spirit and essential worth but not when you're three feet tall.'

THE FILM Though still decidedly a B-movie, this is Jack Arnold's finest film. Having directed camp classics including *It Came from Outer Space* (1953), *Creature from the Black Lagoon* (1954) and *Tarantula* (1955), he took on a project that contained elements of all of these films. The movie is roughly divided into three sections. In the first the perfect American marriage is increasingly affected by the physical practicalities of Scott's changing size. The hero's deep depression is indicative of his sense of his own emasculation. In the central section, having shrunk dramatically, Carey has to re-evaluate his world and come to terms with the change as a cellar floor becomes a vast plain, a chest of drawers a mountain and a harmless spider a

▲ *THE INCREDIBLE SHRINKING MAN* Grant Williams (Scott Carey) about to do battle with a giant spider in the hostile alien landscape that his cellar has become.

deadly predator. The story concludes with Carey's becoming suddenly verbose as he experiences his enlightenment and realizes that he does after all still exist. An effective, surprisingly intelligent film with some neat set designs and serviceable special effects.

ODD/SALIENT FACTS Screenwriter and author of the original novel *The Shrinking Man*, Richard Matheson has written widely in the science fiction and horror genres for the cinema and TV as well as novels. He wrote several screenplays for Roger Corman and, having worked on the original TV series, contributed two of the stories to the portmanteau *Twilight Zone – The Movie* (1983). Also on the credit side he wrote the novel *I Am Legend*, which has been filmed twice, notably as *The Omega Man* (1971) starring Charlton Heston, and he provided the screenplay for Steven Spielberg's breakthrough success the TV movie *Duel* (1971), later released as a feature film. On the

debit side he furnished the regrettable script for *Jaws-3D* (1983) and returned to his own source to pen the sequel *The Incredible Shrinking Woman* (1981), a lightweight vehicle for the talents of Lily Tomlin.

MEMORABLE MOMENTS We cut from Carey, distraught at the revelation that he is now shorter than Clarice and that the shrinking has started again, to him sitting in a normal living room. There is a sudden thundering sound which turns out to be Louise's footsteps descending the stairs. He is now living in a doll's house.

The various adventures he has in his new kingdom in the cellar: the epic climb up the storage unit; lighting the vast match; snatching the stale cheese from the mousetrap; his narrow escape from drowning as he tries to attract the attention of his brother and his departing wife who think him dead; the final conflict with the spider.

KEY LINES

Carey: 'Easy enough to talk of soul and spirit and essential worth but not when you're three feet tall.'

Carey's final speech: 'There was no longer the terrible fear of shrinking. Again I had this sensation of instinct, of each movement, each thought tuned to some directing force. I was continuing to shrink, to become what? The infinitesimal? What was I? Still a human being?... To God there is no zero. I still exist.'

INTOLERANCE

US, 1916, Wark Producing Company, 13 reels, 12,598 ft (in original version)

D SC PR D. W. Griffith; **PH** G. W. (Billy) Bitzer and Karl Brown; **ED** James and Rose Smith; **M** (for original presentation) Joseph Carl Breil and D. W. Griffith
CAST Lillian Gish (Woman who rocks cradle).
A Present Day Town in the American West: Mae Marsh (The Dear One), Fred Turner (Her Father), Robert Harron (Boy), Sam de Grasse (Jenkins, mill owner)
Ancient Jerusalem: Howard Gaye (Jesus Christ, the Nazarine), Lillian Langdon (The Virgin Mary), Olga Grey (Mary Magdalene), Erich von Stroheim (First Pharisee)
Paris ad 1572: Margaret Wilson (Brown Eyes, daughter of a Huguenot family), Eugene Pallette (Prosper Latour, her sweetheart), Frank Bennett (Charles IX, King of France), Josephine Crowell (Catherine de Medici, his mother), Constance Talmadge (Marguerite de Valois, his sister), Maxfield Stanley (Duc d'Anjou, heir to the throne), Joseph Henabery (Admiral Cologny)
Ancient Babylon 539 BC: Constance Talmadge (Mountain Girl), Elmer Clifton (The Rhapsode, her suitor and secret agent of the High Priest of Bel), Alfred Paget (Prince Belshazzar), Carl Stockdale (King Nabonidus, ancient apostle of religious toleration), Tully Marshall (High Priest of Bel), George Siegmann (Cyrus, emperor of the Persians)

The story Introduced by a recurrent image of a mother rocking a cradle, the film interweaves four stories from different historical periods.
1. The modern story set in a contemporary American city, centres on a young working-class couple who have been driven into the slums as a result of a strike. The husband is sent to jail, and after his release he is framed for the murder of a criminal

attempting to rape his wife. He is saved from execution at the last minute by his brave wife's arrival with a confession that clears him.
2. The Judean story, concerned with Christ's struggles with the Pharisees, covers the marriage at Cana, the woman taken in adultery and the Crucifixion.
3. In the French story Charles IX of France is encouraged by his mother, the fanatic Catholic Marguerite of Medici, to issue an edict against the Huguenots, and the St Bartholomew's Day Massacre of 24 August 1972 occurs in Paris the night before Brown Eyes, daughter of a leading Huguenot family, was to marry Prosper Latour.
4. The Babylonian episode in 539 BC pits the scholarly, peace-loving Prince Belshazzar against the rigid High Priest of Bel, who conspires with the Persian King Cyrus to destroy Belshazzar's regime. The Mountain Girl, who secretly loves the Prince, discovers the plot but arrives too late to avert the tragedy.
The film In 1915, the US Supreme Court ruled that movies were a business, not an art, and thus not protected by the First Amendment. Griffith was determined to prove them wrong, though he died in 1948, four years before they reversed that early decision. *Intolerance*, subtitled 'Love's Struggle Through the Ages', is arguably the first American film that can be called truly great. It was the most profitable picture ever made, but the cult it created and maintained was concerned with white supremacists who launched the post-First World War resurgence of the Ku Klux Klan, whose post-Civil War activities Griffith's film had dignified. *Intolerance* was neither as expensive (it cost $386,000) nor as unpopular as legend has it, though it didn't show a profit, but among cinéastes and cinéphiles, this has always been *the* Griffith movie. Shortly after its first screening Griffith released the modern and Babylonian episodes as separate films; the former had in fact been originally made to stand on its own, and the latter had become an obsessive activity involving a huge set and innumerable extras. Dramatically the modern sequence was the best, and the Babylon episode the most specacular, but what makes *Intolerance* so magnificent is the way Griffith brings the stories together within one great personal idea, what he called a 'fugue form'. Combining kitsch and high art, drawing on painting, opera, the Bible, theatrical melodrama, labour disputes, it is an astonishing artistic hybrid and a vivid panorama of intolerance through the ages.

Odd/salient facts This was the first time a film was widely publicised as it was made and became a legend before it was released. Several future great moviemakers assisted Griffith, e.g. W. S. Van Dyke and Tod Browning. Allegedly the only known moment of tension during the lengthy production came when Mae Marsh addressed the imperious Mr Griffith as 'Griff'.

Memorable moments The army opening fire on strikers in the modern sequence.

The innovative crane shots in the Babylon scenes, and the sheer size of the sets.

Key lines

From opening titles: 'Each story shows how hatred and

▲ *Intolerance* Belshazzar entertains on one of the greatest sets in the history of the cinema.

intolerance, through all the ages, have battled against love and charity.'

From a Walt Whitman poem providing the leitmotif *of a mother rocking a cradle:* 'Out of the cradle endlessly rocking.'

Introductory title to modern story: 'Today as yesterday, endlessly rocking, ever bringing the same human passions, the same joys and sorrows.'

INVASION OF THE BODY SNATCHERS

US, 1956, ALLIED ARTISTS, 80 MINS

D DON SIEGEL; **P** WALTER WANGER; **SC** DANIEL MAINWARING (FROM THE NOVEL BY JACK FINNEY); **PH** (BW SUPERSCOPE) ELLSWORTH FREDERICKS; **M** CARMEN DRAGON; **ED** ROBERT S. ELSEN

CAST KEVIN MCCARTHY (MILES BENNELL), DANA WYNTER (BECKY DRISCOLL), KING DONOVAN (JACK), CAROLYN JONES (THEODORA), LARRY GATES (DAN KAUFMAN), JEAN WILLES (SALLY)

AND

INVASION OF THE BODY SNATCHERS

US, 1978, UNITED ARTISTS, 115 MINS

D PHILIP KAUFMAN; **P** ROBERT H. SOLO; **SC** W. D. RICHTER; **PH** MICHAEL CHAPMAN, **M** DENNY ZEITLIN; **ED.** DOUGLAS STEWART

CAST DONALD SUTHERLAND (MATTHEW BENNELL), BROOKS ADAMS (ELIZABETH DRISCOLL), VERONICA CARTWRIGHT (NANCY BELLICEC), JEFF GOLDBLUM (JACK BELLICEC), LEONARD NIMOY (DR DAVID KIBNER)

THE STORY 1956 version: Dr Miles Bennell returns from a conference to the small Californian town of Santa Mira, where he's the local GP, to find the community both quiet and edgy, several patients suspecting relatives of having changed their identities. He and his girlfriend, Becky, gradually discover that seeds long floating in space have landed in local fields and created pods which first replicate humans, then take over their bodies while they are asleep, turning them into emotionless creatures. Eventually Miles and Becky are the only ones left and they elude their pursuers. But in an abandoned tunnel in the hills Becky falls asleep and is taken over, leaving Miles on his own to warn the world of the impending disaster.

In outline the plot of the 1978 version is similar to the earlier one, but now the setting is San Francisco and the central characters, Matthew Bennell and Elizabeth Driscoll, are colleagues at the city's Public Health department. Once again their best friends are a writer and his wife, and a psychiatrist, who initially dismisses the phenomenon as mass hysteria, and turns out to be the ringleader of the replicants. The remake, however,

> '*Don't be trapped by old concepts, Matthew, you're evolving into a new life form.*'

ends with Bennell first attempting to destroy the factory producing the pods, then turning out to be taken over himself.

THE FILMS Siegel's low-budget classic is set in a tight, idealized community where everyone knows each other, and the tension grows as the hero notices the change in those around him, until the once familiar becomes dangerously hostile. The bodies oozing from pods are repellent, but the film uses few shock effects. Appearing at the mid-point of Eisenhower's presidency, the movie was perceived as an allegory about conformity, though it could as easily be interpreted as a warning against socialism or as an attack on the craven behaviour of the McCarthy era. The expensive 1978 film takes place in an alienated city in the wake of the Sixties' revolution and Watergate. People are high on apocalyptic science fiction, conspiracy theory, new religions and therapies, worry about the ecology, and seem ready for some takeover that would have the effect of putting Prozac in the drinking water. Kaufman's picture accepts the cult status of Siegel's original by giving small roles to Kevin McCarthy (who throws himself on to the bonnet of Sutherland's car, shouting out a warning before being killed) and to Don Siegel (as a taxi driver who betrays the hero and heroine to the police).

ODD/SALIENT FACTS Don Siegel didn't like the script's framing device and wanted to end with Bennell standing among the passing traffic pointing at the audience and saying: 'You're next.' Sam Peckinpah worked as dialogue director, did a week-long (uncredited) polish on the script and appears as Charlie the gas-man. The film was shot in 19 days for under $300,000, and designer Ted Haworth (whose credits include Hitchcock's *Strangers on a Train* and *I Confess*) had a budget of $15,000 for special effects. In 1994 Abel Ferrara's *Body Snatchers* transposed the same story to an army base in Alabama, creating the problem of how to suggest the imposition of extraterrestrial conformity on a community of earthlings who had already surrendered their individuality to the military.

MEMORABLE MOMENTS In the 1956 film: Miles's inability to destroy his girlfriend's cloned shape.

Miles's horrified realization that Becky has become a pod person.

In both movies the sound of music (a Spanish love song in

▲ *INVASION OF THE BODY SNATCHERS* Dana Wynter, Carolyn Jones, King Donovan and Kevin McCarthy stare in horror at the pods in the greenhouse.

1956, 'Amazing Grace' in 1978), suggests on-going human life nearby, and turns out to be on a radio owned by pod people.

In the 1978 picture a street musician's dog appears with his master's bearded face after the two have fallen asleep beside a pod.

KEY LINES

Miles, 1956: 'All of us, we've … grown callous. Only when we have to fight to stay human do we realise how precious it is to us.'

Miles, 1956: 'Stop, listen to me, we're in danger, something terrible is happening, they have arrived and you're next.'

Matthew, 1978: 'Do you want to see my friend, he's a

psychiatrist. He'd eliminate a lot of things – whether Geoffrey was having an affair, whether he had become gay, whether he had a social disease, whether he had become a Republican, all the alternatives that could have happened to him.'

David, the psychiatrist, 1978: 'Don't be trapped by old concepts, Matthew, you're evolving into a new life form.'

IT'S A WONDERFUL LIFE
US, 1946, LIBERTY FILMS, 129 MINS

D *FRANK CAPRA;* **PR** *FRANK CAPRA;* **SC** *FRANK CAPRA, FRANCIS GOODRICH, ALBERT HACKETT;* **ADD SC** *JO SWERLING;* **PH** *(BW) JOSEPH WALKER, JOSEPH BIROC;* **M** *DIMITRI TIOMKIN;* **ED** *WILLIAM HORNBECK*

CAST *JAMES STEWART (GEORGE BAILEY), DONNA REED (MARY HATCH), LIONEL BARRYMORE (MR POTTER), THOMAS MITCHELL (UNCLE BILLY), BEULAH BONDI (MRS BAILEY), FRANK FAYLEN (ERNIE), WARD BOND (BERT), HENRY TRAVERS (CLARENCE), H. B. WARNER (MR GOWER), GLORIA GRAHAME (VIOLET), TODD KARNS (HARRY BAILEY), VIRGINIA PATTON (RUTH DAKEN), SAMUEL S HINDS (PA BAILEY), SHELDON LEONARD (NICK)*

THE STORY It is Christmas Eve and the prayers of several residents of Bedford Falls are answered. Trainee angel Clarence is summoned to earn his wings by saving the life of the suicidal George Bailey. In a series of flashbacks Clarence is filled in on the key events of Bailey's life. As a young boy he saved the life of his kid brother Harry, and prevented his pharmacist boss from accidentally poisoning a sick child. George is prevented from leaving his small town by a succession of factors: his father's death, the needs of his family building and loan company, his brother's education and career, a run on the bank. Married with children, and in charge of the company, on the eve of his brother's heroic homecoming from war, George faces disgrace when his Uncle Billy misplaces $8,000. On the verge of suicide, George's life is saved by Clarence, who then shows him how bad things would have been had he never been born. Suddenly back in Bedford Falls after witnessing the nightmare of this parallel world, George is chastened. He returns to his family to find that all is well and that it is, after all, a wonderful life.

THE FILM It's a Wonderful Life was the first film that James Stewart made in nearly six years. During this 'sabbatical', he had become a decorated flying officer in the Second World War but spoke little of his wartime experiences. When Capra first brought the project to Stewart's attention, the director himself described it as: 'The lousiest piece of cheese I ever heard of.' The film was a failure at the box office and was only hailed as a classic when it became a staple of American Christmas TV from the 1960s onwards. When Capra's Mr Deeds Goes to Town (1936) was first shown in the Soviet Union, the censors cut the last twenty minutes so this ultimately patriotic film would instead be seen as a savage indictment of the awful-

> ## 'I wish I'd never been born.'

ness and corruption of American life. The same trick would work in It's a Wonderful Life. George Bailey's life is one of continual disappointment, one in which George himself comes to understand that forces are preventing him from ever leaving his claustrophobic small town. The intensity of his anguish is shocking. This is Capracorn so thoroughly disguised as unrelentingly bleak, existential gloom that it was just too much for a postwar audience. The film requires the repeated viewings allowed by TV reruns, the VCR and cinema re-releases for its

▼ IT'S A WONDERFUL LIFE The Bailey family, their friends and creditors gather to toast George, the richest man in town.

grimly optimistic message to be appreciated – that normal American life is awful and harrowing, built on frustration and disappointment, but it could be a lot worse, so in fact it's great after all.

ODD/SALIENT FACTS Dalton Trumbo, Dorothy Parker and Clifford Odets all did uncredited work on the script. There is a rock band called Zuzu's Petals, named after the petals that George pretends he has glued on to the flower at the bedside of his sick daughter. They disappear when Clarence eradicates all traces of George's existence and it is their return as well as his deaf ear and bleeding mouth that prove that he is alive once more. In the 1980s, a suicidal criminal in America was ordered by the judge passing sentence in his case to watch the film. The cop and cab driver buddies Ernie and Bert inspired the *Sesame Street* characters of the same names.

MEMORABLE MOMENTS George and Mary at Harry's high-school prom, dancing the Charleston wildly and oblivious to the gym floor parting to reveal the pool beneath. When they eventually fall in the pool they just carry on their delirious dancing.

Their tuneless but joyful singing of *Buffalo Girls* as they wander home in borrowed clothes, and throw stones in the ruined old house they will eventually share. Their tryst is interrupted by the news of Pa Bailey's stroke.

The scene we wait for throughout the film, the one that is instantly recognisable and that is used in *Gremlins* (1984), when the nightmare is over and George runs ecstatically through the winter wonderland of Bedford Falls.

KEY LINES

George Bailey to Potter: 'Just remember this, Mr Potter. This rabble you're talking about. They do most of the working and praying and living and dying in this community! Well, is it too much to have them work and pray and live and die in a couple of decent rooms and a bath?'

George to Clarence: 'I wish I'd never been born.'

Clarence: 'Strange, isn't it? Each man's life touches so many other lives, and when he isn't around, he leaves an awful hole, doesn't he?'

THE ITALIAN JOB

UK, 1969, PARAMOUNT/OAKHURST, 117 MINS

D PETER COLLINSON; **PR** MICHAEL DEELEY; **SC** TROY KENNEDY MARTIN; **PH** (COL) DOUGLAS SLOCOMBE; **M** QUINCY JONES; **ED** JOHN TRUMPER

CAST MICHAEL CAINE (CHARLIE CROKER), NOËL COWARD (MR BRIDGER), BENNY HILL (PROFESSOR SIMON PEACH), RAF VALLONE (ALTAHANI), TONY BECKLEY (FREDDIE), ROSSANO BRAZZI (BECKERMAN), MAGGIE BLYE (LORNA), IRENE HANDL (MISS PEACH), JOHN LE MESURIER (GOVERNOR), FRED EMNEY (BIRKINSHAW), JOHN CLIVE (GARAGE MANAGER), GRAHAM PAYN (KEATS), MICHAEL STANDING (ARTHUR), STANLEY CAINE (COCO), BARRY COX (CHRIS), HARRY BAIRD (BIG WILLIAM), GEORGE INNES (BILL BAILEY), JOHN FORGEHAM (FRANK), ROBERT POWELL (YELLOW)

THE STORY Charlie Croker is released from prison and takes on the caper of a lifetime bequeathed to him by a recently deceased fellow con. The plan is to steal a consignment of gold bullion in the centre of Turin and create a backdrop distraction of the biggest-ever traffic jam by sabotaging the computer which controls the city's traffic. Securing funding from the incarcerated criminal bigwig Mr Bridger, aided by a computer whizz-kid with a penchant for large women and with a fleet of getaway minis, the scam goes ahead. Everything goes to plan, the bullion is stolen, the minis evade the police, escape the city and load the gold on to the getaway coach heading for Switzerland. But the overzealous driver careers off the road and the coach, the gang and the gold are left in a literal cliffhanger with Charlie needing just one more great idea.

THE FILM There are some old-fashioned, unpleasant racist undertones to the film with the jingoism of the upper-class and working-class outfit taking on and beating the mafia and the Italian police. The raid is on a security van conveying money to be used in a deal between the Chinese and Fiat. Bridger is a fanatical patriot, obsessed with the Queen. The job, which coincides with a football match between England and Italy, uses three emblematically English Minis, one red, one white, one

'Hang on a minute, lads, I've got a great idea ...'

121

▲ *THE ITALIAN JOB* *The red, white and blue getaway Minis negotiate the narrow streets and stairways of Turin.*

blue, that will be driven on to a red, white and blue coach. The raid goes perfectly but is bungled only by the reckless behaviour of the black driver, 'Known as Big William for very obvious reasons.' Nevertheless this is a perennial favourite, beloved by a generation whose appreciation is instantly communicated by the exchange of a few key lines which have entered the language. Coward was encouraged out of retirement to take the role of the highly patriotic supercriminal Bridger. It was the last film he made and marked an exuberant if unsubtle swan song to the great man's career.

ODD/SALIENT FACTS The screenplay was written by Troy Kennedy Martin who became a regular writer on the TV series *The Sweeney* and also wrote the classic 1980s TV eco-thriller *Edge of Darkness*. The film is perhaps best remembered for its

bold/irritating inconclusive conclusion. This was not always how it was supposed to be as Caine recalls in William Hall's *Raising Caine*:

> There was no ending written. We figured we'd get to an ending when we got there, and that's how we left it. We were going to do a sequel: the coach is teetering on the edge of a cliff, and they have to get the weight from the back where the gold is piled. The idea is that they have to sit there for five hours with the engine running because the petrol tanks are at the back. Then the weight comes up – but as all the guys get off the gold goes over on its own ...

> At the bottom of the cliff is a Mafia leader, who makes off with the gold. He takes it across the border to the South of France, and then we were going to chase him. Instead of using Minis we were to use another British invention which was the two-seater hovercraft, with the motorcycle cops chasing us through the marshes and the roads – a real zoom-zoom ending.

MEMORABLE MOMENTS The euphoric scenes of the minis evading the Italian police, driving over the vast undulating roof, negotiating weirs, bridges, car lots and sewers, intercut with the victory parade of Bridger in prison.

Desperate to secure funding for his little job in Italy, Charlie breaks into prison for an unscheduled meeting with Mr Bridger in his toilet, thus committing the unforgivable crime of upsetting the older man's 'natural rhythm'.

KEY LINES

Peach: 'I like 'em big.'

Charlie: after a series of disastrous dummy runs in which a succession of cars are destroyed, watches his countdown lead to a van being blown to smithereens. He shouts, in Caine's inimitable crescendo:'You're only supposed to blow the bloody doors off.'

Charlie: 'Hang on a minute, lads, I've got a great idea ... er ... er ...'

JAWS★

US, 1975, UNIVERSAL PICTURES, 124 MINS

D STEVEN SPIELBERG; **PR** RICHARD D ZANUCK, DAVID BROWN; **SC** PETER BENCHLEY, CARL GOTTLIEB; **PH** BILL BUTLER; **M** JOHN WILLIAMS; **ED** VERNA FIELDS

CAST ROY SCHEIDER (BRODY), ROBERT SHAW (QUINT), RICHARD DREYFUSS (HOOPER), LORRAINE GRAY (ELLEN BRODY), MURRAY HAMILTON (VAUGHAN), CARL GOTTLIEB (MEADOWS), JEFFREY C. KRAMER (HENDRICKS), SUSAN BACKLINNIE (CHRISSIE), JONATHAN FILLEY (CASSIDY), TED GROSSMAN (ESTUARY VICTIM), CHRIS REBELLO (MICHAEL BRODY), JAY MELLO (SEAN BRODY), LEE KIERRO (MRS KINTNER), JEFFREY VOORHEES (ALEX KINTNER), CRAIG KINGSBURY (BEN GARDNER), DR ROBERT NEVIN (MEDICAL EXAMINER), PETER BENCHLEY (INTERVIEWER)

THE STORY A woman out skinny-dipping at night is attacked and dragged underwater by an unseen beast. Chief Brody, a cop with a fear of water and the new chief of police in the holiday resort of Amity Island, attributes the young woman's death to a shark attack. His attempts to close the beach are blocked by the mayor, and after a second attack a great shark hunt begins. On a night dive off his boat, Hooper, a wealthy ichthyologist discovers that Ben Gardner, one of the fishermen, has also fallen victim to the Great White. Brody, Quint, a local fisherman, and Hooper set out to catch and kill the Great White. After a mighty struggle that costs Quint's life, Brody conquers his fear of the water, blows the shark up, and paddles back to land with Hooper.

THE FILM The film was chaotic in production, with the three fake sharks continually malfunctioning, the project going months behind schedule and millions of dollars over budget, and many, including Dreyfuss, predicted it would be a dismal failure. In post-production Spielberg and his collaborators, seeing the shots of the cross-eyed shark, shifted the focus of the film. They realised that what makes the film so scary is the suggestion of danger, the delay in seeing the shark. It became the most successful film of all time and, like *Easy Rider* (1969), marked a fundamental change in the way in which films were made in Hollywood. Spielberg himself talks of empathizing with Coppola over his experiences with *Apocalypse Now* (1979), having himself courted disaster and eventually suffered panic attacks with *Jaws*. Peter Benchley's crude best-selling novel has been honed into a modern exploitation masterpiece with ele-ments of the group jeopardy film, the Western and the political conspiracy thriller.

ODD/SALIENT FACTS Richard Dreyfuss turned down the role of Hooper three times, and as he recalls in Peter Biskind's *Easy Riders, Raging Bulls*: 'Then I saw *The Apprenticeship of Duddy Kravitz*, and I was just so freaked out, I thought my performance was so terrible, that I called Steven and begged for the job. I went with the fish movie. We started the film without a script, without a cast, and without a shark.'

MEMORABLE MOMENTS The attack sequences – the brilliantly constructed opening, the boy on the lilo, the fishermen on the jetty, the man in the pond.

Roy Scheider on the beach reacting to the second attack (achieved by the camera moving away from him on tracks while simultaneously zooming in on his face).

The head of Ben Gardner suddenly appearing in the port-hole of the sunken boat.

KEY LINES

The enduring cult element of the film surrounds Quint's chilling speech at night aboard the *Orca*. He and Hooper have shown off their scars, when Brody asks him what caused the scar on his arm. He explains that it was a tattoo he had removed of the *USS Indianapolis*. Hooper who had been laughing, falls silent, and Quint recounts the events of the return journey of the boat that had delivered the Hiroshima bomb. It was struck by two Japanese torpedoes on 29 June 1945:

'11,000 men went into the water. The vessel went down in one and a half minutes. Didn't see the first shark for about a half an hour. Tiger. 13-footer. You know how you know that when you're in the water, Chief? You tell by looking from the dorsal to the tail. What we didn't know was our bomb mission had been so secret, no distress signal had been sent. They didn't even list us overdue for a week. Very first night, Chief, sharks came cruising. So we formed ourselves into tight groups like old squares in the battle, like you see in the calendar, like in the Battle of Waterloo, and the idea was: shark comes to the nearest man and he's pounding and hollering and screaming. Sometimes the shark'd go away, sometimes he wouldn't go away. Sometimes that shark, he looks right into you, right into your eyes, and you know a thing about a shark, he's got lifeless eyes, black eyes, like a doll's eyes. When he comes at you he doesn't seem to be living until he bites you and those black eyes roll over white and then you hear that terrible, high-pitched screamin' and the ocean turns red, despite all the pounding and the hollering they all come in and they rip you to pieces ...'

A brilliant piece of writing and acting that provides a depth of fear and history to the action. It suggests that sharks acted as some kind of instant divine or diabolical retribution for the Americans daring to use the bomb. The authorship of the speech was contested, with John Milius having provided an uncredited rewrite and Robert Shaw also claiming to have contributed to it.

▼ *La Jetée The beginning and the end for the unnamed hero of Chris Marker's stunning photo roman.*

LA JETÉE
FRANCE, 1962, ARGOS FILMS, 29 MINS

D *Chris Marker;* **SC** *Marker; BW*

CAST *Hélène Chatelain (The woman), Davos Hanich (The man), Jacques Ledoux (The scholar), André Heinrich, Jacques Branchu, Pierre Joffroy, Etienne Becker, Philbert von Lifchitz, Ligia Borowczyk, Jeannine Klein, Bill Klein, Germano Facetti, Jean Negroni (The storyteller)*

THE STORY A man is chosen for a time-travel experiment in post-apocalyptic subterranean Paris because of the strength and vividness of a memory when as a boy he stood on the pier at Orly airport looking at a young woman. In these experiments, he travels back in time and meets up with this same woman on several disjointed assignations. He also travels into the future from where he receives the secret that is the salvation of life on earth. Offered the chance to live in the future, he asks instead to be sent back to the past to meet up with the woman. Back on the pier at Orly, he sees the woman and starts to run towards

her, but he has been followed by a man from his present who shoots him, and only then does he realize that the memory he has carried with him since childhood is a glimpse of his own death.

THE FILM This haunting, brilliant, bleak 29-minute film is told almost entirely in still photographs. Chris Marker describes it as a *photo roman*. The photographs are all in black and white, some striking and enigmatic, others banal. Sometimes the camera lingers on the image, sometimes there are quick cuts and for one sequence, the man's first journey back in time, the pictures come as a series of pulsing images that quickly fade in from black and equally quickly fade away again.

ODD/SALIENT FACTS The story, loosely of the sci-fi genre, is markedly influenced by Jorge Luis Borges. The notion of a man selected for his remarkably powerful memory brings to mind the central character in the story 'Funes the Memorious'. But the central idea of the child seeing himself die is especially reminiscent of the story 'The Other' from *The Book of Sand*, in which the narrator meets himself as an old man and converses with himself for a short while. This is Chris Marker's only fictional film. A man of mysterious origins and early life, Marker, born in 1921, has worked as a critic, poet and documentary film-maker collaborating with Alan Resnais and Walerian Borowczyk. The film inspired Terry Gilliam's *Twelve Monkeys* (1995) which (with a script by Janet and David Peoples) uses *La Jetée's* basic plot and framing device, and melds it to elements borrowed from *The Terminator* (1984) and T2 (1991) and David Cronenberg's *The Dead Zone* (1983).

MEMORABLE MOMENTS For just one sequence we see a succession of pictures of the woman lying asleep in bed, which ends with a couple of seconds of barely discernible moving film in which she opens her eyes and smiles very slightly.

KEY LINES

'He ran towards her and when he recognized the man who had been trailing him since the camp, he knew there was no way out of time, and he knew that this haunted moment he had been granted to see as a child was the moment of his own death.'

▲ *JULES ET JIM* Jim (at the top), Jules and Catherine form a romantic triangle in the early Midi morning light.

JULES ET JIM

FRANCE, 1962, LES FILMS DU CARROSSE, 105 MINS

D FRANÇOIS TRUFFAUT; **PR** MARCEL BERBERT; **SC** FRANÇOIS TRUFFAUT, JEAN GRUAULT (FROM THE NOVEL BY HENRI-PIERRE ROCHÉ); **PH** (BW, FRANSCOPE) RAOUL COUTARD; **ED** CLAUDINE BOUCHÉ; **M** GEORGES DELERUE

CAST JEANNE MOREAU (CATHERINE), OSKAR WERNER (JULES), HENRI SERRE (JIM), MARIE DUBOIS (THÉRÈSE), VANNA URBINO (GILBERTE), SABINE HAUDEPIN (SABINE), BORIS BASSIAK (ALBERT), MICHEL SUBOR (NARRATOR)

> *'Is her kind made for marriage? I fear she may never be happy on this earth. She is an apparition.'*

THE STORY 1912, PARIS. The German writer Jules meets the French writer Jim on a visit to France; they become close friends, pursue girls together, translate each others' work. After becoming obsessed with the smile on an ancient Mediterranean sculpture, they meet Catherine, a girl with a similar smile. She's the wilful, free-spirited daughter of an aristocratic French father and a working-class English mother, and the three become inseparable. Shortly before the outbreak of the First World War, Jules and Catherine marry, and the two friends serve in the armies of their native countries, hoping never to confront each other. After the war, Jim, now an established novelist, comes to Germany to write a series of articles on the country's troubles. He stays with Jules and Catherine, who now have a six-year-old daughter, and eventually becomes the lover of the sexually liberated Catherine. They break up but meet again when Jules and Catherine move back to a mill on the Seine, and finally Jim elects to marry the stable Gilberte. Some years later, after Hitler's rise to power, Jim meets Jules and Catherine at a Paris cinema showing Nazi book-burning. Re-united, Jim goes for a drive in Catherine's car and they plunge over a broken bridge to their deaths in the river beneath. Jules picks up their ashes in the crematorium.

THE FILM *Jules et Jim* was Truffaut's third feature film, one of his most loved, and possibly his greatest. Raoul Coutard's mobile camerawork gives it a restless, lyrical quality, and the black-and-white images suggest postcards and family snapshots of a bygone time. Truffaut presents an idealized form of male and female friendship, in which passionate intellectuals attempt to control their confused feelings and frustrated desires by elegant articulation and literary allusion. The film contrasts the characters' discussions and the narrator's wise certitudes. Everything centres on Moreau's commanding, destructive heroine, one of the screen's most seductive *femmes fatales*, and through her Truffaut first proposes the major theme of his work – how we confront the attractions, repulsions and inevitability of death.

ODD/SALIENT FACTS Truffaut was nicknamed 'the grave-digger of French cinema' for his critical assaults on established directors in the mid-1950s, but when he came to make movies, death scenes, funerals and cemeteries became his trademark. Roché's semi-autobiographical novel *Jules et Jim* was published in 1953 when the author was seventy-four. In 1980 writer-director Paul Mazursky made *Willie and Phil*, about three free-wheeling New Yorkers (Michael Ontkean, Ray Sharkey, Margot Kidder) who modelled their lives on the trio in *Jules et Jim*.

MEMORABLE MOMENTS Catherine's first appearance descending the outdoor staircase.

Catherine dressing as a boy and drawing a moustache on her upper lip to go out in the streets of Paris with Jules and Jim.

Jules, Jim and Catherine cycling to the beach in Provence.

Jules reciting *La Marseillaise* in perfect French to Jim over the phone on the eve of the Great War.

Catherine singing Boris Bassiak's 'Le Tourbillon' to a guitar accompaniment at the chalet in Alsace.

KEY LINES

Jim: 'Is her kind made for marriage? I fear she may never be happy on this earth. She is an apparition.'

Narrator: 'Jules' country lost the war and Jim's country won it, but the real victory was that Jules and Jim were both alive.'

Jules: 'But she is a queen. To be candid, Catherine is not particularly beautiful, intelligent or sincere – but she is a real woman, and it is this woman we love and all men desire.'

THE KING OF COMEDY★
US, 1983, 20TH CENTURY-FOX, 108 MINS
D MARTIN SCORSESE; **PR** ARNON MILCHAN; **SC** PAUL D. ZIMMERMAN; **PH** (COL) FRED SCHULER; **M** ROBBIE ROBERTSON; **ED** THELMA SCHOONMAKER
CAST ROBERT DE NIRO (RUPERT PUPKIN), JERRY LEWIS (JERRY LANGFORD), DIAHNNE ABBOT (RITA), SANDRA BERNHARD (MASHA), TONY RANDALL (HIMSELF), SHELLEY HACK (CATHY LONG), FRED DE CORDOVA (BERT THOMAS), DR JOYCE BROTHERS (HERSELF), ED HERLIHY (HIMSELF), LOU BROWN (BANDLEADER), VICTOR BORGE (HIMSELF)

THE STORY Rupert Pupkin is a fantasist fixated on Jerry Langford, one of America's leading talk-show hosts. Rupert imagines a friendship blossoming between himself and his idol. He phones and visits Jerry's office, trying to get his big break as a stand-up comic. His fantasies become more elaborate and he dreams of being invited by Jerry to spend the weekend at his country house. Rupert and his reluctant girlfriend Rita are ejected by a furious Langford. Now more determined than ever, Rupert and Masha, a fellow fan, kidnap Jerry and force the show's producers to let Rupert deliver his routine on the programme, while Masha attempts to seduce Jerry. When Jerry eventually escapes, it is too late and the show has aired. Rupert is arrested and sent to jail, but he becomes a *cause célèbre* and when he is released after nearly three years, he is rich, famous and has achieved his dream of becoming the king of comedy.

THE FILM Scorsese came to the project, which had been doing the rounds since the late Sixties, after the rigours of *Raging Bull*

(1980), before, during and after which he was seriously ill from a mixture of stress, cocaine addiction and asthma. While on a superficial level it is a lighter film, it is nevertheless essentially a reworking of the themes and plot of *Taxi Driver* (1976). Both films have central characters who are quiet sociopaths, going about their insanity anonymously in New York. Both have been driven mad by the American experience, one by the Vietnam War and the grotesque morality of urban life, the other by the obsessive cult of fame. Each woos an initially suspicious woman into agreeing to come on a date with him and each time the date ends in horrific embarrassment, one in a pornographic cinema, the other in the home of a TV star. Each is driven to exact violent revenge on an embodiment of what they despise and each film ends with the anti-hero hailed as a hero in the media. The film is pitched as a black comedy, but is in reality a comedy with no jokes and little humour. The ambiguous mood of the film was too confusing and dark for the commercial mainstream. It has, in De Niro and Lewis, two actors each arguably delivering the performance of their career. The leading character's name is so perfect for a deliberately unfunny film, and it is rendered variously Pipkin, Pumpkin, Bodkin and Crupkin. De Niro approached the role with his customary rigour, honing his skills on the stand-up circuit, having hung out with comedians Robin Williams and John Belushi. He perfected the cadence and timing of the comic, which in his climactic sequence he applies to a routine of inspired awfulness. In *Scorsese on Scorsese* (Faber & Faber) the director says of the experience of the film: 'The King of Comedy was right on the edge for us: we couldn't go any further at that time.'

ODD/SALIENT FACTS Scorsese likes to use as many members of his family in his films as possible. Having placed his parents at the centre of his documentary *Italianamerican* (1974) he casts both of them in *King of Comedy*, his mother as the nagging off-screen voice of Rupert's mother, and his father as a man in the bar when Rupert shows off his TV performance to Rita. Scorsese himself makes his Hitchcockian cameo appearance as the director of the Jerry Langford Show. Among the street scum berated by Masha are Ellen Foley and Mick Jones, Joe Strummer and Paul Simenon (credited as Paul Simmion) from The Clash. Scorsese had originally approached Johnny Carson to play the part of Langford. Carson declined, explaining that he couldn't cope with a performance that would entail more than one take, but *The Tonight Show* is given special thanks in the credits: 'For help in researching the ambience of our film.' Other actors considered for the role were Frank Sinatra, Dean Martin and Orson Welles.

MEMORABLE MOMENTS The film's most striking scene is the embarrassing arrival of Rupert and Rita uninvited at Jerry's country home. It makes uncomfortable and disturbing viewing and leaves the audience with no one to sympathize with or root for. In *Scorsese on Scorsese*, the director recalls the shooting of this sequence as 'extremely painful. It took two weeks and it was just so painful because the scene itself was so excruciating.'

KEY LINES

In his daydream, in reply to Jerry's asking him about the secret of his talent, Rupert replies: 'I think it's that I look at my whole life and see the awful, terrible things in my life and turn it into something funny. It just happens.'

KISS ME DEADLY

US, 1955, PARK LANE PICTURES/UNITED ARTISTS, 105 MINS
D/PR ROBERT ALDRICH; **SC** A.I. BEZZERIDES (FROM THE NOVEL BY MICKEY SPILLANE); **PH** (BW) ERNEST LASZLO; **ED** MICHAEL LUCIANO; **M** FRANK DE VOL
CAST RALPH MEEKER (MIKE HAMMER), GABY RODGERS (GABRIELLE/LILY) ALBERT DEKKER (DR SOBERIN), PAUL STEWART (CARL EVELLO), JUANO HERNANDEZ (EDDIE EAGER), WESLEY ADDY (PAT CHAMBERS), MARIAN CARR (FRIDAY), MAXENE COOPER (VELDA), CLORIS LEACHMAN (CHRISTINA BAILEY), NICK DENNIS (NICK), FORTUNIO BONANOVA (TRIVAGO), JACK ELAM (CHARLIE MAX), JACK LAMBERT (SUGAR SMALLHOUSE)

THE STORY Mike Hammer, an unscrupulous Los Angeles private detective, gives a lift to Christina Bailey, a fugitive from a mental hospital. She criticizes his arrogance, he protects her at a police check point and she urges: 'Remember me!' before they are captured by thugs. She provides some information under torture before dying, and her body is placed next to Mike in his car before it goes over a cliff. Mike survives and soon discovers the FBI are interested in the case, and wants part of the action, assisted by his adoring secretary Velda. He comes up against gangsters and thugs and meets Christina's roommate Gabrielle. He is kidnapped and injected with a truth drug; his best friend Nick is murdered; and everyone is after a

128

▲ *KISS ME DEADLY* *Gaby Rodgers recoils as she releases the nuclear horrors from the fateful box.*

lead-lined box of nuclear material that contaminates all who open it. Following up the 'Remember me' clue (a reference to a Christina Rossetti poem) Hammer locates the box in the locker-room of a sports club, but it is seized by sinister Dr Soberin, kingpin of the operation, whose mistress is Gabrielle (aka Lily). Hammer tracks them down to a beach house, where they're holding Velda captive. Gabrielle/Lily kills Soberin, opens his Pandora's Box, and the house goes up in a great nuclear conflagration.

THE FILM This expressionist *film noir* masterpiece was loathed in America (where liberals despised Spillane's novels as symptoms of a culture in decline), subjected to censorship everywhere (nearly ten minutes were cut in Britain), and made Aldrich one of the cult heroes of the *Cahiers du Cinéma* critics

who nicknamed him 'Le Gros Bob'. The jagged style, the narrative short-cuts, the refusal to explain, inspired them four years later, when they became film-makers and created the *Nouvelle Vague*. Aldrich was a master of genre cinema – a great exponent of the Western, the thriller, the war movie – but this remains his wildest, least compromising picture. He was a rebel, an anarchist who never sought respectability. His heroes were outsiders embodied by stars such as Burt Lancaster, Jack Palance and Lee Marvin. In *Kiss Me Deadly* he chose to expose Spillane's right-wing, fascistic private eye Mike Hammer, by showing him going about his work beating up people, exploiting the weak. Apart from the mildly sympathetic cop, Pat Chambers, the film's only attractive characters are the poetry-loving Christina and the cheerful mechanic Nick, both of whom are killed.

The movie's violence is relentless, though most of it is implied. The dialogue (by A. I. Bezzerides, a one-time truckdriver) is stylized rather than plain demotic, and full of classical and literary allusions. In one poolside shot, three of the leading heavies in post-war Hollywood cinema are framed together – Jack Lambert, Jack Elam and Paul Stewart.

ODD/SALIENT FACTS In Spillane's original novel the box in the locker contains a consignment of heroin belonging to the Mafia. Ralph Meeker came to prominence in 1948 when he took over from Brando in *A Streetcar Named Desire* on Broadway; he rarely played sympathetic characters. Spillane apparently liked the film and in an equivocal 1955 article in the *New York Herald Tribune* Aldrich spoke of 'playing fair by Spillane fans'. Never once in the film do we hear the words bomb, thermo-nuclear or atomic.

MEMORABLE MOMENTS Christina and Mike driving through the night in his cramped sportscar.

The blonde Lily Carver sitting up in bed pointing her gun at the camera.

The spinning tapes of Mike's answering machine repeating messages.

Images of nuclear contamination concluding with Lily's final opening of the box.

KEY LINES

Velda: 'They, a wonderful word. Who are they? They are the nameless ones who kill people for the great what's it. Does it exist? Who cares?'

Dr Soberin to the drugged Hammer: 'What is it you are seeking? Diamonds, rubies, gold? Perhaps narcotics. How civilized this earth used to be. But as the world became more primitive, its treasures became more fabulous. Perhaps sentiment will succeed where greed failed. You will die Mr Hammer, but your friend, you can save her, yes you can.'

Dr Soberin to Gabrielle: 'The head of Medusa. That's what's in the box, and who looks on her will be changed not into stone but into brimstone and ashes. But of course you wouldn't believe me, you'd have to see for yourself, wouldn't you?'

LAURA

USA, 1944, TCF, 88 MINS

D/PR OTTO PREMINGER; **SC** JAY DRATLER, SAMUEL HOFFENSTEIN, BETTY REINHARDT (FROM THE NOVEL BY VERA CASPARY); **PH** JOSEPH LASHELLE; **M** DAVID RAKSIN

CAST GENE TIERNEY (LAURA HUNT), DANA ANDREWS (MARK MCPHERSON), CLIFTON WEBB (WALDO LYDECKER), VINCENT PRICE (SHELBY CARPENTER), JUDITH ANDERSON (ANN TREADWELL), DOROTHY ADAMS (BESSIE CLARY)

THE STORY Homicide detective Mark McPherson takes over the investigation of the murder of Laura Hunt, a successful advertising executive found dead by her maid in her New York apartment, blasted in the face by a shotgun and recognizable only from her clothes. McPherson has four suspects. Waldo Lydecker, celebrated columnist and broadcaster, a waspish dandy and Laura's mentor and confidant, introducing her into society, helping her reach the top of her profession, and protecting her from unworthy suitors; Shelby Carpenter, Laura's fiancé, a charming, womanizing, irresponsible, impoverished Southern aristocrat; Ann Treadwell, Laura's rich, amoral aunt, in love with Shelby; Bessie, Laura's devoted maid, an Irish-American with a hatred for the law. Within hours of embarking on the case, McPherson falls in love with Laura's portrait hanging over the fireplace and settles in the apartment. He falls asleep and awakes to find Laura standing before him. She had been spending the weekend at her country cottage reconsidering her engagement to Carpenter. The woman killed in her

place was in fact Carpenter's mistress who answered the door while they were having an assignation. Laura senses the detective's fascination with her. It transpires that Waldo, refusing to let Laura marry Carpenter, had attempted to murder her. After McPherson has exposed him, Waldo is gunned down by the police.

THE FILM *Laura* has the contrived plot of a B-feature whodunnit, but its witty script and production values are those of an A-production, and the picture is less concerned with suspense than with exploring the perversity of the characters. Waldo, a brilliant creation, superbly played, is a Pygmalion obsessed with his Galatea, an impotent crypto-homosexual who cannot physically possess his creation and is convinced that no one else is worthy of her. Laura, the chilly career girl, has made a Faustian pact with Waldo that she attempts to break. Her aunt is drawn to the weak, epicene Shelby by their shared corruption. McPherson, who regards all women as dames or dolls, is attracted to Laura because she is unattainably dead and thus no threat to him. Like a number of 1940s movies (e.g. *Rebecca*, *The Woman in the Window*, *Portrait of Jennie*) *Laura* has as a central erotic image a painting of a woman who obsesses the characters, an effect reinforced by the repeated playing (on the

▼ *LAURA* The protective Waldo (Clifton Webb) looks on disapprovingly as Laura (Gene Tierney), cigarette in hand, is swayed by gigolo Vincent Price.

129

radio, phonograph and by a restaurant orchestra) of the title song by Johnny Mercer and David Raksin. Though always described as a *film noir*, the picture only occasionally goes in for expressionist effects.

ODD/SALIENT FACTS The film was begun by Rouben Mamoulian, who claimed it was essentially his work. Preminger, who initiated the project as producer and took over the direction, said that he brought in a new cameraman and scrapped all Mamoulian's footage. The film made Preminger's reputation and has his characteristic use of elaborate camera movements combined with shooting the dialogue in longish takes in which two or more characters appear together in a single shot so that none is morally favoured by the editing. The character of Waldo Lydecker appears to be based on the columnist, broadcaster and *New Yorker* theatre critic Alexander Woollcott, who was impotent, a repressed gay, a famous wit and, like Waldo, fascinated by murder. Woollcott always dined at the Algonquin Hotel, where Laura first approaches Lydecker. Darrryl F. Zanuck was opposed to casting Clifton Webb in the role because of his known homosexuality, but Preminger prevailed and the 54-year-old Webb (making his first screen appearance since the silent era) was nominated for an Oscar.

MEMORABLE MOMENTS Waldo first seen in his bath, typing his column.

Laura's seemingly luminous portrait dominating every scene in her living room.

Mark awakening to see Laura, slightly out of focus, for the first time.

Waldo turning at the top of the staircase outside Laura's flat, his body and the banister rails casting a shadow on the wall.

KEY LINES

The opening lines: 'I Waldo Lydecker was the only man who really knew her.'

Shelby: 'I can afford a blemish on my character but not on my collar.'

> **'I can afford a blemish on my character but not on my collar.'**

Waldo: 'You'd better watch out McPherson or you'll finish up in a psychiatric ward. I doubt that they've ever had a patient who fell in love with a corpse.'

Laura: 'You forced me to give my word. I never have been nor ever will be bound by anything I don't do of my own free will.'

Waldo: 'If McPherson weren't muscular and handsome in a cheap sort of way you'd see through him in a second.'

LAWRENCE OF ARABIA

UK, 1962, COLUMBIA/HORIZON/SAM SPIEGEL, 222 MINS

D DAVID LEAN; **PR** SAM SPIEGEL; **SC** ROBERT BOLT, ORIGINAL DRAFT BY MICHAEL WILSON; **PH** (COL, SUPER PANAVISION) FREDERICK A. YOUNG; **PR DES** JOHN BOX; **M** MAURICE JARRE **CAST** PETER O'TOOLE (LAWRENCE), ALEC GUINNESS (PRINCE FEISAL), ANTHONY QUINN (AUDA ABU TAYI), JACK HAWKINS (GENERAL ALLENBY), OMAR SHARIF (SHERIF ALI), JOSE FERRER (TURKISH BEY), ANTHONY QUAYLE (COLONEL BRIGHTON), CLAUDE RAINS (MR DRYDEN), ARTHUR KENNEDY (JACKSON BENTLEY), DONALD WOLFIT (GENERAL MURRAY), I. S. JOHAR (GASIM), GAMIL RATIB (MAJID), MICHEL RAY (FARRAJ), JOHN DIMECH (DAUD), ZIA MOHYEDDIN (TAFAS)

THE STORY Following Lawrence's death in a motorbike accident and his memorial service, his adventures in Arabia are recounted in flashback. He was working as a military mapmaker when, with his experience of the land and the people, he was assigned to journey to the encampment of Prince Feisal and 'appreciate the situation'. En route he displays to his guide, Tafas, his strength of will and understanding of Arab ethnicity. Tafas is shot by Sherif Ali for drinking at a well owned by a rival tribe. Finding Feisal's camp under attack from the Turks, and with the British military indifferent to the needs of the Arabs, he suggests a daring attack on Aqaba. He undertakes the dangerous crossing of the Nefud desert with Ali, increasingly a friend and ally, and 50 men. Shortly before completing the journey, he risks his own life saving one of the men, Gasim. He persuades Auda, the leader of a rival tribe, to join in the raid, and shortly before the attack, Lawrence is forced to execute

▲ *LAWRENCE OF ARABIA Auda (Anthony Quinn) looks on as desperate Lawrence (Peter O'Toole) sees his dream of a united Arabia vanish.*

Gasim and so avert a tribal blood feud. Having taken Aqaba, Lawrence crosses the Sinai, in the process losing one of his faithful servants, to inform Allenby of the military success. Lawrence and Ali lead a campaign of sabotage against the Turkish railroad. Increasingly daring, Lawrence is arrested, and presumably raped in a Turkish garrison. Once released, Lawrence has lost heart and wants to leave the army, but is persuaded by Allenby to stay on. Before a successful raid on Damascus, he exacts a bloodthirsty revenge on the Turks. When his attempt to establish a democratic Arab council in Damascus descends into chaos, a disillusioned Lawrence returns to England.

THE FILM One of the most beautiful films ever made, this biopic of a tortured cult figure became, like *Heart of Darkness* and *Nostromo* (a long-cherished but unrealized dream of Lean's), a cult project. Many directors tried to bring the story to the screen – Lewis Milestone, Zoltan Korda, William K. Howard and Powell and Pressburger among others – with numerous stars considered for the leading role, including Robert Donat, Leslie Howard, Laurence Olivier and Cary Grant. With a cast led by the newcomer O'Toole and nearly two years spent shooting in the desert, Lean emerged with a vast and compelling study of Lawrence, an enigma driven apparently as much by his masochism and unconsummated homosexual desires, as by his passion for the land and ambition to foster a united Arabian nation. The film is remarkable for its central character's ambiguous personality, confused motivations and sexuality, his love/hate of violence, as well as its extraordinary design and cinematography. One of Lawrence's biographers said of the film: 'Perhaps this is being frivolous, but in a sense it is a picture not so much about Lawrence as about a love affair between a director, a cameraman and a desert.'

ODD/SALIENT FACTS One of the second unit directors on the film was Nicolas Roeg, co-director of *Performance* (1970). The film was restored by Robert A. Harris in 1989, with lines having to be overdubbed nearly thirty years on in reconstructed sequences in which the original soundtrack had gone missing. This is evident particularly in the sequence in which Feisal has a lengthy meeting with the American journalist Bentley. With no extant copies of the shooting script available, the restorers had to use lip-readers and guesswork to deduce what the characters were saying.

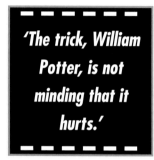

'The trick, William Potter, is not minding that it hurts.'

MEMORABLE MOMENTS Lawrence, about to leave the cartography office in Cairo, holds a match which he blows out in close-up. Cut to the desert at sunrise.

Tafas and Lawrence are at the well, Tafas drinking, Lawrence checking his compass, when he sees a speck on the horizon. The figure approaches along a demarcated path, shimmering as a mirage. As he nears the well, Ali, the rider on camel-back, shoots Tafas. The most famous entrance in cinema, Lean had intended it to be much more drawn out and regretted not sticking to his plan. According to Kevin Brownlow in his biography *David Lean*, the director turned to his designer John Box, after completing the second and final day of filming this sequence and said: 'You'll never do a better bit of design in films, ever!'

KEY LINES

Lawrence extinguishs a match with his fingertips without flinching. Potter, who has repeated this but got burnt asks: 'Well, what's the trick, then?'

Lawrence: 'The trick, William Potter, is not minding that it hurts.'

Lawrence, reporting to Allenby after the capture of Aqaba, talking of his responsibility for the deaths of Gasim and

Daud: 'There was something about it I didn't like.'
Allenby: 'Well, naturally …'
Lawrence: 'No, something else.'
Allenby: 'I see. Well, that's all right. Let it be a warning.'
Lawrence: 'No, something else.'
Allenby: 'What then?'
Lawrence: 'I enjoyed it.'

M

GERMANY, 1931, NERO-FILM, 101 MINS

D FRITZ LANG; **PR** SEMOUR NEBENZAL; **SC** LANG AND THEA VON HARBOU; **PH** FRITZ ARNO WAGNER (BW); **M** ADOLF JANSEN

CAST PETER LORRE (FRANZ BECKERT), OTTO WERNECKE (KARL LOHMAN), GUSTAV GRÜNDGENS (SCHRAENKER), THEODOR LOOS (COMMISSIONER GROEBER), ERNST STAHL-NACHBAUER (CHIEF OF POLICE), THEO LINGEN (BAURENFAENGER), ELLEN WIDMAN (MRS BECKMAN), INGE LANDGUT (ELSIE BRECKMAN), GEORG JOHN (PEDDLER)

THE STORY A psychopathic child-killer murders his ninth victim, Elsie Beckman, and writes another unsigned letter to the press about his inability to control his impulses. Terror and mutual suspicion create panic among the citizens of Düsseldorf and Inspector Lohmann, head of homicide, cracks down on the city's criminals. The threatened underworld bosses organize beggars to patrol every section of the city. Checking released mental patients the police deduce that Franz Beckert is their man, while simultaneously a blind balloon seller recognizes Beckert as the man who bought a balloon for Elsie, the clue being the same whistled tune. He alerts people and someone chalks an M (for Mörder) on the back of his coat. Beckert flees to an office block pursued by criminals who capture him and take him off to an abandoned distillery. The police arrest the single burglar left behind and trick him into revealing Beckert's whereabouts. At a kangaroo court the assembled criminals demand that the prisoner be 'put down like a mad dog', but the terrified Beckert claims they have chosen a life of crime, but he is driven by irresistible impulses. The police arrive to arrest Beckert, and the film ends with a panel of official judges assembling in court and a grieving mother saying: 'we should keep a closer watch on our children'.

▲ *M* A horrified Peter Lorre realizes he has been branded as a murderer.

THE FILM *M* is the first sound film by Fritz Lang (1890–1976), one of the half-dozen greatest artists the cinema has produced. A pioneer of the epic, the paranoid conspiracy thriller, the SF movie, the *film noir*, and a major exponent of the Western, he produced two equally important bodies of work addressing the same theme of men struggling with fate and destiny – in the German silent cinema of the 1920s and in the American sound film of the 1930s, '40s and '50s. *M* is possibly his masterpiece, an exciting and provocative thriller, the first about a serial killer long before the term existed. It treats Beckert with sympathy without losing sight of the suffering he inflicts. It is also a seminal police-procedural thriller, with montages of cops conducting routine enquiries, blow-ups of fingerprints, the psychological interpretation of Beckert's letter by a graphologist. Lang used sound imaginatively: the children's grisly counting-out game in the opening scene anticipates the murders; Elsie's mother saying the time to worry is when you don't hear your children; a blind man hearing a whistled tune identi-

fying the killer. The film captures the Weimar Republic just before the Nazi takeover. The responses to Beckert by the angry public, a disoriented officialdom and the criminal community, constitute a paradigm of the society that sent Hitler to power. Weirdly the underworld's kangaroo court and its readiness to wipe out social undesirables anticipates the Nazi legal system and the extermination camps. The great sequence in which Lang cross-cuts between the two smoke-filled rooms where the complementary sides of society discuss their problems – a long rectangular table for the forces of law and order, a small round table for the heads of the underworld – creates a devastating image. What ultimately makes the film so compelling and gives it a deeply tragic dimension is Peter Lorre's performance. Like Shylock in *The Merchant of Venice*, he dominates the drama despite his frequent absences from the stage. Each appearance is charged by guilt, anxiety and a nervous charm, until he turns on his persecutors with his final anguished speech.

ODD/SALIENT FACTS Peter Lorre (1904–64) became a world star in *M* and worked steadily until the day he died, despite problems with drugs and alcohol. He appeared in two Hitchcock pictures, became a cult double-act with Sydney Greenstreet in the 1940s, and ended up in Roger Corman productions, and as a foil to Jerry Lewis (*The Patsy*, 1964). When Lang fled Germany after Goebbels offered him the post as head of the Nazi Film Industry, his wife, screenwriter Thea von Harbou, remained behind to serve the Nazis. Gustav Gründgens (1899–1963), the greatest German actor of his generation and Thomas Mann's son-in-law, remained in Germany and inspired Claus Mann's novel *Mephisto*, filmed in 1981 by Istvan Szabo. Lang became an iconic figure, and played himself with immense dignity as a director from the golden age in Jean-Luc Godard's *Le Mépris* (1963).

MEMORABLE MOMENTS Elsie bouncing her ball against the 'Who is the Murderer?' poster and Beckert's shadow falling upon it.

Beckert's reflection in a mirror as he discovers the letter M on the back of his overcoat.

Beckert shrinking into the corner of the attic like a trapped rat.

KEY LINES

Leading criminal: 'A non-member is ruining our respective businesses. If the situation is not restored to order we'll be ruined.'

133

Ditto: 'We're just doing a job but this man is beyond the pale and has no right to live.'

Beckert: 'You have chosen to be criminals, but I can't help myself. I can't control the evil within me.'

MAD MAX – THE ROAD WARRIOR★

US, 1981, KENNEDY MILLER, 96 MINS

D GEORGE MILLER; **PR** BYRON KENNEDY; **SC** GEORGE MILLER, TERRY HAYES, BRIAN HANNANT; **PH** (COL) DEAN SEMLER; **M** BRIAN MAY; **ED** DAVID STIVEN, TIM WELLBURN, MICHAEL BALSON

CAST MEL GIBSON (MAX), BRUCE SPENCE (THE GYRO CAPTAIN), PAPPAGALLO (MIKE PRESTON), MAX PHIPPS (THE TOADIE), VERNON WELLS (WEZ), KJELL NILSSON (THE HUMUNGUS), EMIL MINTY (THE FERAL KID), VIRGINIA HEY (WARRIOR WOMAN), WILLIAM ZAPPA (ZETTA), ARKIE WHITELEY (THE CAPTAIN'S GIRL), STEVE J. SPEARS (MECHANIC), HAROLD BAIGENT (VOICE OF NARRATOR)

THE STORY Having lost his wife and child in the first film, the sequel sees Max still battling road nasties and searching for fuel in the post-apocalyptic near-future. After a battle over a container truck, he escapes with a little more fuel and a music box that plays 'Happy Birthday to You'. Max encounters a comical helicopter man who shows him a compound which contains a supply of precious fuel. From their mountain view they see a rival group of thugs, including those with whom Max had the opening fight, terrorizing those leaving the compound. Max rescues one man and takes him back to the fuel depot, but the man dies before he can fulfil his promise of giving Max some petrol. Instead Max helps the people, among them a wild child, who are led by Pappagallo, withstand an attack from The Humungus and his troops. Max then offers to bring them a rig with which they can transport their stock of fuel to the coast. This he does and then takes some fuel and attempts to escape. He is pursued and driven off the road, his dog is killed and when his car blows up he is left for dead. The helicopter man rescues him

> '**You're a scav-enger, Max, you're a maggot. D'you know that? Living off the corpse of the old world.**'

and brings him back to the compound where at last he resolves to drive the rig himself. After a protracted chase in which many people are killed on both sides, the rig is crashed and is seen to be filled with sand. The surviving members of Pappagallo's community, among them the kid who will grow up to be the film's narrator, head off, leaving Max to travel the road.

THE FILM Less than twenty years after its release it is hard to see exactly why *The Road Warrior* caused such a stir. A loose reworking of *Shane*, it was influential but unlike, say, *Blade Runner* it is no better than many of the films it influenced. Apart from Gibson himself, the cast is pretty ordinary, but the editing is slick and the direction keeps the action ticking along at a good pace. The film ends on a high point with the protracted and chaotic climactic chase. Its big features are its star and its design. It was, like the first Mad Max film, enormously popular in Japan and in its presentation of a desolate, post-apocalyptic cartoon future world it helped shape the character of video games. It established Gibson as an international star and along with *Mad Max* set the template for what would become his stock role – the committed family man confronting the death of, or threat to, his family.

ODD/SALIENT FACTS In Brian Pendreigh's *Mel Gibson and His Movies*, the star recalls the atmosphere and the pricking of his tough guy persona on the film's New South Wales location: 'There were some pretty tough lads there but we got along very well. I used to have a pair of pinkish bedroom slippers and I wore them everywhere. They thought it was a great joke, Mad Max wearing pink bedroom slippers. One night I went into the local pub and one of the boys showed me that on the roof of the pub he had written "Mad Max drives a Mini and wears pink bedroom slippers". Well, I got on his shoulders and crossed out the word "pink" and wrote "red". That could have been a situation that got out of hand but it turned out to be good fun.'

MEMORABLE MOMENTS Apart from the lengthy chase at the end with its brilliant stunt work, the film's signature image is the iconic stance of the road warrior with which the film opens and closes.

KEY LINES

From the opening narration: 'I remember a time of chaos, ruined dreams and wasted land. But most of all I remember the road warrior, the man we called Max.'

Classic loner, light-travelling anti-hero Max, on his dog, his car and some fuel: 'I got all I need here.'

Pappagallo on Max: 'You're a scavenger, Max, you're a maggot. D'you know that? Living off the corpse of the old world.'

'Lasso's a ghost town Dock, and that's what you are Dock, a ghost.'

MAN OF THE WEST

US, 1958, UNITED ARTISTS/ASHTON PRODUCTIONS, 100 MINS

D ANTHONY MANN; **PR** WALTER M. MIRISCH; **SC** REGINALD ROSE (FROM THE NOVEL BY WILL C. BROWN); **PH** (COL CINEMASCOPE), ERNEST HALLER; **M** LEIGH HARLINE; **ED** RICHARD HEERMANCE

CAST GARY COOPER (LINK JONES), LEE J. COBB (DOCK TOBIN), JULIE LONDON (BILLIE ELLIS), ARTHUR O'CONNELL (SAM BEASLEY), JACK LORD (COALEY), JOHN DEHNER (CLAUDE TOBIN), ROYAL DANO (TROUT), ROBERT WILKE (PONCH), JACK WILLIAMS (ALCUTT), CHUCK ROBERSON (RIFLEMAN ON TRAIN)

THE STORY On a journey across Texas to hire a schoolteacher for Fort Worth, reformed outlaw Link Jones is stranded in the wilds with cardsharp Sam Beasley and saloon singer Billie Ellis when their train speeds off after a botched hold-up. Link leads Beasley and Billie to an abandoned farmhouse once used by Dock Tobin, who treated his mob as a family and Link as a son. There he finds the aged demented Dock surrounded by psychopaths and it transpires they are the train robbers and have Link's carpet-bag containing the money for the teacher. Link pretends to be returning to the gang, and Dock believes him, though Dock's son, Claude, is suspicious. The party set out to rob the bank at Lasso and Link creates dissension in the gang, leading to the death of Beasley, who takes a bullet intended for Link; Dock kills the man who fired the shot. Link and the vicious Trout discover Lasso is a ghost town, Trout shoots the only inhab-

itant and Link kills him. There is a shootout in which the two remaining gang members die. Returning to the camp, Link discovers that Dock has raped Billie. Link threatens to take him in, and Dock provokes a gun fight. Link discovers his township's money on Dock's corpse and rides off with Billie.

THE FILM Anthony Mann made cult classics in three genres – the *film noir T-Men* in the 1940s, a string of Westerns in the 1940s, the epic *El Cid* in the 1960s. His most celebrated Westerns are the six with James Stewart, but the one closest to the hearts of his admirers is *Man of the West*, the story of a reformed man drawn back into his past and forced to employ the violence and low cunning he has renounced to defeat his captors and confirm his redemption. It is an unromantic film – the love between Billie the saloon girl and Link, a married man with two young children, is one-sided – but there is considerable erotic tension when he attempts to prevent Billie's striptease, and pretends to be her lover to halt Dock's advances. Mann is unsurpassed in his use of the widescreen and in the way he uses the landscape. Link's journey takes him first from civilization to the wilderness, then from the verdant countryside to the parched desert around the ghost town. Although Beasley the gambler is a comic figure, his demise is sudden and tragic, and the picture is relentlessly tense, with death a constant threat. The first person to be killed (the shots heard off-stage) is a gang member wounded during the robbery and thereafter everyone dies except Link and Billie.

ODD/SALIENT FACTS This was the penultimate Western for both Mann and Cooper. The professional relationship between Mann and James Stewart came to an end when Mann refused to direct Stewart in *Night Passage* (1957) or give him the role that he coveted in *Man of the West*, and Mann died in 1967 before the friendship could be renewed. *Man of the West* is the only Western to be scripted by Reginald Rose, who wrote *Twelve Angry Men* (1957) and created the TV series *The Defenders*. Reviewing the film in *Cahiers du Cinéma* (February 1959) Jean-Luc Godard wrote: 'I have seen nothing so completely new since – why not? – Griffith. Just as the director of *Birth of a Nation* gave one the impression that he was inventing the cinema with every shot, each shot of *Man of the West* gives one the impression that Anthony

Mann is reinventing the Western, exactly as Matisse's portraits reinvent the features of Piero della Francesca'.

MEMORABLE MOMENTS Coaley with his knife to Link's throat as Billie is forced to strip.

Coaley humiliated when Link strips him down to his long johns.

Dock Tobin on a peak above the gang's camp, ranting like an Old Testament patriarch before Link kills him.

KEY LINES

Beasley: 'You've changed since you walked into that shack. You're a different man all of a sudden. You act like you belong with these people.'

Link: 'I never had a family, just that man down there. He

▲ *MAN OF THE WEST* Arthur O'Connell (Sam), Royal Dano (Trout) and Julie London (Billie) keep their distance as Gary Cooper (Link) humiliates outlaw Jack Lord (Coaley).

took care of me, he taught me killing and stealing. I didn't know any better. Then one day I grew up. You either grow up and become something or you rot like that bunch. So I busted away. I found something better. I made myself a home.'

Link: 'Lasso's a ghost town Dock, and that's what you are Dock, a ghost. You've outlived your kind and outlived your time and I'm coming to get you.'

THE MAN WITH THE MOVIE CAMERA

USSR, 1929, 66 MINS

D Dziga Vertov; **PH** Mikhail Kaufman; **ED** Elizaveta Svilova

THE STORY A dawn-till-dusk documentary on life in Moscow in the mode that became known as the 'city symphony,' after Walter Ruttmann's *Berlin: Symphony of a Big City* (1927). The city awakens, trams come out, people go to work, an ambulance speeds to the scene of an accident, a fire engine is called out. A couple gets married, another is divorced, a child is born, a funeral takes place. After work people exercise, engage in sport and games, drink in bars, play chess in clubs. But the film also includes material from the beach at Odessa and of coal miners underground. We see the cameraman shooting the film we are watching and the editor assembling it, and the film begins and ends in a cinema, where we and an audience are watching it. *Man With a Movie Camera*, which is accompanied by music that follows instructions written by Vertov, uses virtually every device available to the cinema before sound (except for inter-titles, which it assiduously avoids), including slow and accelerated motion, split screen, freeze-frame and superimposition.

THE FILM A virtuoso film that remains as fresh and as puzzling as the day it was made, *Man with a Movie Camera* purports to be a social documentary but is in fact a fascinating examination of the nature of film and its relation to reality, as well as a political and aesthetic manifesto. Dziga Vertov (Ukrainian for spinning top) was the *nom de guerre* of Denis Kaufman (1896–1954), poet and polemicist, who became a leading film-maker during the Russian Revolution and Civil War, specializing in propagandistic documentaries. To him the 'camera-eye' was a new way of seeing the world, but he despised fiction films and persuaded Lenin to decree that a fixed proportion of state-supported movies should be documentaries.

137

▼ *THE MAN WITH THE MOVIE CAMERA Superimposition linking the mind of man to the operation of the machine.*

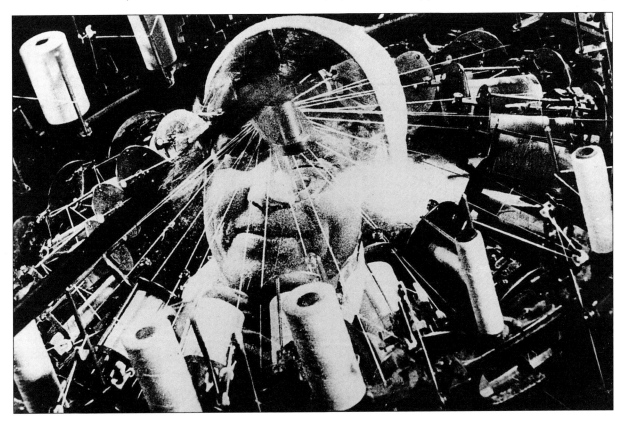

The opening titles state that this 'excerpt from the diary of a cameraman' is 'a manifesto expressed in celluloid', that it has no inter-titles or scenario, that it sets out to create an international language that owes nothing to theatre or literature. Each of the film's eight reels pursues a different theme, every single image is dense with meaning about cinema, society and the revolution, many of them (e.g. visualizations of precepts by Trotsky) in need of explication.

ODD/SALIENT FACTS Like most Soviet avant-garde films, *The Man with the Movie Camera* was not a success with popular audiences in Russia, but for 70 years it has been one of the most discussed and analysed pictures ever made, a hypnotic work to be watched again and again. The film's editor, Elizaveta Svilova, was Vertov's wife and its cinematographer, Mikhail Kaufman, was his brother. Another brother, Boris Kaufman (1906–80), emigrated to France in 1927, where he photographed Jean Vigo's *À Propos de Nice*, *Zéro de conduite* and *L'Atalante*, and then moved on to Canada and the United States, where he lit several films for Elia Kazan (winning a 1954 Oscar for *On the Waterfront*) and Sidney Lumet (including *Twelve Angry Men*).

MEMORABLE MOMENTS A couple getting a divorce followed by a split screen of trams going in different directions.

The film stopping to show strips of film that have yet to be seen being viewed by the film editor.

The cameraman in an iron foundry drawn back from the flames by a worker.

The hand-held coverage of a football match in which the cameraman appears to be taking part.

Cross-cutting between workers and machines that makes them interdependent.

THE MAN WITH TWO BRAINS
US, 1983, WARNER/ASPEN, 93 MINS

D CARL REINER; **PR** WILLIAM E. MCEUEN, DAVID V. PICKER; **SC** CARL REINER, STEVE MARTIN, GEORGE GIPE; **PH** MICHAEL CHAPMAN; **M** JOEL GOLDSMITH; **ED** BUD MOLIN

CAST STEVE MARTIN (DR MICHAEL HFUHRUHURR), KATHLEEN TURNER (DOLORES BENEDICT), DAVID WARNER (DR NECESSITER), PAUL BENEDICT (BUTLER), RICHARD BRESTOFF (DR PASTEUR), JAMES CROMWELL (REALTOR), GEORGE FURTH (TIMON), PETER HOBBS (DR BRANDON), EARL BOEN (DR CONRAD)

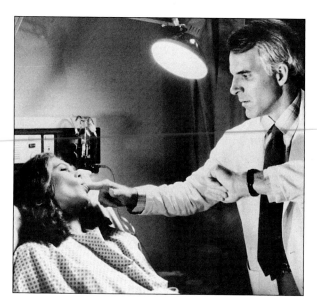

▲ *THE MAN WITH TWO BRAINS* Dr Hfuhruhurr (Steve Martin) acts as a human thermometer while he checks on Dolores (Kathleen Turner) recovering from his cranial screw-top brain surgery.

THE STORY Dr Michael Hfuhruhurr, a brilliant brain surgeon, falls in love at first sight with Dolores, a deceitful woman whom he has just knocked down and whose life he saves using his revolutionary cranial screw-top method of entry into the brain. He marries her in hospital, but she refuses to consummate the marriage. Michael accepts an invitation to lecture in Vienna, hoping that a honeymoon will inspire some marital romance. But there his work is interrupted by the activities of 'the elevator killer' who is murdering women by injecting them with window cleaner. He discovers that Dr Necessiter is keeping the brains of the killer's victims alive in jars, and falls telepathically in love with the brain of Anne Uumellmahaye. Dolores finds out that Michael has inherited $15 million and decides to stick around. Michael moves with Anne's brain and Dolores to the country, where he finally splits with Dolores. Finding that Anne's brain is starting to die, Michael returns to the city where he searches for a fresh corpse into which Dr Necessiter can transplant Anne's brain. At last he stumbles upon the body of Dolores, the most recent victim of the elevator killer, who turns out to be Merv Griffin. The operation is performed in the nick of time and Michael and Anne in Dolores's body arrive at the 'House of Hfuhruhurr'.

THE FILM *The Man With Two Brains* marks the third of the four collaborations between Steve Martin and writer/director and sometime actor Carl Reiner. The films they made together – *The Jerk* (1979), *Dead Men Don't Wear Plaid* (1982), and *All of Me* (1984) – were of consistently brilliant comic inventiveness and perfect vehicles for Martin at the height of his talent. But the middle two performed poorly at the box office to the extent that in the UK *The Man With Two Brains* was not granted a theatrical release, but instead quietly put out directly on video. Particularly compared to *Dead Men Don't Wear Plaid*, a superb, affectionate spoof on *film noir* which weaves scenes from classic movies of the 1930s and '40s into its story of Steve Martin's quest for the inventor of a dangerously potent cheese, this is not a slick piece of film-making. But although relentless and artless it is crammed with visual and verbal gags and is simply one of the funniest films of the decade. It slowly gathered a reputation as a lost gem and eventually received a limited arthouse release in the UK in 1986. By the mid-1980s Martin seems to have consciously abandoned the pure, inspired approach to comedy that had made him an enormously wealthy star of rock stadia, TV and LP recordings before he reached the big screen. He began to appear in more conventional, generally tedious, mainstream fare which allowed him, if nothing else, to add to his impressive private collection of twentieth-century art.

ODD/SALIENT FACTS The central idea of the story in which a self-centred man wants to have the perfect brain in the perfect body within a comic framework must have been unconsciously borrowed from *Stardust Memories* (1980). The voice of Anne Uumellmahaye is supplied, uncredited, by Sissy Spacek. The pop group The Pointy Birds take their name from the poem by John Lillith, Britain's greatest one-armed poet, and the first person to be hit by a car. It goes:

A pointy birds
A-pointy-pointy
Anoint my head
Anointy-nointy

MEMORABLE MOMENTS Dr Hfuhruhurr is stopped by the Austrian police and made to do some drunk tests. He has to walk along the white line in the middle of the road, then back on his hands, then on one hand, then roll over, turn over and flip, then juggle three balls, do a tap dance while singing the Catalina Magdalena, Lupensteiner, Wollendeiner

song. As he says: 'Damn, your drunk tests are hard.' He gets back into the car and Dolores's body slumps across him. The policeman shouts: 'She's not drunk, she's dead.' To which Dr Hfuhruhurr replies: 'Dead?! My God! I better get her to a cemetery right away.'

KEY LINES

Dr Hfuhruhurr, to the journalist interviewing him: 'Will you read that back to me. I'm afraid that might make me sound pompous to your readers.'
Journalist: 'My brilliant research into brain transplantation is unsurpassed and will probably make my name live beyond eternity.'
Dr Hfuhruhurr: 'No, that's fine. Take out the "probably". It makes me sound wishy-washy.'

As the newly wed Dr Hfuhruhurr and Dolores drive up to his home, Ramon and his wife are waiting on the porch, surrounded by potted plants.
Dolores: 'What are those assholes doing on the porch?'
Dr Hfuhruhurr: 'Those aren't assholes. It's pronounced azaleas.'

THE MANCHURIAN CANDIDATE
US, 1962, UNITED ARTISTS/MC PRODUCTIONS, 126 MINS

D JOHN FRANKENHEIMER; **PR** GEORGE AXELROD, JOHN FRANKENHEIMER; **ART DIR** RICHARD SYLBERT; **SC** GEORGE AXELROD, BASED ON THE NOVEL BY RICHARD CONDON; **PH** LIONEL LINDON; **M** DAVID AMRAM; **ED** FERRIS WEBSTER **CAST** FRANK SINATRA (BENNETT MARCO), LAURENCE HARVEY (RAYMOND SHAW), JANET LEIGH (ROSIE), ANGELA LANSBURY (RAYMOND'S MOTHER), HENRY SILVA (CHUNJIN), JAMES GREGORY (SENATOR JOHN ISELIN), LESLIE PARRISH (JOCIE JORDAN), JOHN MCGIVER (SENATOR THOMAS JORDAN), KHIGH DIEGH (YEN LO), JAMES EDWARDS (CORPORAL MELVIN), DOUGLAS HENDERSON (COLONEL), ALBERT PAULSEN (ZILKOV), BARRY KELLEY (SECRETARY OF DEFENCE), LLOYD CORRIGAN (HOLBORN GAINES), MADAME SPIVY (BEREZOVO)

THE STORY Raymond Shaw, a deeply unpopular officer in Korea, is led along with his platoon into a trap. Returning to America he is granted the Congressional Medal of Honor, and takes a job as the assistant to a decent Republican journalist, Holborn Gaines, against the wishes of his scheming mother and crude, commie-bating stepfather, Senator Iselin. Meanwhile his former fellow soldiers Bennett Marco and Al Melvin are suffering almost identical recurring nightmares in which the members of the troop are hypnotized and Shaw turned into an emotionless killer. In New York the brainwashed Shaw is activated with the use of a queen of diamonds playing card by the communist conspirators. His effectiveness as an assassin is tested by having him kill Gaines. Marco at last persuades the authorities that his dreams are flashbacks to the troop's capture in Korea, and is employed to investigate Shaw's activities. Shaw marries his old sweetheart, the daughter of a liberal senator and arch enemy of Iselin. After a brief honeymoon, Shaw is induced by the conspiracy's American chief, his mother, to kill his wife and father-in-law. Marco tracks Shaw down to an eyrie in Madison

▼ THE MANCHURIAN CANDIDATE *A brainwashed Raymond Shaw (Laurence Harvey) about to blow the brains of his comrade over a portrait of Stalin.*

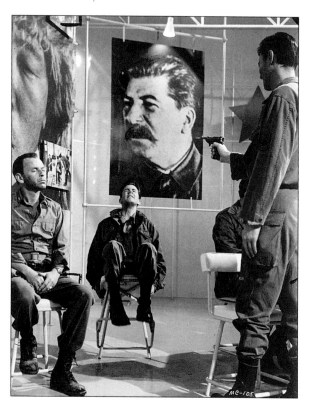

Square Garden, where Shaw is due to kill the presidential nominee, thus dramatically advancing his stepfather's political career. At the last moment Shaw breaks the spell, shooting his mother and stepfather, then himself.

THE FILM The outstanding film of Frankenheimer's career, this faithful screen version of Richard Condon's conspiracy thriller is a remarkable prediction of the mood that would overtake the US and elsewhere in the wake of the century's most famous assassination. It is a strange thriller, one that manages to maintain its delicately balanced mood of dark political foreboding and black humour. The script is sharp, the direction taut, the production design excellent. Part of its skill is the unshowy way it presents complex visual scenes, such as the superb nightmare flashbacks and the sequence in which Iselin provokes his rival in a live TV debate. The film not only marks career highpoints for the director and Laurence Harvey, but was also the last noteworthy movie of Sinatra's career. It was made as Hollywood was recovering from the self-inflicted wounds of McCarthyism and was, unwittingly, gearing itself up for the sudden, violent end of the Kennedy presidency. In Gerald Pratley's *The Films of John Frankenheimer*, the director says: 'I wanted to do a picture that showed both how ludicrous McCarthy-style far right politics are and how dangerous the far left is also, how they were really exactly the same thing, and the idiocy of it all. I wanted to show that and I think we did.'

ODD/SALIENT FACTS President Kennedy himself played a role in the film's genesis. Arthur Krim, president of United Artists and national finance director of the Democratic Party, considered the novel too politically inflammatory. Sinatra, by this stage being forced into the background of the presidential set, took the matter directly to JFK, who liked the idea and agreed to persuade Krim to give the project the go-ahead. As Richard Condon recalled: 'That's the only way the film ever got made. It took Frank going directly to Jack Kennedy.' Later Sinatra arranged a private screening of the film for Kennedy, and after the president's assassination, denied permission for a re-release of the movie. The film contains one of the traditional Hollywood parent–child relationships in which the 37-year-old Angela Lansbury, who had appeared in Frankenheimer's *All Fall Down* (1962), played the mother of the 34-year-old Laurence Harvey.

MEMORABLE MOMENTS The nightmares of Marco and Melvin. The camera pans smoothly around the set in 360-degree shots which interchange the various versions of the audience – the black women, the white women and the communist soldiers who were really there. Having already strangled one of his men, Shaw is ordered to shoot the young soldier Bobby Limbeck. After close-ups of the barrel of the gun and Bobby smiling we see the scene from the gallery. The gun is fired, Limbeck flies back in his chair as his brains splatter over a large portrait of Stalin that forms part of the stage's back-drop.

The assassination of Senator Jordan. Shot through the carton of milk he is removing from the fridge, the liberal politician is shown to bleed milk.

KEY LINES

Yen Lo to the assembled audience: 'I'm sure you've all heard the old wives' tale that no hypnotized subject may be forced to do that which is repellent to his moral nature, whatever that may be. Nonsense of course.'

MANHUNTER

US, 1986, RECORDED RELEASING/RED DRAGON/DE LAURENTIIS ENTERTAINMENT, 120 MINS

D MICHAEL MANN; **PR** RICHARD ROTH; **SC** MICHAEL MANN, BASED ON THE NOVEL RED DRAGON BY THOMAS HARRIS; **PH** DANTE SPINOTTI; **M** THE REDS AND MICHAEL RUBINI; **ED** DOV HOENIG

CAST WILLIAM PETERSEN (WILL GRAHAM), KIM GREIST (MOLLY GRAHAM), DENNIS FARINA (JACK CRAWFORD), JOAN ALLEN (REBA), BRIAN COX (DR HANNIBAL LECTER), STEPHEN LANG (FREDDIE LOUNDS), TOM NOONAN (FRANCIS DOLLARHYDE), DAVID SEAMAN (KEVIN GRAHAM), BENJAMIN HENDRICKSON (DR CHILTON), MICHAEL TALBOT (GEEHAN), DAN E. BUTLER (JIMMY PRICE), MICHELE SHAY (BEVERLY KATZ), ROBIN MOSELEY (SARAH), PAUL PERRI (DR SIDNEY BLOOM), PATRICIA CHARBONNEAU (MRS SHERMAN)

THE STORY Will Graham is tempted out of early retirement to help catch the 'Tooth Fairy', a serial killer operating on nights of a full moon, in the southern states of America. He visits his incarcerated nemesis Dr Lecter to get some advice and refamiliarize himself with the psychotic mindset. Will also watches

> *Have you seen blood in the moonlight, Will? It appears quite black*

home movies of the two dead families, and visits the murder scenes. It is discovered that Lecter is communicating with the 'Tooth Fairy' using an indecipherable code. Graham employs Lounds, a sleazy tabloid journalist, to set himself up as human bait for the killer. But the killer, styling himself after Blake's Red Dragon, kidnaps and kills Lounds. When it emerges that Lecter has informed the killer of Graham's address, his family is moved into a safe house. Red Dragon, Francis Dollarhyde, begins an affair with Reba, a blind woman, in the film labs where they both work. It is the night of the full moon. Dollarhyde misconstrues Reba's innocently kissing a co-worker, kills the man and takes Reba back to his house. Meanwhile Graham finally realizes that the 'Tooth Fairy' must have seen the same films that he has. Flying to St Louis, they identify Dollarhyde as the killer just before landing. Dollarhyde kills two policemen before being killed himself by Graham. Graham returns to his family's peaceful beachfront home.

THE FILM The project was caught up in the producer's legal wranglings. This delay in release led it to be perceived as a problem film and it became an instant cult movie, apparently incapable of mainstream appreciation because of its uncompromising approach to its unpalatable subject matter. Yet four years later *The Silence of the Lambs* (1990), a sequel of sorts, was a smash hit. Will Graham is an older version of Clarice Starling, a dedicated professional who has risked his life and soul to track down murderous psychopaths. In both films, Lecter, played by a Celtic actor, is around to steal the show with his darkly comic cameos. Both films feature modern takes on the battle of good versus evil and the dangers of good people entering the minds of their prey. Each film has a sequence in which the net of law enforcement is apparently being tightened around the killer, only for a sudden twist to reveal that they are on the wrong track, and instead an unsuspecting party encounters the killer. Each ends with the killer attacking a woman who is actually or effectively blind. Michael Mann earlier created the mainstream TV success *Miami Vice* and went on to *The Last of the Mohicans* (1992) and *Heat* (1995). He employs his trademark slick visuals and a very eighties synth-rock soundtrack. Timing, technique and mood ensure that this remains a dark cult favourite.

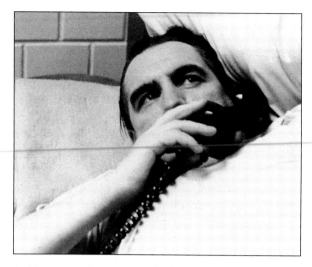

▲ MANHUNTER *Brian Cox as the fiendishly clever Dr Hannibal Lecter, establishing contact from his top security cell with his newest disciple, the Red Dragon.*

ODD/SALIENT FACTS Dennis Farina, then a serving police officer, began as an advisor to Mann on police matters, before moving into acting himself on TV and in films, notably as the irascible crime boss in *Midnight Run* (1988). The notorious sequence in *Henry: Portrait of a Serial Killer* (1986), in which the killer watches his own work on a video set at a skewed angle, is based on the killer's-eye-view opening sequence of *Manhunter*.

MEMORABLE MOMENTS Graham's intuition of the killer's modus operandi leading him to instruct the forensic scientists to check for fingerprints on the victims' fingernails, toenails and their corneas.

Lecter's casual ingenuity in short-circuiting the phone and then getting hold of Graham's address.

Graham's being woken on his plane journey by the screams of the young girl sitting next to him who has caught sight of the grisly photos that have spilled out of his case file.

With time running out Graham's climactic realization that the 'Tooth Fairy' has seen the same films that he has.

KEY LINES

Lecter: 'By implication you think you're smarter than me since you caught me.'
Graham: 'No, I know that I'm not smarter than you.'

Lecter: 'Then how did you catch me?'
Graham: 'I had advantages.'
Lecter: 'What advantages?'
Graham: 'You're insane.'

Lecter: 'Have you seen blood in the moonlight, Will? It appears quite black.'

Lecter: 'Do you know how you caught me? The reason you caught me, Will, is we're just alike. You want the scent, smell yourself.'

THE MASQUE OF THE RED DEATH

UK, 1964, AMERICAN INTERNATIONAL PICTURES/ALTA VISTA, 86 MINS

D/PR ROGER CORMAN; **SC** CHARLES BEAUMONT, R. WRIGHT CAMPBELL (FROM THE STORIES 'THE MASQUE OF THE RED DEATH' AND 'HOP-FROG' BY EDGAR ALLAN POE); **PH** (COL SCOPE) NICOLAS ROEG; **ED** ANN CHEGWIDDEN; **M** DAVID LEE

CAST VINCENT PRICE (PRINCE PROSPERO), HAZEL COURT (JULIANA), JANE ASHER (FRANCESCA), PATRICK MAGEE (ALFREDO), SKIP MARTIN (HOP TOAD), DAVID WESTON (GINO), NIGEL GREEN (LUDOVICO), JOHN WESTBROOK (MAN IN RED), PAUL WHITSUN-JONES (SCARLATTI), JOHN LODGE (SCARLATTI'S WIFE), VERINA GREENLAW (ESMERALDA)

THE STORY In medieval Italy, Prince Prospero, worshipper of Satan, withdraws into his castle with his mistress Juliana, chosen friends and corrupt courtiers, as the Red Death plague sweeps his province. He takes along a peasant girl, Francesca, a virginal Christian, whose father Ludovico and fiancé Gino he has sentenced to death for their insolence. Juliana, handmaid of Satan, is jealous of Francesca and arranges for her to escape with her father and Gino, but all three are recaptured. Prospero's cruel lieutenant Alfredo has humiliated Esmeralda, a dwarf dancer, whose lover Hop Toad swears revenge. At a feast Prospero produces five knives, one of them bearing a deadly poison, and forces Ludovico and Gino to cut themselves. Ludovico attempts to stab Prospero and is killed; Gino is expelled to catch the plague but Death's emissary, the masked Man in Red, tells him to return and rescue Francesca. Juliana is punished by being ripped to death by Prospero's falcon. At the great ball the Man in Red appears, and Prospero mistakes him for Satan. In a *danse macabre,* the blood-spattered guests die of the plague, and Prospero sees that the Man in Red's face is his own. The Man in Red ensures that Francesca's and Gino's lives are spared.

THE FILM Made in England on a slightly larger budget and longer shooting schedule (25 days instead of 15) than his earlier films, *Red Death* is the seventh and best of Roger Corman's Poe movies, and sticks more closely to the two tales it draws on. It features the finest performance in a Corman movie of Vincent Price, whose Prince Prospero is a witty dandy, a thoughtful connoisseur of evil, who has found God's creation wanting and opted to serve Satan.

Less shocking than its predecessors, much influenced by Ingmar Bergman's *Seventh Seal,* using an eloquent script, *Red Death* is more poetic than horrific. Sets and costumes are more opulent than before (Corman's Hollywood designer worked on

▼ *THE MASQUE OF THE RED DEATH* Evil Prince Prospero communes with fellow predator in his somber courtyard.

the picture uncredited): the castle's chequered floor ballroom and the suite of identical rooms Juliana walks through after meeting Satan are beautifully conceived. The dramatic lighting drew attention to the then little-known cinematographer Nicolas Roeg. Corman used some distinguished local actors, most especially the Irishman Patrick Magee as the sadistic Alfredo. He was shortly to appear as the Marquis de Sade in Peter Brook's production of *The Marat Sade* for the Royal Shakespeare Company.

The film is not without its imperfections. The hallucinatory sequence of Juliana's marriage to the Devil is arty and pretentious. The choreography is stiffly formal, tepid when it should be orgiastic, and the final dance of death fails to chill in the way intended.

ODD/SALIENT FACTS The former child actress Jane Asher, then seventeen, had her first starring role in *Red Death*; she was the girlfriend of Paul McCartney, whose first film, *A Hard Day's Night,* opened the same month. Corman, always noted for ingenious ways of squeezing his budgets, used the set of a monastery left over from the British comedy *Crooks in Cloisters*; Robert Jones is credited as designer on both pictures. John Trevelyan, the Secretary of the British Board of Film Censors, was so worried about recrudescence of devil worship in Britain that he insisted on Juliana's Satanic dream being cut from the British release print. Corman couldn't find a suitable dwarf to play Esmeralda, so he used a young girl and dubbed her with an adult voice.

MEMORABLE MOMENTS The Man in Red's presenting a white rose speckled with blood to a peasant woman at the beginning of the film, telling her: 'Take this to your village and tell the people that the day of their deliverance is at hand.'

Prospero's first appearance to sneer at the villagers.

Juliana's branding her breast with an inverted cross to become Satan's handmaiden.

Prospero's sticking five daggers into the banqueting table as he speaks to his guests.

The Man in Red's presenting a Tarot card to Gino in the forest.

Prospero's seeing his own face beneath the cowl of the Man in Red.

KEY LINES

Alfredo: 'Can such eyes ever have known sin?'

Prospero: 'They will, Alfredo, they will.'

Prospero: 'Not *corrupting*, Alfredo, *instructing*.'

Prospero: 'If a God of love and light did exist, he is long since dead. Someone, something rules in his place.'

Man in Red: 'There is no face of Death until the moment of your own death and I am one of many messengers.'

MONTY PYTHON'S LIFE OF BRIAN★

UK, 1979, HandMade Films, 93 mins

D *Terry Jones;* **PR** *John Goldstone;* **SC** *Graham Chapman, John Cleese, Terry Gilliam, Eric Idle, Terry Jones, Michael Palin;* **PH** *(Eastman Color) Peter Biziou;* **M** *Geoffrey Burgon;* **ED** *Julian Doyle*

CAST *Terry Jones (Mandy, Mother of Brian et al.), Graham Chapman (Brian et al.), Michael Palin (Pontius Pilate et al.), John Cleese (Dirk Reg, Leader of Judean People's Front et al.), Eric Idle (Mr Cheeky et al.), Terry Gilliam (Revolutionary et al.), Ken Colley (Jesus), Gwen Taylor (Mrs Big Nose), Carol Cleveland (Mrs Gregory), Sue Jones-Davies (Judith), Spike Milligan (Spike), George Harrison (Mr Papadopoulis)*

THE STORY Three Wise Men bring gifts of gold, frankincense and myrrh to the stable in Bethlehem where Mandy Cohen has just given birth to her son Brian. Realizing their error, they retrieve the gifts and present them to Joseph and Mary in the manger down the road. Thirty-three years later ('Judea AD 33 – Saturday Afternoon – About Teatime') Brian and Mandy are in the crowd listening to Christ's Sermon on the Mount, though she would rather be at a stoning. Brian, who sells sweetmeats at the Jerusalem Colosseum, is shocked to learn his father was a Roman Centurion, and joins the People's Front of Judea, an anti-Roman liberation movement. Captured during an attempt to kidnap Pontius Pilate's wife, he is brought before Pilate but escapes. Posing as a speaker at Prophets Corner he attracts a following who proclaim him the Messiah.

'He's not the Messiah, he's a very naughty boy.'

He is recaptured and added to 139 other people sentenced to be crucified at Passover. His mother, the leaders of the People's Front, and his revolutionary girlfriend Judith all make their self-serving farewells, and he dies with his fellow victims, cheerfully singing Eric Idle's song 'Always Look on the Bright Side of Life'.

THE FILM A film of the 1970s that wittily criticizes the 1970s, *Life of Brian* gives the team a firm line on which to peg their gags and is the most sustainedly funny, the most daringly irreverent, and the most stylistically consistent of the Python movies. It sends up the pious, sadistic, bogusly uplifting tradition of run-of-DeMille religious epics from the silent era down to *Ben Hur* (whose credit titles it parodies). But it isn't truly blasphemous and lacks the bruised resignation of Jewish humour on the one hand and the Catholic fascination with the liturgical and sacerdotal on the other. It is a very C of E approach by a group of middle-class, public-school-educated agnostic rationalists who have come to find the historical context of the gospels and the theology they contain comic, ludicrous and absurd. Through the competing revolutionary movements in Judea, the film mocks the pomposity and hypocrisy of the trade unions (then exerting a stranglehold on British life) and the ineffectuality of Marxist revolutionary groups that had such an appeal for the students of the 1970s. Christ, however, in the two scenes in which he appears, is treated with respect if not reverence. One of the movie's great attractions is that between them the six members of the Monty Python team play some forty characters, populating a whole world.

ODD/SALIENT FACTS *Life of Brian* was largely shot on sets built in Tunisia for the reverential, star-studded Lew Grade TV production, *Jesus of Nazareth*, directed by Franco Zeffirelli. Lord Grade's brother, the impresario Sir Bernard Delfont, withdrew the support of his distribution chain from *Life of Brian* on the grounds that it would offend audiences. Fortunately George Harrison's HandMade company picked up the film.

MEMORABLE MOMENTS Brian caught by a Roman centurion daubing the graffito 'Romanes eunt domus' (Romans Go Home) on Pontius Pilate's palace and being instructed, with ear-pulling sadism as if by a traditional Latin master, to construe the language and come up with the correct 'Romani ite domum' and write it out a hundred times on Pilate's wall.

The naked Brian opening his front door to find himself confronted by a crowd of devoted followers.

Pilate confronted by a crowd mocking his speech impediment and introducing his friend Bigus Dickus as a hero who 'wanks as high as any in Wome'.

KEY LINES

Misheard beatitude passed on during the Sermon on the
Mount: 'Blessed are the cheese-makers.'

Leader of Judea People's Front: 'All right. *Apart from the*
aquaducts, the sanitation, the roads, the medicine, the
irrigation, the education, the wine, the public order,
what have the Romans ever done for us?'

Brian: 'All right, I'm the Messiah. Now fuck off!'
His followers: 'How shall we fuck off, O Lord?'

Mandy: 'He's not the Messiah, he's a very naughty boy.'

Brian: 'You don't need to follow me, you don't need to
follow anyone, you've got to think for yourselves, you're
all individuals.'
His followers, in unison: 'We are all individuals.'

THE MOST DANGEROUS GAME (UK TITLE: THE HOUNDS OF ZAROFF)

US, 1932, RKO, 63 MINS

D *ERNEST B. SHOEDSACK, IRVING PICHEL;* **PR** *ERNEST B.*
SHOEDSACK, MERIAM B. COOPER; **SC** *JAMES A. CREELMAN*
(FROM A STORY BY RICHARD CONNELL); **PH** *(BW) HENRY*
GERRARD; **M** *MAX STEINER;* **ED** *ARCHIE F. MARSHEK*
CAST *LESLIE BANKS (COUNT ZAROFF), JOEL MCCREA (BOB*
RAINSFORD), FAY WRAY (EVE), ROBERT ARMSTRONG (MARTIN)
NOBLE JOHNSON (IVAN), STEVE CLEMENTO (TARTAR), WILLIAM
DAVIDSON (CAPTAIN)

THE STORY Count Zaroff, a rich Cossack who escaped the Soviet Revolution with his fortune intact, has tired of hunting big game and retired to a small island in the Malayan archipelago to hunt humans. Using fake lights he lures ships to their destruc-

tion and treats survivors as guests at his castle until they are ready to become his prey as he stalks them through the jungle with a long-bow. The latest to be marooned is celebrated American big-game hunter Bob Rainsford, who has been preceded to the island by Eve and her drunken brother, Martin. Martin becomes Zaroff's next victim. Refusing Zaroff's invitation to join him in the hunt, Rainsford is given a knife and let loose in the jungle with Eve, who will go to the victor. The chase escalates from bow to telescopic rifle as the resourceful Rainsford fights back, and finally Zaroff brings out his pack of hounds. But the American turns the tables on his pursuer, and as Rainsford and the girl escape by motorboat, the fatally wounded Zaroff is savaged by his own hounds.

THE FILM This intense, economical thriller gives a principled big-game hunter a taste of his own medicine and in his fight for survival makes him as ruthless a killer as his enemy. Suave, decadent European is pitted against resourceful American and the picture pre-figures the conflict between the totalitarianism (Zaroff dresses like an Italian fascist) and democracy of the Second World War. The Count is an early example of the criminal as sadistic, world-weary aesthete, living in a private world in the manner of Dr No and other Bond villains, and the way he strokes his scarred forehead anticipates Ernst Stavro Blofeld. The film has been remade twice and much imitated, most famously in the Geoffrey Household novel *Rogue Male* that Fritz Lang adapted as *Manhunter*, and was much admired by the European surrealists, with Georges Franju evoking it in his *Les Yeux Sans Visage*.

ODD/SALIENT FACTS Many members of the production team (producer, writer, co-director, composer and several actors) were simultaneously engaged on the making of another cult movie, *King Kong*, though the latter's script was still being written. Both films concern terrible occurrences on uncharted islands, and the same jungle set was used for both. Some scenes for *Kong* involving Fay Wray and Robert Armstrong were shot between takes on *The Most Dangerous Game*. The original idea was to have Zaroff use leopards to track his prey, but when this didn't work the company borrowed a pack of Great Danes from comedy star Harold Lloyd. This was the first film of British stage star Leslie Banks who, as a result of a wound received during the Great War, had a partially paralysed face that made his right profile peculiarly sinister, producing a Jekyll and Hyde effect.

▲ *THE MOST DANGEROUS GAME Fay Wray and Joel McCrea flee from Leslie Banks on the set where she and Bruce Cabot will later flee from King Kong.*

MEMORABLE MOMENTS The knocker on the door of Zaroff's castle depicting a wounded satyr clutching a maiden.

Zaroff at his grand piano in a silk dressing gown.

The mounted human heads on the walls of the Count's trophy room.

Rainsford fleeing through the jungle dragging the heroine after him à la James Bond.

KEY LINE

Zaroff: 'He talks of wine and women as a prelude to the hunt. We barbarians know that it is after the chase, and then only, that man revels. You know the saying of the Ogandi chieftains: "Hunt first the enemy, then the woman." It is the natural instinct. The blood is quickened by the kill. One passion builds upon another. Kill, then love! When you have known that, you have known ecstasy.'

MYSTERY TRAIN

US, 1989, PALACE/VC, 110 MINS

D/SC JIM JARMUSCH; **PR** JIM STARK; **PH** ROBBIE MÜLLER (COLOUR DUART); **M** JOHN LURIE; **ED** MELODY LOUDUN

CAST MASATOSHI NAGASI (JUN), YOUKI KUDOH (MITZUKO), SCREAMIN' JAY HAWKINS (DESK CLERK), CINQUÉ LEE (BELLBOY), NICOLETTA BRASCHI (LUISA), ELIZABETH BRACCO (DEE DEE), JOE STRUMMER (JOHNNIE), STEVE BUSCEMI (CHARLIE), RICK AVILES (WILL), TOM NOONAN (CONMAN IN DINER), TOM WAITS (DISK-JOCKEY)

THE STORY Three parallel narratives centre on foreigners in Memphis, Tennessee, who spend the night at a seedy hotel away from the spruce new city centre and leave the following morning by train, plane and truck. In each story the same disk-jockey is heard playing Elvis's 'Blue Moon', the same gunshot rings out, the same train is seen passing over a bridge at night. FAR FROM YOKOHAMA: Two young Japanese rock fans, the cheerful Mitzuko and the morose Jun, make a pilgrimage to Memphis to visit Sun Studios and Graceland. They trail around town, and finally book into a cheap hotel where they talk about rock music, make love and leave the following day.

A GHOST: Luisa, an attractive Italian widow, is escorting her husband's coffin to Rome. A conman in a diner tells her Elvis's ghost wants him to give her his comb and collect a delivery fee of $20. She gives him $10 for the comb and $10 to go away, but when he menaces her she takes refuge in the same hotel as the Japanese. In the foyer she meets Dee Dee, who cannot

afford a room, but the desk clerk suggests they share one. The flighty Dee Dee tells Luisa she is quitting Memphis, leaving behind her English common-law husband Johnny and her brother Charlie, a hairdresser. Luisa tells Dee Dee the conman's story and learns he's a well-known trickster. When Dee Dee goes to sleep, Elvis's ghost appears to Luisa.

LOST IN SPACE: Dee Dee's husband, Johnnie, hates Presley since people keep calling him Elvis because of a slight resemblance. Having lost his job he sits around in a black bar with a friend, getting drunk and flashing a loaded gun. Another black friend, Will, owner of a pick-up truck, and his brother-in-law Charlie are summoned to take him away. Visiting a liquor store, the drunken Johnnie shoots the manager and the three go on the run, drinking steadily and ending up in the same seedy hotel, where the desk clerk is Will's brother-in-law. In the morning Charlie discovers that Johnnie isn't his real brother-in-law because Dee Dee never actually married him. When Johnnie attempts suicide there is a scuffle over the gun and Charlie is

▼ *MYSTERY TRAIN* Japanese Elvis fans relax in their hotel room after a day's sightseeing in Memphis.

wounded in the knee by the shot that is heard by all in the hotel.

THE FILM *Mystery Train* is a witty look at different aspects of one of the crazes of our time, the worship of Elvis Presley. The third of its stories, Lost in Space, takes its title from the cult television series of the 1960s, which the characters discuss. The cast includes cult performers like Tom Noonan (the serial killer in Michael Mann's *Manhunter*), Steve Buscemi and singer Tom Waits (heard on the radio), and the movie is directed by one of America's leading independent directors. *Mystery Train* is possibly Jarmusch's most immaculate film, and though the movie gets steadily darker in its comic tone, it is his least bleak work to date. The patterning is precise, the film growing richer as the three strands are finally woven together, or perhaps unwoven, as the people go their different ways. Robbie Müller, the great Dutch cameraman who lit Alex Cox's *Repo Man* and Wim Wenders' *Paris Texas*, once more brings an outsider's perceptive eye to the American landscape, giving the night scenes and hotel interiors a Hopperesque look and endowing a dilapidated section of Memphis with an elegiac sadness.

ODD/SALIENT FACTS *Mystery Train* signalled a new departure in US film financing, being subsidized entirely, and rather aptly, by the Japanese electronics company JVC. Jarmusch calls the film 'a modern mimimalist's version of *The Canterbury Tales*' and at one point the Japanese tourists walk down Chaucer Street. Jarmusch, Waits and singer Nick Cave (himself a 'cultist' par excellence) formed and exclusive ad hoc appreciation society for the actor Lee Marvin.

MEMORABLE MOMENTS The Japanese couple, their red suitcase slung on a stick between them, passing a row of rickety, wooden houses in the early morning.

A tour guide at Sun Studio delivering her spiel at such speed that the Japanese visitors cannot understand a word.

The Japanese girl going through her scrap book, demonstrating Elvis's resemblance to the Buddha, the Statue of Liberty and Madonna.

Elvis's ghost appearing to Luisa.

Johnny demanding that the Presley portraits be turned to the wall, saying a black hotel should have Otis Redding – only to be told that it's a white-owned hotel that employs blacks.

> **'You fucking shot me. You ain't even my brother-in-law and you've fucking shot me.'**

KEY LINES

Jun: 'You know, Memphis *does* look like Yokohama.'

Jun: 'It feels cool to be in Memphis.'

Mitzuko: 'Was that a gun?'
Jun: 'Probably, this is America.'

Johnnie: 'We didn't choose to be white – right Charlie?'

Charlie: 'You fucking shot me. You ain't even my brother-in-law and you've fucking shot me.'

THE NARROW MARGIN
US, 1952, RKO, 71 MINS

D *RICHARD FLEISCHER;* **PR** *STANLEY RUBIN;* **SC** *EARL FENTON (FROM A STORY BY MARTIN GOLDSMITH AND JACK LEONARD);* **PH** *GEORGE E. DISKANT;* **ED** *ROBERT SWINK*

CAST *CHARLES MCGRAW (WALTER BROWN), MARIE WINDSOR ('MRS NEIL'), JACQUELINE WHITE ('ANN SINCLAIR'), GORDON GEBERT (TOMMY SINCLAIR), QUEENIE LEONARD (MRS TROLL), DAVID CLARKE (KEMP), PETER VIRGO (DENSEL), DON BEDDOE (GUS FORBES), PAUL MAXEY (JENNINGS), HARRY HARVEY (TRAIN CONDUCTOR)*

THE STORY Tough, cynical LAPD Sergeant Walter Brown and his older partner, Gus Forbes, arrive in Chicago to escort Mrs Neil, widow of a leading mobster, who is to submit her husband's secret pay-off list to a grand jury in Los Angeles. Neither mobsters nor police have ever seen her, and she turns out to be a tough, chain-smoking broad. As they leave Mrs Neil's sordid apartment block Gus is killed by an assassin who is out to silence her. On the train, Walter conceals Mrs Neil in his compartment. In the dining car he meets Ann Sinclair, a middle-class woman travelling to California. Mobsters on the train threaten Walter and try bribing him to hand over Mrs Neil, who mocks him for his incorruptibility. Meanwhile Brown suspects the obese Jennings of being a gangster, and he deliberately distracts the crooks by paying attention to Ann Sinclair. But it turns out that Jennings is a railway detective, Ann Sinclair is the dead gang

148

▲ *THE NARROW MARGIN* Femme fatale *Marie Windsor* *tempts police minder Charles McGraw on the train to LA.*

boss's real widow, and 'Mrs Neil' is a woman cop from Internal Affairs, working as a decoy to throw the crooks off the scent and test Brown's probity. She is killed, and Brown goes into action to protect Ann Sinclair, shooting Densel, her would-be assassin, and seeing his accomplice arrested by state policemen. While Jennings blocks the press at Union Station, Brown escorts 'Ann Sinclair' to the Los Angeles Department of Justice.

THE FILM *The Narrow Margin* is one of the great claustrophobic thrillers and one of the great train movies. Everything happens in a confined space – a taxi, a seedy apartment, a transcontinental train with its narrow corridors, cramped compartments, small washrooms. There are just two stops between Chicago and Los Angeles for cables to be sent and new passengers to get on, though porters can drop off messages en route. The movie is trimmed to the bone, every shot tells, and the only music comes from the 78s on 'Mrs Neil's' portable gramophone and the muzak in the train's dining car. One of the sleepers of the early 1950s, this modest RKO picture was

embraced by serious moviegoers. Richard Fleischer suddenly became a hot name, going straight on to big-budget action films, first with Disney's *20,000 Leagues Under the Sea* (1954) and then such cult epics as *The Vikings* (1958) and *Barabbas* (1962). A certain casual sadism underlies all his best work. Ostensibly, the respectable major theme of *The Narrow Margin* is the cynic Brown learning not to judge by appearances. But the movie's strength derives from the way its tone and plot reflect some darker contemporary issues – the fear that organized crime (as being exposed by Senator Estes Kefauver's crime commission) was all-pervasive, its corruption irresistible; the feeling that the threats to national security during the McCarthy Era had created a climate where everyone was being investigated and no one was trusted.

ODD/SALIENT FACTS Howard Hughes admired *The Narrow Margin* and had to be dissuaded from remaking it with Robert Mitchum and Jane Russell. Several scenes in *North By North West* (1959) show that Hitchcock had studied Fleischer's film. It was remade none too well by Peter Hyams as *Narrow Margin* (1990) where some contrivance was needed by Earl Fenton Jr (son of the original screenwriter) to get Gene Hackman and Anne Archer on a train. The 1952 picture cost under $230,000; the remake $25 million. Neither of the 1952 film's leads became major stars, which helps preserve its freshness and unpredictability. Marie Windsor, who specialized in treacherous broads, had her two finest hours in this movie. Charles McGraw never had as good a role again.

MEMORABLE MOMENTS Gus descending a staircase ahead of Walter and Mrs Neil, whose necklace breaks and white beads cascade down the steps landing by the highly polished black shoes of a man (Densel) hiding in the shadows.

Man shoots Gus; Walter, pursuing him, gets entangled in some pegged-out washing.

Walter watching a reflection of Densel preparing to shoot Ann Sinclair.

KEY LINES

Gus: 'Bet you're wondering the same thing I am. What's she look like?'

Walter: 'I don't have to wonder. I know … A dish.'

Gus: 'What kind of dish?'

Walter: 'Sixty cent special. Cheap. Flashy. Strictly poison under the gravy.'

Gus: 'Amazing, and how d'you know all this?'
Walter: 'Well, she married a hoodlum, didn't she? What
    kind of a dame … would marry a hood?'
Gus: 'All kinds.'

Walter to 'Mrs Neil': 'My partner's dead and it's my fault.
    He's dead and you're alive. Some exchange.'

THE NIGHT OF THE HUNTER

US, 1955, UNITED ARTISTS, 93 MINS

D *CHARLES LAUGHTON;* **PR** *PAUL GREGORY;* **SC** *JAMES AGEE,
CHARLES LAUGHTON, FROM THE NOVEL BY DAVIS GRUBB;*
PH *(BW) STANLEY CORTEZ;* **M** *WALTER SCHUMANN;* **ED** *ROBERT
GOLDEN;* **ART DIR** *HILYARD BROWN;* **SETS** *AL SPENCER*
CAST *ROBERT MITCHUM (HARRY POWELL), SHELLEY WINTERS
(WILLA HARPER), LILLIAN GISH (RACHEL), BILLY CHAPIN (JOHN),
PEARL (SALLY JANE BRUCE), PETER GRAVES (BEN HARPER), EVELYN*
*VARDEN (ICEY SPOON), DON BEDDOE (WALT SPOON), JAMES
GLEASON (UNCLE BIRDIE), GLORIA CASTILLO (RUBY)*

THE STORY Harry Powell, a murderer and fake preacher, is
jailed for the theft of a car. He shares a cell with Ben Harper,
who has secreted a stolen $10,000 in his daughter Pearl's doll.
Harper is executed. On his release, Powell charms his way into
the life of Ben's widow, Willa. The two are soon married, and
Powell tries to discover the whereabouts of the cash, but John
(Ben and Willa's young son) mistrusts him and makes Pearl
promise not to tell him. Powell kills Willa, but the children manage to escape down-river. Powell pursues them on horseback.
John and Pearl seek refuge with Rachel who looks after other
waifs and strays. Rachel sees off Powell who tries to snatch the

▼ *THE NIGHT OF THE HUNTER Robert Mitchum as preacher
Harry Powell brings the wrath of God down upon his
innocent wife Willa (Shelley Winters).*

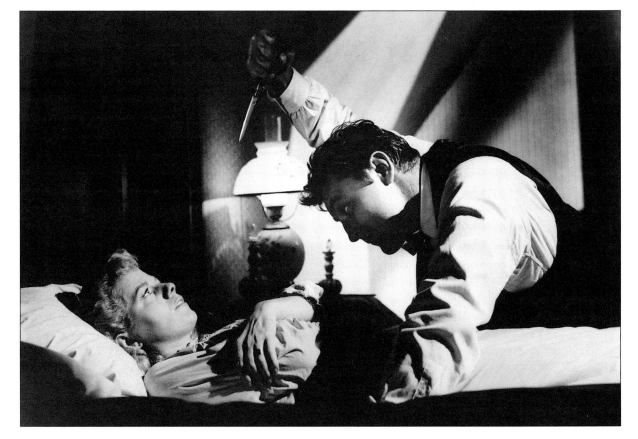

children, and only when Powell is being arrested does John give him the money from the doll.

THE FILM The role of Powell is perfect for Mitchum, who imbues it with a mixture of broad humour and menace. According to Simon Callow in *Charles Laughton: A Difficult Actor*, when the director first spoke of the project to his proposed star, he explained: 'This character I want you to play is a complete shit.' Mitchum replied: 'Present.' Mitchum's phony preacher dominates the film, with his singing, his sinister presence, and humorous psychosis. He is a ruthless killer, who prays sincerely but only for personal gain and in the finest performance of his career Mitchum turns him into one of the greatest of all cinema's charismatic psychopaths. Laughton also turned his hand to writing and entirely reshaped James Agee's 350-page script. Cinematographer Stanley Cortez lends the film its distinctive look, with every shot adding to the dark fairy-tale atmosphere. Cortez himself said: 'Every day I consider something new about light, that incredible thing that can't be described. Of the directors I've worked with, only two have understood it: Orson Welles and Charles Laughton.'

The film like *The Window* (1949) skilfully derives its horror from the impotence of children in the face of violent, devious, vindictive adults. It is only John who instantly sees through the obviously phony Powell. He senses from the outset that Powell is after the money, but his mother is blinded by love, indeed the whole town is taken in. The children try to get help from their uncle Birdie, who has discovered Willa's body but he tells no one to avoid being blamed for it himself. Birdie is hopelessly drunk, and John has to look out for himself and Pearl. As they travel down the river, John has temporarily to become an adult, until he can resume his childishness in his new surrogate family. Apart from his tremendous performance, Mitchum lent Laughton further assistance, as he recalled: 'Charles loathed those children. He made *me* direct them.' Laughton briefly flirted with the idea of adapting Norman Mailer's *The Naked and the Dead* for the screen, but was so dismayed at the failure of this highly personal work that he never directed another film.

ODD/SALIENT FACTS Winters was cast as Willa by her friend Laughton. She writes in her autobiography, *Shelley*, of her problems at having to retrieve her natural Southern accent that she had so studiously lost. Laughton encouraged her: 'In this life we never forget our bad habits, Shelley. They stay around somewhere and are easily recalled when we need them.' Mitchum was unimpressed by his co-star, commenting bluntly: 'Shelley got what she deserved, lying there dead at the bottom of the river.'

MEMORABLE MOMENTS John winces as his father is arrested. He repeats the empathic gesture when Powell, his evil stepfather is in turn arrested.

Powell telling the story of the eternal battle between Love and Hate, via the tattoos on his knuckles.

The off-screen execution of Ben Harper. The camera follows the executioner as he returns home to his wife and children. Cut to John and Pearl being teased about their dead father.

Willa's body strapped into a car in the river, with her hair flowing with the tide. The body is discovered by the feckless Uncle Birdie.

As the children sleep in a barn by the side of the river, Powell is seen in silhouette passing on a nearby road, riding his stolen horse and singing.

KEY LINES

Powell, praying in prison: 'Lord, I reckon you knowed what you was doing when you put me in this very cell at this very time – a man with $10,000 hidden somewhere and a widow in the making.'

Rachel: 'It's a hard world for little things.'

NOSFERATU (EINE SYMPHONIE DES GRAUENS)

GERMANY, 1922, PRANA FILMS, APPROX. 72 MINS

D *F.W. MURNAU;* **SC** *HENRIK GALEEN (LOOSELY BASED ON THE NOVEL DRACULA BY BRAM STOKER);* **PH** *(BW) FRITZ ARNO WAGNER;* **DES** *ALBIN GRAU;* **M** *(FOR ORIGINAL PRESENTATION) HANS ERDMAN*

CAST *MAX SCHRECK (COUNT ORLOK, NOSFERATU THE VAMPIRE), ALEXANDER GRANACH (KNOCK, AN ESTATE AGENT), GUSTAF VON WANGENHEIM (HUTTER, KNOCK'S ASSISTANT), GRETA SCHRÖDER (ELLEN, HUTTER'S WIFE), G. H. SCHNELL (HARDING, A SHIPBUILDER), RUTH LANDSHOFF (ANNE, HIS WIFE), JOHN GOTTOWT (PROFESSOR BULWER, A PARACELSAN), GUSTAV BOTZ (PROFESSOR SIEVERS, TOWN MEDICAL OFFICER), MAX NEMETZ (SHIP'S CAPTAIN), GUIDO HERZFELD (INNKEEPER)*

THE STORY In 1838 in the German port of Wisberg the eccentric estate agent Knock receives a letter from a Count Orlok enquiring about some property. Knock sends Hutter, his young, recently married assistant, to the Count's castle in Transylvania. Hutter stops at an inn nearby; the locals are shocked to learn his destination, and next to the bed he discovers a book about Nosferatu, the Vampire. At the castle he finds only one occupant, the weird Orlok who is in fact Nosferatu, and the following morning Hutter finds two bites in his neck. Back home his wife Ellen has premonitions of the dangers facing him. After seeing a picture of Ellen, Orlok decides to buy the house next door to the Hutters and packs three coffins full of earth to be shipped there. Hutter has discovered Orlok's identity and a race is on to see who reaches Wisberg first. Spreading the plague via rats from his coffins, Orlok sails into the town just ahead of Hutter and the plague strikes immediately. The citizens believe that Knock is to blame, but Ellen has

▲ *NOSFERATU Count Orlok rises from his coffin, terrifying a sailor on the boat to Wisberg.*

learnt Nosferatu can be destroyed by a virtuous woman who freely gives him her blood and keeps him from his coffin until dawn. This she achieves, saving the town but sacrificing her life.

THE FILM Subtitled 'A Symphony of Horror', *Nosferatu* is the first and best of many movies inspired by Bram Stoker's *Dracula* by one of the cinema's true poets, who created the language of the horror flick. It is a dreamlike picture where much is left unexplained, the geography is marvellously vague, and several characters such as the Van Helsing figure, Professor Bulwer, have little connection with the main action. From the start there is a sense of unease and menace, but everything is done by suggestion without any explicit violence. Blood is constantly mentioned but none actually seen. Plague overtakes a city

> **'Your wife has such a beautiful neck.'**

but we are left to imagine the state of its victims. When the townspeople chase Knock over the countryside they seem to be tearing their victim apart, but the object of their frenzy turns out to be a scarecrow.

The film's climax has a gentle sensuality. Instead of a phallic stake being driven through the vampire's heart, a self-sacrificial heroine holds him in her bed to ensure his death. Sex and death, blood and contamination, are the film's themes. Max Schreck's Orlok is a truly grotesque iconic figure, both frightening and moving, with his bat ears, his aquiline nose, hunched shoulders, hairless dome, flaring eyebrows, black-ringed eyes, white skin and clawlike hands.

Instant culthood was conferred on the picture when it became the subject of legal action by Bram Stoker's estate for breach of copyright. Many prints were destroyed and the film has circulated in numerous versions, some giving the British novel as the source and the characters the names from the book. The film has always had the reputation of a controversial classic.

ODD/SALIENT FACTS Like James Whale, the director of the first two *Frankenstein* movies, F. W. Murnau was homosexual, and both died somewhat bizarrely in California. Murnau was already working in Hollywood on his masterly *Sunrise* (1927) before a mutilated version of *Nosferatu* was released in the States. The only version of *Dracula* that was a remake of the Murnau movie is Werner Herzog's 1979 *Nosferatu The Vampire*. In Peter Bogdanovich's *Targets*, Boris Karloff is called Byron Orlok. The restored version shown at the 1997 London Film Festival was accompanied by an admirable new score by James Bernard, house composer to Hammer Films.

MEMORABLE MOMENTS The Transylvanian innkeeper and his patrons cowering when Hutter announces his destination.

The speeded-up carriage ride (several frames in negative) taking Hutter to Orlok's castle.

Nosferatus emerging from a gothic doorway into Hutter's bedroom, his shadow imposed on Hutter in Ellen's dream.

Nosferatu stalking the deck of the death ship as seen from below.

Nosferatu's giant shadow approaching Ellen's bedroom, his elongated hand reaching out to the door like some monstrous creature of the deep.

Ellen's expression of lust and self-sacrifice as she awaits the Vampire's visit to her bed.

KEY LINES

Opening narrative: 'Nosferatu – does this word sound like the midnight call of the Bird of Death?'

Orlok: 'During the day I sleep my friend, the deepest sleep of all.'

Orlok: 'Your wife has such a beautiful neck.'

Knock: 'Blood is life! Blood is life!'

ODD MAN OUT
UK, 1946, GFD/TWO CITIES, 115 MINS
D CAROL REED; **PR** CAROL REED; **SC** F. L. GREEN, R. C. SHERRIFF, BASED ON GREEN'S NOVEL; **PH** (BW) ROBERT KRASKER; **M** WILLIAM ALWYN; **ED** FERGUS MCDONNELL
CAST JAMES MASON (JOHNNY), ROBERT NEWTON (LUKEY), ROBERT BEATTY (DENNIS), F. J. MCCORMICK (SHELL), FAY COMPTON (ROSIE), BERYL MEASOR (MAUDI), CYRIL CUSACK (PAT), DAN O'HERLIHY (NOLAN), ROY IRVING (MURPHY), MAUREEN DELANY (THERESA), KITTY KIRWAN (GRANNY), MIN MILLIGAN (HOUSEKEEPER), JOSEPH TOMELTY (CABBIE), W. G. FAY (FATHER TOM), ARTHUR HAMBLING (ALFIE), KATHLEEN RYAN (KATHLEEN), DENNIS O'DEA (HEAD CONSTABLE), WILLIAM HARTNELL (FENCIE), ELWYN BROOK JONES (TOBER)

THE STORY Johnny McQueen, the recently escaped leader of the Organisation in an unnamed city in Northern Ireland, plans a fund-raising raid on a mill. Making his escape he wrestles with an employee, is shot by him and finally shoots and kills his assailant. Falling from the escape car, Johnny is left behind by his companions Pat, Nolan and Murphy. Slowly bleeding to death and hallucinating, Johnny comes across, is cared for and exploited by a variety of the city's inhabitants: a little girl, a courting couple, some recent arrivals from England, a cabbie, and three eccentrics sharing a grand but derelict house. Meanwhile Dennis, a friend and colleague, and later Kathleen, who is in love with Johnny, set out to look for him. Murphy escapes to his mother's house while Pat and Nolan are betrayed by Theresa, the wealthy owner of a supposed safe house, and shot dead by the police. Dennis, acting as a decoy for Johnny, is arrested. At last Johnny meets up with Kathleen who leads him to the docks and to a ship which she hopes will take him to safety. As Johnny and Kathleen arrive at the docks in the heavy snow, the police close in on them. Kathleen fires towards the police and she and Johnny are shot dead.

THE FILM The film, based on a novel by F. L. Green, marks Reed's first collaboration with the cinematographer Robert Krasker. Krasker, born in Australia, had his view of films shaped by the German Expressionist cinema. The stylized lighting effects that would be such a feature of *The Third Man* (1948), the third of Reed's great trilogy after *The Fallen Idol* (1947), are quite evident here. The Organization and the city are never named but clearly stand for the IRA and Belfast. In *The Man Between*, Nicholas Wapshott's biography of Reed, Joseph Tomelty of the Group Theatre, Belfast, recalls the director as a stickler for the film's authentic detail, demanding of his researchers: 'Describe an armoured car. Do the letters GPO appear on Belfast pillar boxes? Is a police car a Ford, Vauxhall or Morris? What is the uniform of a prison warder in Northern Ireland?' Yet there are some obvious flaws to the film. The main one is the unevenness of the accents with most of the cast speaking in an Irish brogue which stands in stark contrast when heard against the genuine Belfast accents of the film's IRA-worshipping street kids. Despite the overblown eccentricities of Robert Newton's performance as the artist Lukey, the film is beautifully worked out and, in David Thomson's assessment 'one of the greatest Irish films ever made'.

ODD/SALIENT FACTS Although the chief source for *Reservoir Dogs* (1992) is *City on Fire* (1989), it must also have been partly inspired by *Odd Man Out*, with its plot of a well-planned heist going badly wrong, and one of the raiders spending the entirety of the action apparently bleeding to death before being shot at the very last. The pub, the Four Winds, in which Johnny

▼ **ODD MAN OUT** *Fatally wounded Johnny McQueen (James Mason) and Kathleen (Kathleen Ryan) meet up at last at Belfast's snow-covered docks.*

hides, was an almost exact replica of the Belfast pub The Crown. The last time the latter was all but destroyed by a terrorist attack, its interior was rebuilt using the production designs for the film.

MEMORABLE MOMENTS The various shootings – the man outside the mill and Johnny, Pat and Nolan, Kathleen and Johnny – before all of which the camera pans away.

The shots of Murphy, Pat and Nolan, and later Dennis running through the streets, filmed with a wide lens and lit from below to show them with their vast distorted shadows pursued across a menacing cityscape.

Johnny's hallucinations of the girl with the football in the shelter as a prison warder, and later seeing the faces of figures from his past in the bubbles of his spilt beer.

KEY LINES

Dennis to Kathleen on Johnny: 'As long as he lives he'll belong to the Organization.'

Shell, hoping to get a reward for Johnny from Father Tom: 'A fella was telling me, I heard tell that his Reverence the Pope is quare and rich.'

Lukey on Johnny: 'I'd paint him and it would all be there, the truth of life and death.'

Johnny, having his epiphany in Lukey's studio, on Father Tom: 'We've always drowned your voice with our shouting, haven't we, Father?'

ON THE WATERFRONT

US, 1954, COLUMBIA/HORIZON PICTURES, 108 MINS

D *ELIA KAZAN;* **PR** *SAM SPIEGEL;* **SC** *BUDD SCHULBERG (BASED ON ARTICLES BY MALCOLM JOHNSON);* **PH** *(BW) BORIS KAUFMAN;* **ED** *GENE MILFORD;* **M** *LEONARD BERNSTEIN*

CAST *MARLON BRANDO (TERRY MALLOY), EVA MARIE SAINT (EDIE DOYLE), KARL MALDEN (FATHER BARRY), LEE J. COBB (MICHAEL J. SKELLY, AKA JOHNNY FRIENDLY), ROD STEIGER (CHARLEY MALLOY), PAT HENNING (KAYO DUGAN), JOHN HAMILTON (POP DOYLE), LEIF ERICKSON (GLOVER, CRIME COMMISSION AGENT), JAMES WESTERFIELD (BIG MAC), TONY GALENTO (TRUCK), TAMI MAURIELLO (TILLIO), FRED GWYNNE (SLIM)*

▲ *ON THE WATERFRONT Marlon Brando as Terry Malloy seeks redemption in the arms of Eva Marie Saint.*

THE STORY Terry Malloy, a slow-witted young ex-boxer, works for racketeer Johnny Friendly who runs a branch of the Longshoremen's Union on the docks of Hoboken, New Jersey. Terry's educated older brother, Charley, is Friendly's chief lieutenant, and he and Friendly, through fixing fights, were responsible for Terry quitting the ring. Joey, a friend of Terry's and fellow pigeon-fancier, is about to appear before the Waterfront Crime Commission, when Terry unwittingly lures him to the roof of their tenement from which he is thrown to his death by Friendly's goons. Joey's sister Edie, a trainee teacher, gets together with Father Barry, a local parish priest, to investigate Joey's death, and Charley tells Terry to spy on their activities. Another protesting docker, Dugan, is 'accidentally' killed by a falling crate. After saving Edie from some thugs, Terry is drawn to her, his conscience is touched, and he confesses his involvement to Edie. After Charley is murdered Terry testifies before the Commission. The next day he is savagely beaten up by Friendly and his thugs. The longshoremen, Edie's father among them, turn on the corrupt union leader and agree to enter the dock only if Terry leads them in. Urged on by Father Barry, the badly injured Terry staggers through the gate followed by his fellow workers.

THE FILM On the Waterfront swept the board at the 1954 Oscars with twelve nominations and eight major awards and gained a reputation for gritty realism and hard-hitting social comment. But what has made it endure as a cult movie is Brando's highly mannered performance, the rhetorical dialogue and the wildly melodramatic style. For all Schulberg's research, the movie hardly hints at the scale of the corruption or the way the Mafia was working hand-in-glove with the capitalists. This isn't actually a realistic movie, but more a throwback to the poetic 1930s theatre glorifying the struggles of the common man but without the politics. It's a tale of one simple-minded man's redemption through the love of a good woman and a tough priest, and of how he becomes a martyr and saviour of his community. From the opening scene of Joey's murder to the final near crucifixion, it is a movie of relentless violence. The major love scene is prefaced by Terry smashing down Edie's door, Friendly lashes out at Terry in the court-room, Terry's pigeons are killed. The movie exalts the forceful men of action who can lead the masses to challenge the forces of evil. It is also a defence of the informer, made at the height of McCarthyism – Kazan, Schulberg and Lee J. Cobb had all appeared before the House Un-American Activities Committee to confess their party membership and name friends and associates. The masochistic ending of On The Waterfront is echoed in later Brando movies. In One-Eyed Jacks he is whipped and has his trigger finger broken; in The Appaloose (a.k.a. Southwest to Sonova) he is dragged behind a galloping horse; in The Chase he is beaten to a pulp by vigilantes.

ODD/SALIENT FACTS During the making Kazan and his crew were protected by armed ex-policemen from strong-arm men

employed by the unions. The movie began life as The Hook, a collaboration between Kazan and Arthur Miller but they fell out after Kazan's appearance before HUAC and didn't work together again until 1964. Budd Schulberg, a great writer on boxing, wrote an earlier version of Terry Malloy in his short story 'The Pride of Tony Colucci'. The novel Waterfront, that Schulberg published in 1955, ends with Terry murdered by the mob and Father Barry assigned to another parish. On the Waterfront was the first American feature to be shot by the cult cinematographer Boris Kaufman (1906–80), the brother of the Soviet film-maker Dziga-Vertov. He left the Soviet Union in 1927, and photographed all Jean Vigo's pictures (À Propos de Nice, Zéro de conduite, L'Atalante) before settling in the States in 1942.

MEMORABLE MOMENTS The skyscrapers of Manhattan seen through the mist across the Hudson River from grimy Hoboken.

Father Barry being harassed by goons as he preaches a sermon over the dead Kayo Dugan in the ship's hold and is then hauled up with the corpse by a crane, as if ascending into heaven.

Terry finding Charley's corpse hanging on a longshoreman's hook from a piece of pipe in an alleyway.

Terry and Charley's dialogue in the back of the taxi.

KEY LINES

Charley asking Terry to spy on Father Barry: 'Stooling is when you rat on your friends.'

Terry: 'It was you Charley. You and Johnny. Like the night the two of youse come in the dressing room and says, "Kid, this ain't your night. We're going for the price on Wilson." It ain't my night. I'd of taken Wilson apart that night! I was ready – remember the early rounds throwing them combinations. So what happens – this bum Wilson he gets the title shot – outdoors in the ball park, and what do I get – a couple of bucks and a one-way ticket to Palookaville. It was you Charley. You was my brother. You should've looked out for me ... I could've been a contender. I could've had class and been somebody. Real class. Instead of a bum, let's face it, which is what I am. It was you Charley.'

> **'Stooling is when you rat on your friends.'**

ONCE UPON A TIME IN THE WEST★

ITALY, 1968, RAFRAN CINEMATOGRAFICA/EURO INTERNATIONAL FILMS, 165, 132 OR 144 MINS

D SERGIO LEONE; **PR** BINO CICOGNA, FULVIO MORSELLA; **SC** SERGIO LEONE, SERGIO DONATI; STORY BY DARIO ARGENTO, BERNARDO BERTOLUCCI, SERGIO LEONE; **PH** TONINO DELLI COLLI; **M** ENNIO MORRICONE; **ED** NINO BARAGLI

CAST HENRY FONDA (FRANK), CLAUDIA CARDINALE (JILL MCBAIN), JASON ROBARDS (CHEYENNE), CHARLES BRONSON (HARMONICA), FRANK WOLFF (BRETT MCBAIN), GABRIELE FERZETTI (MORTON), KEENAN WYNN (SHERIFF), PAOLO STOPPA (SAM), MARCO ZUANELLI (WOBBLES), LIONEL STANDER (BARMAN), JACK ELAM (KNUCKLES), JOHN FREDRICK (MEMBER OF FRANK'S GANG), WOODY STRODE (STONY), ENZIO SANTIANELLO (TIMMY), DINO MELE (HARMONICA AS A BOY)

THE STORY Three men employed by arch-villain Frank wait at a small-town station for the arrival of a train. The train pulls away to reveal Harmonica, who kills the men in a gunfight. Brett McBain, his two sons and a daughter, are gunned down by Frank and his men. Meanwhile Jill McBain, recently married to Brett, arrives. At a trading post she encounters Harmonica and Cheyenne, an escaped prisoner, who has been framed for the McBain killings. Jill finds her new family dead, but decides to stay on. Frank, an employee of the railway, is trying to force the tenants of the farm off the land before a small town can be built on the site. Harmonica fends off an assassination attempt on Jill and helps her keep possession of the land by collecting the bounty on Cheyenne. In a final shootout Harmonica shoots Frank. Just before Frank dies Harmonica reveals his motivation. In flashback we see Frank placing Harmonica's elder brother, a noose round his neck, on Harmonica's shoulders. He shoves a harmonica in his mouth and the young Harmonica plays it until he collapses to the ground, so killing his brother. Cheyenne dies from wounds inflicted when once again escaping. Jill stays as the work on her new town continues and the railway approaches, while Harmonica rides off with the body of Cheyenne.

THE FILM Sergio Leone had, along with the star he created, Clint Eastwood, revolutionized and revived the Western. His dark, existential myths of 'the man with no name' fundamentally altered the moral world of the genre and brought it up to date with a more cynical age. In Once Upon a Time in the West he created his masterpiece which, despite a starry cast, failed at the box office in America. One obvious reason for the signal failure of Leone's great fable of the death of the American West is that it is profoundly anti-American. Leone had been appalled by the sudden and disastrous departure of American money from the Italian film industry. He uses this film to tell the story of how the forces of the modern industrial world are indistinguishable from those of the bandits they were superseding, other than being more powerful, indeed inexorable. He employs a cast of faces familiar from the Westerns of John Ford (Fonda, Elam, Strode), places them in the iconic landscape of the great Westerns, Monument Valley, the instantly recognizable vista framed by the arch from which Harmonica's brother is hanged, and creates a succession of breathtakingly composed set-pieces, all within a narrative framework that subverts the traditions of the genre.

ODD/SALIENT FACTS Ennio Morricone, the composer and Leone's longtime collaborator, endeared himself to the director by not taking his films too seriously. According to Christopher Frayling, Morricone 'used to shriek with laughter' during screenings. The score for Once Upon a Time in the West, composed before a frame of the film had been shot, quotes from Don Giovanni, and in Frank's approach to the final, fateful gunfight with Harmonica, from Beethoven's Seventh Symphony. In his autobiography Henry Fonda, Leone's first choice for 'The Man with No Name', recalls the impact of Frank's first appearance in the film: The camera cuts to a long shot and from behind the sagebrush on the desert come five ominous figures, all wearing grey dusters, black, wide-brimmed hats, and they're carrying rifles and side arms. Slowly, they converge on this little boy. Cut to him. Cut to the advancing men. Cut to the terror in the kid's eyes. Cut to the back of the central figure of the five desperados. Very slowly the camera comes around and that's what Sergio Leone was going for all the time. The main heavy, Jesus Christ, it's Henry Fonda!

MEMORABLE MOMENTS The prolonged opening sequence leading to the sudden, very quick gunfight.

The gunning down of the McBains.

The final confrontation between Harmonica and Frank in which Frank, at the very last, understands who Harmonica is. All these display the qualities that led Leone's films to be described as 'operas in which the arias are starred'.

KEY LINES

Harmonica: 'No Frank?'
Knuckles: 'Frank sent us.'
Harmonica: 'Did you bring a horse for me?'
Knuckles: 'Looks like we're shy one horse.'
Harmonica: 'You brought two too many.'

Before Frank and Harmonica's final shootout.
Frank: 'Nothing matters now, not the land, not the money, not the woman. I came to see you because I know that you'll tell me what I'm after.'
Harmonica: 'Only at the point of dying.'
Frank: 'I know.'

ORPHÉE

FRANCE, 1950, LES FILMS DU PALAIS ROYAL, 112 MINS

D/SC JEAN COCTEAU; **PR** ANDRÉ PAULVÉ; **PH** (BW) NICOLAS HAYER; **M** GEORGES AURIC; **ED** JACQUELINE SADOUL
CAST JEAN MARAIS (ORPHÉE), FRANÇOIS PÉRIER (HEURTEBISE), MARIA CASARÈS (THE PRINCESS), MARIE DÉA (EURYDICE), ÉDOUARD DERMITHE (CÉGISTE), JACQUES VARENNE (THE FIRST JUDGE), JULIETTE GRECO (AGLAONICE), ROGER BLIN (THE WRITER)

▲ *ORPHÉE Jean Marais as the questing Orpheus clutches a mirror, the gateway to the Underworld.*

THE STORY At the Café des Poètes in Paris the celebrated poet Orphée runs into fans of his young rival Cégiste, whom he despises. The Princess arrives in a Rolls-Royce driven by Heurtebise; there is a riot and Cégiste is killed by two motorcyclists.

'Mirrors are the doors by which death comes?'

The Princess drives him away, persuading Orphée to come along as a witness. She is Death, the motorcyclists are her aides, and she takes Cégiste through a mirror into the next world leaving Orphée to wake up in a sand quarry. Heurtebise drives Orphée home where his wife Eurydice is being comforted by a police inspector and Eurydice's friend Aglaonice, leader of women and owner of the nightclub Les Bacchantes. Orphée becomes obsessed by the cryptic messages coming from the car radio in the Rolls-Royce (e.g. 'The bird sings with its fingers, once', 'Silence is twice as fast backwards, three

times') and is indifferent to his wife. It transpires that Orphée and Death are in love with each other, and Heurtebise loves Eurydice. When Eurydice is killed while cycling, Heurtebise takes Orphée through a mirror into the Zone, an underworld of ruins, where they appear with Death before a tribunal that allows Eurydice to return to life provided Orphée doesn't look at her, but he does and she's taken away. Orphée is attacked and killed by Aglaonice's followers, who believe Orphée has stolen Cégiste's poems (the gnomic lines heard on the car radio). Death and Heurtebise decide to sacrifice themselves so that Orphée and Eurydice can be free, and are led away by the two motorcyclists.

THE FILM *Orphée* is still one of the most magical fantasy movies, despite the technical advances made in special effects. The journeys through mirrors (achieved by using doubles, vats of mercury, troughs of water and unsilvered glass) have a dreamlike quality and the Zone beyond them has the haunted nightmare feeling of a 1940s neo-romantic painting. A versatile poet, playwright, artist, essayist and film-maker, Cocteau (1889–1963) made this, his fifth and best movie, in his sixtieth year. He identified with the egotistical, death-loving Orphée, and the hostility that people in the movie have towards the poet represents the homosexual, dilettante, politically uncommitted Cocteau's own resentment of the attacks made upon him by the Surrealists and communists in the 1920s, and after the war by younger critics. The tribunal in the underworld is a combination of wartime resistance meetings and postwar courts set up to judge collaborators The cryptic snatches of poems on the car radio were inspired by the coded messages sent by the BBC to the French Resistance. The casting of Jean Marais as the fading poet and Édouard Dermithe as the rising one reflects the position the two actors had in Cocteau's life. The film is at once timeless and a reflection of Paris in the postwar years.

Orphée has its weaknesses, but generally it has worn well and while it may seem less obscure today it has lost little of its poetic charm. Some of its particular grace comes from the performances of the handsome Marais, the striking Casarès, and François Perier.

ODD/SALIENT FACTS Orphée won First Prize at the 1950 Venice Festival. The request 'Astonish us', spoken to Orphée at the café, was originally addressed to the young Cocteau by Sergei Diaghilev in the form 'Étonne-moi'. Most of the underworld scenes were shot in the blitzed ruins of the St Cyr military academy. Roger Blin became famously associated with Beckett's plays. Georges Auric (whose score incorporates themes from Glück's Orpheus and Eurydice) composed the music for many French, American and British films, e.g. Passport to Pimlico (1949) and The Lavender Hill Mob (1951).

MEMORABLE MOMENTS The first glimpse of Death's Rolls-Royce stopping outside the café.

Orphée's opening the avant-garde magazine Nudisme to discover that all its pages are blank.

The handpiece of the telephone floating back into the holder after Heurtebise takes a call from the police inspector.

Heurtebise and Orphée floating along a wall in the Zone.

Death and Heurtebise being led away at the end.

KEY LINES

Man in café to Orphée: 'Your trouble is knowing just how far to go too far.'

The Princess: 'The role of the dreamer is to accept his dreams.'

The Princess: 'What are you staring at, Cégiste? Did you expect a shroud and a scythe?'

Heurtebise: 'Mirrors are the doors by which death comes?'

The Princess: 'Perhaps he sleeps and dreams us. We are his bad dreams.'

OUT OF THE PAST (UK TITLE: BUILD MY GALLOWS HIGH)

US, 1947, RKO, 96 MINS

D JACQUES TOURNEUR; **SC** GEOFFREY HOMES (FROM HIS NOVEL BUILD MY GALLOWS HIGH); **PH** (BW) NICHOLAS MUSURACA; **M** ROY WEBB; **ED** SAMUEL E. BEETLEY

CAST ROBERT MITCHUM (JEFF BAILEY), JANE GREER (KATHIE MOFFETT), KIRK DOUGLAS (WHIT STERLING), RHONDA FLEMING (META CARSON), STEVE BRODIE (FISHER), VIRGINIA HUSTON (ANN)

'You started this and you'll end it. Besides Joe couldn't find a prayer in a Bible.'

THE STORY World-weary ex-private-eye Jeff Bailey, attempting to start a new life with Ann, a small-town girlfriend in California's Sierra Nevada, is tracked down by a henchman of sadistic gambler Whit Sterling. Flashbacks reveal that Sterling had hired Bailey to trace his mistress, Kathie, who had shot him and fled with $40,000. Pursuing her to Mexico, Jeff falls for her and together they go on the run to San Francisco where the treacherous Kathie kills Jeff's crooked partner and involves Jeff in a complex intrigue that leads to the grave.

THE FILM One of the great film noir thrillers, it contrasts (in the manner of eighteenth-century English fiction) the wholesome, boring countryside against the wicked, alluring town; the cold, repressive United States against the torrid, liberating Mexico.

Insidiously presenting the world of nightclubs, irregular occupations and unsanctified relationships as more desirable than settled, middle-class family life, the movie goes to the cruel heart of American *noir*. The moral retribution demanded by Hollywood's Hays Office Code happily coincides with the filmmakers' world view, leading to an ending of tragic finality far more satisfying than most American movies.

ODD/SALIENT FACTS Dick Powell was originally announced to play the leading role. Geoffrey Homes is a pseudonym for the left-wing novelist Daniel Mainwaring who wrote several screenplays under his own name, including those for *The Lawless* (Joseph Losey, 1950), *Invasion of the Bodysnatchers* (Don Siegel, 1956) and *Baby Face Nelson* (Don Siegel, 1957). Jane Greer has a cameo role in *Against the Odds* (Taylor Hackford, 1984), a remake of *Out of the Past* in which Jeff Bridges and James Woods replace Robert Mitchum and Kirk Douglas.

MEMORABLE MOMENTS Kathie's first appearance, wearing a white broad-brimmed hat, entering from the sun-drenched street into the dark Acapulco bar where Jeff awaits her.

The couple on a silvery moonlit beach, framed by fishing nets that symbolize both the trap they are in and the spider's web into which Kathie has lured Jeff.

▼ *OUT OF THE PAST* Brunette enchantress Jane Greer emerges from the shadows to re-enter private eye Mitchum's life.

KEY LINES

Jeff: 'I never saw her in the daytime. We seemed to live by night. What was left of the day went away like a pack of cigarettes you smoked.'

Whit: 'You started this and you'll end it. Besides Joe couldn't find a prayer in a Bible.'

Kathie: 'Jeff, you ought to have killed me for what I did a moment ago.'
Jeff: 'There's time.'

PANDORA'S BOX
GERMANY, 1929, NERO FILM A.G., 140 MINS (ALTERNATIVE VERSIONS 120 AND 131 MINS)
D *G. W. PABST;* **PR** *GEORGE C. HORSETZKY;* **SC** *LADISLAUS VAJDA, JOSEPH R. FLIESNER FROM THE PLAYS* ERDGEIST *AND* DIE BÜCHSE DER PANDORA *BY FRANK WEDEKIND;* **PH** *(BW) GÜNTHER KRAMPF;* **M** *CURTIS IVAN SALKE;* **ED** *JOSEPH R. FLIESLER*
CAST *LOUISE BROOKS (LULU), FRITZ KORNER (DR PETER SCHÖN), FRANZ LEDERER (ALWA SCHÖN), CARL GÖTZ (SCHIGOLCH, PAPA BROMMER), ALICE ROBERTS (COUNTESS ANNA GESCHWITZ), DAISY D'ORA (MARIE DE ZARNIKO), KRAFFT RASCHIG (RODRIGO QUAST), MICHAEL VON NEWLINSKY (MARQUIS CASTI-PIANI), SIEGFRIED ARNO (STAGE MANAGER), GUSTAV DIESSL (JACK THE RIPPER)*

THE STORY Lulu, a prostitute, hopes to marry the prosperous newspaper owner, Schön, and is upset by his engagement to Marie Adelaide de Zarniko. At the theatre where she is due to appear in a revue, Lulu is inflamed with jealousy and refuses to go on. Schön appeases her and the two are discovered in a passionate embrace by Marie and Alwa. Schön and Lulu marry, but on their wedding night Lulu shoots and kills Schön. The subsequent trial descends into chaos and Lulu escapes with the help of Schigolch, Rodrigo and Alwa. This mismatched quartet survive blackmail and a three-month stay on a gambling boat before ending up in a seedy garret in London. There, Lulu, working as a prostitute is killed by Jack the Ripper.
THE FILM This film, distilled from two Wedekind plays, is remarkable for several reasons, first for being the only film for which a gifted director and iconic star are widely remembered. Pabst's use of an elliptical narrative technique, brilliant lighting

▲ *PANDORA'S BOX Louise Brooks as Lulu, the role that both defined and effectively finished her career.*

and complex sight-lines create an unsettling effect but his film would hardly be talked of today were it not for an inspired piece of casting in the central role. Louise Brooks was a 23-year-old former dancer who had appeared in a handful of Hollywood films, one alongside W. C. Fields, before appearing in what she saw as an 'unimportant part' in Howard Hawks's *A Girl In Every Port* (1928). This role brought her to the attention of Pabst who saw her as perfect for the role of the destructive and self-destructive prostitute, Lulu. Her performance retains its erotic charge and created the cult of Lulu, or Loulou. Brooks herself would work hard for the rest of her life to cultivate this enigmatic persona.

ODD/SALIENT FACTS Brooks returned to Hollywood after making one more film for Pabst and another in France but found that her status there had been harmed by her having abandoned her contract with Paramount, and she gradually withdrew from films, making her last appearance in 1938. She slipped into obscurity working as a storegirl in New York before her repu-

tation was revised and her cult status assured by the revival of several of her films in the 1950s. She studied cinema and began to publish autobiographical and critical pieces for film journals, a collection of which were published as *Lulu in Hollywood*. Louise Brooks's status as an icon was enhanced in a series of profiles, most notably by Kenneth Tynan (whose wife, the late Kathleen Tynan, wrote a screenplay about their affair, soon to be filmed), and cemented by cult director Jonathan Demme's *Something Wild* (1986). One of the best of the mid-eighties mini-genre of 'yuppie nightmare' movies, this tells the story of Jeff Daniels' urban wimp being transported on an ever more dangerous adventure by fantasist Lulu played by Melanie Griffiths, complete with Louise Brooks black bob wig.

MEMORABLE MOMENTS Backstage at the theatre, Schön and his fiancée are enjoying the frenetic action. Marie and then Schön stare at Lulu and she stares back, suddenly so upset that she refuses to go onstage: 'I'll dance for the whole world, but not in front of that woman.' Pabst ignores the grammar of film here to have the characters captured from different angles making it appear as if they are all three staring in the same direction.

When Marie finds her fiancé kissing in the back room, Lulu can't suppress her delighted smile and Schön declares: 'This is my execution.'

The murder scene itself is filmed with Schön's back filling almost the entire screen, so that we see Lulu's head and realize the shot has been fired only from the wisp of smoke rising between the two of them.

KEY LINES

Louise Brooks wrote: 'The finest job of casting G. W. Pabst ever did was casting himself as the director, the Animal Trainer of his adaptation of Wedekind's "tragedy of monsters".'

This insinuation of director into the story is echoed in the film. Directly after the murder scene we cut to the last words of the defence speech which suggests what the film has shown: 'Honoured Court: in a rapid series of pictures I have shown you a fearful destiny.' The prosecution responds: 'Honoured court – gentlemen of the jury. The Greek gods created a woman, Panndora. She is beautiful, enticing, well versed in the arts of flattery.'

PEEPING TOM

UK, 1960, ANGLO-AMALGAMATED, 103 MINS

D/PR MICHAEL POWELL; **SC** LEO MARKS; **PH** OTTO HELLER;
M BRIAN EASDALE; **ED** NORMAN ACKLAND
CAST CARL BOEHM (MARK LEWIS), MOIRA SHEARER (VIVIAN),
ANNA MASSEY (HELEN STEPHENS), MAXINE AUDLEY (MRS
STEPHENS), ESMOND KNIGHT (ARTHUR BADEN), BARTLET MULLINS
(MR PETERS), BRENDA BRUCE (DORA), MARTIN MILLER (DR
ROSEN), PAMELA GREEN (MILLIE), MICHAEL POWELL (PROFESSOR
A. N. LEWIS), SHIRLEY ANNE FIELD (PAULINE SHIELDS), MICHAEL
GOODLIFFE (DON JARVIS), JACK WATSON (CHIEF INSPECTOR
GREGG), NIGEL DAVENPORT (DET. SGT. MILLER), MILES
MALLESON (CUSTOMER IN NEWSAGENT'S)

THE STORY The reclusive Mark Lewis's tenants in his London
house include Helen, a librarian attracted to Mark, and her
blind mother, who distrusts him. Mark works at a film studio and
aims to eventually direct movies, and has a projection room and
laboratory at home. He has two clandestine projects: taking
nude photographs in a sleazy studio above a newsagent's, and
filming women at the moment of death; they see their faces in
a mirror as the knife in the camera tripod plunges into their
throats. The death of a prostitute in Central London, and of
Vivian, a stand-in at 'Chipperfield Studios', alert Scotland Yard
to the presence of a serial killer. It is revealed that Mark's father
was a biologist interested in the physiology of fear. He experi-
mented on the young Mark, observing his reactions when
suddenly finding a lizard on his bed, seeing his mother's corpse,
or meeting his father's new young wife. Mark is told by a psychiatrist that his father was doing research into voyeurism or
scopophilia, 'the morbid desire to gaze', only curable with
years of treatment. That night Mark, now under police surveil-
lance, murders his third victim, and returning home finds Helen
horrified at the film of Vivian's death. Mark tells her all and com-
pletes his film by photographing the arrival of the police and
his own suicide using the method employed on his victims. The
last words are from a tape-recording of Mark the child saying:
'Goodnight Daddy'.

THE FILM Peeping Tom retains its capacity to shock, disgust,
slyly amuse, and to shame us, the movie audience, into recog-
nizing that every time we enter the cinema we become voyeurs.
This is Hitchcock's *Rear Window* with the velvet glove removed
from the steel fist. It's a bizarre collaboration between one of

the great geniuses of the cinema and a British studio known for
low-budget exploitation flicks, that had just launched a series of
low-brow farces with *Carry On Sergeant*. For nearly thirty years
Powell, the romantic Englishman, had collaborated with Emeric
Pressburger, the ironic Mittel-European, on some of the most
sophisticated pictures ever made in Britain, *A Matter of Life and
Death* and *The Red Shoes* among them. The partnership was
dissolved in 1956 and neither did anything of consequence in
the last three decades of life apart from *Peeping Tom*, one of
the most savage works ever made about film and the film business, by someone fascinated and disgusted by film in equal
measure.

Peeping Tom is deliberately cheap-looking, glibly edited,
and much of the acting is coarse-grained. It is a picture about
a film company run by a cost-cutting studio boss with contempt
for his own product. Mark's friend frequents the Everyman
Cinema in Hampstead and reads *Sight and Sound*, but is also

▼ PEEPING TOM *Duffel-coated homicidal photographer Carl
Boehm returns to the scene of the crime.*

162

a connoisseur of porn photographs. Mark's other employer, the newsagent, sells obscene pictures to respectable readers of *The Times* and *Daily Telegraph*.

The film divided critics, most of whom loathed it ('this beastly picture', C. A. Lejeune, *Observer*), some admired it ('a masterpiece', *Sunday Times*), and it rapidly developed a cult following. The idea that the vilification ended Powell's career is a myth.

ODD/SALIENT FACTS Powell put himself at the centre by playing Mark's father and using his own son as the young Mark. The screenwriter Leo Marks was apparently trying to exorcise demons from his role in wartime espionage when he had to send people to their deaths. Powell chose Newman Passage (off Upper Rathbone Place, north of Oxford Street) for the pre-credit sequence murder of the prostitute because that was where he shot the first scene on location in his directorial debut, *Two Crowded Hours* (1931). Anna Massey had her first substantial film role in *Peeping Tom*.

MEMORABLE MOMENTS The prostitute realizing that she is the cameraman's victim just as the spectator recognizes that the camera eye resembles the assassin's beady lens.

The monochrome home-movie footage of the lizard dropped on young Mark's bed like a creature in *Jurassic Park*.

The blind Mrs Stephens standing between screen and projector, sensing something evil.

Mark showing Helen his instrument of death, her face hideously distorted in the mirror.

KEY LINES

Helen: 'I like to understand what I'm shown. What was your father trying to do?'

Helen: 'Mark are you crazy?'
Mark: 'Yes, do you think they'll notice?'

Mrs Stephens: 'All this filming isn't healthy. Get some help Mark.'

Mark: 'Do you know what the most frightening thing in the world is? It's fear.'

Two cops in final sequence: 'It's only a camera.'
'Only?'

PERFORMANCE★
UK, 1970, WARNER BROS/GOODTIME ENTERPRISES, 105 MINS

D DONALD CAMMELL, NICOLAS ROEG; **PR** SANFORD LIEBERSON; **SC** DONALD CAMMELL; **PH** (COL) NICOLAS ROEG; **M** JACK NITZSCHE; **ED** ANTHONY GIBBS, BRIAN SMEDLEY-ASTON
CAST JAMES FOX (CHAS), MICK JAGGER (TURNER), ANITA PALLENBERG (PHERBER), MICHELLE BRETON (LUCY), ANN SIDNEY (DANA), JOHN BINDON (MOODY), STANLEY MEADOWS (ROSEBLOOM), ALAN CUTHBERTSON (THE LAWYER), ANTHONY MORTON (DENNIS), JOHNNY SHANNON (HARRY FLOWERS), ANTHONY VALENTINE (JOEY MADDOCKS), KEN COLLEY (TONY FARRELL), JOHN STERLAND (THE CHAUFFEUR), LARRAINE WICKENS (LARRAINE)

THE STORY Chas is an enforcer working for gay gangster Harry Flowers. When Chas kills Joey, he

'*I am a bullet.*'

goes into hiding in the basement flat of decadent, reclusive pop star Turner. Turner, involved in a sexual *ménage à trois*, sees the violent Chas as a kind of alter ego, and sets about dismantling him with drugs and mind games. Just before Chas is taken away by his old cronies, he shoots Turner, but as the car pulls away, it is Turner's face that looks out at the camera.

THE FILM *Performance* marks the directorial debut for both Cammell and Roeg. The former was a successful painter who turned to film-making as a more vibrant art form. Roeg was a distinguished cinematographer who had shot, among others *The Masque of the Red Death* (1964), *Fahrenheit 451* (1966) and *Far From the Madding Crowd* (1967). The background to the story is the new social fluidity of the time in England. Sex, drugs and money facilitated a coming together of the aristocracy, show business, particularly actors and rock stars, and gangsters in a hip new demi-monde. Early cuts of the film had a clear two-part structure of roughly equal weight given to the gangster material and the sex and drugs and rock 'n' roll, with the actors on either side knowing little or nothing of the rest of the film. The need to trim the first half helped reinforce a quality that was already in the later scenes and would mark the few remaining Cammell and Roeg movies of the 1970s. Cammell's belief that time itself was an illusion is conveyed by sudden jump-cuts and jarring temporal juxtapositions. The other central thrust of the film is the notion of spiritual twinning, diametrically opposed characters being halves of a whole, parallel to the social mixing, a blurring of the distinctions in gender, sexuality, light and dark. The relationship between Chas and Turner is symbiotic and destructive, a dark melding of the personalities of two performers.

ODD/SALIENT FACTS During the shoot, the Notting Hill house set became a scene for the blurring of the barriers between art and life. In this closed environment, the actors were kept away from natural light and Cammell and Jagger set about the deconstruction of Fox's ego in replication of the on-screen drama. This they achieved so effectively that Fox withdrew first from their social milieu, but then from acting itself. He worked as a Christian evangelist throughout the 1970s, only returning to the screen in the mid-1980s. Off-screen tensions arose between Jagger and his own glimmer twin, Keith Richards, over the authenticity of the intimate sex scenes between Jagger and Pallenberg, Keef's then girlfriend. There was a persistent rumour that the bullet's-eye shot as Chas shoots Turner was achieved by placing a camera between Pallenberg's legs and doing a zoom shot of her vagina. The myth is apparently unfounded, although its spread was presumably encouraged by the filmmakers themselves. A further rumour has it that the shot was achieved by a zoom shot into the bullet wound of a corpse. Cammell's own post-*Performance* career was one largely of frustration, with only two completed films, *The Demon Seed* (1977) and *White of the Eye* (1987). *Performance* is the work of a man obsessed with mirrors, questions of identity and death. Cammell had always planned to end his life by suicide, unable to contemplate the randomness of a natural death. In 1995, professionally frustrated by the post-production problems with *Wild Side* (1996), Cammell shot himself in the head, and survived without pain for perhaps 45 minutes, during which time he asked for a mirror so that he could watch himself die.

MEMORABLE MOMENTS Turner, Pherber and Lucy share a bath and plaster on to one another the notes that Chas has given them.

As Pherber questions Chas about his identity she holds a mirror against his chest, so that it looks as if he has her breast, and against his face, so that he seems to have half of her face.

The climactic shooting in which the fatal bullet enters Turner's head, travelling along some apparently pre-existing tunnel before smashing through a photograph of the great Argentinian writer Jorge Luis Borges.

It is said that Cammell's dying words were: 'Did you see Borges?'

KEY LINES

Chas to Harry Flowers: 'I know who I am, Harry.'

Chas, just before killing Joey: 'I am a bullet.'

Turner to Chas: 'The only performance that makes it, that really makes it, that makes it all the way, is the one that achieves madness.'

PIMPERNEL SMITH
UK, 1941, BRITISH NATIONAL, 121 MINS

D LESLIE HOWARD; **PR** LESLIE HOWARD; **SC** ANATOLE DE GRUNWALD, ROLAND PERTWEE BASED ON A STORY BY A. G. MCDONELL AND WOLFGANG WILHELM; **PH** MUTZ GREENBAUM; **M** JOHN GREENWOOD; **ED** SIDNEY COLE

CAST LESLIE HOWARD (PROFESSOR HORATIO SMITH), MARY MORRIS (LUDMILLA KOSLOWSKI), FRANCIS L. SULLIVAN (GENERAL VON GRAUM), HUGH MCDERMOTT (DAVID MAXWELL), RAYMOND HUNTLEY (MARX), MANNING WHILEY (BERTIE GREGSON), DAVID TOMLINSON (STEVE), PETER GAWTHORNE (SIDIMIR KOSLOWSKI), ALLAN JEAYES (DR BECKENDORF), DENNIS ARUNDELL (HOFFMAN), PHILIP FRIEND (SPENCER), JOAN KEMP-WELCH (SCHOOLTEACHER), LAWRENCE KITCHIN (CLARENCE ELSTEAD), BASIL APPLEBY (JOCK MCINTYRE), PERCY WALSH (DVORAK), ROLAND PERTWEE (SIR GEORGE SMITH), CHARLES PATON (STEINHOF), AUBREY MALLALIEU (THE DEAN), GEORGE STREET (SCHMIDT), A. E. MATTHEWS (EARL OF MEADOWBROOK), BRIAN HERBERT (JAROMIR), ARTHUR HAMBLING (JORDAN)

THE STORY Berlin, spring 1939. A scientist is rescued from Nazi Germany by a mystery man who whistles 'There Is a Tavern in the Town' and carries a calling card that reads: 'The mind of man is bounded only by the universe.' Cut to Cambridge University where the dreamy, misogynist Professor Horatio Smith teaches archaeology. He takes six of his students along with him on a trip to Germany to investigate an ancient Aryan civilization. They spend a night at a chalet by the Swiss border across which another man escapes the Nazis late one night with the help of the mysterious, whistling benefactor.

▲ PIMPERNEL SMITH *Professor Smith explains the finer points of British humour to an uncomprehending General von Graum (Francis L. Sullivan).*

Meanwhile General von Graum hatches a plot to catch him. The man disguised as a scarecrow is shot in the arm while helping a pianist escape. Smith's pupils finally realize that Smith is the hero and insist on helping him. Von Graum tries to trap the mystery man with the help of Ludmilla, the daughter of a prisoner of the Nazis. She identifies Smith, but the two fall in love and he resolves to help her father escape. This he does with the aid of his students, under the noses of the Germans and, having disproved the existence of an Aryan civilization, escapes himself.

THE FILM Leslie Howard went into acting largely as therapy to help him counter the shell shock he suffered in the First World War. Having established himself as a major star on both sides of the Atlantic, he returned to England at the outbreak of the Second World War. The character of Smith is a fusion of two of his most popular pre-war roles, Sir Percy Blakeney from *The Scarlet Pimpernel* (1935) and Professor Higgins from *Pygmalion* (1938). The heroism of the former is joined to the intellect and initial misogyny of the latter. It remains a sparklingly entertaining piece of propaganda which, apart from its influence on the mood of the audience at the time, had a major effect in shaping one of the most popular franchises of modern Hollywood. The idea of an archaeologist hero who leads a double life as a staid professor and a bold adventurer battling the Nazis

inspired George Lucas and Steven Spielberg to invent their own character, Indiana Jones.

ODD/SALIENT FACTS The impact of Howard's propaganda work in general, and particularly with *Pimpernel Smith* and his subsequent film *First of the Few* (1942), was tremendous. It remains unclear whether Howard's plane, returning from a secret mission to Lisbon on 1 June 1943, was shot down because the Nazis believed that Churchill was aboard, or simply to eradicate Howard himself, who was, according to his son Ronald 'Britain's most powerful and effective propagandist'. The film has been interpreted as a specifically Christian fable with Smith described by his students as 'the greatest man in the Universe', being identified by his wounded wrist and finally vowing to return. But its culthood lies in the iconic status and death of Howard and the striking effect the film had on the young Swedish diplomat Raoul Wallenberg, who went on to save the lives of thousands of Hungarian Jews from the Nazis (Howard's own father was a Hungarian Jew). In *Righteous Gentile*, his biography of Wallenberg, John Bierman writes of how in the winter of 1942 Wallenberg went with his half-sister to a special screening of the film at the British embassy in Stockholm: 'Wallenberg identified strongly with Howard's quiet, pipe-smoking Professor Smith, whom he physically resembled. "On the way home he told me that was just the kind of thing he would like to do," Nina Lagergren recalls. By an astonishing twist of fate, Wallenberg was to get his chance.'

MEMORABLE MOMENTS The shooting of the scarecrow followed by silence and the discreet trickle of blood from its wrist.

Smith's final escape from under the spotlight at the station, gone with a wisp of smoke.

KEY LINES

Smith: 'No I hate violence. It seems such a paradox to kill a man before you can persuade him what's right.'

Smith, explaining his reasons for helping others escape: 'You see, when a man holds the view that progress and civilization depend in every age upon the hands and brains of a few exceptional spirits, it's rather hard to stand by and see them destroyed.'

Smith's final assurance to von Graum: 'Don't worry. I'll be back. We'll all be back.'

PINK FLAMINGOS★

US, 1972, SALIVA FILMS, 95 MINS

D JOHN WATERS; **PR** JOHN WATERS; **SC** JOHN WATERS;
PH JOHN WATERS; **M** VARIOUS; **ED** JOHN WATERS

CAST DIVINE (DIVINE/BABS JOHNSON), DAVID LOCHARY
(RAYMOND MARVEL), MINK STOLE (CONNIE MARVEL), MARY
VIVIAN PEARCE (COTTON), EDITH MASSEY (MAMA EDIE), DANNY
MILLS (CRACKERS), CHANNING WILROY (CHANNING), COOKIE
MUELLER (COOKIE), PAUL SWIFT (EGGMAN), SUSAN WALSH (FIRST
KIDNAPPED WOMAN), LINDA OLGEIRSON (SECOND KIDNAPPED
WOMAN)

THE STORY Divine/Babs Johnson, lives with her super-trailer-trash family – the relatively normal Cotton (her egg-obsessed mother) and mentally retarded son Crackers – and rejoices in her reputation as the filthiest person alive. This title is challenged by her rivals, the homicidal, drug and porn-peddling Marvels. They track down Divine by arranging for Cookie to have sex with Crackers and a live chicken. They send Divine a turd as a birthday gift. At the party, Mama Edie marries the eggman, and when the police, who have been called by the Marvels, arrive, they are killed and eaten. Divine and Crackers get revenge on the Marvels by licking their furniture, and release Channing, who had been locked in a closet for spying on the Marvels having sex. Channing is in turn castrated by the two pregnant women who had been locked in the Marvels' basement. When she finds that the Marvels have burnt down the family's trailer, Divine tars and feathers them and, in front of journalists, shoots them. Moving to Boise, Idaho, Divine cements her reputation as the filthiest person in the world by eating dog shit.

THE FILM John Waters was born in Baltimore and dropped out of NYU's film school to begin his career as a genius of painstakingly tasteless low-budget film-making. He has proved himself, whatever the people behind *Serial Mom* (1994) may have thought, incapable of working within the mainstream. *Pink Flamingos* is the purest expression of his unique talents and was trumpeted by the director himself as 'the most disgusting picture of all time'. The film's and the director's desire to appal with every scene is somehow infantile, but the film has an undeniable potency and a unique brand of humour. The final sequence is still genuinely disgusting, as is the perverse chicken-fucking scene. *Pink Flamingos* is the film that launched Waters and Divine as major cult figures. It remains a kind of masterpiece of

schlock, an essay in gross-out, an exercise in defining and then surpassing limits of tastelessness.

ODD/SALIENT FACTS Waters is Quentin Crisp's favourite current director. The mayor of Baltimore declared 7 February 1985 as 'John Waters Day'. Dedicated to trash in all its forms, Waters attempted to revive the short-lived Fifties cinematic vogue for smellovision. *Polyester* (1981) was released in Odorama, with a scratch and sniff card for each member of the audience with its smells including gas, smelly socks and, inevitably, a fart. In a recent questionnaire in *Vanity Fair* magazine, Waters' response to the question, 'If you could choose what to come back as, what would it be?', was: 'A mirror in a Douglas Sirk film.'

MEMORABLE MOMENTS The one scene for which Waters will always be remembered, and for which his and Divine's names will go down in the annals of grotesqueness, is the shit-eating climax. Divine said in an interview for Image in 1977 of having to perform for the sequence: 'Well, I thought about it and checked with doctors and things and they said it really wouldn't hurt me or do anything to me. It was strictly done for shock value. I threw up afterward, and then I used mouthwash and brushed my teeth. There was no aftertaste of anything. I just forgot about it as quickly as I could.'

KEY LINES

Connie: 'There are two kinds of people, my kind and
    assholes.'

*Divine, on discovering her birthday present from the
    Marvels:* 'Someone has sent me a bowel movement.'
Crackers: 'No one sends you a turd and expects to live.'

PLAN 9 FROM OUTER SPACE

US, 1959, WADE WILLIAMS PRODUCTIONS, 79 MINS

PR/D/SC/ED EDWARD D. WOOD JR; **PH** WILLIAM THOMPSON;
M SUPERVISOR GORDON ZAHLER

CAST TOR JOHNSON (INSPECTOR CLAY), VAMPIRA (VAMPIRE GIRL),
BELA LUGOSI (GHOUL MAN), GREGORY WALCOTT (JEFF TRENT),
MONA MCKINNON (PAULA TRENT), TOM KEENE (COL.
EDWARDS), DUKE MOORE (LT. HARPER), DUDLEY MANLOVE
(EROS), JOANNA LEE (TANNA), JOHN 'BUNNY' BRECKINRIDGE
(THE RULER), LYLE TALBOT (THE GENERAL), DAVID DEMEEERING
(DANNY, CO-PILOT), CRISWELL (HIMSELF)

THE STORY Criswell, the TV clairvoyant, tops and tails the movie, assuring the audience that 'future events like these will affect your future' and that every 'incident is based on sworn testimony'. Extraterrestrials Eros and Tanna descend on earth in their flying saucer at the behest of their Ruler to prevent the earthlings destroying the universe by harnessing sunlight. They are observed flying into Los Angeles by airline pilot Jeff Trent, but he is sworn to silence by Federal authorities, who rally the army to repel the invasion from outer space. At a San Fernando Valley cemetery, near the home of Jeff and his wife Paula, the aliens activate the bodies of a recently dead couple, who become the Vampire Girl and the Ghoul Man, and kill the detective, Inspector Clay, who is investigating the deaths of two gravediggers. Trent, a police lieutenant and an army colonel are lured into the flying saucer, debate with the visitors, and escape just before it takes off and explodes in the air over Los Angeles.

THE FILM By general agreement *Plan 9 From Outer Space* (aka *Graverobbers From Outer Space*) is the worst movie by the world's worst director, Edward D. Wood Jr. (1922–78), the cult director of all time, promoted by Harry and Michael Medved on TV and in their influential book *The Golden Turkey Awards* (1980) and apotheosized by Tim Burton in his cinebiography *Ed Wood* (1994) starring Johnny Depp as the producer/director/writer/editor. The movie has a mesmerising awfulness: wooden acting, performers bumping into the flimsy sets, incoherent plotting and ludicrous dialogue. It takes a genius of sorts to make a movie so badly and Wood's admirer Burton is incapable of matching it, just as he could only improve on the 1950s SF films he sends up in *Mars Attacks* (1996). Oddly, Depp is less attractive on screen than the conventionally good-looking Wood. Yet the issues it touches on are those of the angst-ridden SF films of the time and Wood thought of himself as an auteur, a follower of Orson Welles. An alcoholic transvestite, Wood is surrounded by a cast of similar ineptitude including the ex-wrestler Tor Johnson, the camp TV personality Criswell, and the flagrantly gay Bunny Breckinridge, who was on his way to Mexico for a sex-change operation when he was drawn into playing the extraterrestrial Ruler. The film's 'music supervisor' selected the music from available records. Every expense was spared; the same wall with different curtains was used for the cabin in an airliner and the flying saucers were painted hub-caps. Bela Lugosi, a cult figure from the moment he appeared in Tod Browning's *Dracula* (1931), was a drug addict whose career was in terminal decline when he met his admirer Wood and appeared in *Glenn or Glenda* and *Bride of the Monster*. He is billed as a Guest Star in *Plan 9* because he died after one day's shooting and only appears in two early scenes before being killed in an off-screen road accident. As a corpse resurrected by aliens he is played by a stand-in (Tom Mason, a hypnotist and chiropractor), his face covered by a cloak.

ODD/SALIENT FACTS *Plan 9* was financed by Southern Baptists in order to raise funds for a series of religious movies and at their insistence Wood and his cast were baptised by full immersion in a swimming pool. Wood ended his career making hardcore porn films and writing pornographic novels, one of them called *Captain Fellatio Hornblower*.

MEMORABLE MOMENTS Tor Johnson's arrival to investigate the killings at the cemetery, his thick accent and stiff movements matched only by the woodenness of the cops.

The effete alien Ruler in an office that resembles a fortune-teller's tent being greeted by his two followers with a cross-armed salute.

KEY LINES
Jeff Trent: 'I saw a flying saucer.'
Paula Trent: 'Saucer – you mean the kind up there?'

▼ *PLAN 9 FROM OUTER SPACE* Ed Wood regulars Tor Johnson and Vampira succumb to extra-terrestrial powers.

Lt. Harper: 'One thing's for sure. Inspector Clay is dead. Murdered. And someone's responsible.'

The Ruler: 'Plan 9? Ah, yes. Plan 9 deals with the resurrection of the dead. Long distance electrodes shot into the pineal and pituitary gland of the recently dead.'

POINT BLANK

US, 1967, MGM, 92 MINS

D *JOHN BOORMAN;* **PR** *JUDD BERNARD, ROBERT CHARTOFF;* **SC** *ALEXANDER JACOBS, DAVID NEWHOUSE, RAFE NEWHOUSE (FROM THE NOVEL* THE HUNTER *BY RICHARD STARK);* **PH** *(COL, PANAVISION) PHILIP H. LATHROP;* **M** *JOHNNY MANDELL;* **ED** *HENRY BERMAN*

CAST *LEE MARVIN (WALKER), ANGIE DICKINSON (CHRIS), KEENAN WYNN (YOST), CARROLL O'CONNOR (BREWSTER), LLOYD BOCHNER (CARTER), MICHAEL STRONG (STEGMAN), JOHN VERNON (MAL REESE), SHARON ACKER (LYNNE), JAMES B. SIKKING (HIRED GUN)*

THE STORY Walker, a professional criminal, is double-crossed by his wife, Lynne, and his best friend, Reese, and left to die in a cell in the abandoned Alcatraz where they have hi-jacked a cash drop for the crime syndicate. But the badly wounded Walker makes his way to the sea and two years later on a tourist boat circumnavigating Alcatraz he meets Yost, a mystery man, who tells him that Reese is now working for the Organization and living with Lynne in Los Angeles. He pursues them there, and with Yost hovering in the background, he works his way up rung-by-rung through the anonymous Organization in search of the $93,000 he's owed. His wife commits suicide shortly after he's tracked her down; her sister Chris is used as bait to get to Reese, who falls naked from the balcony of his penthouse while grappling with Walker. Eventually Brewster, number two man in the Organization, leads Walker back to Alcatraz to pick up his money. But Brewster is shot, Yost reveals himself as Fairfax, head of the Organization, and Walker withdraws into an empty cell.

THE FILM This seminal thriller, one of the first to be made after Hollywood abandoned the Hays Office Code, introduced the techniques of the French New Wave to American cinema and most particularly flashback techniques associated with Alain

Resnais, who in *La Guerre est fini* used flash-forwards to suggest alternative routes the hero's life might take. It may well be that, as with Ambrose Bierce's Civil War story 'An Occurrence at Owl Creek Bridge', *Point Blank* might be going on in the mind of the dying Walker. The film is a devastating account of an angry, lone avenger up against a criminal syndicate, the Organisation, run by neatly dressed men with Waspish names who work in polished boardrooms behind the reflective facades of skyscrapers, carry credit cards, and support worthy causes. It is in fact an image of American corporate society that was prospering while an insane war was being fought in Vietnam and violence raged in the cities across the nation.

ODD/SALIENT FACTS Director John Boorman (whose only previous work for the big screen was the 1965 Dave Clark Five picture, *Catch Us If You Can*) became involved in the project while gathering material in Los Angeles for a BBC documentary on D. W. Griffith. He established immediate rapport with Lee Marvin (then making *The Dirty Dozen* in England), who used his position as number one box-office attraction to have Boorman get carte blanche to rewrite the script and direct and edit in an innovative fashion. It was Marvin's idea that in the reunion scene with his wife she alone would speak, giving answers to Walker's unspoken questions. This was the first film to use Alcatraz Island after the prison was closed in 1963 and possibly the first to

▼ *POINT BLANK World-weary avenger Lee Martin between worried sister-in-law Angie Dickinson and anxious gang boss Carroll O'Connor.*

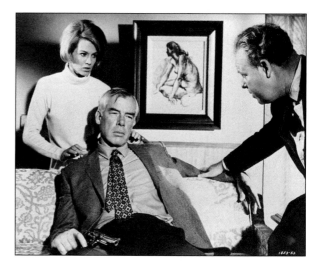

have a major scene (a double killing) set in the Los Angeles storm drains. Underlying much of Boorman's work is the story of the Grail legend and he saw Walker, Lynne and Reese as modern versions of Arthur, Guinevere and Lancelot. James B. Sikking, who plays a cool, pipe-smoking assassin, found fame on TV in *Hill Street Blues* and the film had a considerable influence on other moviemakers, most notably Walter Hill and Michael Mann. *The Hunter* is one of a series of books about a gangland loner called Parker, written by Donald E. Westlake under the pseudonym of Richard Stark. Jean-Luc Godard filmed Stark's *The Jugger* as *Made in U.S.A.* (1966).

MEMORABLE MOMENTS Cross-cutting between Walker striding along a corridor at Los Angeles airport and his wife visiting a beauty parlour, the only sound being his pounding footsteps.

Walker blasting away with his pistol at the empty bed his wife and best friend have shared.

Walker extracting information from a car salesman by taking him on a destructive, bone-shaking drive without a seat belt in one of his own cars.

Walker with a gun to Reese's head in the foreground as the naked Chris hastily dresses in the background.

KEY LINES

Lynne: 'How good it must be being dead. Is it?'

Chris: 'What's my last name?'
Walker: 'What's my first name?'

Fairfax to the dying Brewster: 'You should have stayed an accountant.'

THE PRODUCERS

US, 1967, SPRINGTIME/MGM/CROSSBOW, 88 MINS

D MEL BROOKS; **PR** SIDNEY GLAZIER; **SC** MEL BROOKS;
PH JOSEPH COFFEY; **M** JOHN MORRIS; **ED** RALPH ROSENBLUM
CAST ZERO MOSTEL (MAX BIALYSTOCK), GENE WILDER (LEO BLOOM), KENNETH MARS (FRANS LIEBKIND), ESTELLE WINWOOD ('HOLD ME, TOUCH ME'), RENÉE TAYLOR (EVA BRAUN), CHRISTOPHER HEWETT (ROGER DEBRIS), LEE MEREDITH (ULLA), ANDREAS VOUTSINAS (CARMEN GIYA), DICK SHAWN (LORENZO ST DUBOIS), JOSEPH ELLIC (VIOLINIST), MADLYN CATES (CONCIERGE), JOHN ZOLLER (DRAMA CRITIC), BILL HICKEY (FAILURE)

THE STORY Max Bialystock is a once-successful Broadway producer fallen on hard times. Leo Bloom, a neurotic accountant doing Bialystock's books, gives him the idea of over-financing a production that would be a guaranteed flop. After an exhaustive search the new partners find their play, *Springtime for Hitler*, and secure the rights from its unreconstructed Nazi author, Franz Liebkind. Bialystock visits his many elderly girlfriends and raises 25,000% of the play's budget. They hire the inept Roger DeBris as director and cast Lorenzo St DuBois, a spaced-out hippie, to play Hitler. Despite all their careful planning the play is a surprise smash. In desperation Bialystock, Bloom and the incensed Liebkind blow up the theatre in which the play is on. They are sent to prison where they repeat their fraudulent scam for the production of *Prisoners of Love*.

THE FILM Mel Brooks launched himself from the realm of the sketch (on film, television and record) into the world of the feature film with this brilliant near disaster about a failed disaster. In *When the Shooting Stops … the Cutting Begins*, his memoirs of a life in film-editing, Ralph Rosenblum outlines the chaotic, sometimes hostile atmosphere that Brooks engendered on his first film. What emerged from this chaos was an intermittently inspired comic near-masterpiece. The central plot of the deliberate, calculated courting of failure is an old one. The film plays with tastelessness, but its satirical intent is somehow diffused. It won't quite admit that its whole point is that it is tastelessness that succeeds, that there is nothing too base to be a triumph. The audience watching the film is allowed the sophisticated pleasure of laughing at the appallingness of the idea of the musical, 'a gay romp with Adolf and Eva at Berchtesgaden'. But not the people watching the play. As the camera moves across the audience, in a recreation of the famous Charles Addams cartoon, each member is frozen in open-mouthed shock, except for Franz Liebkind who is loving every moment. The success of the play comes via a technicality, the odd fact that the audience suddenly finds funny the anachronistic, hippie presentation of a fascist fantasy that has apparently been rewritten according to the whim of Lorenzo, a man so stoned that he can't remember his own name. Brooks himself has acknowledged that the film should have ended with the 'Springtime for Hitler' number. This is a crucial, but not fatal flaw in what remains a wonderfully funny film. Zero Mostel is hammy and large and genuinely misanthropic as the desperate, unlikely gigolo Bialystock. He and Wilder are hilarious in their first scene

together. In fact Gene Wilder has never been better than as Bloom, the role that made him, although his tendency towards sentimentality is already evident in the courtroom scene. With *Blazing Saddles* (1974) and *Young Frankenstein* (1974) Brooks would make slicker, smarter films but as a director he would never again come so close to genius.

ODD/SALIENT FACTS The film had the working title *Springtime for Hitler*, but Joseph E. Levine persuaded Brooks that this would mean commercial suicide. A compromise title of *Springtime for Mussolini* was rejected. The title was retained for the Swedish release and has been used for all Brooks's subsequent films (e.g. *Springtime for the Sheriff*, 1974; *Springtime for Frankenstein*, 1974). Dustin Hoffman was originally sought to play Liebkind, but instead opted to appear in *The Graduate* (1967).

MEMORABLE MOMENTS The elaborately staged Busby Berkeley-style musical number *Springtime for Hitler*. The couplet:

Don't be stupid, be a smarty
Come and join the Nazi party

is dubbed by Brooks himself. Brooks used the joke of the inappropriate musical treatment again in *History of the World – Part I*

▲ **THE PRODUCERS** *A chorus line of glamorous storm-troopers in full high-kicking glory for the film's musical show-stopper 'Springtime for Hitler'.*

(1981), in which he stages a musical version of the Spanish Inquisition.

KEY LINES

Bialystock soliciting Bloom's help: 'You can do it, you're in a noble profession. The word "count" is part of your title.'

Bialystock: 'What's the matter with you?'
Bloom: 'I'm hysterical. I'm having hysterics. I'm hysterical. I can't stop when I get like this. I can't stop. I'm hysterical. [Bialystock takes a glass of water and throws it at Bloom] I'm wet. I'm wet. I'm hysterical and I'm wet. [Bialystock slaps him in the face.] I'm in pain and I'm wet and I'm still hysterical.'
Liebkind: 'Hitler was a great painter. He could paint an entire apartment in one afternoon. Two coats.'

Bloom on DeBris: 'Is he good? I mean is he bad?'
Bialystock: 'He stinks. He is perhaps the worst director that ever lived. He's the only director whose plays close on the first day of rehearsals.'

Jury foreman: 'We find the defendants incredibly guilty.'

QUADROPHENIA

UK, 1979, THE WHO FILMS, 120 MINS

D *FRANC RODDAM;* **PR** *ROY BAIRD, BILL CURBISHLEY;* **EXEC PR** *THE WHO;* **SC** *DAVE HUMPHRIES, MARTIN STELLMAN, FRANC RODDAM;* **PH** *(COL) BRIAN TUFANO;* **M** *THE WHO PLUS VARIOUS ARTISTS;* **ED** *SEAN BARTON, MIKE TAYLOR*

CAST *PHIL DANIELS (JIMMY), MARK WINGETT (DAVE), PHILIP DAVIS (CHALKY), LESLIE ASH (STEPH), GARRY COOPER (PETE), TOYAH WILCOX (MONKEY), STING (ACE), TREVOR LAIRD (FERDY), KATE WILLIAMS (JIMMY'S MOTHER), MICHAEL ELPHICK (JIMMY'S FATHER), KIM NEVE (YVONNE), RAYMOND WINSTONE (KEVIN), GARY SHAIL (SPIDER)*

THE STORY By day Jimmy works as a mail boy for an advertising company, but at night and on weekends his life revolves around music, drugs, girls, his scooter and his Mod mates. He and his friends pop pills, gatecrash a party and have skirmishes with Rockers. On the Bank Holiday weekend Jimmy and his friends go to Brighton. The increasingly erratic Jimmy gets kicked out of a club. He spends the night staring at the sea. The next day everyone meets up and the gang wanders along the seafront. They set upon a gang of Rockers in a café. This leads to an all-out battle between the two groups and the police when they arrive in force. In the midst of the action, Jimmy and Mod-girl Steph sneak down an alley and have sex. Returning to the riot, Jimmy is arrested and shares a paddy wagon with Ace, the leader of the Mods. Back in London, Jimmy walks out of his job, and finds that Steph has now hooked up with Dave, one of his mates. He is kicked out of his home by his mum. Finally rejected by Steph, and having smashed up his scooter, he takes a load of pills and booze on the train to Brighton. Everything is quiet and he discovers that his idol, Ace, is working as a hotel bell-boy. He steals Ace's scooter and rides it along the chalk

▼ *QUADROPHENIA The gang's all here, l-r: Ferdy (Trevor Laird), Monkey (Toyah Wilcox), Chalky (Philip Davis), Ace (Sting), Steph (Leslie Ash), Jimmy (Phil Daniels), Spider (Gary Shail), Pete (Garry Cooper), Dave (Mark Wingett).*

cliffs. Suddenly he turns the bike and speeds towards the cliff. We see only the bike fly over the edge and land on the rocks below.

THE FILM This film came just four years after Ken Russell's dismal attempt to bring The Who's other rock opera, *Tommy* (1975), to the screen. Where that remained a musical, this is a narrative developed from the themes and central character devised by Pete Townshend. It is about growing pains and youth culture, with Jimmy an updated version of his namesake in *Rebel Without a Cause* (1955). He is torn between the need to belong and the need to establish his own identity. He seeks calm, spending much time staring into the canal or out to sea, but he is never happier than when speeding, riding his beloved Lambretta with his mates, dancing and fighting Rockers. His already split personality is further divided by drugs and his post-adolescent confusion leading to the four-way psychic split of the musically punning title. The film is an exhilarating expression of disaffection but also a touching story about the aimlessness and pointlessness of divisions among youth cults. In the scene in the baths where Jimmy and Kevin duel between 'Be-Bop-a-Lula' and 'You Really Got Me', the schism between Mods and Rockers is seen to be absurd. Kevin has been in the army, is unimpressed with artificial regimentation and is uninterested in mutually hostile cults. Jimmy tries to explain his philosophy: 'It isn't the bikes, is it? It's the people ... I don't wanna be the same as everybody else. That's why I'm a Mod, see. I mean, you gotta be somebody, ain't ya, otherwise you might as well jump in the sea and drown.' The two are essentially good friends and the revelation that Kevin is one of the Rockers being beaten up by his mates, deeply affects Jimmy. It represents the folly of a civil war with sides being allotted and families divided arbitrarily. This is another factor in Jimmy's mental ill health. Jimmy's sense of loss of identity leads him to contemplate jumping in the sea at the end, but the change of heart suggests a sudden epiphany, an optimistic turn towards adulthood.

ODD/SALIENT FACTS The alley in Brighton where Steph and Jimmy retreat for their quickie in the middle of the riot has itself become a cult place, a shrine to the film. Fans of the film have travelled from all over Europe to pay their respects and leave graffiti messages commemorating their visit.

MEMORABLE MOMENTS The film achieves a rare thing, convincing crowd sequences and even more remarkable, realistic

'Nothing seems right apart from Brighton

riots. The sense of excitement and immediacy was achieved by Roddam simply making them as real and unchoreographed as possible. The director recalls telling the actors: "Those fucking police are fucking up the scene, go for them for real." And so when they mix these people are almost fighting for their lives. Phil Daniels himself remembers laying into one of the policemen: 'It seemed as real as you can get.'

KEY LINES

Jimmy's mum, on her son's habit of riding around at night with his mates: 'It's not normal.'
Jimmy: 'Oh yeah, what's normal, then?'

Jimmy to Steph: 'Nothing seems right apart from Brighton.'

Jimmy to the van driver who has smashed his Lambretta: 'You've killed me scooter.'

THE QUIET MAN

US, 1952, REPUBLIC/ARGOSY PICTURES, 129 MINS
D JOHN FORD; **PR** JOHN FORD, MERIAN C. COOPER; **SC** FRANK S. NUGENT (FROM A STORY BY MAURICE WALSH); **PH** (TECHNICOLOR) WINTON C. HOCH AND (SECOND UNIT) ARCHIE STOUT; **ED** JACK MURRAY; **M** VICTOR YOUNG
CAST JOHN WAYNE (SEAN THORNTON), MAUREEN O'HARA (MARY KATE DANAHER), VICTOR MCLAGLEN (RED WILL DANAHER), BARRY FITZGERALD (MICHAELEEN OG FLYNN), WARD BOND (FATHER LONERGAN), MILDRED NATWICK (MRS SARAH TILLANE), FRANCIS FORD (DAN TOBIN), ARTHUR SHIELDS (REVD CYRIL PLAYFAIR), EILEEN CROWE (MRS ELIZABETH PLAYFAIR), SEAN MCCLORY (OWEN GLYNN), JAMES LILBURN (FATHER PAUL), JACK MCGOWRAN (FEENEY), KEN CURTIS (DERMOT FAHY)

THE STORY Irish-American boxer Sean Thornton returns to Innisfree whence his family emigrated when he was a child. Sean became the prizefighter 'Trooper Thorn', but his championship bid was cut short when he killed an opponent in the ring, and he has vowed never to fight again. Back in Innisfree he's taken under the wing of Michaeleen, the village's crafty,

▲ THE QUIET MAN *Wayne courts O'Hara in a shot reprised by Steven Spielberg in* E.T.

drunken bookie and matchmaker. He falls in love with the spirited Mary Kate Danaher, but crosses her boorish brother Will when he outbids him to buy the old family cottage from the wealthy widow Tillane. Will Danaher opposes the match, but a benign conspiracy between the Catholic priest, the vicar, and Michaeleen persuades him that giving Mary Kate to Thornton will ease his path to marrying the widow Tillane. Sean and Mary Kate cut short the elaborate courting ceremonies and marry, but when the widow rejects Danaher's proposal, he reneges on the agreement. Mary Kate, humiliated, refuses to consummate the marriage unless her dowry is paid, and they spend their wedding night in separate rooms. The Reverend Playfair, the only person to rumble Sean's identity and the reason he won't fight Danaher, encourages him to do so for Mary Kate's sake. Sean drags her over to confront Danaher, they get – and burn – the dowry, and an epic cross-country fist-fight between Sean and Danaher ensues. Followed from pub to pub by the whole village, and a visiting bishop, they arrive drunk, battered and reconciled at Mary Kate's dinner table.

THE FILM A re-working of *The Taming of the Shrew*, this is Ford's most joyous movie, a celebration of marriage and community, in which his favourite actor and actress engage in a courteous love affair between America and Ireland, and traditional preconceptions are turned on their heads. Wayne represents the search for the anti-material simple life; O'Hara is

obsessed with material possessions. *The Quiet Man* is one of the most gloriously romantic pictures ever made, apparently free-wheeling but in fact carefully patterned. Its Ireland is an Irish-American idyll, but it quietly mocks the pretensions of the IRA and sees Protestants and Catholics living happily together in the unforgettable scene where Father Lonergan encourages the villagers to cheer the Church of Ireland bishop and thus ensure the tenure of the Reverend Playfair. *The Quiet Man*, once Ford's most popular film, but subsequently rejected as politically incorrect, has become the cult picture in his oeuvre. The melodies on the soundtrack and the communal singing trump most musicals.

ODD/SALIENT FACTS Maurice Walsh's story appeared in the *Saturday Evening Post* in 1933, and Ford optioned it for $10 in 1936. Many years later the British writer Richard Llewellyn, author of *How Green Was My Valley*, expanded the tale for Frank S. Nugent to write a screenplay, but didn't take a credit. The film brought Ford his fourth Oscar as Best Director. The film is a family affair that took Ford back to Ireland and gave work, behind and in front of the camera, to numerous members of his repertory company, two of his brothers, several of John Wayne's children, two of Maureen O'Hara's brothers, Victor McLaglen's son, as well as Barry Fitzgerald's brother Arthur Shields. Mae Marsh, the heroine of D. W. Griffith's *Intolerance* and several Ford pictures, appeared as the priest's housekeeper.

MEMORABLE MOMENTS Sean's first sighting of Mary Kate tending the sheep.

Sean and Mary Kate escaping on a tandem from Michaeleen, their chaperone, for a lyrical ride through the countryside.

The expressionistic flashback from Danaher's attack on Sean at the wedding breakfast to the fatal knock-out in the boxing ring.

The epic, ten-minute fight.

KEY LINES

Sean: 'I'm Sean Thornton and I was born in that little cottage over there and I'm coming home and that's where I'm going to stay.'

Michaeleen (reacting to Sean's first sight of Mary Kate): 'It's only a mirage brought on by your terrible thirst.'

Sean: 'Some things a man doesn't get over so easily – like the sight of a girl coming through the fields with the sun on her hair, and kneeling in church looking like a saint.'

Michaeleen (to Mary Kate): 'Have the good manners not to hit the man until he's your husband and entitled to hit back.'

Michaeleen (misinterpreting the collapsed bridal bed on which Sean has thrown Mary Kate): 'Impetuous! Homeric!'

Father Lonergan (rallying the villagers to impress the protestant Bishop): 'Now, when the Reverend Playfair comes down, good man that he is, I want you all to cheer like Protestants.'

RASHOMON

JAPAN, 1950, DAEIE, 88 MINS

D *AKIRA KUROSAWA;* **PR** *JINKICHI MINOURA;* **SC** *KUROSAWA AND SHINOBU HASHIMOTO (FROM TWO STORIES BY RYUNOSUKE AKUTAGAWA);* **PH** *KAZUO MIYAGAWA;* **M** *TAKASHI MATSUYAMA* **CAST** *TOSHIRO MIFUNE (TAJAMURU, THE BANDIT), MACHIKO KYO (THE WIFE), MASAYUKI MORI (THE HUSBAND), TAKASHI SHIMURA (THE WOODCUTTER), MINORU CHIAKI (THE PRIEST), KICHIJIRO UEDA (THE COMMONER)*

THE STORY In the countryside of war-torn medieval Japan three men – a priest, a woodcutter and a cynical traveller – shelter from the rain in the ruins of the Rashomon gate. Three days earlier the priest and the woodcutter appeared as witnesses at the trial of a notorious bandit, Tajamuru, charged with murdering a nobleman, raping his wife and stealing his horse, and they seem deeply disturbed by the experience. Questioned by the traveller, they describe the trial and in flashbacks, and flashbacks within flashbacks, the film presents the events as recounted by the woodcutter who claims to have found two hats and the dead body; by the priest who passed the married couple on the road; the bandit, who admits to rape and murder; the now-widowed wife who fled from the scene; and (through a female medium) the dead man, who says he committed suicide. The stories are in sharp conflict, and eventually under pressure from the stranger, the woodcutter admits to having spied on the events but having concealed this because he subsequently stole a valuable knife belonging to the wife. His account shows that everyone has been lying. Suddenly an

▲ **RASHOMON** *Bandit Toshiro Mifune gives his version of what happened in the woods.*

abandoned baby is found among the ruins and the priest's faith in humanity is restored when the woodcutter offers to take it home to be reared with his five children.

THE FILM One of the most beautifully crafted films ever made, *Rashomon* has three distinctive settings – the rain-lashed ruin of a once grand building in which the framing narrative takes place; the idyllic woods where the sun shining through the trees casts delicate shadows on the encounter between the bandit and the married couple; the courtyard with a sand-covered floor and a wall that bisects the screen laterally where the trial is held. In the court scenes, the magistrate is neither seen nor heard; the characters address the camera turning the cinema audience into judges. We are all familar with the fact that through imperfect memory, dishonesty and self-interest subjective reports on events rarely tally, and this has been the basis of such works as Browning's *The Ring and the Book* and the modest British crime movie *The Woman in Question* (1949), which was shown in the US as *Five Angles on Murder*. But none before had approached the subject with such subtle irony, psychological insight and moral force, and almost immediately the film's title entered the language in the phrase 'a *Rashomon* situation' as a dozen years later *Catch-22* did. Moviegoers would discuss the meaning of the movie and the issues it raises as earlier they talked of Rosebud in *Citizen Kane* and later whether the couple in *Last Year in Marienbad* had actually met before.

ODD/SALIENT FACTS *Rashomon* won the Gold Lion at the 1951 Venice Festival and an Oscar as the best foreign language film (it was also nominated for best art direction) and was the first Japanese movie to be shown widely in the West, opening the eyes of the West to a hitherto neglected national cinema. As such it played a key role in the healing process after the Second World War, helping citizens of the allied nations to look sympathetically on Japan, recognize the Japanese as individuals and to appreciate the country's culture. Machiko Kyo, a dancer playing her first important dramatic role, became an international star as did Toshiro Mifune, the first Japanese actors to do so since Sessue Hayakawa became a Hollywood star in 1914. *Rashomon* was presented on Broadway as a play in 1959 (starring Claire Bloom and Rod Steiger) and was re-made as the Western *The Outrage* (1964) and as *Iron Maze* (1991), a US-Japanese thriller set in Pittsburgh produced by Oliver Stone. In *Easy Riders, Raging Bulls* (1998) Peter Biskind remarks: 'Kurosawa's *Rashomon* remains one of the truest movies about the movies and people who make them.'

MEMORABLE MOMENTS The bandit seeing the wind raise the veil hanging from the wife's straw hat as she rides by on her horse.

The look of cold contempt on the husband's face as he looks at his wife after the rape in her flashback.

The wife's knife glinting at the edge of the clearing as the husband approaches it contemplating suicide.

The female medium, her hair blowing in the wind, speaking in the nobleman's voice to the court.

KEY LINES

The commoner: 'Men are only men, they can't tell the truth, not even to each other.'

The priest: 'It's because men are so weak, that's why they lie, that's why they must deceive themselves.'

REBEL WITHOUT A CAUSE
US, 1955, WARNER BROS, 111 MINS

D NICHOLAS RAY; **PR** DAVID WEISBART; **SC** STEWART STERN; **PH** (COL, CINEMASCOPE) ERNEST HALLER; **M** LEONARD ROSENMAN; **ED** WILLIAM ZIEGLER

CAST JAMES DEAN (JIM STARK), NATALIE WOOD (JUDY), JIM BACKUS (JIM'S FATHER), ANN DORAN (JIM'S MOTHER), ROCHELLE HUDSON (JUDY'S MOTHER), WILLIAM HOPPER (JUDY'S FATHER), SAL MINEO (PLATO), COREY ALLEN (BUZZ), DENNIS HOPPER (GOON), ED PLATT (RAY), STEFFI SYDNEY (MIL), MARIETTA CANTY (PLATO'S NURSE-MAID), VIRGINIA BRISSAC (JIM'S GRANDMOTHER), BEVERLEY LONG (HELEN), FRANK MAZZOLA (CRUNCH), ROBERT FOULK (GENE), JACK SIMMONS (COOKIE), NICK ADAMS (MOOSE)

THE STORY The paths of three adolescents – Jim, Judy and Plato – cross one night in a police station. Jim, newly arrived in town, has been arrested for public drunkenness, Plato for shooting some puppies, while Judy has been found wandering the streets alone late at night. At his new school Jim and Buzz, a gang leader, have a knife fight. When this is broken up they agree to settle the score with a 'Chickie run' in their cars. During this contest Buzz plunges to his death over a cliff. Misunderstood by his parents and ignored by the police, Jim gets together with Judy, who dated Buzz, and Plato at an abandoned mansion. Jim and Judy become surrogate parents to Plato. When Plato

▼ *REBEL WITHOUT A CAUSE* Rebels Judy (Natalie Wood) and Jimmy (James Dean) create their own perfect nuclear family.

falls asleep Judy and Jim sneak off to consummate their love. A disoriented Plato is woken by angry members of Buzz's gang. He shoots one of them and flees to a planetarium, pursued by the police. Jim and Judy follow Plato and persuade him to give himself up. But as they leave Plato, upset by the blinding lights from the police cars, makes a run for it and is fatally shot.

THE FILM The film and its central examination of the alienation of the American adolescent, is a companion piece to *The Wild One* (1953), the film that confirmed Dean's great rival Marlon Brando as the star of his generation. In that film, Brando's character responds to the question of what he is rebelling against with the famous line: 'Whatcha got?' In *Rebel Without a Cause*, the rebellion is inspired by the decline of the conventional nuclear family. All three leading characters come from conspicuously wealthy families and are driven to rebellion by specific things lacking in their domestic lives. Plato is upset because his parents have abandoned him, and replace love with a maid and cash. Judy wants her father to be physically affectionate to her, something he hasn't been since she became a woman. Jim is sent crazy by the fact that his mother is strong and confident, his father weak – given to wearing a pinny around the house. Jim is very clear about how things should change and believes that a gentle beating should get his mother back in line. Together the three teenagers improvise the perfect family. *Rebel Without a Cause* remains a cult film despite a dated and reactionary story and script. Visually it is brilliantly composed throughout. It has three fascinating and iconic leading players all of whom died prematurely (Dean, 24; Mineo, 37; Wood, 43) of unnatural causes, respectively car crash, murder and drowning. Its lingering resonance comes from Dean. This was one of only three films in which he starred – after *East of Eden* (1955) and before *Giant* (1956). The film works better in the memory or with the sound turned down and offers a tantalizing view of Dean's potential.

ODD/SALIENT FACTS In *Hollywood Babylon* Kenneth Anger claims that the odd twitchiness of Dean's performance was the result of the crabs from which he suffered through much of the production. The homoerotic overtones of the script's relationship between Plato and Jimmy were matched in real life, at least in an attraction between the two actors. When questioned on the subject by Boze Hadleigh in *Conversations With My Elders*, Mineo answered: 'I might tell you some people I had affairs with – maybe. But Jimmy was special, so I don't want to say.'

During the shoot Dean had a long-standing girlfriend, and a possibly platonic relationship with Ursula Andress, as well as a brief liaison with Natalie Wood, which was uncomfortably consummated in his Porsche. Wood was simultaneously having affairs with Dennis Hopper and Nicholas Ray. Crunch is played by Frank Mazzola, who was employed as an advisor on gang life and later worked as editor alongside Donald Cammel on the final cut of *Performance*.

MEMORABLE MOMENTS The film is memorable for its use of red in the transference of red jackets, first to Judy, then Jimmy and finally, fatally, to Plato. The film's two great scenes are the choreographed knife fight in which Jimmy is wounded and the chicken race in which Buzz is killed.

KEY LINES

Jimmy, contorted with psychic rage, to his bickering parents in the police station: 'You're tearing me apart.'

Jimmy to Judy: 'You live here, don't you?'
Judy: 'Who lives?'

Jim's father: 'You can't be idealistic all your life, Jim.'
Jimmy: 'Except to yourself.'

RESERVOIR DOGS★
US, 1992, RANK/LIVE AMERICA/DOG EAT DOG, 99 MINS
D QUENTIN TARANTINO; **PR** LAWRENCE BENDER; **SC** QUENTIN TARANTINO; **PH** (COL) ANDRZEJ SEKULA; **M** VARIOUS; **ED** SALLY MENKS
CAST HARVEY KEITEL (MR WHITE, LARRY), TIM ROTH (MR ORANGE, FREDDY NEWENDYKE), MICHAEL MADSEN (MR BLONDE, VIC VEGA), CHRIS PENN (NICE GUY EDDIE), STEVE BUSCEMI (MR PINK), LAWRENCE TIERNEY (JOE CABOT), RANDY BROOKS (HOLDAWAY), KIRK BALTZ (MARVIN NASH), EDDIE BUNKER (MR BLUE), QUENTIN TARANTINO (MR BROWN), MICHAEL SOTTILE (TEDDY), ROBERT RUTH (SHOT COP), LAWRENCE BENDER (YOUNG COP)

THE STORY A diamond heist goes badly wrong. The surviving gang members make their way back to the rendezvous – Mr White, the badly wounded Mr Orange, Mr Pink, Mr Blonde and later the leaders Joe and his son Eddie. Mr Blue

PERFORMANCE

ABOVE: Decadent sixties rock 'n' roll troilism as Turner (Mick Jagger), Lucy (Michele Breton) and Pherber (Anita Pallenberg) take to the bath in the scene that really upset the suits at Warner Brothers.

ONCE UPON A TIME IN THE WEST

RIGHT: Charles Bronson as Harmonica, another mysterious Spaghetti gunfighter with no name, confronts an opponent in a characteristically striking Leone composition.

PINK FLAMINGOS

Divine (Divine), eager to prove him/herself the filthiest person in the world, prepares to tuck in. If you think this is disgusting, you ain't seen nothing yet.

RESERVOIR DOGS

Things are looking increasingly bad and bloody for
Mr Orange (Tim Roth) despite the tender ministrations of
Mr White (Harvey Keitel).

THE ROCKY HORROR PICTURE SHOW
LEFT: Tim Curry as transvestite scientist Dr Frank-N-Furter stands in front of the tower of RKO Radio Pictures, ready to celebrate the glories of classic horror films with Brad, Janet and Rocky.

SINGING IN THE RAIN
RIGHT: Cathy Selden (Debbie Reynolds) and Don Lockwood (Gene Kelly) are the new romantic team that rescues R. J. Simpson's Monumental Pictures as sound comes to Hollywood.

THIS IS SPINAL TAP

ABOVE: *Nigel Tufnel (Christopher Guest) and David St Hubbins (Michael McKean) rock it on stage as 'the Tap' crank it up to eleven on their uneven American tour.*

THE TERMINATOR

RIGHT: *The terminator (Arnold Schwarzenegger) single-handedly takes out a police precinct, having assured the desk sergeant 'I'll be back'.*

WITHNAIL AND I

ABOVE: I (Paul McGann) and Withnail (Richard E, Grant), with the rubber-boot money generously given to them by Monty (Richard Griffiths), have the means to demand the finest wines available to humanity.

THE WICKER MAN

RIGHT: Scottish copper Edward Woodward pays the ultimate price for preserving his virginity as the eponymous sacrificial pyre goes up in smoke.

and Mr Brown are dead. In a frenzy of accusations and panic, the story unfolds at the warehouse and in flashback. We see the plans for the raid, the recruitment of the gang, and the immediate aftermath of the heist. Mr Orange is an undercover cop who kills Mr Blonde as he in turn is about to kill a cop whom he has taken hostage and is torturing. Eddie, Mr White and Mr Pink and finally Joe arrive back at the warehouse. After a brief Mexican stand-off, Joe shoots Mr Orange, Mr White shoots and kills Joe, Eddie shoots Mr White, and Mr White shoots and kills Eddie. Mr Pink, who had been hiding under a ramp, escapes with the diamonds but his exit is followed by the sound of police sirens and gunfire. Mr Orange tells Mr White that he is a cop. As the police arrive Mr White shoots Mr Orange and is himself blown off the screen.

THE FILM Quentin Tarantino, a movie obsessive, came to his feature debut, with his sum total experience being, by all accounts, a wretched short film *My Best Friend's Birthday* on his CV. He had however recently sold his script of *True Romance* (1993) to Tony Scott. The script for *Reservoir Dogs* was written in just three weeks and is a blend of originality, enthusiasm and homage. Tarantino worked in a video store and turned himself into a sponge and encyclopaedia of cult, often violent, marginal and sometimes classic cinema. The film is dedicated to, among others, the cult figures Jean-Luc Godard, Jean-Pierre Melville, Chow Yun Fat and Roger Corman. The taut screenplay is filled with references to Tarantino's favourite films: *The Killing* (1956), *White Heat* (1949), *Rififi* (1955), *Ocean's Eleven* (1960) and *Straight Time* (1977) – based on a book by Eddie Bunker, aka Mr Blue – among many, many others. The concept of a gang of mutual strangers known only by colours appears in the New York Subway train heist movie, *The Taking of Pelham 123* (1974), one of Tarantino's favourite films. A key source was another Tarantino favourite, Ringo Lam's *City on Fire* (1989), which features Chow Yun Fat as an undercover cop infiltrating a jewel gang, scenes in a café, a sequence where the cool-looking gang walk in hip, bedraggled unity towards the camera, and concludes with an identically composed Mexican stand-off. Another source was *Odd Man Out*. The film is fascinating for its complex borrowings but most admirable for the profane poetry of the dialogue, the complexity of the

> **'You gonna bark all day, little doggy, or are you gonna bite?'**

narrative structure (itself similar to *Rashomon* [1951]), and the stylishly camp soundtrack. It is supremely cool, and gained an instantly devoted following. Everything about it was taken from somewhere else, and yet it had a style of dialogue that immediately established the Tarantino signature, and a look and sound all its own.

ODD/SALIENT FACTS The film was executive produced by cult director Monte Hellman, who had initially wanted to come out of his semi-retirement to direct the project himself. Steve Buscemi had at first wanted to play Mr Blonde. Mr Blonde, Vic Vega is the brother of Vincent Vega, the John Travolta character in *Pulp Fiction* (1994). The film created an added buzz by its narrative ambiguities. In the Mexican stand-off, which ends with four men being shot, only three guns are seen being fired. Similarly, the shot by which Mr Orange is supposedly killed is not shown on screen. Of the latter it would just seem hard for Mr White to miss. Of the end of the stand-off, if Mr White's swivel and shooting of Eddie weren't already visible, Tarantino's screenplay makes it clear that Mr White does in fact shoot Eddie after shooting Joe and being shot himself.

MEMORABLE MOMENTS The gang, plus Eddie and Joe, walking towards the camera in the credit sequence.

The torture and ear-cutting scene – 'It's amusing to me to torture a cop' – accompanied by the cheerful sounds of Stealer's Wheel playing 'Stuck in the Middle with You'.

KEY LINES

Mr White to Mr Blonde: 'You shoot me in a dream, you better wake up and apologize.'

Mr Pink, in the midst of his reasons for not tipping waitresses: 'And this non-college bullshit you're telling me. I got two words for that: "Learn to fuckin' type."'

Pink, seeing Mr Orange in a pool of his own blood: 'It's bad. It's bad. Is it bad?'
Mr White: 'As opposed to good?'

Mr Blonde to Mr White: 'You gonna bark all day, little doggy, or are you gonna bite?'

THE REVENGE OF FRANKENSTEIN

UK, 1958, HAMMER FILMS, 89 MINS

D TERENCE FISHER; **PR** ANTHONY HINDS; **SC** JIMMY SANGSTER (ADDITIONAL DIALOGUE BY HANFORD JANES); **PH** (TECHNICOLOR) JACK ASHER; **ED** ALFRED COX; **M** LEONARDO SALZEDO

CAST PETER CUSHING (DR VICTOR STEIN), FRANCIS MATTHEWS (DR HANS CLEVE), EUNICE GAYSON (MARGARET CONRAD), MICHAEL GWYNN (THE CREATURE), OSCAR QUITAK (KARL, THE DWARF), JOHN WELSH (BERGMAN), LIONEL JEFFRIES (FRITZ), RICHARD WORDSWORTH (UP PATIENT), CHARLES LLOYD PACK (PRESIDENT OF THE MEDICAL COUNCIL), JOHN STUART (INSPECTOR), MARGERY CRESLEY (COUNTESS BARSCYNSKA), ARNOLD DIAMOND (MOLKE), ANNA WARMSLEY (VERA BARSCYNSKA), GEORGE WOODBRIDGE (JANITOR), MICHAEL RIPPER (CURT), IAN WHITTAKER (BOY), AVRIL LESLIE (GERDA, THE GIRL)

THE STORY 1860: Baron Frankenstein is led to the scaffold for the murders committed by his monster. However, Frankenstein, with the assistance of his servant, the hunchback Karl, manages to have a Catholic priest executed and buried in his place. Three years later Frankenstein has established himself in Carlsbrück as Dr Victor Stein, the town's most prosperous general practitioner and devoted surgeon in charge of the workhouse hospital. Stein is invited to join Carlsbrück's medical

▼ *THE REVENGE OF FRANKENSTEIN Dr Stein instructs his new assistant Cleve in the Promethean arts.*

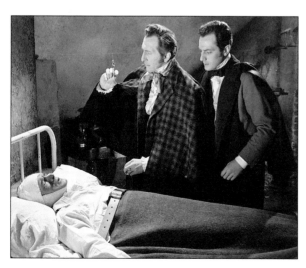

council, he refuses their offer, but one council member, the brilliant young Hans Cleve, recognizes Frankenstein and asks to become his assistant. Stein is determined to avenge himself on the medical establishment and his first major project is to transplant the brain of the deformed Karl into a perfect body he has cobbled together from parts taken from his indigent patients. Stein and Cleve perform the operation successfully. But Cleve reveals to the Creature that he is to be an exhibit alongside the ugly body of Karl to demonstrate Frankenstein's brilliance to medical science. While the Creature is strapped down to recover from the operation, Margaret, an altruistic aristocrat working at the hospital, unwittingly releases his bonds. He first thrusts Karl's corpse into the furnace, then kills Stein's janitor, and murders a peasant girl. Finally he crashes into an elegant party and dies at the feet of his creator. The Medical Council demands Stein's arrest, but before this can be affected, vengeful victims of Stein's experiments are alerted and inflict fatal injuries on him. Reacting rapidly, Dr Cleve shows Stein's corpse to the authorities, then transplants Frankenstein's brain into a waiting body. The film ends with Cleve and Frankenstein (moustachioed, monocled, and called Dr Franck) running a fashionable practice in London's Harley Street.

THE FILM Founded in 1948, Hammer Studios spent eight years producing B-feature schlock until establishing its identity with sexy, elegantly staged, Technicolor horror flicks that, like Roger Corman's Edgar Allan Poe movies being made in Hollywood, looked far more costly than their low budgets would have suggested. They were set in a stylized nineteenth century where graveyards loomed out of the fog and red gore flowed freely. Hammer's cult period lasted half-a-dozen years and though the studio ventured into most genres, the key works were horror movies starring Peter Cushing (1913–96) and Christopher Lee (b. 1922), minor British character actors who became international icons. Their names are forever linked as Frankenstein and the Creature, and Van Helsing and Dracula, though they played together in other movies. Whereas Karloff had dominated the 1930s James Whale movies, to the extent that the name Frankenstein became popularly associated with the monster rather than his creator, Cushing's Frankenstein is at the centre of the Hammer movies. The 1957 *Curse of Frankenstein* was generally excoriated by the critics, but this sequel, following in the wake of *Dracula*, proved that Cushing was a star and his polite, coldly fastidious, quietly sadistic

Frankenstein became a new kind of mad scientist for the second part of the twentieth century, a sort of stiff-upper-lip Anglo-Saxon brother to Dr Mengele. *Revenge* also introduced the strong element of dark humour and camp that was to be a part of the Hammer tradition. The women in the movies are invariably pallid.

ODD/SALIENT FACTS Universal Studios had copyright in the appearance of Karloff's Monster and after playing a new-style Monster in *The Curse of Frankenstein*, Christopher Lee refused to play the role again. The first British critic to recognize the merits of Hammer films was the screenwriter Paul Dehn, movie reviewer of the now defunct *News Chronicle*, who happened to be the long-time companion of James Bernard, Hammer's house composer. The American censors intervened to prevent the results of the creature's cannibalism being shown on screen.

MEMORABLE MOMENTS Frankenstein using a Bunsen burner to show Dr Cleve how eyes and hands suspended in glass tanks react to heat.

The Creature seeing himself in the mirror.

The Creature putting Karl's corpse into the furnace.

KEY LINES

Frankenstein: 'That's the arm of a pickpocket. You need sensitive fingers to be a member of that profession. It will be very useful to me.'

The Creature's last words: 'Frankenstein, help me!'

Dr Franck in his Harley Street surgery: 'You were an excellent pupil Hans. These scars will hardly show.'

RIDE LONESOME

US, 1959, RANOWN/COLUMBIA, 73 MINS

D BUDD BOETTICHER; **PR** HARRY JOE BROWN; **SC** BURT KENNEDY; **PH** (COL, CINEMASCOPE) CHARLES LAWTON JR.; **M** HEINZ ROEMHELD; **ED** JEROME THOMAS

CAST RANDOLPH SCOTT (BEN BRIGADE), KAREN STEELE (CARRIE), PERNELL ROBERTS (SAM BOONE), JAMES BEST (BILLY JOHN), LEE VAN CLEEF (FRANK), JAMES COBURN (WID), DYKE JOHNSON (CHARLIE), BOYD STOCKMAN (INDIAN CHIEF)

THE STORY Bounty hunter Ben Brigade captures fugitive killer Billy John and aims to take him to Santa Cruz to stand trial. He is joined by Carrie, whose husband has been captured by marauding Indians, and by two young outlaws, Sam and Wid, who believe they can obtain an amnesty if they turn in the wanted Billy. They can then give up their life of crime and start a new life as ranchers. At a staging post Brigade attempts to keep an Indian war party at bay by pretending to sell Carrie to them as a squaw, but she breaks down and panics when she notices that the Indians have her husband's horse. Brigade and his party head off across holy Indian land pursued by Indians and feuding among themselves. It transpires that Brigade is using Billy as bait to capture his brother Frank, a vicious outlaw who has abducted and murdered Brigade's wife. Using the same tree on which his wife was hanged, Brigade strings up Billy to draw Frank into a gunfight. Frank is killed. Brigade hands over Billy to Wid and Sam so they can obtain their amnesty, and Carrie rides off with them. Brigade sets fire to the hanging tree and rides off alone.

THE FILM Two of the screen's great collaborations between star and director took place in the 1950s. Starting with *Winchester 73* in 1950, James Stewart and Anthony Mann made eight films together, five of them Westerns. Beginning in 1956 with *Seven Men From Now*, Randolph Scott and Budd Boetticher made seven pictures together, all of them Westerns. The Scott-Boetticher pictures are taut, ironic fables either set in corrupt townships or on journeys in which the impassive Scott, his face weathered and leathery, is invariably a widowed ex-lawman, confronting or reluctantly travelling with outlaws. Andrew Sarris has called the films 'floating poker games' and they involve serious games-playing in which cards are concealed and people are invited to call their opponents' bluff. All the films last under 80 minutes (four exactly 77 minutes) and the best are the four written by Burt Kennedy (who would himself direct Westerns in the 1960s): *Seven Men From Now* (1956), *The Tall T* (1957), *Ride Lonesome* (1959) and *Comanche Station* (1960). They're shot in the same arid, rocky landscapes and not only have similar plots, but incidents and lines of dialogue recur. They are Westerns pared down to their essential moral core in the manner of Samuel Beckett's plays and it is significant that Monte Hellman's pair of spare cult Westerns of 1967, *Ride in the Whirlwind* and *The Shooting*, were influenced both by Boetticher and Beckett.

The withdrawn, slightly mysterious probity of Scott brings out the character of the outlaws, giving colour and substance to

180

▲ *RIDE LONESOME* Karen Steel and Randolph Scott negotiate with hostile Indians in the Mojave Desert.

their villainy. Mann's Westerns with James Stewart suggest that the hero will settle down in a community he has helped create. Boetticher's Westerns on the other hand imply that we are essentially isolated beings who live and die alone and that society is a sham. Thus we are faced with the certainty that the Scott character will proceed on his way unaccompanied.

ODD/SALIENT FACTS *Ride Lonesome* and most of the other Scott-Boetticher films were shot at Big Pines, a recreational area north of Los Angeles in the south-west section of the Mojave Desert. James Coburn made his screen debut as the wise-cracking outlaw in *Ride Lonesome*; Pernell Roberts, who played his partner, became famous two years later as Adam Cartwright in the long-running TV series *Bonanza*. Budd Boetticher was trained as a matador before entering the cinema as technical adviser on *Blood and Sand*, and there is a resemblance between his films and the rituals of bullfighting. After their final collaboration on *Comanche Station* (1960), Scott and Boetticher made a single feature film each, Scott

appearing in Peckinpah's *Ride the High Country* (1962) and Boetticher directing the Audie Murphy Western *A Time For Dying* (1969).

MEMORABLE MOMENTS Scott emerging through the rocks to corner his prey in the opening shot.

The widescreen image of the five travellers being followed by an Indian war party across medicine country.

The shootout with Indians at an abandoned coach station.

KEY LINES

Brigade, after the burial of a stagecoach driver: 'Hang on to that shovel because likely enough you're going to be needing it again, soon.'

Sam: 'The way I look at it, it's half so hard if a man knows the way he's going to die.'

Frank: 'There's no hurry, he'll be waiting.'

Sam (a line also spoken by Scott as Pat Brennan in The Tall T): 'There are some things a man can't ride around.'

THE ROCKY HORROR PICTURE SHOW★

US, 1975, TCF, 100 MINS

D JIM SHARMAN; **PR** MICHAEL WHITE; **SC** JIM SHARMAN, RICHARD O'BRIEN FROM RICHARD O'BRIEN'S PLAY THE ROCKY HORROR SHOW; **PH** PETER SUSCHITZKY; **M** RICHARD O'BRIEN; **ED** GRAEME CLIFFORD

CAST TIM CURRY (DR FRANK N. FURTER), BARRY BOSTWICK (BRAD MAJORS), SUSAN SARANDON (JANET WEISS), RICHARD O'BRIEN (RIFF RAFF), JONATHAN ADAMS (DR EVERETT MAJORS), NELL CAMPBELL (COLUMBIA), PETER HINWOOD (ROCKY), MEATLOAF (EDDIE), PATRICIA QUINN (MAGENTA), CHARLES GRAY (NARRATOR/THE CRIMINOLOGIST), HILARY LABOW (BETTY MUNROE), JEREMY NEWSON (RALPH HAPSCHATT)

THE STORY Brad and Janet, travelling from a wedding to seek the blessing for their own marriage from their favourite professor, Dr Scott, stumble upon a big creepy house. They meet the inhabitants, the butler Riff Raff, the maid Magenta, the owner Frank N. Furter and their party guests. Their host shows them his latest creation, a man called Rocky whom he has created as a prospective lover for himself. But Rocky is scared and hides. Eddie, who is adored by another maid, Columbia, arrives but is brutally murdered by Frank. That night Frank seduces first Janet and then Brad. Janet who sees Brad and Frank on a TV monitor, makes love to Rocky. Dr Scott arrives at the castle having been alerted to strange goings-on by his nephew, Eddie. Everyone sits down to a feast, the meat course of which turns out to be Eddie. Frank turns Brad, Janet, Dr Scott, Columbia and Rocky to stone and brings them back to life for a stage performance. Riff Raff and Magenta turn on and kill Frank. Janet, Brad and the doctor escape the house which flies as a massive spacecraft back to the planet Transylvania.

THE FILM Watched coldly it is easy to see why *The Rocky Horror Picture Show* was a commercial flop when it first opened. A confused musical pastiche of horror and sci-fi movies in an atmosphere of sexual ambiguity, it is approximately half an entertaining film that goes badly out of control in its later stages. There are some very catchy tunes and a spectacular performance from Curry. In the many revivals of the stage show, the central role has become irresistible to a succession of actors and pop stars who want to show that they have an edge and a sense of humour. But there is no point in watching the film in other than ideal circumstances, that is in a late-night screening with an audience of aficionados who know the routine. The year after its disappointing opening it was given a tactical re-release at strictly targeted venues as a late-night event movie. It began to attract a devoted following of fans who developed a set of responses to the actions on screen. This phenomenon that began in New York City spread across the US and eventually to Britain. The audience arrive in costume, and throughout the film comment on the events of the movie. The lines are spoken simultaneously with the characters, or mocked, or treated to prepared or improvised responses. Water pistols are fired, toast, loo rolls and playing cards thrown at the screen. The audience response has turned each screening into an event where what the audience is getting up to is almost guaranteed to be more entertaining than what is happening on the screen. Perhaps the archetypal cult film.

ODD/SALIENT FACTS The film recreates Grant Wood's *American Gothic* in the opening scene with Richard O'Brien taking the place of the farmer. In the song 'Science Fiction Double Feature' there are references to several seminal B-movies: *The Day the Earth Stood Still* (1951), *When Worlds Collide* (1951), *Tarantula* (1955) and *The Forbidden Planet* (1956), as well as *King Kong* (1933). The latter inspires the climactic sequence in which Rocky carries Frank's body up the RKO tower. In this scene Magenta's hair is in the style of Elsa Lanchester's from *The Bride of Frankenstein* (1935). One of the film's unique boasts is that it features both Christopher Biggins and Koo Stark in supporting roles.

MEMORABLE MOMENTS Frank's entrance and performance of 'Sweet Transvestite'.

His arrival in Janet's bed disguised as Brad, and subsequent seduction of her, followed by his arrival in Brad's bed disguised as Janet, and subsequent seduction of him using the identical words.

KEY LINES

Brad to Janet, on arriving at Frank's castle: 'It's probably some kind of convention for rich weirdos.'

> **'It's probably some kind of convention for rich weirdos.'**

181

Janet to Brad: 'If only we were amongst friends or sane persons.'

Frank, Brad and the recently arrived Dr Scott discover
   Janet and Rocky in a compromising position.
Dr Scott: 'Janet!'
Janet: 'Dr Scott!'
Brad: 'Janet!'
Janet: 'Brad!'
Frank: 'Rocky!'
Dr Scott: 'Janet!'
Janet: 'Dr Scott!'
Brad: 'Janet!'
Janet: 'Brad!'
Frank: 'Rocky!'
Dr Scott: 'Janet!'
Janet: 'Dr Scott!'
Brad: 'Janet!'
Janet: 'Brad!'
Frank: 'Rocky!'

▲ *LE ROMAN D'UN TRICHEUR At a café table the Cheat
recollects his scandalous life in tranquillity.*

LE ROMAN D'UN TRICHEUR (UK TITLE: THE STORY OF A CHEAT)

FRANCE, 1936, CINÉAS, 80 MINS

D/SC *SACHA GUITRY;* **PR/PH** *(BW) MARCEL LUCIEN;* **M** *ADOLPHE
BORCHARD*

CAST *SACHA GUITRY (THE CHEAT), SERGE GRAVE (THE CHEAT AS
A BOY), PIERRE ASSY (THE CHEAT AS A YOUNG MAN), JACQUELINE
DELUBAC (THE WIFE), MARGARET MORENO (THE COUNTESS),
ROASINE DÉREAN (THE THIEF), PAULINE CARTON (THE AUNT, MME
MORIOT), FRÉHEL (THE SINGER)*

THE STORY A distinguished middle-aged man, The Cheat, is
writing his memoirs in a restaurant while providing a voice-over
right through the film in lieu of dialogue. Flashback to his childhood and his large family of twelve, parents who are grocers,
grandparents, aunts and uncles. One day he steals a few sous
from the shop and that evening, as punishment, he has to go
without supper while the others enjoy their mushrooms, which
turn out to be poisonous and they all die. This incident becomes
the moral fulcrum of his future life. Honesty goes unrewarded,

dishonesty pays off. Unwanted and cheated out of his inheri-
tance by distant relatives, he runs off to make his own fortune,
first as a bellboy at a smart hotel. There follows an interlude in
Montmartre (at this point in the flashback Assy takes over the role
from Grave) with Russian revolutionaries. Then to Monte Carlo,
where he works as a lift operator and is picked up by a countess twenty years his senior. The film returns to the restaurant
where the memoir-writing Cheat is approached by an elderly
woman whom he recognizes as the countess of long ago but
he doesn't acknowledge their acquaintance. Another flashback:
The Cheat returns to Monte Carlo and becomes a croupier.

In 1914 he goes off to war, is injured at the front and saved
by an ambulance driver who loses his arm in the process.
Shaving off his enormous beard before returning to civilian life
he sees the use of disguises. (Here Sacha Guitry takes over the
character.) Using card tricks and, often in disguise, he starts
making money at the gaming tables of Monte Carlo. A woman
jewel thief involves him in a heist, and there's a brief marriage
to a fellow gambler. One evening he runs into the one-armed
ambulance driver who is an addicted but honest card-player.

They team up and he becomes a straight gambler, losing all his money and possessions. Back at the restaurant.the countess has returned and has discovered The Cheat's identity. She invites him to become her partner in crime, starting by robbing the big private residence opposite. The Cheat tells her there are two reasons he won't do this: first, the house used to belong to him and it would be like robbing himself; second, he joined the Security Police two months previously. She runs off and he concludes his memoirs.

THE FILM Guitry (1885–1957), author of over a hundred plays, was widely regarded as the director of *théâtre filmé*, but this dazzling *tour de force* demonstrates that he was not only a great man of the theatre but had mastered the medium of film. Unlike Chaplin's *City Lights* and *Modern Times*, which are silent films with sound effects, *Roman d'un Tricheur* is a sound film without spoken dialogue. Some contemporary critics were puzzled but others were enthusiastic and the film become a cult favourite among the critic-directors who launched the French *Nouvelle Vague*, and had a major influence on François Truffaut. Earlier it had undoubtedly inspired the form and tone of *Kind Hearts and Coronets* (1949), directed by the francophile Robert Hamer.

ODD/SALIENT FACTS For what are thought of as daringly original closing credits of *The Magnificent Ambersons* (1942) Orson Welles drew directly on Guitry's innovative opening credit titles. A pack of cards spread out face down and lifted seemingly at random to reveal the film's title is followed by Guitry suavely and wittily introducing his collaborators and actors in person (speaking in voice-over). Guitry ran into a little moral trouble himself eight years after *Roman d'un Tricheur* when he was arrested following the liberation of Paris and accused of collaboration during the Occupation.

MEMORABLE MOMENTS The young Cheat coming to terms with the deaths in his family ('There were too many of them for me to actually mourn them').

Guitry repeatedly coming through revolving doors in various disguises which fool the security staff who are on the lookout for the Cheat.

KEY LINES

People in the village: 'You know why the boy didn't die? Because he had stolen. And the others who were honest died.'

The Cheat to waiter: 'I'm talking about rich people. Mind you, what I call rich people are those who spend, not those who save their money. Money only becomes valuable when it leaves your pocket. If you don't you simply disrupt the general circulation of money, and that causes trouble.'

SALVATORE GIULIANO
ITALY, 1961, LUX/VIDES/GALATEA, 125 MINS

D FRANCESCO ROSI; *PR* FRANCO CRISTALDI; *SC* FRANCESCO ROSI, SUSO CECCHI D'AMICO, ENZO PROVENZALE, FRANCO SOLINAS; *PH* (BW) GIANNI DI VENANZO; *ED* MARIO SARANDREI; *M* PIERO PICCIONI

CAST FRANK WOLFF (GASPARE PISCIOTTA), SALVO RANDONE (PRESIDENT OF THE VITERBO ASSIZE COURT), FEDERICO ZARDI (PISCIOTTA'S DEFENCE COUNSEL), PIETRO CAMMARATA (SALVATORE GIULIANO), FERNANDO CICERO (A BANDIT), SENNUCCIO BENELLI (A REPORTER), BRUNO EKMAR (A SPY), MAX CARTIER (FRANCESCO), COSIMO TORINO (FRANK MANNINO), GIUSEPPE TETI (THE PRIEST OF MONTELPRE)

THE STORY In 1950, Salvatore Giuliano, a young Sicilian Robin Hood, is found shot dead in a courtyard in the impoverished town of Castelvetrano. In flashbacks the film shows how Giuliano, turned bandit

'Who are they – bandits or partisans?'

after shooting a *carabiniere* at the age of 21, has been employed by Sicilian separatists in 1945 to conduct a terrorist campaign against the national government. This leads to the granting of regional autonomy though not to an independent Sicily. Bandits are given amnesty for polical crimes, but Giuliano's gang reverts to kidnapping and robbery under the protection of the Mafia. When the communist-dominated People's Alliance wins free elections for the island and demands major reforms, the landowners and the Mafia hire Giuliano to harass them. This culminates in the deaths of unarmed innocents, mown down while attending a 1947 May Day rally. Giuliano returns to orthodox crime, but a campaign by the *carabinieri* leads to his 1950 assassination. A confused trial at Viterbo puts

over a dozen members of his gang in the dock, charged with participation in the May Day massacre. Giuliano's right-hand man, Pisciotta, admits to having betrayed and killed Giuliano under pressure from the Mafia and the *carabinieri*. He threatens to expose the links between politicians, the Mafia and the police, and after he and various associates are given life sentences, Pisciotta is poisoned in jail. In a 1960 postscript, the farmer who led the police to Pisciotta is killed by unknown assailants at a horse fair.

THE FILM Rosi came out of Italian neo-realism and shot this film on Sicilian locations using a largely non-professional cast. Gianni Di Venanzo's photography has a documentary feel in its hard-contrast monochrome and the positioning of the camera as a conscious observer, beginning with a scene in which a police spokesman addresses himself to the recording lens in describing the (as we later learn, highly dubious) scene of

▲ *SALVATORE GIULIANO The white-jacketed Salvatore (far right) and his cohorts command the Sicilian high ground.*

the crime. But *Salvatore Giuliano* goes far beyond neo-realism. It is a Marxist take on *Citizen Kane*, in which a society is anatomized through a single individual. But Rosi isn't interested in Giuliano's individual psychology. The social bandit's mother grieves for him, he's revered as a local hero, but his public status is that of a social and political pawn at the disposal of the allied invaders during the war, the Mafia, the Sicilian aristocracy and the National government in Rome. There is no psychological 'Rosebud' to explain his actions In life, he's seen in the middle-distance wearing his regulation flat cap and white coat, a gun on his shoulder, or from behind observing his enemies through binoculars. In death he's a handsome corpse.

Salvatore Giuliano was the first of Rosi's complex political thrillers, followed by *The Mattei Affair*, *Lucky Luciano*, and *Illustrious Corpses*. It shaped the paranoid style in Hollywood pursued by John Frankenheimer (*Seven Days in May*) and Alan J. Pakula (*The Parallax View*, *All the President's Men*) and initiated a new kind of open-ended thriller. It was the springboard for the cycle of socially contextualized American Mafia movies that began a decade later with *The Godfather*.

ODD/SALIENT FACTS The discussion provoked by the film forced the Italian government to re-open the never-ending investigation of collusion between politicians and criminals in Sicily. Frank Wolff, who plays Pisciotta, was a Jewish American actor based in Rome; he later appeared in Spaghetti Westerns. The Marxist writer Franco Solinas went on to script Gillo Pontecorvo's cult classic *The Battle of Algiers*.

MEMORABLE MOMENTS The opening inventory of the dead Giuliano as if he's just been taken off the cross.

The later scene where his mother comes to identify his corpse on a slab as if she were the Virgin Mary.

The attack on the police headquarters at Castelventrato and the May 1947 communist rally; confused, chillingly violent assaults in which the assailants are not seen.

Shots of the mysteriously charismatic Giuliano leading his men into battle.

The courtroom confrontations between bemused judges on the bench and aggressive defendants behind bars.

KEY LINES

Narrator: 'Giuliano's rural kingdom, protected by a conspiracy of silence and terror.'

Conscript soldier, 1946: 'Who are they – bandits or partisans?'

Pisciotta's Defence Counsel: 'Nobody has realized the true nature of this tragic event. Because, Your Honour, to understand how a bandit can become a great political figure … one must have the courage to spotlight the sad life of misery, of ignorance, and feudal subjugations of so many poor people, the varied acts of political meddling and the nature of the Mafia. One must have the courage to pursue matters to the end.'

SEBASTIANE
UK, 1976, MEGALOVISION/CINEGATE/DISCTAC, 86 MINS

D DEREK JARMAN, PAUL HUMFRESS; **PR** HOWARD MALIN, JAMES WHALEY; **SC** JAMES WHALEY, DEREK JARMAN, LATIN BY JACK WELCH; **PH** (COL) PETER MIDDLETON; **M** BRIAN ENO; **ED** PAUL HUMFRESS

CAST LEONARDO TREVIGLIO (SEBASTIAN), BARNEY JAMES (SEVERUS), NEIL KENNEDY (MAXIMUS), RICHARD WARWICK (JUSTIN), DONALD DUNHAM (CLAUDIUS), KEN HICKS (ADRIAN), JANUSZ ROMANOV (ANTHONY), STEFFANO MASSARI (MARIUS), DAEVID FINBAR (JULIAN), GERALD INCANDELA (LEOPARD BOY), LINDSAY KEMP AND TROUPE (EMPEROR'S DANCE)

THE STORY Sebastian, captain of the palace guard and a favourite of the Emperor Diocletian, is dispatched to a distant garrison in a crack-down on the spread of Christianity. There he immerses himself in his spirituality as his comrades have fun in the sun. The centurion Severus is agonized in his unrequited love for Sebastian and becomes ever more vindictive towards him. The other men have contempt for Sebastian's self-absorption as they toss a frisbee, dance, fight, frolic in the surf, bathe and just sit around discussing sex and politics. After Sebastian mocks and humiliates Severus in a final rejection of his drunken sexual advances, Severus sentences him to death. Sebastian is taken on to a cliff-top, tied to a stake and shot repeatedly with arrows.

THE FILM Like *Lawrence of Arabia* (1962) this is an extended study of homosexual repression, frustration and extreme masochism in the desert. Jarman came to the project after a fruitful collaboration with Ken Russell, designing the sets for *The Devils* (1971) and *Savage Messiah* (1972). Jarman said: 'One of the things that most fascinates me about film-making, is its recreating the past in terms of the present.' The jarring, often humorous anachronism is a feature of his work, from the jokily modern references in *Sebastiane* to the time-travelling Elizabeth of *Jubilee* (1978). Jarman was an uncompromising film-maker, not so much or not only in his portrayal of homosexuality, which was central to his movies, but in his particular vision which often had him wilfully adhering to a vision of cheap, grainy, self-conscious artifice. His continuing devotion to Super 8 was unaccountable, perhaps symptomatic of a kind of nostalgia. *Sebastiane* is in many ways an impressive film, but its very serious ideas sit uneasily beside the Fire Island/Sardinian gay idyll sequences and the film's puerile humour. It does have a style that is instantly recognizable as Jarman's and that would remain intact throughout his career to his last and best film, *Blue* (1993).

ODD/SALIENT FACTS Richard Warwick played one of Mick's gang of schoolboy renegades in *if ...* (1969). The film is entirely in Latin and shares the schoolboy humour of *Carry On Cleo* (1965) with the use of the language ranging from soldiers shouting 'Sinister. Dexter'. as they run to the childish jokes like the expletive 'Excrementum!' for 'Shit!' The verb 'facere' (do or make) and the plural noun 'faces' (torches) proved irresistible to the writers in a slightly more risqué level of the *Carry On*-style *double entendre* in expressions like 'nihil facere' and reaching

▼ *SEBASTIANE* Roman soldiers enjoy some r'n'r in Derek Jarman's singular vision of life in a colonial outpost.

its height with the joyously uttered 'faciebam'. The discussion in the steam room ends with a jokey series of allusions to previous historical Roman and gladiator movies with references to *Fellini-Satyricon* (1969), the films of Cecil B. De Mille, and *Ben Hur* (1959) – in the obscure classical joke of the charioteer Stephanon Paidon, paidon being the Greek for boy, hence Stephen Boyd, the rival charioteer to Charlton Heston in that film.

MEMORABLE MOMENTS The execution of Sebastian in which Jarman himself plays one of the Roman archers. This was the image familiar to him from many works of art that drew Jarman to the project. While viewing the film for classification, James Ferman noticed in the background of this sequence a naked actor with a very obvious erection. When this was pointed out to Jarman, he assured Ferman that having viewed the film only on small-scale editing screens, he was unaware of this minor detail.

KEY LINES

Sebastian: 'Christiani non pugnant' ['Christians don't fight.']

The pejorative term 'Oedipus!' translated simply as 'Motherfucker!'

THE SERVANT
UK, 1963, WARNER-PATHÉ /SPRINGBOK-ELSTREE, 115 MINS
D JOSEPH LOSEY; **PR** JOSEPH LOSEY, NORMAN PRIGGEN;
SC HAROLD PINTER (FROM THE NOVEL BY ROBIN MAUGHAM);
PH (BW) DOUGLAS SLOCOMBE; **ED** REGINALD MILLS; **M** JOHN DANKWORTH
CAST DIRK BOGARDE (HUGO BARRETT), JAMES FOX (TONY), WENDY CRAIG (SUSAN STEWART), SARAH MILES (VERA), CATHERINE LACEY (LADY MOUNSET), RICHARD VERNON (LORD MOUNSET), ANN FIRBANK (SOCIETY WOMAN), DORIS KNOX (OLDER WOMAN), PATRICK MAGEE (BISHOP), ALUN OWEN (CURATE), HAROLD PINTER (SOCIETY MAN), JILL MELFORD (YOUNG WOMAN)

THE STORY Tony, a wealthy upper-class Englishman involved in nebulous schemes to build cities in the Brazilian jungle, hires Barrett, a Yorkshire valet, to run the Georgian house he has

▲ **THE SERVANT** *Dirk Bogarde burnishes the mirror that diminishes his master James Fox in their Chelsea retreat.*

bought in a Chelsea square off the King's Road. The wheedling, manipulative Barrett comes into conflict with Tony's aggressive, lower-middle-class fiancée Susan. He introduces into the household as a new maid his sexy young mistress Vera, passing her off as his sister, and gets her to seduce Tony. But when Tony and Susan return early from a weekend in the country they discover Vera and Barrett frolicking in the master bedroom, and they are fired. Susan exits in high dudgeon, and the house and Tony steadily decay. Barrett contrives an accidental meeting with the demoralized Tony in a pub, and returns to the house to assume the role of dominant partner, casually addressing his employer as 'Tone', all deference abandoned. Vera attempts to return, but is somewhat ambiguously shown to the door by Barrett, and some time later Susan turns up just as a rather demure drug orgy is about to begin. Tony collapses on the floor, and Barrett orders Susan and the other guests to leave.

THE FILM *The Servant* was the first of three movies (the others were *Accident* and *The Go-Between*) about class, sex and domination that the left-wing American exile director Joseph Losey and the working-class Jewish playwright Harold Pinter

adapted from very literary, sexually ambivalent novels by upper-middle-class English writers. The film was made on a small budget, but with complete artistic freedom (though subject to censorship) and employing some of the best artists in the British film industry. Stylistically the film constantly contrasts foreground figures in extreme close-up against people to the rear of the shot who seem to be in command. Tony and Barrett invariably have half their faces in shadow. This was the first time that Losey's baroque talent was allowed to express itself untrammelled, though within the constraints of a Pinter script. It's a subtle study of sado-masochism, of the battle for power between master and servant, and the bi-sexual character of relationships between the classes in England. *The Servant* is a Buñuel nightmare treatment of Wodehouse's Wooster and Jeeves ménage. In 1963 it dramatized the ongoing Profumo scandal, and the erotic scene in which Tony and Vera make love on a swivel chair anticipated, indeed coincided with, the famous picture of a naked Christine Keeler straddling a chair. Dirk Bogarde, who had appeared nine years earlier in Losey's first, pseudonymous British film, *The Sleeping Tiger*, had his career burnished by this movie and went on to make three more pictures with Losey. Cinematographer Douglas Slocombe and designer Richard Macdonald advanced into the big time, the former ending up shooting the Indiana Jones pictures, the latter creating the sets for the first Addams family film.

ODD/SALIENT FACTS The screenplay was originally commissioned by Michael Anderson, the British director of *The Dam Busters* and *Around the World in 80 Days*. Losey claims that the film became possible because he was the only person who remained sober at a mammoth 1962 drinking session at the Connaught Hotel. Losey also claims that the restaurant scene was shot in a day, with the numerous well-known actors being paid largely in booze.

MEMORABLE MOMENTS Barrett's first appearance on the King's Road beneath the royal coat of arms dignifying the fact that Thomas Crapper provides lavatories to the Royal Family.

Barrett's first appearance in his dark coat and hat standing over Tony, drunkenly slumped in a deckchair.

The numerous shots in the convex mirror over the mantelpiece.

The restaurant sequence in which various decadent dialogues are going on around Tony and Susan.

KEY LINES

Tony: 'He may be a servant, but he's still a human being.'

Susan: 'What do you want from this house?'
Barrett: 'I'm a servant, miss.'

Tony: 'Do something about it, you're supposed to be the bloody servant.'

Tony: 'I don't know what I'd do without you.'
Barrett: 'So go and pour a glass of brandy. Don't just stand there.'

THE SET-UP

US, 1949, RKO, 72 MINS

D *ROBERT WISE;* **PR** *RICHARD GOLDSTONE;* **SC** *ART COHN (BASED ON THE POEM BY JOSEPH MONCURE MARCH);* **PH** *(BW) MILTON KRASNER;* **ED** *ROLAND GROSS*

CAST *ROBERT RYAN (BILL 'STOKER' THOMPSON); AUDREY TOTTER (JULIE THOMPSON), GEORGE TOBIAS (TINY), PERCY HELTON (RED), ALAN BAXTER ('LITTLE BOY'), WALLACE FORD (GUS), HAL FIEBERLING ('TIGER' NELSON), DARRYL HICKMAN (SHANLEY), KENNY O'MORRISON (MOORE), JAMES EDWARDS (LUTHER HAWKINS), DAVID CLARKE ('GUNBOAT' JOHNSON), PHILIP PINE (TONY SOUZA), EDWIN MAX (DANNY)*

THE STORY 9.05pm, a hot summer night in Paradise City. Boxing fans are filing into the sleazy stadium. Across the street at Hotel Cozy, the tired, punchy 35-year-old heavyweight Bill 'Stoker' Thompson is resting before his four-round bout with 23-year-old 'Tiger' Nelson. Stoker's wife Julie wants him to quit, but Stoker believes he might win and earn a better billing. Meanwhile, his manager Tiny has taken fifty dollars from the minor racketeer managing Nelson, for Stoker to take a dive in the third round. Convinced Stoker will lose, Tiny doesn't tell him about the set-up and squares Stoker's squalid second.

During three brutal rounds Stoker is more than holding his own. Before the bell for the fourth round, Tiny reveals the set-up, but a battered Stoker knocks out his opponent. Trying to escape he's cornered in an alleyway by Little Boy and his henchmen and is pinned down so that Little Boy can smash his right fist to a pulp. He staggers out into the street where Julie

cradles him before the ambulance arrives. A clock shows the time as 10.16pm

THE FILM *The Set-Up* is one of the great boxing movies, using the game as a metaphor for the illusory nature of the American Dream, with one of the screen's most realistic scraps, staged by John Indrisano. In the symbolically named Paradise City, Thompson and his wife stay at the sordid Hotel Cozy, and Julie cradles her husband under the neon sign of the Dreamland dance hall in the final scene. In the seedy dressing room Stoker meets a range of boxers – a teenager making his debut, a demented no-hoper going into the ring for the last time, a handsome black determined to box his way out of the ghetto. The film is not an attack on boxing itself, and ultimately the doomed Stoker snatches victory from his defeat.

The Set-Up was shot entirely in a studio and has a stylized, expressionistic *noir* atmosphere. There is only source music from

▼ *THE SET-UP* Typical 1940s production still shows Ryan's Stoker Thompson standing stoic, isolated and alone.

radios, bars and clubs. The film lasts exactly the 72 minutes from the opening to the closing shot (unlike *High Noon*, for instance, which is rather shorter than the time stated by the clocks).

Robert Wise edited *Citizen Kane* and *The Magnificent Ambersons* before he made his directorial debut with Val Lewton's low-budget horror movie unit at RKO and became a versatile genre director. *The Set-Up*, his ninth film, completed his RKO contract, after which he entered the big time, which ultimately led to such pictures as *West Side Story* and *The Sound of Music*.

> '**Doesn't that guy get enough shut-eye in the ring?**'

ODD/SALIENT FACTS The film was based on a narrative poem published in 1928 by William Moncure March, who gave up his job as the first managing editor of *The New Yorker* to devote himself to writing. On the strength of it he went to Hollywood as a screenwriter, remaining there for a dozen years. In 1948 he volunteered to work on Wise's film of *The Set-Up* 'but they didn't want me around'. The rhythms and rhymes of his poem anticipate rap music and March was incensed that his black boxer Pansy Jones was changed into the white Stoker Thompson. Robert Ryan (1909–73) was a boxing champion while a student at the Ivy League college, Dartmouth.

MEMORABLE MOMENTS Tiny, the corrupt manager, striking a match across Stoker's name on the poster outside the stadium to relight the stub of his cigar.

The pained face of Stoker waking up in his shabby hotel.

Julie's walk through the garish, neon-lit urban hell of Paradise City.

Stoker's desperate glances from the ring at his wife's empty seat.

The shadow of a jazz band playing behind a barred window thrown on the alley wall as Little Boy advances to smash Stoker's hand.

KEY LINES

Tiny, on being told Stoker is resting: 'Doesn't that guy get enough shut-eye in the ring?'

Julie: 'I remember the first time you told me that. You were just one punch away from the title shot. Don't you see Bill, you'll always be one punch away ... What kind of a life is this, how many more beatings do you have to take?'

Little Boy: 'I paid for something tonight, Stoker. I didn't get it.'

Stoker: 'I won tonight.'
Julie: 'You won tonight. We both won tonight.'

SE7EN

US, 1995, NEW LINE CINEMA, 127 MINS

D *David Fincher;* **PR** *Arnold Kopelson, Phylis Carlyle;* **SC** *Andrew Kevin Walker;* **PH** *Darius Khondji;* **PR DES** *Arthur Max;* **M** *Howard Shore;* **ED** *Richard Francis-Bruce* **CAST** *Morgan Freeman (Somerset), Brad Pitt (Mills), Kevin Spacey (John Doe), Gwyneth Paltrow (Tracy Mills), Richard Roundtree (Talbot), R. Lee Ermey (Police Captain), Bob Mack (Gluttony victim), Hawthorne (George, library guard), Gene Borkan (Eli Gould), Julie Araskog (Mrs Gould), Alfonso Freeman (Fingerprint forensic man), Michael Reid MacKay (Victor), Martin Serene (Wild Bill), Michael Massee (Man in Massage Parlour booth), Cat Mueller (Hooker), Heidi Schanz (Beautiful woman), Richmond Arquette (Delivery man)*

THE STORY The young Detective Mills, on his new assignment in a big city, and the soon-to-retire Detective Somerset investigate a series of murders based on the seven deadly sins. After Gluttony, Greed and Sloth, Somerset, who shares the killer's love of literature, tracks him down, but the man, John Doe, evades capture. Somerset and Mills search the killer's flat and find evidence of his connection to the crimes as well as 2,000 journals. After the bodies of a prostitute and model are found for the sins of Lust and Pride, Doe gives himself up to Mills and Somerset. He strikes a deal whereby he will sign a full confession on the condition that the detectives go with him to find the bodies of his final two victims. The three of them drive into the desert where a package is delivered to them. When he finds that it is the head of his pregnant wife, Mills shoots Doe repeatedly thus completing the themed killings with Envy and Wrath.

▲ *SE7EN Mills (Brad Pitt) and Somerset (Morgan Freeman) are confronted with the grim interior of John Doe's apartment.*

THE FILM *Se7en* somehow ought to have been a minor success at best. It is the video director David Fincher's follow-up to his inauspicious debut *Alien 3* (1992). The notion of a serial killer working with a specific theme is straight out of the camp horror of the Vincent Price *Dr Phibes* films. The basic structure is hackneyed with the cynical veteran cop on the eve of retirement resisting his final case and mismatched with his new, 'gung-ho, rookie' partner. Somerset works by getting into the mind of the villains he tracks down. The film is such a surprising triumph and was a box-office smash, because of the ingenuity of the plotting, the performances of the three leads and perhaps chiefly because of the consistency of the vision, the sheer brilliance of the design and the unrelenting bleakness of the atmosphere. It pits a cultivated, civilized man who is a hardened pessimist against a philistine who wants to make a difference. Somerset instantly recognizes the literary and biblical allusions of the killer. Mills thinks that *Of Human Bondage* is about bondage, and snaps at his partner about the killer: 'Just because the fucker's got a library card, doesn't make him Yoda.' His idea of the most erudite man in the universe is the mystic muppet from *Star Wars* (1977). The film's dull lighting, with shady interiors and perma-raining exteriors and the muffled sound, force the audience to lean towards the screen, getting closer to the grim, ingeniously devised and realized action. It will remain as a cult favourite.

ODD/SALIENT FACTS Writer Andrew Kevin Walker plays the part of the murder victim in the scene in which Somerset and Mills first meet. Kevin Spacey was due to have star billing but insisted on not being listed in the opening credits so his appearance would remain a surprise for audiences. To compensate he appears first in the final credits which go against tradition, scrolling up rather than down. While filming the chase sequence, Brad Pitt slipped and put his arm through a car's windscreen, causing an injury which required surgery. This injury was worked into the script.

MEMORABLE MOMENTS The clues deliberately left at the murder scenes: the plastic shavings found in the Gluttony victim's stomach which reveal that the fridge was moved, behind which is written 'Gluttony' in grease; the upside-down hanging of the painting in Gould's office, behind which is written 'Help Me' using Victor's fingerprints.

The discovery of John Doe's flat with its links to the crimes, 2,000 journals and the photograph which shows that Doe was the photographer who approached Somerset and Mills outside Victor (Sloth)'s apartment.

The final scene with the sudden realization of the contents of the box.

KEY LINES

Mills on his introduction to poetry: 'Fuckin' Dante, God-damned poems, rhyming faggot, piece of shit fucker.'

The Doctor on why Victor won't spill the beans: 'Even if his brain weren't mush, which it is, he chewed his own tongue off long ago ... He's experienced about as much pain and suffering as anyone I've encountered, give or take, and he's still got Hell to look forward to.'

Somerset to Mills: 'You know this isn't gonna have a happy ending.'

Somerset to Mills: 'If we catch John Doe and he turns out to be the devil. I mean if he's Satan himself, that might live up to our expectations. But he's not the devil. He's just a man.'

John Doe: 'I'm setting the example and what I've done is gonna be puzzled over and studied and followed forever.'

SHADOWS

US, 1959, GENA PRODUCTION/FACES INT., 87 MINS

D JOHN CASSAVETES; *PR* MAURICE MCENDREE, NIKOS PAPATAKIS; *SC* JOHN CASSAVETES (BASED UPON IMPROVISATIONS BY THE CAST); *PH* (BW) ERICH KOLLMAR; *ED* MAURICE MCENDREE; *M* SHAFI HADI, CHARLES MINGUS

CAST BEN CARRUTHERS (BEN), LELIA GOLDONI (LELIA), HUGH HURD (HUGH), ANTHONY RAY (TONY), DENNIS SALLAS (DENNIS), TOM ALLEN (TOM), DAVID POKITILLOW (DAVID), RUPERT CROSSE (RUPERT), DAVEY JONES (DAVEY), VICTORIA VARGAS (VICKI), JACK ACKERMAN (JACK), JACQUELINE WALCOTT (JACQUELINE)

THE STORY Black nightclub jazz singer Hugh lives in a Manhattan apartment, supporting his younger brother Ben, an unemployed trumpeter, and his sister Lelia, a twenty-year-old painter, both of whom can pass for white. Hugh does some work in Philadelphia, which involves telling jokes and introducing the dancers. Ben hangs out with his white friends Dennis and Tom, picking up girls in bars. Lelia is taken by a novelist friend to a Greenwich Village party attended by smart intellectuals, where she meets Tony, who takes her virginity on their second meeting. Meeting her brothers, Tony is shocked by their colour and Hugh orders him to leave. After a destructive party thrown by Hugh, the trio go in different directions. Lelia accepts an invitation to go dancing with a handsome black musician. Hugh and his manager catch a train at Grand Central for an ill-paid week's engagement in Chicago. Ben and his friends get beaten up by the boyfriends of some girls they've moved in on, and Ben decides to change his ways.

THE FILM One of the most influential films of its time, *Shadows* ends with the credit 'THE FILM YOU HAVE JUST SEEN WAS AN IMPROVISATION'. It was in fact devised by actors – mostly unemployed – in John Cassavetes' drama workshop and the film has the raw, quality of two movements that sprung up at this time, the French New Wave and the cinéma vérité documentarists. Like them, Cassavetes was reacting against the contrivance of orthodox cinema and very precisely against the kind of Hollywood movies in which he continued to appear, so as to finance his personal movies. *Shadows* is anti-star, anti-plot, and his most extreme work. It helped inspire and define American independent cinema. It made possible Martin Scorsese's *Mean Streets*; indeed Scorsese recognized Cassavetes as his mentor. But the film divided critics and was rejected by the general public.

Shot with a hand-held camera in Manhattan diners, bars and apartments, around Times Square and in Central Park, the movie captures the vivacity of New York bohemian life in the Fifties. The improvised jazz score by saxophonist Shafi Hadi and bassist Charlie Mingus are an essential part of the atmosphere. The improvisational technique suggests the characters' searching for identities; and the title refers apparently to people being shadows of future selves. Although Cassavetes' later pictures dug deeper they tended to be burdened with longueurs. The later movies featured familiar stars (Peter Falk, Ben Gazzara) whereas none of the actors in *Shadows* went on to stardom. Surprisingly, the mercurial, provocative Lelia Goldoni failed to find fame, though she had the odd role, most memorably in the remake of *Invasion of the Body Snatchers* and Ben Carruthers appeared in two cult films of the mid-1960s, Robert Rassen's *Lilith* and Alexander Mackendrick's *A High Wind in Jamaica*, billed in the latter as 'Benito'. While some aspects of the film lack subtlety, race is treated with great skill and intelligence. There were no Hollywood movies at that time in which whites and blacks mixed with social ease, and *Shadows* reflected the tensions and limitations involved in inter-racial relationships.

ODD/SALIENT FACTS The movie was shot over two years on 16mm for a total of $40,000. The seed money came in 1957

▼ *SHADOWS Innocent Lelia Goldoni bristles as hip Village bohemian Anthony Ray makes his conventional amorous advances.*

when John Cassavetes was appearing on a late-night radio chat show in New York and appealed to listeners to send in cash if they wanted to see him make a truly realistic picture dealing with racial issues in everyday life. The station received $2,000 in small sums. All the actors in the film used their own names for the characters they created. Anthony Ray, who played Tony, is the son of Nicholas Ray, director of *Rebel Without a Cause*, a film for which Cassavetes auditioned.

MEMORABLE MOMENTS Lelia walking down 42nd Street looking at the ads outside movie houses.

> 'We went out to have a ball. You pay the price. If you get beat up, you get beat up.'

Ben, Tom and Dennis in the Museum of Modern Art sculpture court where Tom rails against culture and mocks Dennis.

Tony and Lelia running away from David in Central Park.

Hugh and Rupert's long, conciliatory dialogue at Grand Central Station.

KEY LINES

Lelia: 'David's writing a new novel all about you Ben.'
Ben: 'It had better not be any of that Beat Generation jazz like the last one.'

Lelia, after losing her virginity: 'I didn't know it could be so awful … I thought being with you would be so important and that afterwards two people would be as close as it was possible to get, but instead we're just two strangers. It's over. I know that much about life.'

Tom: 'We went out to have a ball. You pay the price. If you get beat up, you get beat up.'

SHERLOCK JR

US, 1924, METRO PICTURES/BUSTER KEATON PRODUCTIONS, 45 MINS

D BUSTER KEATON; **PR** JOSEPH M. SCHENK;. **SC** CLYDE BRUCKMAN, JEAN HAVES AND JOSEPH MITCHELL; **PH** (BW) ELGIN LESSLEY, BRYON HOUCK; **ED** BUSTER KEATON

CAST BUSTER KEATON (THE PROJECTIONIST/SHERLOCK JR.), KATHRYN McGUIRE (THE GIRL), WARD KRANE (THE RIVAL), JOSEPH KEATON (THE GIRL'S FATHER), HORACE MORGAN, JANE CONNELLY, ERWIN CONNELLY, FORD WEST, GEORGE DAVIS, JOHN PATRICK, RUTH HOLLEY

THE STORY A projectionist in a small town movie theatre dreams of becoming a detective. Short of money he buys his beloved a $1 box of chocolates. His rival, seeing the threat posed by the projectionist, steals the girl's father's watch, pawns it, buys a bigger box of chocolates with the proceeds and plants the pawn ticket in the projectionist's pocket. The projectionist briefly trails the cad before having to go to work in the projection booth where he falls asleep. Meanwhile the girl goes to the pawn shop and discovers the truth. As he sleeps, the projectionist's ghostly alter-ego leaves his body and enters the screen, first chaotically then suavely, as 'The World's most renowned crimebuster – Sherlock Jr.' Pursuing the cad who has kidnapped the girl, he rescues her and defeats the gang before waking up again in the projection booth. Inspired by events on the screen he kisses her. Fade to babies. The projectionist is left scratching his head.

THE FILM Like his great rival Chaplin, Keaton's most productive period had passed by the time sound had arrived. But while Chaplin continued to produce major films and his fortunes were improving, Keaton's luck changed and he faced poverty and alcoholism. By the late Forties the cult of the cinema's second great clown was reestablished and he found regular and lucrative work in films and on television and travelled the festival circuit. The film, originally titled *The Misfit* and made by an already established and independently creative star, came in the midst of Keaton's golden era which included *The Navigator* (1924), *Go West* (1925) and his great masterpiece *The General* (1927). He uses the opportunity to explore with wit and no pretentiousness the nature of film and film-making. This is one of cinema's first exercises in post-modernism, a brilliantly innovative and imaginative minor masterpiece which investigates and toys with the boundaries of the screen.

ODD/SALIENT FACTS Buster Keaton was famous for inventing and performing the stunts in his own films. In *Sherlock Jr* when he did the first take of the sequence in which he runs along the tops of the railway cars and grabs hold of the spout of the water tower, Keaton seriously underestimated the force of the gushing water. He was knocked to the ground but, with the bounce and spirit that, according to legend, had him nick-named 'Buster' as a kid by Houdini, he got straight back up and carried on with the work. Only in a medical examination many years later was it discovered that he had broken his neck in this fall. The scene in which Keaton escapes the gangsters by driving into the suitcase of ties his disguised accomplice is holding in front of his stomach, was accomplished without camera trickery. It was an old vaudeville gag which Keaton replicated for Ed Sullivan on his TV show *Toast of the Town* in 1957. Keaton employed his old pal Roscoe 'Fatty' Arbuckle to work as a co-director on the film at a time after his infamous murder/rape case when he could find no other work. Arbuckle was to be credited as William Goodrich, a pseudonym he used for his directorial work over the next decade, but was so irascible with the actors that Keaton removed him from the picture.

MEMORABLE MOMENTS Keaton shadowing his rival, matching him pace for pace as they walk down the pavement. The cad picks up a cigarette, takes three drags, tosses it over his shoulder where Keaton catches it and takes a drag himself before discarding it. The two trip up on the same paving stone and simultaneously swerve to avoid a passing car before entering a railway yard.

▼ *SHERLOCK JR The projectionist (Buster Keaton) is faced with the awful truth that his one dollar is not going to stretch to a three-dollar box of chocolates.*

Keaton's first moments in the film within the film when he finds himself tossed about in various jump-cutting scenes from the front of a house, to a garden bench, to the middle of a busy road, to the edge of a cliff, to between two lions, to a desert through which a train speeds, to a rock in the sea, to a snow-covered forest, and back to the garden.

Buster's escape from the gang's lair. His sidekick has supplied him with a hoop containing a concertinaed dress. This Buster places in the window frame before entering the house. The side wall is removed to reveal that the stunt is achieved without special effects. Having suddenly to flee, Buster dives out of the window, through the hoop and into the dress, in which he walks away, so when the gang rush straight out of the house, the only person they see is an innocent old lady.

KEY LINE
The card on Sherlock's performance in the fantasy film: 'His mind solved everything about the mystery except identifying the thieves and recovering the pearls.'

SHOCK CORRIDOR

US, 1963, FROMKESS-FIRKS/ALLIED ARTISTS, 110 MINS
D/PR/SC *SAMUEL FULLER;* **PH** *STANLEY CORTEZ;* **ED** *JEROME THOMS;* **M** *PAUL DUNLAP*

CAST *PETER BRECK (JOHNNY BARRETT), CONSTANCE TOWERS (CATHY), GENE EVANS (BODEN), JAMES BEST (STUART), HARI RHODES (TRENT), LARRY TUCKER (PAGLIACCI), WILLIAM ZUCCART ('SWANEE' SWANSON), PHILIP AHN (DR FONG), JOHN MATHEWS (DR CHRISTO), CHUCK ROBERSON (WILKES), JOHN CRAIG (LLOYD)*

THE STORY The film opens and closes with the title: Whom God wishes to destroy he first makes mad – Euripedes 425 BC. Reporter Johnny Barrett, ambitious to win a Pulitzer Prize, is coached by a psychiatrist and his editor to feign insanity so that he can be admitted to a state mental hospital and crack the unsolved murder of an inmate. Johnny's girlfriend Cathy, a stripper, pretends to be his sister and accuses him of attempted incest. He's admitted to the institution where he is under the supervision of Dr Christo and two male attendants, the caring Wilkes and the brutal Lloyd. Johnny identifies three psychotic witnesses to the murder and wins their confidence. Stuart, a Southern redneck who was brainwashed while a PoW in

Korea, now lives in a fantasy world where he believes himself to be the Civil War General Jeb Stuart. The second witness is Trent, a black student who cracked under pressure of being the first black student in an all-white university in the Deep South. His self-hatred has turned him into a Ku Klux Klan racist. The third witness is the guilt-ridden Dr Boden, a Nobel Prize-winning physicist, one of the creators of the A-bomb, who has reverted to childhood. Johnny eventually discovers that the killer was Wilkes, whom his victim was about to expose as a sexual predator. Cathy observes Johnny's steady deterioration, as he does himself. By the time he extracts a confession from Wilkes, he is as far gone as the other patients and is kept inside.

THE FILM The maverick Sam Fuller's forceful movie style was shaped by his experiences as a tabloid journalist and as an infantryman in the Second World War. In *Shock Corridor* he wanted to expose the conditions in American mental hospitals, but this startling low-budget movie has little to do with the American treatment of the nation's mentally sick. *Shock Corridor* (like *The Cabinet of Dr Caligari*) uses a mental hospital as a metaphor for the nation itself. Eschewing subtlety and good taste, the movie is about a society driven mad by the Cold War, racial prejudice and nuclear angst. Driven on by blind ambition, Johnny merely pretends to sympathize with Stuart, Trent and Boden, and in consequence joins them in madness. From the office walls of the psychologists and the newspaper editor, photographs of Freud, Jung and Pulitzer look down on men who have betrayed their professions. As in Fuller's *Pickup on South Street*, where a pickpocket and a whore emerge as hero and heroine in a story of Cold War espionage, the voice of sanity is a stripper. A photograph of Fuller is pinned to the mirror in the strippers' changing room.

ODD/SALIENT FACTS Fuller was steeped in American newspaper lore and his plot was inspired by the intrepid muck-raking journalist Nelly Bly (1867–1922) who got herself committed to a New York asylum in the 1880s to write about the appalling treatment of inmates for Joseph Pulitzer's *New York World*. The British Board of Film Censorship banned *Shock Corridor* for seven years on the grounds that its depiction of mental hospitals was irresponsible. The film's dream sequences are from 16mm CinemaScope colour footage that Fuller shot in Japan (while making *House of Bamboo*) and Brazil (for the unfinished picture *Tigrero*). The cinematographer, Stanley Cortez, shot Orson Welles's *The Magnificent Ambersons* and Charles

▲ *SHOCK CORRIDOR Constance Towers clutches Peter Breck's knee as he goes round the bend in pursuit of a Pulitzer Prize.*

Laughton's *Night of the Hunter*. The art director, Eugene Lourie, worked for Jean Renoir, e.g. on *La Grande Illusion* and *La Règle du Jeu*, and directed several SF horror pictures, among them *The Beast From 20,000 Fathoms* (1953). Shortly after *Shock Corridor*, Fuller appeared as himself in Jean-Luc Godard's *Pierrot le Fou*, and subsequently had walk-on and cameo roles in other pictures, including Dennis Hopper's *The Last Movie* (as the director of the film-within-the-film), and Wim Wenders's *The End of Violence* (his final appearance, playing the hero's father).

MEMORABLE MOMENTS The first scene of the asylum's corridor, stretching out into infinity.

The vulgar shots of Cathy doing her strip routine superimposed on the sleeping Johnny, her feather boa tickling his ear.

The deranged Johnny's waking nightmare of a thunderstorm occurring indoors along the corridor.

KEY LINE

Dr Christo: 'A man can't tamper with his mind and expect to come out of it sane. Johnny is a catatonic schizophrenic. What a tragedy – an insane mutt will win the Pulitzer Prize.'

SHOWGIRLS

US, 1995, CAROLCO, 131 MINS

D *PAUL VERHOEVEN;* **PR** *ALAN MARSHALL;* **SC** *JOE ESZTERHAS;*
PH *(COL) JOST VACANO;* **M** *DAVID STEWART;* **ED** *MARK GOLDBLATT, MARK HELFRICH*

CAST *ELIZABETH BERKLEY (NOMI MALONE), KYLE MACLACHLAN (ZACK CAREY), GINA GERSHON (CRISTAL CONNORS), GLENN PLUMMER (JAMES SMITH), ROBERT DAVI (AL TORRES), ALAN RACHINS (TONY MOSS), GINA RAVERA (MOLLY ABRAMS), LIN TUCCI (HENRIETTA BAZOOM), GREG TRAVIS (PHIL NEWKIRK), AL RUSCIO (MR KARLMAN), PATRICK BRISTOW (MARTY JACOBSEN), WILLIAM SHOCKLEY (ANDREW CARVER), MICHELLE JOHNSTON (GAY CARPENTER), DEWEY WEBER (JEFF), RENA RIFFEL (PENNY)*

THE STORY Nomi, a drifter with a mysterious past, arrives in Las Vegas with dreams of becoming a dancer. She works as a lap dancer but aspires to dance beside Cristal Connors at the Stardust club where Molly works backstage. Nomi catches Cristal's eye and one night Cristal takes her boyfriend Zack, the entertainment director at the Stardust, to the club where Nomi works. She pays $500 for Nomi to do a private lap dance for Zack, which turns into a dry hump. Nomi gets a job in the chorus line at the Stardust, Nomi has sex with Zack and wins the job of Cristal's understudy. Cristal vetoes this appointment so Nomi pushes Cristal down a flight of stairs after a show. Nomi becomes the star of the show but at her celebration party her friend Molly is raped by Andrew Carver, a singer on whom she had a crush. When she finds out from Zack that the attack is going to be hushed up, Nomi, who it turns out is a former prostitute and crack addict, whose father killed her mother and then himself, beats up Carver, and visits both Molly and Cristal in hospital. She heads out of town towards Los Angeles, catching a lift with Jeff, the man with whom she had hitched into Vegas in the first place.

THE FILM *Showgirls* is an hilariously terrible film. In his book *Paul Verhoeven*, Rob Van Scheers writes of the 'story which will make Verhoeven's previous film *Basic Instinct* look like *Bambi*, as one of the director's assistants puts it'. *Showgirls* makes *Basic Instinct* look like *Citizen Kane*. Van Scheers captures the director's approach on set:

> A patient mentor, he explains what he intends to do with the scene, and is not ashamed to whisper words of encouragement into the actress's ear. He caresses her,

cracks jokes with her – all of which is intended to put Elizabeth, his material, at her ease. If necessary, Verhoeven does exactly the same with her opposite number Gina Gershon.

We begin to see the project's appeal for the director – beyond, no doubt, his desire to present a searing satire on American culture. The film was, as Janet Maslin wrote in *The New York Times*, an 'instant cult classic'. A disaster at the box office, soon after release it became a favourite on American college campuses, and works very well as a comedy. In his American work Verhoeven has explored levels of tastelessness, deliberately or otherwise. Fans of *Showgirls* should proceed directly to *Starship Troopers* (1997), another camp masterpiece,

'She's dazzling! She's exciting! She's also very sexy.'

with lashings of fascist ideology and mixed-sex group shower scenes. Hollywood makes some big mistakes. Who thought that it would be a good idea for the man who had directed the worst disco sequence in Hollywood history in *Basic Instinct* (1992) to make a film all about dancing? For connoisseurs of turkeys it is a good idea that they did.

ODD/SALIENT FACTS Screenwriter Joe Eszterhas, a flamboyant ex-Rolling Stone journalist proved with *Jagged Edge* (1985), *The Music Box* (1989) and *Basic Instinct* (1992) that he had mastered at least one narrative structure and he would keep reworking it until someone told him to stop or, worse, stopped paying him to rewrite it under different titles. With *Showgirls* he proved that he could also write soft-core pornographic melodrama every bit as bad as Jacqueline Susann's. Paul Verhoeven modelled the hand-held camera sequences capturing the backstage life of the showgirls on Fellini's *8½* (1963).

MEMORABLE MOMENTS Nomi and Zack first make love in Zack's pool. After drinking champagne, Nomi disrobes and wanders into the pool. Zack soon follows with the champagne which he pours over Nomi and licks off her. She submerges for some very brief, underwater oral sex, and then some water sports in the fountain. Finally she mounts him at the water's edge, and becomes a wave machine before going into alarming spasms.

▲ *SHOWGIRLS Elizabeth Berkley grapples with the greasy pole of success that is the world of Las Vegas glamour dancing.*

KEY LINES

Mr Karlman on Cristal (he says the same of Nomi after her debut as Goddess): 'She's dazzling! She's exciting! She's also very sexy.'

Al Torres, giving new girl Penny some career advice: 'If you wanna last longer than a week, give me a blow-job. First I get you used to the money, then I make you swallow.'

Nomi and James are getting steamy as they dance together, but when things go too far, Nomi cautions: 'It's my period.'
James, incredulous: 'Oh, right!'
Nomi: 'Check. [He checks.] See.'

James, to the departing Nomi: 'It's all right, I got towels.'
Al and Mama (Ms Bazoom) visit Nomi at the Stardust. Al suggests that maybe Nomi misses them.
Mama: 'She misses us like I miss that lump on my twat that I had taken off last week.'

SID AND NANCY

UK, 1986, ZENITH/INITIAL, 114 MINS
D *ALEX COX;* **PR** *ERIC FELLNER;* **SC** *ALEX COX, ABBE WOOL;*
PH *(COL) ROGER DEAKINS;* **M** *JOE STRUMMER, THE POGUES, PRAY FOR RAIN;* **ED** *DAVID MARTIN*
CAST *GARY OLDMAN (SID VICIOUS), CHLOE WEBB (NANCY SPUNGEN), DAVID HAYMAN (MALCOLM), DEBBY BISHOP (PHOEBE), ANDREW SCHOFIELD (JOHN), XANDER BERKELEY (BOWERY SNAX), PERRY BENSON (PAUL), TONY LONDON (STEVE), SANDY BARON (HOTELIER – USA), SY RICHARDSON (METHADONE WORKER), EDWARD TUDOR-POLE (HOTELIER – UK)*

THE STORY In the aftermath of Nancy Spungen's death, Sid Vicious recalls their meeting and romantic life together. They meet at the flat of a mutual friend, a dominatrix, just after Sid joined the Sex Pistols. Nancy introduces Sid to heroin and hangs around during the group's brief spell in the limelight. The other members of the band resent Nancy's presence and the effects of drugs on Sid's abilities. Nancy, banned from coming along on the disastrous tour of America, stays in London and works as a prostitute. When Sid collapses on a plane, Nancy travels to New York to meet him and they spend time together in Paris where Sid does some recording. They move into the Chelsea Hotel in New York, and Nancy arranges a few gigs for Sid. They attend a methadone clinic, and spend a disastrous thanksgiving with Nancy's family. All the time their dependence on heroin becomes increasingly desperate. Having made a pact to go out together, Nancy dies from stab wounds, presumably inflicted by Sid. Sid is arrested, undergoes cold turkey in jail, and is released on bail. Sid is dancing with some kids on a wasteland outside a diner, when a cab pulls up. A smiling Nancy is sitting inside. Sid gets into the cab and it drives off.

THE FILM The working title for the film was *Love Kills*. It was not intended to be a film about music, a biopic of The Sex Pistols. It is a love story. Then why is there all that embarrassing stuff about punk that makes much of the first half of the film unwatchable, but unwatchable in a completely different way from the last section which is even harder to sit through. It has a lot to do with the writer/director. Cox began with the promising, flawed cult debut, *Repo Man* (1984), starring Harry Dean Stanton, a man of impeccable cult standing. By this, his second film, things were already starting to unravel and would go utterly pear-shaped in his disastrous third film, *Straight to Hell* (1986). Whatever the shortcomings of the film, and its lack of control, the central performances are remarkably raw, naked and courageously unsympathetic, and deserve to feature in some minor modern masterpiece rather than a fascinating cult failure.

ODD/SALIENT FACTS Thus far, Chloe Webb's post-Nancy career has featured only two notable roles, in Peter Greenaway's *The Belly of an Architect* (1987) and opposite Danny De Vito in *Twins* (1988). The role of Sid Vicious launched Gary Oldman as one of the Hollywood cult psycho character actors of the nineties, in *State of Grace* (1990), *JFK* (1991), Bram Stoker's *Dracula* (1992), and *True Romance* (1993). The film is the first in the new wave of cinematic heroin chic, blazing the way for such distinguished druggy cult works as *Pulp Fiction* (1994), *Trainspotting* (1995) and *Fear and Loathing in Las Vegas* (1998). The supporting cast features: Kathy Burke, later to star in Oldman's grim, autobiographical debut as writer-director, *Nil by Mouth* (1997); Courtney Love who plays one of Nancy's friends and appeared in *Straight to Hell*, no stranger to the sex and drugs and rock 'n' roll lifestyle, and herself married to Kurt Cobain, a successor, if much more talented, to Sid Vicious's place in the 'live fast, die young and leave a pale body' stakes; and, as one of the prospective guests of the Chelsea Hotel put off by Sid and Nancy's antics, Iggy Pop, who must have been one of the models for the part of Rock-Head, the self-confessed 'Godfather of punk'.

MEMORABLE MOMENTS As their relationship collapses with their addiction to heroin, Sid and Nancy kiss on a New York

▼ *SID AND NANCY With vacant eyes and scars of self-mutilation, Gary Oldman in the performance that launched his career as Hollywood's favourite psychotic outsider.*

street as rubbish falls all around them.

They huddle together on a subway train as Sid salivates and blows a snot bubble from a nostril.

In their zonked-out state, they lie on their bed, unbothered by the fire started when a cigarette is discarded among the junk detritus of their lives.

KEY LINES

Sid: 'You know I was so bored once that I fucked a dog.'

Malcolm: 'But Sidney's more than a mere bass player. He's a fabulous disaster. He's a symbol, a metaphor, he embodies the dementia of a nihilistic generation. He's a fuckin' star.'

Nancy: 'I hate my fuckin' life.'

Sid: 'This is just a rough patch. Things'll be much better when we get to America, I promise.'

Nancy: 'We're in America. We've been here a week. New York is in America, you fuck.'

SINGIN' IN THE RAIN★

US, 1962, MGM, 102 MINS

D *STANLEY DONEN, GENE KELLY;* **PR** *ARTHUR FREED;* **SC** *BETTY COMDEN, ADOLPH GREEN;* **PH** *(TECHNICOLOR) HAROLD ROSSON;* **ED** *ADRIENNE FAZAN;* **M** *NACIO HERB BROWN, ARTHUR FREED*

CAST *GENE KELLY (DON LOCKWOOD), DONALD O'CONNOR (COSMO BROWN), DEBBIE REYNOLDS (KATHY SELDEN), JEAN HAGEN (LINA LAMONT), MILLARD MITCHELL (R. F. SIMPSON, HEAD OF MONUMENTAL PICTURES), DOUGLAS FOWLEY (ROSCOE DEXTER), RITA MORENO (ZELDA ZANDERS), KING DONOVAN (ROD, PUBLICIST), MADGE BLAKE (DORA BAILEY), KATHLEEN FREEMAN (PHOEBE DINSMORE), CYD CHARISSE (DANCER IN 'BROADWAY MELODY')*

THE STORY Friends since childhood, Don Lockwood and Cosmo Brown were a burlesque song-and-dance act before trying their luck in Hollywood in the mid-1920s. Cosmo plays mood music on the set of silent films; after working as a stunt-man Don became a swashbuckling star, appearing opposite Lina Lamont, a vain beauty with a grating Bronx accent. Don

loathes Lina but the fan magazines suggest they are virtually engaged. After the premiere of their latest picture, Don is rescued from a mob of admirers by Kathy Selden, an aspiring actress who claims to despise movie stars. Later that night at a party given by J. R., the studio boss, there is a demonstration of a talking picture followed by a floor show with Kathy jumping out of a cake. Don makes a joke about Kathy's job and a cream cake she aims at him strikes Lina and Kathy flees. Sound arrives in Hollywood, and the new Lockwood-Lamont picture is turned into a talkie. Don has been looking for Kathy and spots her in a chorus on the set; they make it up, Kathy admitting to being a long-time fan. Lina's appalling voice contributes to a disastrous sneak preview of *The Duelling Cavalier,* and

'I can't make love to a bush.'

Cosmo suggests re-doing it as a musical with Kathy dubbing Lina. Lina threatens to sue the studio if Kathy's role is revealed. But at the triumphant premiere, Lina is tricked into revealing her lack of vocal talent and Don and Kathy become the studio's new stars.

THE FILM If Billy Wilder's *Sunset Boulevard* is the most vitriolic poison pen letter ever posted by a Hollywood insider, *Singin' in the Rain* is the most seductive Valentine card Tinseltown ever sent itself. Wilder's film is Hollywood as tragedy, the Donen-Kelly movie is Hollywood as comedy. Both deal with victims of the first Hollywood crisis – the coming of sound and the Wall Street crash that immediately followed – and were made during Hollywood's second great crisis – the McCarthyite witchhunts and the impending break-up of the studio system. At the time the movie was being made, Gene Kelly and his then wife, actress Betsy Blair, were being investigated by the House Un-American Activities Committee. *Singin' in the Rain* is, in the opinion of the authors of this book, the greatest musical ever made. The script is witty, the performances endearing (Kelly, O'Connor and Reynolds have never been better), and an unbroken succession of evergreen numbers embody the action and advance the story. This is an idealized Hollywood of likeable eccentrics and benevolent tycoons. The film's quality was not immediately recognized by critics or by the makers' peers (the only Oscar nominations were Lennie Hayton for his musical arrangements and Jean Hagen as best supporting actress). But it immediately found a place in the hearts of those who responded to the lure of musicals, Westerns and horror flicks and to the magical notion of Hollywood itself. In the crucial number when Don declares his love for Kathy, he deconstructs the movie-making process, as he takes her on to an empty sound stage, places her on a stepladder like Juliet on the balcony, conjures up a sunset on the cyclorama, creates a gentle breeze with a wind machine before singing 'You Were Meant For Me'.

ODD/SALIENT FACTS The screenwriters were invited by producer Freed to concoct a script using existing hits he had written with composer Nacio Herb Brown in the 1920s and '30s, and decided to set it in the period the songs were written, mostly for forgotten pictures. The only new songs were 'Moses Supposes' (by the scriptwriters and Roger Edens) and Freed's 'Make Em Laugh', which is more-or-less a copy of 'Be a Clown', the Cole Porter number Kelly performed in *The Pirate* (1948). The singing voice with which Debbie Reynolds dubs Jean Hagen is Hagen's own voice, while Reynolds' tap-dancing in 'Good Morning' was dubbed by Gene Kelly. Two numbers were cut before release to speed up the picture, Kelly's *pas seul* of 'Dreaming of You' and Reynolds singing 'Lucky Star'. The featureless dummy O'Connor flirts with in 'Make Em Laugh' was designed to be dressed up as a battlefield corpse in action movies and was brought in with a random selection of props to inspire his improvisations.

MEMORABLE MOMENTS Don's flashback account of his show-business career.

Don meeting cute with Kathy when he leaps from a streetcar into her convertible.

Roscoe Dexter trying to get Lina to speak into a concealed microphone.

The sound going out of sync at the preview of *The Duelling Cavalier*.

Every song but especially 'Make Em Laugh', 'You Were Meant for Me', 'Good Morning', 'Singin' in the Rain'.

KEY LINES

Don's voice-over accompanying the indignities of his career: 'Dignity, always dignity.'

Lina to Dexter: 'I can't make love to a bush.'

Lina: 'I earn more than Calvin Coolidge – put together.'

SOME LIKE IT HOT
US, 1959, ASHTON/MIRISCH, 120 MINS

D BILLY WILDER; **PR** BILLY WILDER, DOANE HARRISON, I. A. L. DIAMOND; **SC** BILLY WILDER, I. A. L. DIAMOND; **PH** CHARLES LANG; **M** ADOLPH DEUTSCH, SONGS VARIOUS; **ED** ARTHUR SCHMIDT

CAST MARILYN MONROE (SUGAR CANE), TONY CURTIS (JOE/JOSEPHINE), JACK LEMMON (JERRY/DAPHNE), GEORGE RAFT (SPATS COLOMBO), PAT O'BRIEN (MULLIGAN), JOE E. BROWN (OSGOOD FIELDING III), NEHEMIAH PERSOFF (LITTLE BONAPARTE), JOAN SHAWLEE (SWEET SUE), BILLY GRAY (SIG POLIAKOFF), GEORGE STONE (TOOTHPICK), DAVE BARRY (BEINSTOCK), MIKE MAZURKI AND HARRY WILSON (SPATS'S HENCHMEN), BEVERLEY WILLS (DOLORES), BARBARA DREW (NELLIE), EDWARD G. ROBINSON JR. (PARADISE)

THE STORY Joe, a saxophonist, and Jerry, a double-bass player, are down on their luck. The speakeasy where they are playing is raided, and they lose their coats on a dog race. When they witness Spats Colombo and his gang carry out the St Valentine's Day massacre, they are forced into hiding. They get into drag as Josephine and Daphne and join Sweet Sue and Her Society Syncopators for a three-week booking in Florida. Both men fall for Sugar, the band's singer who has a history with saxophonists. In Florida Joe poses as a millionaire to woo Sugar while the real millionaire Osgood falls for Daphne. The two men are unmasked by the gangsters who are in town. Joe and Jerry are witnesses to another slaughter, this time of Spats and his boys at the hands of Little Bonaparte. The two odd couples flee to safety aboard Osgood's yacht.

THE FILM Billy Wilder came to this project having already built up, as writer and director, an impressive and diverse roster of credits. Here he and his writing partner I. A. L. Diamond created a dizzy blend of violence and gender confusion, subtle humour and broad farce. The film was a triumph despite David O. Selznick's warning to Wilder: 'Blood and jokes do not mix.' Joe and Jerry are established as heterosexual men – crude, selfish, inept chancers. When in desperation they assume female identity, they both instantly, as Dustin Hoffman would in the near remake *Tootsie* (1982), become better people. Part of the film's strange power comes from the comfort with which the men assume their new identities. Josephine, although the less developed character, is still the hidden positive side of the cynical

200

▲ *SOME LIKE IT HOT* Daphne (Jack Lemmon) is struck by something familiar about Sugar's (Marilyn Monroe) new friend Junior (Tony Curtis).

Joe, someone whom Sugar can rely on and confide in. Daphne is luckier and happier than Jerry could ever be. Even before the famous punchline, the romantic Daphne wants to go ahead with the wedding despite Joe's appealing to Jerry about the union's central hitch. At the heart of the film is Marilyn Monroe in one of her signature performances. Her husband Arthur Miller was a lot more impressed with her than the role: 'She had so assiduously worked on this small worthless part, and she couldn't get a part worth working on.' But this misses the point that the role defines Monroe's continuing cult status. She is a supremely gorgeous woman who should be unattainable to a sleaze-ball like Joe. But from the start she tells Josephine, the person whom she judges the most trustworthy, that Joe is precisely the kind of man she is attracted to, an unreliable saxophone-playing Lothario. Sugar and Joe don't meet until the final sequence, by which

stage he has been redeemed by being Josephine and by the innocence of Sugar's affection. Regardless of Curtis's famous comment that kissing Monroe was like 'kissing Hitler', their scenes together, in which both are lying but only Joe knows it, are truly romantic. Monroe was not invited to Billy Wilder's end-of-shoot party on 6 November 1958. The start of filming was delayed as Monroe was suffering from depression after a miscarriage. She had another miscarriage that began just hours after her final day of shooting. In marked contrast to the conditions under which it was made, *Some Like It Hot* remains one of the most joyous and strangest comedies to have come out of Hollywood.

ODD/SALIENT FACTS Billy Wilder initially acceded to the wishes of United Artists who wanted Frank Sinatra for the role of Joe. Director and prospective star made a positive start to negotiations but the deal fell through when Sinatra failed to show up for a subsequent meeting. The production was beset by delays, most of which were caused by Monroe. The scene in which the disconsolate Sugar goes into Josephine and Daphne's hotel room and asks 'Where's that bourbon' is said to have required 59 takes.

MEMORABLE MOMENTS The first appearance of Sugar at Chicago's railway station, carrying her ukulele and wiggling along in her tight skirt, being startled by a jet of steam. She moves, according to Jerry 'like jello on springs'.

Sugar's seduction of the 'frigid' Josephine on Osgood's yacht, in which her increasingly passionate kisses eventually steam up his glasses, intercut with Daphne and Osgood's tango.

KEY LINES

Joe's mantra as a 'brand new' girl: 'I'm a boy.'

Sugar to Josephine: 'I 'm tired of getting the fuzzy end of the lollipop.'

Joe/Josephine having kissed the crying Sugar: 'None of that, Sugar. No guy is worth it.'

Daphne's final reason why the proposed marriage can't go ahead: 'You don't understand, Osgood. [He removes his wig] I'm a man.'
Osgood: 'Well, nobody's perfect!'

SONS OF THE DESERT

US, 1933, MGM, 68 MINS

D WILLIAM A. SEITER; **PR** HAL ROACH; **SC** FRANK CRAVEN, BYRON MORGAN; **PH** KENNETH PEACH; **ED** BERT JORDAN

CAST STAN LAUREL (STAN LAUREL), OLIVER HARDY (OLIVER HARDY), CHARLEY CHASE (CHARLEY CHASE), MAE BUSCH (MRS LOTTIE CHASE HARDY), DOROTHY CHRISTIE (MRS BETTY LAUREL), LUCIEN LITTLEFIELD (DR HORACE MEDDICK), JOHN ELLIOT (EXALTED/EXHAUSTED RULER), CHARLEY YOUNG, JOHN MERTON, WILLIAM GILLESPIE, CHARLES MCAVOY, ROBERT BURNS, AL THOMPSON, EDDIE BAKER, JIMMY AUBREY, CHET BRANDENBERG, DON BRODIE (SONS OF THE DESERT)

THE STORY Stan and Ollie make a solemn oath to travel to the annual convention of their fraternity, the 'Sons of the Desert', in Chicago the following week. When Ollie's wife refuses permission for him to go, he hatches a plan. He and Stanley hire a doctor to declare Ollie sick and recommend a break in Hawaii, and instead sneak off to Chicago. There they meet up with Charley Chase who turns out to be Ollie's brother-in-law. Betty and Lottie are distraught to learn that the boat on which their husbands were due to be travelling from Hawaii has sunk. Sneaking back to their neighbouring homes, Stan and Ollie hide out in the loft. When they finally confront their furious wives, Ollie is punished for inventing an elaborate cover story, while Stanley comes clean and is immediately forgiven and rewarded by Betty.

THE FILM Having been brought together by Max Roach in 1926, Laurel & Hardy established themselves as the most popular comedy double act in the history of cinema. Laurel was the creative force behind their films, devising many of their gags, constantly coming up with new ideas, and even working on the editing of the films. The pair always play childish, unsophisticated men struggling to get ahead, and striving to control the inevitable chaos that results from their schemes. They share an unspoken bond – they will always be friends and partners – and are perfectly matched. Stanley is utterly at sea in the world while Ollie is marginally less clueless, but always has his pride dented as a result of his and Stanley's mistakes and ends up suffering some kind of physical injury and indignity.

The duo had already used the basic plot of Sons of the Desert in Be Big (1930), in which Ollie feigns sickness in order that he and Stanley can avoid a trip to Atlantic City with their wives, and instead go to a club. Here as ever the women in their lives are ferocious creatures, stronger and smarter than their bumbling, ineffectual husbands. They manage to get away with their terribly executed plan, in which Stan hires a vet to confirm Ollie's illness, and then give the game away in an hilarious sequence. Betty and Lottie are trying to distract themselves from concern over their husbands' fate with a visit to the cinema. Just as they pray to see them one more time, there is a newsreel report from the Chicago convention. Stan and Ollie are in their Order's parade when they see the camera. Rather than hiding they approach the camera looking deliriously happy and carefree. It is the essence of the cinema's most enduringly loveable team.

ODD/SALIENT FACTS The film was released in Britain under the title *Fraternally Yours*. Oliver Hardy was a master mason in real life. Charley Chase, who plays Ollie's brother-in-law, was the brother of James Parrott, a seasoned director of comedy shorts who made several with Laurel & Hardy including their Oscar-winning *The Music Box* (1932). The film gave its name to the fan club started by the team's own biographer John McCabe, that to this day continues to celebrate Laurel & Hardy. He approached Stanley asking for his blessing for the enterprise and permission to use the title. As he recalls in *The Comedy World of Stan Laurel*: 'Stan made only one proviso. The group *must*, he insisted, maintain at all times a "half-assed dignity".'

▼ *SONS OF THE DESERT* Stan and Ollie trying to convince their wives they've indeed been to Hawaii.

MEMORABLE MOMENTS Stan, sitting in the Hardy living room, struggling to eat a wax apple. Lottie reveals that it is the third piece of fruit she has missed that week.

While trying to convince Lottie of his illness Ollie scalds his feet. Stanley loses an aspirin, forcing Ollie to sit down in a tub of boiling water. Stan takes the tub away and Lottie slips into it, sitting on Stan's head. Stan gets rid of the tub in the kitchen, but when Lottie goes to change she trips up over it. In anger she throws it at Stanley who ducks, and it hits Ollie instead who ends up with his head sticking out of its ripped open bottom.

KEY LINES

Ollie: 'Do you have to ask your wife everything?'
Stan: 'Well, if I don't ask her, I wouldn't know what she wanted me to think.'

Ollie: 'Why do you get a veterinarian?'
Stan: 'Well, I didn't think his religion would make any difference.'

Ollie: 'To catch a Hardy they've got to get up pretty early in the morning.'
Stan: 'What time?'
Ollie: 'Oh about half past … [pushes Stan] "What time?"'

Ollie: 'Well, here's another fine mess you've gotten me into.'

STARDUST MEMORIES

US, 1980, UNITED ARTISTS, 88 MINS

D WOODY ALLEN; **PR** ROBERT GREENHUT, JACK ROLLINS, CHARLES H. JOFFE; **SC** WOODY ALLEN; **PH** (BW) GORDON WILLIS; **M** DICK HYMAN; **ED** SUSAN H. MORSE

CAST WOODY ALLEN (SANDY BATES), CHARLOTTE RAMPLING (DORRIE), JESSICA HARPER (DAISY), MARIE-CHRISTINE BARRAULT (ISOBEL), TONY ROBERTS (TONY), DANIEL STERN (ACTOR), AMY WRIGHT (SHELLEY), HELEN HANFT (VIVIAN ORKIN), JOHN ROTHMAN (JACK ABEL), ANNE DE SALVO (DEBBIE, SANDY'S SISTER), JOAN NEUMAN (SANDY'S MOTHER), KEN CHAPIN (SANDY'S FATHER), LEONARDO CIMINO (SANDY'S ANALYST), LOUISE LASSER (SANDY'S SECRETARY), ROBERT MUNK (YOUNG SANDY), SHARON STONE (GIRL ON THE TRAIN)

THE STORY Sandy Bates is a film-maker trying to break away from the shackles of a career in comedy. While being encouraged by the studio to recut his latest downbeat film, he reluctantly agrees to attend a weekend festival of his films where he is continually approached by fans. He flirts with Daisy, a violinist he meets who reminds him of Dorrie, a depressive woman he used to be in love with. His girlfriend Isobel arrives with her two kids and tells him that she has left her husband. Sandy and Daisy are stranded in the nearby countryside and join a gathering of Ufologists. There Sandy fantasizes about meeting extra-terrestrials and being shot by a crazed fan. As Isobel is about to leave on a train, Sandy vows to rewrite life and make her stay. We cut to the festival screening room where the cast walk out while discussing the film.

THE FILM Woody Allen has a core, cult following – a group of people around the world who are fans to the extent that they will go and see whatever film Allen delivers in the year, and Allen reliably produces one film per year. More than any other director's films Allen's inspire a game for his fans and anyone writing about him – assessing the autobiographical nature of his work. Despite Allen's repeated and understandable denials that his movies are simply autobiographical, it is impossible not to see his cinematic persona as an alter ego, a native New Yorker obsessed with himself, New York, sex, sport, death, films and music and, dithering between mocking pretentiousness in others and edging towards pretentiousness himself, a miserable, hypochondriac neurotic with a matchless gift for one-liners. The key film in this cult of the Woodman is *Stardust Memories* in which he addresses this issue in a brilliant, self-indulgent and self-consciously Felliniesque masterpiece. With nods towards *8½* (1963) and *Sullivan's Travels* (1941), Allen presents the mindscape of a film-maker at a crossroads in his career. Should he go straight? Whom should he love? What is the point of anything when all matter is crumbling anyway? The title of the film refers to a memory he has, while staying at the Stardust hotel, that is inspired by Louis Armstrong's version of Hoagy Carmichael's 'Stardust', of a perfect moment when he stared at Dorrie's face. It is something that keeps the Allen character going, like Isaac's list (including Tracy's face and Louis Armstrong's 'Potato-Head Blues') in *Manhattan* (1979) and Mickey watching *Duck Soup* (1933) in *Hannah and Her Sisters* (1986). The jokes Sandy makes are versions of material from Allen's previous work, but with the humour taken out. But still the

audience laps it up and laughs automatically. Bates if not Allen has contempt for his stupid fans, for all the sycophants who approach him for autographs, with ideas for scripts or other odd requests; for the grotesques in his dream in the film within the film from whom he dissociates himself and for people in general. In Stig Björkman's *Woody Allen on Woody Allen*, the director responds to the question of whether Bates's attitude to his audience reflected his own: 'If I did think that, which I don't, I would be smart enough not to say it in a movie.'

ODD/SALIENT FACTS The film began with the working title *Woody Allen No. 4*, because as Allen explained to Marie-Christine Barrault: 'I am not even half of the Fellini of 8½.' After their brief appearance opposite one another, if not quite together here, Allen and Sharon Stone worked together but did not appear in the computer animation *Antz* (1998). Jack Rollins, Allen's long-time producer/manager, appears as one of the film company directors. Rollins appeared as himself as one of the regulars of the deli in the framing scenes of *Broadway Danny Rose* (1984).

MEMORABLE MOMENT The opening scene of the nightmare in Sandy Bates's latest film in which the character is trapped on

▲ *STARDUST MEMORIES* Jaded film-maker Sandy Bates (Woody Allen) has his faith restored by violinist Daisy (Jessica Harper).

a train with ugly people when he wants to be on the beautiful train going in the opposite direction.

KEY LINES

Sandy: 'What do you want me to say? I don't want to make funny movies any more. They can't force me to. I don't feel funny. I look around the world and all I see is human suffering.'

Manager: 'Human suffering doesn't sell tickets in Kansas City.'

Mr Payson: 'We love your work. My wife has seen all your films.'

Mrs Payson: 'I especially like your early, funny ones.'

Og, the alien: 'And incidentally, you're also not Superman, you're a comedian. You wanna do mankind a real service, tell funnier jokes.'

SULLIVAN'S TRAVELS

US, 1941, PARAMOUNT, 91 MINS

D PRESTON STURGES; **SC** STURGES; **PH** (BW) JOHN F. SEITZ; **M** LEO SHUKMAN, CHARLES BRADSHAW; **ED** STUART GILMORE **CAST** JOEL MCCREA (JOHN L. SULLIVAN), VERONICA LAKE (THE GIRL), ROBERT WARWICK (MR LEBRAND, HEAD OF STUDIO), MR HADRIAN (PORTER HALL), MR JONES (WILLIAM DEMAREST), ERIC BLORE (SULLIVAN'S VALET), ROBERT GREIG (SULLIVAN'S BUTLER), MARGARET HAYES (SECRETARY)

THE STORY John L. Sullivan, ace Hollywood comedy director of such hits as *So Long Sarong, Hey Hey in the Hayloft* and *Ants In Your Pants* 1939, wants to confront the big issues of the time in a film of 'stark realism' called *O Brother, Where Art Thou?* Defying the studio bosses he goes on the road dressed as a tramp to gain authentic experience, and they send a back-up bus manned by PR men and a doctor to follow him. He gives them the slip, is briefly ensnared by an amorous widow and hitches a ride from a truckdriver who drops him back in Hollywood where a disenchanted actress (never identified by name) generously buys him breakfast. After discovering his identity, she accompanies him, disguised as a boy, when he dons a hobo outfit and goes on the road again, another unsatisfactory experience which he concludes, and offers to introduce the actress to Lubitsch. Sullivan then goes out for a third excursion, to distribute $5 bills to the poor. An old tramp mugs him, steals his money and the shoes that contain identification cards, and is then crushed by a train, leading to national press headlines like 'Strange Death of Hollywood Director'. Meanwhile the concussed Sullivan, stepping out of a freight car, reacts to a brutal railway policeman by hitting him with a rock and drawing a six-year sentence on a rural chain gang. After seeing a silent Mickey Mouse comedy, shown to an audience of convicts in a black baptist church, Sullivan secures his release, but determines to make more comedies rather than *O Brother, Where Art Thou?*

THE FILM This double-edged satire manages, like most of Sturges's comedies, to have it both ways, simultaneously attacking Hollywood's crassly commercial escapism and the patronizing left-wing artists who attempt to make politically relevant films (a parody of one such opens the movie). Sullivan is both pretentious and pathetic (like the aristocrat in J. M. Barrie's *The Admirable Crichton* he's far less smart than his butler). Technically interesting (1) for the long takes of dialogue scenes

▲ *SULLIVAN'S TRAVELS Rangy Joel McCrea and diminutive Veronica Lake hit the road in search of reality.*

and (2) for a couple of lengthy montage sequences where Sturges dispenses with speech and sound effects and there's only music on the soundtrack.

ODD/SALIENT FACTS The film that director Sullivan and his producers watch in the opening sequence is deliberately ambiguous: is this someone else's picture, a rough-cut of a proposed Sullivan film, or a fantasy created in their minds from the director's conference pitch? This is, like much else in the movies, post-modernism *avant la lettre*. Veronica Lake riding the rods as a hobo was almost certainly inspired by Louise Brooks's posing as a boy to accompany Richard Arlen on the road in William Wellman's early Depression film *Beggars of Life* (1928). In his posthumous autobiography (*Sturges on Sturges*, 1991), the director said: 'I wrote *Sullivan's Travels* to satisfy an urge to tell [my fellow-comedy directors] that they were getting too deep-dish; to leave the preaching to the preachers.' Joel McCrea (1905–90), an uneasily definable talent, competed with Gary Cooper and James Stewart in the middle-ground of American innocence, working thrice with Sturges, twice with Tourneur, once with Hitchcock, and finally with Sam Peckinpah in *Ride the High Country/Guns in the Afternoon* (1962) .

MEMORABLE MOMENTS Sullivan being instructed by his valet and butler on poverty. The luxurious studio back-up bus with short-wave and shower. Sullivan and the Girl suddenly facing a darker world and getting afflicted by fleas and lice in a hobo village. Sullivan, after his horrific days on a chain gang, laughing with fellow prisoners at a silent cartoon.

KEY LINES

The Girl: 'If you were a casting director I'd be staring into your bridgework saying "Yes Mr Smearcase".'

Sullivan: 'Wherever I start out I always end up back here in Hollywood.'

SWEET SWEETBACK'S BAAD ASSSSS SONG

US, 1971, A YEAH PRODUCTION, 97 MINS

D/PR/SC/ED/M *MELVIN VAN PEEBLES;* **PH** *(COL) BOB MAXWELL* **CAST** *'STARRING THE BLACK COMMUNITY AND BRER SOUL'*

THE STORY Reared in an all-black brothel and given his nickname by its girls in awe of his sexual prowess, Sweet Sweetback is a prodigious stud who performs sexual acts for admiring black audiences in a Los Angeles underground circus. One night two white detectives providing protection to the establishment's owner ask if they can take someone into the police station for the night, just to show their boss they've collared a suspect. Sweetback goes along, but when they pick up and assault a young black radical, Sweetback beats them unconscious and goes on the run. The rest of the movie is a single chase in which Sweetback has sex with virtually every woman he meets, is arrested several times, kills some policemen in self-defence, and helps the young radical to escape. Meanwhile the white police and a pair of reluctant black cops are urged to bring in Sweetback, who becomes a revolutionary hero to the black community. Sweetback's friends and supporters are shot and tortured by the cops, though he is briefly helped by Hells Angels impressed by his courage and sexual successes. Eventually he staggers across the desert, tending his own wounds, and kills two police dogs in the Rio Grande as he crosses into Mexico.

THE FILM Melvin Van Peebles' rebarbative one-man-show, a low-budget film, is part crude exploitation skin-flick, part European art movie. It combines soft-core sex with slow-motion, speeded-up camerawork, jump cuts, shots in negative and a total disregard for conventional narration. Born in 1932 in Chicago, Van Peebles is an authentic maverick, who was one of the first blacks given a commission in the US Air Force but refused to join the Establishment. After his military service he became a San Francisco trolley driver and writer, before relocating to Paris, where he was a local hero as journalist, actor and film-maker. His movie, *Story of a Three Day Pass*, brought an invitation to the 1969 San Francisco Film Festival and then a Hollywood contract to make him one of the first trio of black directors to work within the system, the others being Ossie Davies *(Cotton Comes to Harlem)* and *Life* photographer Gordon Parks *(The Learning Tree)*. Van Peebles's *The Watermelon Man*, a feeble tale about a complacent white middle-class professional waking up black, was a mild success, and he formed his own company and, using his own money, made the aggressive, transgressive *Sweet Sweetback*, which set out to offend both white society and respectable middle-class blacks. The film's long chase is a bitter poem of injustice in which the only sympathetic whites are fascistic bikers. Sweetback is neither a servile black like the characters in films of the 1930s and '40s, nor one of the saintly blacks of the 1950s and '60s. He's a stud who stands up for himself and is

▼ *SWEET SWEETBACK'S BAAD ASSSSS SONG Black activist Melvin Van Peebles reveals his superstud virility to a counter-cultural white chick.*

politicized by the brutality he sees. Black audiences responded to the picture's raw power, and it made a fortune but was excluded from normal distribution, and although Van Peebles was made modestly rich the movie was rarely seen outside the States. He refused to allow it to be shown in South Africa until 1994. *Sweet Sweetback* helped create the 'blaxploitation' movement of the 1970s, which Van Peebles believes turned his liberating movie on its head. It also gave a generation of African-American film-makers their vocation. Van Peebles subsequently worked in the theatre, but made no more movies.

ODD/SALIENT FACTS Van Peebles refused to submit the film for certification to what he called 'an all-white jury' and gave the film his own X-Certificate. The director's son Mario made his movie debut at the age of 13 in *Sweet Sweetback*. He later worked as a film-maker, directing his father in *Posse and Panther*. Melvin Van Peebles worked for a time in the 1980s on the New York Stock Exchange and wrote *Bold Money*, a bestselling book on investment.

MEMORABLE MOMENTS The erotic title sequence in which the teenage Sweetback is initiated into sex is a sly exercise in ethnic sexuality.

The second half is a sustained montage of pursuit, oppression and cruelty, accompanied by a choral commentary that anticipates rap music.

KEY LINES

The film's epigraph given in French and English: 'Sire these
    lines are not a homage to brutality that the artist has
    invented, but a hymn from the mouth of reality.'

Opening title: 'This film is dedicated to all the Brothers and
    Sisters who had enough of the man.'
Final title: 'Watch out – a baad assss nigger is coming
    back to collect some dues'.

TARGETS

US, 1967, PARAMOUNT, 100 MINS
D PETER BOGDANOVICH; **SC** BOGDANOVICH, FROM A STORY BY
POLLY PLATT AND HIMSELF; **PH** LASZLO KOVACS
CAST BORIS KARLOFF (BYRON ORLOK), TIM O'KELLY (BOBBY
THOMPSON), NANCY HSUEH (JENNY), PETER BOGDANOVICH
(SAMMY MICHAELS)

THE STORY Ageing British horror movie star Byron Orlok decides that *The Terror*, his latest film for a minor Hollywood studio, will be his last because the gothic pictures with which he's associated are hopelessly old-fashioned in a world of random daily violence. 'I'm an antique, out of date, an anachronism', he says and refuses to read writer-director Sammy Michaels's latest script. But he reluctantly agrees to attend the premiere of *The Terror* at a drive-in in San Fernando Valley. Meanwhile Bobby Thompson, a seemingly well-adjusted insurance salesman married to a telephonist and living with his conformist, lower-middle-class parents, is turning the boot of his car into an arsenal. He's first seen holding the distant Orlok in the telescopic sights of a rifle he's buying at a gun-shop. The following day Bobby murders his wife, mother and a delivery boy, before taking up a position on a gas tank overlooking a freeway to pick off passing motorists. Fleeing from the police he takes refuge in the drive-in movie house where *The Terror* is to be shown. As dusk falls and the movie starts, Bobby returns to the rampage from a position high-up behind the movie screen, picking off isolated members of the audience in their cars and killing the projectionist. As panic reigns in the cinema, Orlok, immaculately dressed in a dinner jacket, walks intrepidly towards the screen. Despite being wounded he disarms the deranged Bobby.

THE FILM *Targets* is the first time a cinéaste critic comparable with the French New Wave directors was let loose on a Hollywood movie and the result is a minor masterpiece, a self-

▼ *TARGETS* Gun-crazy all-American boy Tim O'Kelly picks a target on the LA freeway.

conscious postmodernist work. There are allusions to Hitchcock, Welles and Preminger, and Orlok and Sammy watch Hawks's *The Criminal Code* (Karloff's first major film) on TV. The movie is about the thin line between art and reality, the relationship between life and film-making (e.g. the projectionist loading his projector parallels the assassin loading his rifle). It is also about the decline of values and banalization of American life by the media and how the availability of guns gives deadly expression to underlying frustration and anger. The ultimate postmodernist aspect of this astute picture is that clearly the script that Orlok refuses to read (i.e. the picture that will take his career in a new direction) is the movie written by Bogdanovich/Michaels in which he is appearing.

> 'All the best movies have been made.'

ODD/SALIENT FACTS Producer Roger Corman gave his protégé Bogdanovich twenty minutes from his 1963 film *The Terror* (on which Monte Hellman and Francis Coppola did second-unit work), a twelve days' schedule and two days remaining from a contract with Boris Karloff who died in 1969 not long after it was released. Bogdanovich showed the draft of his screenplay to Samuel Fuller, who worked it over without credit. The film was inspired by an incident on 1 August 1966 in Austin, Texas, when honours student Charles J. Whitman, after murdering his wife and mother, locked himself in the University of Texas tower from which he shot 44 people, killing 14 of them, before himself being gunned down by the police. Roger Corman sold the movie to Paramount instead of releasing it via the AIP exploitation company, and following the assassinations of Martin Luther King and Bobby Kennedy, Paramount put out only six prints and prefaced the picture with a statement that it was a demand for gun control. Count Orlok was used for the central character of *Nosferatu*, FW Murnau's seminal 1922 version of Bram Stoker's *Dracula*. *Targets* has no written score, just source music, and the subtle soundtrack is credited to Verna Fields, who was to win an Oscar as editor on Spielberg's *Jaws* (1975) and the reputation (challenged by its director) of having salvaged the film.

MEMORABLE MOMENTS Karloff reciting Death's speech from Somerset Maugham's *Sheppey* about 'an appointment in Samarra'.

Bobby tidying up after his picnic while preparing to shoot passing drivers from his eyrie overlooking the freeway.

Bobby unable to distinguish between Byron Orlok on screen in *The Terror* and the real Orlok walking towards him.

KEY LINES

Sammy: 'All the best movies have been made.'

Orlok: 'God what an ugly town this has become.'

Orlok on the drive-in audience: 'Strange not hearing any reaction.'

Orlok on Bobby: 'Is *that* what I was afraid of?'

Bobby to police: 'I hardly ever missed, did I?'

TARZAN AND HIS MATE
US, 1934, MGM, 103 MINS

D CEDRIC GIBBONS, (UNCREDITED) JACK CONWAY; **PR** BERNARD K. HYMAN; **SC** JAMES KEVIN MCGUINNESS, **ADAPT** HOWARD EMMETT ROGERS AND LEON GORDON (BASED ON CHARACTERS CREATED BY EDGAR RICE BURROUGHS); **PH** CHARLES G. CLARKE, CLYDE DE VINNA; **M** (UNCREDITED); **ED** TOM HELD

CAST JOHNNY WEISSMULLER (TARZAN), MAUREEN O'SULLIVAN (JANE PARKER), NEIL HAMILTON (HARRY HOLT), PAUL CAVANAGH (MARTIN ARLINGTON), FORRESTER HARVEY (BEAMISH), NATHAN CURRY (SAIAI)

THE STORY In *Tarzan the Ape Man* (1932), Jane Parker comes to Africa to join her father, and his assistant, Harry Holt, in search of the ivory in a remote elephant's graveyard. When they're attacked by pygmies, Tarzan, a verbally challenged European reared by apes, comes to their rescue and following her father's death from battle wounds, Jane remains with Tarzan, and Harry, who's in love with her, returns to civilization. A year later, in *Tarzan and His Mate*, Harry recruits his British friend, the penniless, womanizing adventurer Martin Arlington, in a scheme to win back his fiancée with European perfumes and a modish wardrobe, and to get rich through the secret ivory hoard. On their journey, Harry and Martin's rival hunters are killed by ferocious tribesmen, and are saved from death by

Tarzan and Jane, whom they tempt with European clothes. When Tarzan refuses to help them find the elephants' graveyard, Martin kills an elephant to make him take them there. He then shoots Tarzan, claiming the Ape Man died fighting a crocodile. But Cheetah, Jane's personal monkey, comes to Tarzan's aide. Harry and Martin die when a native tribe calls on lions to kill them, and Tarzan, his elephants and his chimpanzees arrive in time to rescue Jane.

THE FILM Like *The Godfather Part II*, *Tarzan and His Mate* is that rare thing, a sequel that is superior to the original. Johnny Weissmuller was the best of all screen Tarzans and this was his best film. Its Africa is pure Hollywood, or European fantasy, and the ethos of a place populated by dangerous animals, reptiles and natives readily subjugated by the right white man is nowadays politically incorrect. The film-makers, however, underplay Edgar Rice Burroughs's racism by not insisting on Tarzan's aristocratic background. Their movie is violent, sexy, funny and fast-moving and much livelier than any Tarzan movies before or after. The rigid application of the Hollywood Production Code shortly after this picture was made ruled out from later pictures the sexual innuendo, the nudity and Jane's scanty clothing. Subsequent films make far less of her sexual attraction to Tarzan or of the way she is torn between the city and the jungle.

ODD/SALIENT FACTS This is the only film on which Cedric Gibbons, long-time head of MGM's design department, is credited as director, but in fact much of it was directed by Jack Conway who took over from Gibbons. Johnny Weissmuller, who made ten Tarzan movies, was Olympic swimming champion in 1924 and 1928, and in 1950 was voted the greatest swimmer of the first half of this century. A parallel series of Tarzan movies were produced by Sol Lesser and his son Julian, leading to one critic calling one of their films 'the evil of two Lessers'. The Irish-born Maureen O'Sullivan, who played Jane five times, was the mother of Mia Farrow, whose screen mother she played in Woody Allen's *Hannah and Her Sisters*.

MEMORABLE MOMENTS Tarzan saving Jane from a lion, a rhino, a leopard and a crocodile.

Harry and Martin's party battling with a gang of gorillas as they climb an escarpment.

Tarzan, Jane and Cheetah performing acrobatic feats as they swing through the jungle.

Harry and Martin looking at Jane's naked silhouette as

▲ *TARZAN AND HIS MATE Me Jane, you Tarzan, she Cheetah — the whole family until Tarzan Finds a Son (i.e. Johnny Sheffield).*

she changes in the tent into the European clothes they have brought her.

Tarzan puzzling out the workings of a gramophone.

KEY LINES

Martin Arlington: 'She's priceless — a woman who's learnt the abandon of a savage and yet would be at home in Mayfair.'

Arlington: 'It's the survival of the fittest.'
Harry Holt: 'Up here the fittest is Tarzan and he wouldn't let her go.'

Arlington: 'You're the first woman I've ever had to coax *into* a dress.'

Tarzan: 'Jane loves Tarzan — Tarzan loves Jane.'

The line 'Tarzan — Jane' (*not* 'Me Tarzan — you Jane') appears in *Tarzan the Apeman*.

THE TERMINATOR★

US, 1984, CINEMA '84/GREENBERG BROTHERS/PACIFIC WESTERN/EURO FILM FUNDING/ORION PICTURES, 107 MINS

D JAMES CAMERON; **PR** GALE ANNE HURD; **SC** JAMES CAMERON AND GALE ANNE HURD; **PH** (COL) ADAM GREENBERG; **M** BRAD FIEDEL; TERMINATOR CREATED BY STAN WINSTON; **ED** MARK GOLDBLATT

CAST ARNOLD SCHWARZENEGGER (TERMINATOR), MICHAEL BIEHN (KYLE REESE), LINDA HAMILTON (SARAH CONNOR), PAUL WINFIELD (TRAXLER), LANCE HENRIKSEN (VULOVICH), RICK ROSSOVICH (MATT), BESS MOTTA (GINGER), EARL BOEN (SILBERMAN), DICK MILLER (PAWN SHOP CLERK), SHAWN SCHEPPS (NANCY), FRANCO COLUMBU (FUTURE TERMINATOR), BILL PAXTON (PUNK LEADER)

THE STORY We cut from Los Angeles AD 2029 to LA in 1984. Two naked men arrive separately, each with a blinding flash of light, in the city at night, both in pursuit of Sarah Connor. The bigger man, the Terminator, steals an arsenal of hi-tech weaponry and kills the first Sarah Connor to be listed in the phone book. Meanwhile the real Sarah, a waitress, is freaked out by this first death but terrified when she learns that the second Sarah has also been killed. The Terminator kills Sarah's flatmate and the flatmate's boyfriend and tracks Sarah down to a nightclub. There, Sarah's life is saved by the other man, Reese, who explains that Sarah's unborn (unconceived) son will in the future save the planet from the machines that have taken over, that the machines have sent a Terminator back in time to kill her before she can produce her son, and that her grown-up son has in turn sent him, Reese, back in time to protect her, and as it turns out to father him, John. Pursued through the city, and then to a police station the couple at last seek refuge in the country. Having killed Sarah's mother, the Terminator finds them and in a final confrontation in some indeterminate automated factory, Reese is killed and the Terminator destroyed. Sarah, newly pregnant, heads off to Mexico assured of her own crucial role in the post-apocalyptic future.

THE FILM James Cameron came to The Terminator after the unpromising directorial debut with Piranha II: The Spawning (1981). His real preparation had been his degree in physics and early work in the art departments of films such as Battle Beyond the Stars (1980) and John Carpenter's Escape From New York (1981). What this culminated in was the film that launched the movie career of Arnold Schwarzenegger and is arguably the best, most imaginative and interesting action film of the last twenty years. Coming from the subsequently profligate Cameron, the most striking aspect of The Terminator is its budget – $8 million. It is the film's beautifully constructed plot and its surprisingness at the time, coming unheralded as it did, that lend it an enduring cult status. The effects are jerky and grainy, whereas the sequel, which ultimately negates the entire story of the first film, has slick, computerized liquid-metal effects which Cameron first exploited in The Abyss (1989). Never has Arnold Schwarzenegger been better used on screen, with an economical script requiring him to deliver fewer than 200 words.

ODD/SALIENT FACTS The central idea of the film, perhaps borrowed unconsciously from a comic strip, of two men travelling back in time to battle for the future, is brilliantly neat. But in this compact, roller-coaster script, the exploration of the notion of time travel is just one of three big ideas toyed with. The club in which Sarah takes refuge is called the Tech Noir, pointing at another of the main strands of the film. In his direction, as well as within his scripts, Cameron has consistently involved himself in technical developments and pushed the boundaries of computer effects. It is ironic that this technophile should achieve his first great success with one of the most obsessively technophobic films of all time. The film is an extended essay on the dangers of unrestricted technological advance. Reese explains: 'It was the machines, Sarah.' In The Terminator, everything bad that happens, does so because of some machine or other: answerphones, telephones, walkmans. The film also marks the beginning of perhaps the most consistent strand in Cameron's work – the centrality of women in the action film and the idea that women are ultimately tougher, better equipped to survive crises than men. Sarah's surface ordinariness (like the Arnie character in True Lies, 1994) masks her natural abilities, her innate strength. Within twenty-four hours of being informed of her awesome destiny, she is preparing field dressings, and showing herself as a motivator, a fighter and a survivor impervious to pain. Her character foreshadows the natural superwomen of Aliens (1986) and The Abyss.

MEMORABLE MOMENTS The Terminator performing eye surgery on himself.

'I'll be back.'

Having arrived in the film with a bad Seventies haircut, the Terminator finds himself with his hair burnt into shape, wearing shades and riding a motorbike.

KEY LINES

Reese to Sarah: 'Come with me if you want to live.'

Soon afterwards, he explains: 'Listen and understand. That terminator is out there. It can't be bargained with, it can't be reasoned with. It doesn't feel pity or remorse or fear and it absolutely will not stop, ever, until you're dead.'

Terminator to desk sergeant: 'I'll be back.'

THE TEXAS CHAIN SAW MASSACRE

US, 1974, VORTEX/A HENKEL-HOOPER PRODUCTION, 83 MINS

D *TOBE HOOPER;* **PR** *JAYE PARSLEY;* **SC** *KIM HENKEL, TOBE HOOPER;* **PH** *(COL, CFI) DANIEL PEARL; M. HOOPER, WAYNE BELL;* **ED** *SALLYE RICHARDSON, LARRY CARROLL*
CAST *MARILYN BURNS (SALLY HARDESTY), ALLEN DANZIGER (JERRY), PAUL A. PARTAIN (FRANKLIN HARDESTY), WILLIAM VAIL (KIRK), TERI MCMINN (PAM), EDWIN NEAL (HITCH-HIKER), JIM SIEDOW (OLD MAN), GUNNAR HANSEN (LEATHERFACE), JOHN DUGAN (GRANDFATHER), PERRY LORENZ (PICKUP DRIVER)*

THE STORY Hearing that vandals have been desecrating graveyards in a remote corner of Texas, Sally Hardesty decides to visit her grandfather's grave and sets off in the family van with her wheelchair-bound brother Franklin and their friends Pam, Kirk and Jerry. Finding the grave undisturbed, they decide to drop in on the grandfather's abandoned farm. A demented hitchhiker tells them he's been made redundant by the mechanization of a slaughterhouse. When he draws a knife and cuts the crippled Franklin for not buying a photograph they eject him. While Sally and Franklin inspect the old farm (which is full of bones), Kirk and Pam investigate a run-down house nearby, also full of human remains. Kirk is murdered by a masked man with a sledgehammer, Pam is killed with a meat hook. When Jerry goes to search for them he too is killed. Later the masked man slaughters Franklin with a chain saw. Sally flees after finding a

mummified old couple, but falls into the hands of an elderly filling station owner, the hitchhiker and Leatherface, the masked chain-saw wielder, all mad brothers formerly employed at the slaughterhouse. One of the mummies is their grandfather, who is revived by drinking Sally's blood. Sally escapes and catches a lift from a lorry driver, leaving Leatherface on the highway with his chain saw.

THE FILM *The Texas Chain Saw Massacre* was produced around Austin, Texas, for a mere $300,000 and made twenty times that through a shrewd advertising campaign. In the wake of *Night of the Living Dead*, George Romero's low-budget classic shot in Pennsylvania, it showed that you didn't have to go to Hollywood to make exploitation horror flicks. Inspired by the real-life story of Wisconsin mass murderer and skin-fetishist Ed Gein that sparked off *Psycho*, Hooper's film is aggressively upfront where Hitchcock's is subtle. Its quintet of heroes and heroines are an unattractive, ill-kempt bunch. The movie takes place over a single day, the sets are littered with skin and bones like an ancient ossuary. But unlike the slasher films that followed in its wake there is surprisingly little blood and no close-ups of fatal blows. What then has made this a cult movie?

First of all *The Texas Chain Saw Massacre* has one of the great exploitation titles and became immediately notorious in Britain by being refused even an X-Certificate, though it was licensed for screening in the metropolis by the Greater London Council. At the 1974 London Film Festival, a debate was staged that divided the critics. Some thought it a challenging, deeply disturbing work that dramatized (or melodramatized) problems of rural deprivation, of people driven mad by social change. To others it was a mindlessly sensational horror flick that failed to provide a social context for its monsters' conduct. Yet others thought it a black comedy about dysfunctional families. The critic of the *Daily Mail* expressed a viewed shared by many who hadn't seen the film: 'What appals me about this film is its lack of purpose; if ever a film should be banned this is it'.

ODD/SALIENT FACTS Tobe Hooper got a Hollywood contract but his biggest movie, *The Poltergeist* (1982), looked so much like the works of its producer, Steven Spielberg, that critics asked: 'Tobe or not Tobe? That is the question.' None of the actors came to anything, and the two long-delayed sequels, *Texas Chain Saw Massacre 2* (1986) and *Leatherface: Texas Chain Saw Massacre III* (1989) featuring such stars as Dennis Hopper and Viggo Mortensen are long forgotten. In a local bid

▲ *THE TEXAS CHAIN SAW MASSACRE Leatherface wielding the Lone Star State's favourite garden implement.*

for respectability, Hooper persuaded Dr W. E. Barnes, a leading plastic surgeon, to devise the grandfather's make-up. Hooper also got the distinguished broadcaster, John Henry Faulk, a famous victim of McCarthyism who successfully sued a right-wing propagandist organization for getting him blacklisted from the national airways, to be the film's introductory narrator.

MEMORABLE MOMENTS A dead armadillo, the semi-official emblematic Texas mascot, on its back in the middle of the road.

Leatherface's sudden appearance to give Kirk the *coup de grâce*.

Leatherface at the end, standing in the road, spinning his chain saw.

KEY LINES

Drunk at the violated cemetery: 'Things happen hereabouts, I see things sometimes.'

Hitchhiker: 'Our family has always been in meat.'

Pick-up driver: 'I take no pleasure in killin'. There's some things you gotta do. Don't mean you gotta like it.'

THIS ISLAND EARTH
US, 1955, U-I/WILLIAM ALLAND, 86 MINS

D JOSEPH NEWMAN; **PR** WILLIAM ALLAND; **SC** FRANKLIN COEN, EDWARD G. O'CALLAGHAN; **PH** (TECHNICOLOR) CLIFFORD STINE; **M** JOSEPH GERSHENSON; **ED** VIRGIL VOGEL

CAST JEFF MORROW (EXETER), FAITH DOMERGUE (RUTH ADAMS), REX REASON (CAL MEACHAM), LANCE FULLER (BRACK), RUSSELL JOHNSON (STEVE CARLSON), DOUGLAS SPENCER (THE MONITOR), ROBERT NICHOLS (JOE WILSON), KARL L. LINDT (DR ADOLPH ENGELBORG)

THE STORY Cal Meacham, a nuclear research scientist, experiences a mysterious loss of control while flying his jet. Back at his lab, his work is interrupted by the arrival of advanced new fuses, and a catalogue from which he orders the components to build an 'interoceptor', a combined weapon and communications machine, by which he is invited by the white-haired, high-browed Exeter to join a specialized research team at an isolated institute. Ruth, an old flame, is one member of the international group of scientists assembled to work in the production of nuclear power, ostensibly with the aim to end all wars. Ruth and Steve, a fellow worker, confide in Cal their suspicions about Exeter and his physically similar assistant Brack. Ruth, Cal and Steve attempt to escape but Steve is killed. Meanwhile Exeter and Brack have been summoned to return to their planet by their leader, The Monitor, and ordered to bring Cal and Ruth with them. The institute is destroyed as a flying saucer takes off from a hollowed-out hill nearby, and the plane in which Cal and Ruth are trying to get away is sucked into the spaceship. As the saucer speeds away from Earth, Exeter explains to Ruth and Cal that the work was necessary to find out how to generate the nuclear energy to sustain the ionized layer protecting his home planet, Metaluna, engaged in war with the planet Zagon and facing imminent destruction. As they arrive there, the protective layer is being breached, and the end is minutes away. They meet The Monitor who plans to colonize Earth with the remaining Metalunans and orders Exeter to reprogramme the brains of Cal and Ruth. They escape and as Cal, Ruth and Exeter flee to the spaceship, the latter is wounded by a mutant. They make it on to the ship, but so does the wounded mutant. They survive a final close-call with the beast, and as the spaceship re-enters the Earth's atmosphere, Ruth and Cal escape in the plane while Exeter stays in the flying saucer which plunges into the ocean.

▲ *THIS ISLAND EARTH* Metalunan mutant menacing Cal, Ruth and Exeter (off-screen) on the return journey to earth.

THE FILM A classic Fifties science-fiction movie, *This Island Earth* is distinct from most of the films of its period and genre in that it enthusiastically champions the ideals of the nuclear age. Professor Meacham is a square-jawed, all-American hero: macho, romantic, incredibly smart and practical and wholeheartedly dedicated to the development of improved nuclear power. The film has a camp mixture of ridiculously cheap special effects, shaky flying saucers and iffy explosions, with great colours, beautifully designed sets and backdrops, especially the interior of Metaluna. There are the cheesily enjoyable Fifties attitudes showing through in the script. Although both hero and heroine are eminent scientists, Exeter reassures Cal that Ruth is 'just a step behind you'. Later when they are kidnapped on the spaceship, Exeter (who looks and sounds uncannily like Robin Williams) appeals to their scientific curiosity about the journey they are embarked upon. When this fails to appease them he says: 'Ruth, don't tell me that as a woman you're not curious

about our destination.' Sure enough, she instantly asks: 'Where are we going?' The scene in which the mutant, with the looks of an insect with an exposed brain, attacks Ruth as all three of them are in the cocooned depressurizing chambers on the return to Earth clearly inspired the final encounter between Sigourney Weaver and her nemesis in *Alien* (1979).

ODD/SALIENT FACTS The film was produced for Universal Pictures by William Alland. Alland started out as a member of Orson Welles's Mercury Theater, and played the reporter attempting to find the meaning of the dying word 'rosebud' in *Citizen Kane* (1941). His second career was as a producer, mainly of cheap science-fiction films, with his credits including *It Came from Outer Space* (1953), *The Creature from the Black Lagoon* (1955), *Revenge of the Creature* (1955), *The Mole People* (1956) and *The Deadly Mantis* (1957). Faith Domergue, who plays Ruth Adams, entered films as a protégée of Howard Hughes but never made it beyond B-movies.

MEMORABLE MOMENTS The scene in which Exeter struggles with the mutant and is eventually saved by Meacham encapsulates all that is simultaneously terrible and great about Fifties science-fiction B-movies.

KEY LINES

Looking at the newly assembled interceptor, Cal's assistant Joe comments: 'You know what my kids would say: "Dig this crazy, mixed-up plumbing."'

While Ruth and Steve are showing Cal around his new lab, a cat leaps up on to the lead slab suspended in front of them. Ruth says: 'It's only Neutron. We call him that because he's so positive.'

THIS IS SPINAL TAP★
US, 1983, MAINLINE/EMBASSY, 82 MINS
D ROB REINER; **PR** KAREN MURPHY; **SC** CHRISTOPHER GUEST, MICHAEL MCKEAN, HARRY SHEARER, ROB REINER; **PH** PETER SMOKLER; **M** CHRISTOPHER GUEST, MICHAEL MCKEAN, HARRY SHEARER, ROB REINER; **ED** KIM SECRIST, KENT BEYDA
CAST CHRISTOPHER GUEST (NIGEL TUFNEL), MICHAEL MCKEAN (DAVID ST HUBBINS), HARRY SHEARER (DEREK SMALLS), ROB REINER (MARTY DEBERGI), JUNE CHADWICK (JEANINE PETTIBONE), TONY HENDRA (IAN FAITH), PATRICK MACNEE (SIR DENIS ETON-HOGG),

THE STORY Director Marty DeBergi presents his 'rockumentary' of The Tap, 'one of England's loudest bands' who have been going since 1966. The film follows their tour of lesser American arenas, in the course of which the band face a succession of rock 'n' roll nightmares: cancelled gigs, faulty stage equipment, internal band frictions, interfering girlfriends, incompetent publicists, temperamental management, inadequate backstage refreshment, rows about their album covers, an indifferent public and spontaneously combusting drummers. Just when things seem to be hopeless the band discover that they are once more big in Japan.

THE FILM One of the sharpest films ever made about the music business, both hilarious and accurate. It presents every cliché of life on the road but, as it is cited by almost every rock star as their favourite film, gets them right. Many of the ideas in the film are based on the archetypes of rock history: the emergence of rock 'n' roll bands in Britain in the sixties, moving through skiffle and psychedelia to heavy rock; the tensions and homosexual undertones in the relationships between singer and lead guitarist; the craziness and limited lifespan of drummers; the pretentiousness of concept albums and tours, especially those involving old English/Celtic mythology. The lasting power of the film is shown by the fact that it is almost impossible to discuss the history of rock music without referring to some moment being Tap-like.

ODD/SALIENT FACTS This was Rob Reiner's first film as director. One of the stars of TV's *All in the Family*, he is the son of Carl Reiner, the director of *The Man with Two Brains* (1982). He went on to make *When Harry Met Sally* (starring Billy Crystal and Bruno Kirby who both have small roles here). Christopher Guest, married to Jamie Lee Curtis, is now Lord Haden-Guest. Harry Shearer claims to have discovered the *double entendre* of 'smalls' only after deciding on the name for his character. The film not only reflects a barely exaggerated version of rock mythology, but seems to have influenced events after its release. On their Pop-Mart tour, the members of U2 were trapped onstage inside a giant lemon. Similarly during Black Sabbath's 1984 Born Again tour, their stage set was Stonehenge. Bassist Geezer Butler requested a full-scale version of the monument, but was supplied with one three times the actual size. Only three of the

> '*My baby fits me like a flesh tuxedo, I'd like to sink her with my pink torpedo.*'

monitors were used, and during the set a dwarf in a crimson leotard would dance on top of them.

MEMORABLE MOMENTS Nigel Tufnel showing Marty his collection of guitars and his special amp that goes up to 11: 'It's one louder.'

The band visiting Elvis Presley's grave and attempting 'Heartbreak Hotel' with harmonies (Tufnel: 'It really puts perspective on things.' St Hubbins: 'Too much, too much fuckin' perspective.')

Tufnel playing an extract from his trilogy in D minor, influenced by Mozart and Bach: 'This piece is called "Lick My Love Pump".'

The band getting lost on the way from their dressing room to the stage. The dwarfs trampling over the 18-in stage model of Stonehenge. Derek Smalls's foil-wrapped trouser cucumber setting off the security alarm at the airport.

KEY LINES

Lyrics from 'Big Bottom':
> My baby fits me like a flesh tuxedo
> I'd like to sink her with my pink torpedo

Nigel Tufnel, reacting to the accusation of sexism re the cover for 'Smell the Glove' which features a greased naked woman on all fours: 'What's wrong with being sexy?'

Tufnel on the restyled all-black cover of 'Smell the Glove': 'How more black could it be? The answer is none. None more black.'

Derek Smalls on the contrasting personalities of Tufnel and St Hubbins: 'It's like fire and ice basically. I feel my role in the band is to be somewhere in the middle of that, kind of like lukewarm water.'

Marty, reading a review of 'Intravenous De Milo': 'This tasteless cover is a good indication of the lack of musical invention within. The musical growth rate of this band cannot even be charted. They are treading water in a sea of retarded sexuality and bad poetry.'
Tufnel responds: 'That's just nit-picking, isn't it?'

213

214

TOP HAT

US, 1936, RKO, 99 MINS

D MARK SANDRICH ('ENSEMBLES STAGED BY HERMES PAN');
PR PANDRO S. BERMAN; **SC** DWIGHT TAYLOR, ALLAN SCOTT
(BASED ON AN ORIGINAL STORY BY TAYLOR); **PH** (BW) DAVID ABEL;
ED WILLIAM HAMILTON; **M DIR** MAX STEINER; **M/LYR** IRVING
BERLIN

CAST FRED ASTAIRE (JERRY TRAVERS), GINGER ROGERS (DALE
TREMONT), EDWARD EVERETT HORTON (HORACE HARDWICK),
ERIC BLORE (BATES), ERIK RHODES (ALBERTO BEDINI), HELEN
BRODERICK (MADGE HARDWICK)

THE STORY American musical comedy star Jerry Travers is in
London to open in a new show when he wakes up Dale
Tremont by dancing in the hotel room above hers. They meet
and he falls in love, but she mistakes him for Horace Hardwick,
the prissy impresario putting on Jerry's show, who's married to
her older confidante, Madge. Escaping from a man she
believes to be a heartless philanderer, she goes to Venice with
Bedini, a preening Italian couturier whose dresses she is mod-
elling. After their show's successful first night, Jerry and Horace
fly out to Venice, where Horace's manservant Bates has been
sent to follow Dale. The misunderstanding continues, and before
Jerry can explain to her the case of mistaken identity, Dale has
married Bedini. But Jerry contrives to keep Dale and Bedini
apart, and before the ceremony is consummated, Bates reveals
that he performed the marriage disguised as a clergyman.

THE FILM The nine RKO musicals featuring Astaire and Rogers
are among the triumphs of world cinema, and *Top Hat*, despite
being almost a remake of *The Gay Divorcee*, is the most per-

▲ *TOP HAT* Fred and Ginger are in heaven as they move
together dancing cheek to cheek.

fect. The art deco sets by Van Nest Polglaze are symphonies in
white and the shimmering, fantasy Venice created in a
Hollywood studio has a dreamlike quality. The book is witty with
scarcely a serious line in it, and the supporting cast of Edward
Everett Horton (master of the double-take), Eric Blore and Erik
Rhodes, virtually reprising their roles from *The Gay Divorcee*,
milk every camp line and became special favourites of gay
moviegoers. Graham Greene, writing in 1935 in *The
Spectator*, commended the film for being 'quite earnestly
bawdy'. Irving Berlin wrote five excellent numbers – 'Top Hat
and Tails', 'No Strings', 'Isn't It a Lovely Day', 'Cheek to Cheek',
'The Piccolino' – all seamlessly worked into the story, the first
performed on stage by Astaire with a chorus, the second as an
Astaire solo, the other three as love duets by Fred and Ginger.
All are beautifully choreographed by Hermes Pan, though the
chorus work on 'The Piccolino' is somewhat kitschy. Finally
everything comes down to Fred and Ginger, the simplicity,
grace, warmth and sublimated passion they brought to their
work together. 'I did everything that Fred did,' Ginger once
observed, 'but backwards and in high heels.'

ODD/SALIENT FACTS By some way the most profitable
Astaire–Rogers musical, *Top Hat* made a profit of $1,325,000.
It was also the first specially written for Astaire, and initially he
didn't like it. Pandro S. Berman, who produced this and most
of the other Astaire–Rogers musicals, was the favourite producer
of Gore Vidal's *Myra Breckinridge*, who believed that 'in the
decade between 1935 and 1945 no irrelevant film was made

in the United States'. Lucille Ball, while still a bit player, makes a brief appearance as an assistant in a London flower shop. The greatest tribute to the cult of the Astaire–Rogers musicals is Federico Fellini's *Ginger e Fred* (1985), in which Marcello Mastroianni and Giulietta Masina play elderly Italian entertainers whose career in music hall was based on imitating the American duo.

MEMORABLE MOMENTS All the dance numbers, but especially Fred putting Horton and Rogers to sleep with his sand dance reprise of 'Fancy Free'.

Fred using his cane as a gun to mow down the chorus in 'Top Hat'.

Fred and Ginger falling in love as they dance apart from each other while sheltering from the rain in 'Isn't It a Lovely Day'.

The gleaming art-deco Venice.

KEY LINES

All the lyrics.

Ginger: 'I don't know you from Adam.'
Fred: 'Maybe it's the way I'm dressed.'

Fred, after being slapped by Ginger for a second time:
  'She loves me.'

TOUCH OF EVIL

US, 1958, UNIVERSAL-INTERNATIONAL, 108 MINS (ORIG. RELEASED AT 93 MINS)

D ORSON WELLES; **PR** ALBERT ZUGSMITH; **SC** ORSON WELLES (FROM THE NOVEL BADGE OF EVIL BY WHIT MASTERSON; **PH** (BW) RUSSELL METTY; **ED** VIRGIL VOGEL, AARON STELL; **M** HENRY MANCINI

CAST CHARLTON HESTON (MIGUEL 'MIKE' VARGAS), JANET LEIGH (SUSAN VARGAS), ORSON WELLES (HANK QUINLAN), JOSEPH CALLEIA (PETE MENZIES), AKIM TAMIROFF ('UNCLE JOE' GRANDI), VALENTIN DE VARGAS ('PANCHO'), JOANNA MOORE (MARCIA LINNEKAR), VICTOR MILLAN (MANELO SANCHEZ), RAY COLLINS (ADAIR, D. A.), MORT MILLS (ED SCHWARTZ, ASSISTANT D. A.), DENNIS WEAVER (NIGHT CLERK, MIRADOR MOTEL), MARLENE DIETRICH (TANYA), HARRY SHANNON (POLICE CHIEF), JOSEPH COTTEN (POLICE DOCTOR), GUS SCHILLING (EDDIE FARNHAM, CONSTRUCTION WORKER), ZSA ZSA GABOR (NIGHTCLUB DANCER)

THE STORY Mexican police officer Mike Vargas of the Pan-American Narcotics Commission is honeymooning with his American bride Susie at the border town of Los Robles. He's to be a key witness at the Mexico City trial of the head of the criminal Grandi clan. Vargas and Susie witness the blowing-up of a car carrying Linnekar, an influential American businessman, and his girlfriend. The film unfolds over the next fraught twenty-four hours through two initially unrelated plots. The obese detective Hank Quinlan investigates the killings with Vargas as observer. The Grandi family start harassing Susie until she's on the verge of a breakdown. Mike leaves her at a remote motel and continues to work on the Linnekar case. Quinlan suspects Sanchez, his daughter's lover, plants dynamite in his apartment and arrests him for murder. When Vargas threatens to reveal the frame-up, Quinlan is lured by 'Uncle Joe' Grandi into framing Vargas and his wife as drug addicts. Susie is drugged and abandoned in a sleazy hotel room, Quinlan strangles Grandi and leaves him beside her bed, and she's arrested for murder. Assistant D. A., Schwartz, and Quinlan's assistant, Sgt. Pete Menzies, come to Vargas's assistance. Bugged to a tape-recorder, Pete gets Quinlan to incriminate himself. Quinlan realizes Pete has trapped him, shoots him, and is himself shot dead by the dying Pete.

'A policeman's job is only easy in a police state.'

THE FILM Made a decade after *Macbeth*, *Touch of Evil* was the fifth and last movie Welles directed in Hollywood. It came about by accident. He was signed to play the corrupt cop Hank Quinlan in a routine Universal thriller, produced by Albert Zugsmith, who made a handful of memorable pictures in the Fifties before going into sleazy freefall. Heston would appear only if Welles directed; Welles wrote the script in a fortnight.

Citizen Kane usually heads polls of the ten greatest pictures ever made, though some think *The Magnificent Ambersons* as good or better. But the weird and wonderful *noir* pulp thriller, *Touch of Evil* is the cult Welles movie. From the elaborate opening single take to the final exchange as Quinlan's body sinks into the swamp, it demonstrates the cinema's ability to make a melodramatic story plausible by creating a baroque expressionist style of deep focus, high and low angles, heavy shadows, sweeping crane shots, fast tracking movements, garish hotel rooms and sordid neon-lit streets, creating a mood that embodies the lives of the character. The tormented Quinlan, his wife murdered, himself crippled by a gangster's bullet, is a tragic figure, as complex as Kane, Macbeth or Falstaff. He is an evil man, yet he intuitively knows the guilty from the innocent, and he is destroyed by breaching his own twisted code. The movie is populated by grotesques like Grandi with his ill-fitting wig, the blind woman shopkeeper, the deranged motel clerk. Vargas is perhaps the only normal, untainted character, and he's the voice of decency, though dull and unimaginative.

Most of the cast are familiar faces from earlier Welles pictures. Notably there are four actors from *Kane* – the credited Ray Collins and Harry Shannon, the uncredited Joseph Cotten and Gus Schilling. *Kane* is evoked by Quinlan's cane. 'His cane. I forgot to give him his cane', Menzies shouts, and it is

the cane left at the scene of Grandi's murder that does for Quinlan.

ODD/SALIENT FACTS The film was cut and scenes added after Welles left Hollywood, but it has since been restored in two versions. The sequence where Janet Leigh encounters a disturbed young night clerk at the motel where she's the only guest anticipates *Psycho*, which Hitchcock was to make two years later at the same studio. The veteran cinematographer Russell Metty did some of his best work on *Touch of Evil*. In 1960 Metty won an Oscar for *Spartacus*.

MEMORABLE MOMENTS The virtuoso three and a half-minute opening take from the priming of the bomb to its explosion off screen.

▼ *TOUCH OF EVIL* Good cop Charlton Heston goes eyeball to eyeball with bad cop Orson Welles.

216

Quinlan's first appearance, shot from ground level as he levers himself out of a police car with his cane.

The murder of Grandi, the only light source being a flashing neon sign from the street.

The final pursuit of Quinlan in a Mexican wasteland beneath oil derricks looking like creatures feeding in a primeval swamp.

KEY LINES

Quinlan: 'I'm no lawyer – all they think about is the law.'

Vargas: 'This isn't the real Mexico. All border towns bring out the worst in people.'

Vargas: 'A policeman's job is only easy in a police state.'

Schwartz: 'Hank was a great detective alright.'
Tanya: 'And a lousy cop.'

TWO-LANE BLACKTOP

US, 1971, UNIVERSAL, 102 MINS

D MONTE HELLMAN; **PR** MICHAEL S. LAUGHLIN; **SC** RUDOLPH WURLITZER, WILLY CORRY; **PH** (TECHNICOLOR WIDESCREEN) JACK DEERSON; **M SUP** BILLY JAMES; **ED** MONTE HELLMAN
CAST WARREN OATES (GTO), JAMES TAYLOR (THE DRIVER), DENNIS WILSON (THE MECHANIC), LAURIE BIRD (THE GIRL), BILL KELLER (TEXAS HITCHHIKER), H. D. STANTON (OKLAHOMA HITCH-HIKER), KATHERINE SQUIRE (OLD WOMAN), MELISSA HELLMAN (CHILD)

THE STORY The Driver and the Mechanic, both laconic, long-haired and in their twenties, win a Californian drag race in their souped-up Chevrolet and head east for more races. In Arizona they are passed by GTO, a middle-aged man in an orange Pontiac. At Flagstaff a young girl quits her psychedelic van and climbs into the back of their Chevy. In Santa Fe they beat a local driver, and the Girl sleeps with the Mechanic. GTO meets up with them at a filling station, they taunt each other, and agree to race to Washington DC, the winner taking the other's car. GTO adopts a different identity – war veteran, test pilot, TV producer – for everyone he meets. He and the boys alternately help and hinder each other as they race through Texas and Oklahoma. The Girl drives a wedge between the

▲ *TWO-LANE BLACKTOP* Chameleon GTO warily sizes up the Driver, the Girl and the Mechanic.

Mechanic and the Driver, before moving over to GTO's car and he offers to take her places after the race. Suddenly, however, she rides off with a young motorcyclist, and the race is abandoned. GTO takes two GIs aboard and spins them a yarn. The Driver and the Mechanic compete in a race but as the car is accelerating the film burns up in the projector.

THE FILM This is arguably the best, most austere of the pessimistic road movies of the late 1960s; pictures like Coppola's *The Rain People*, Hopper's *Easy Rider*, Spielberg's *Duel*, all reflecting the tensions of the divisive years of Nixon and the Vietnam War, when the counter-culture was pitted against the Establishment, the hip against the square.

The film's images are bleached out to prevent the West from looking romantic, the car races aren't exciting, the characters have no histories, and they work in the margins of a disturbed nomadic society, identifying themselves through their relationship with their cars. The Girl undermines their alliance. The relationship between the boys and GTO is illuminated by a passage in Tony Tanner's 1970 study of American fiction, *City of Words:*

In many recent American novels we will find the hero in quest of identity confronting a Protean figure whose quick metamorphoses seem to make him enviably well adapted to reality; but the hero seldom takes him for a model, no matter how he may learn from him, for that way lies chaos, the nightmare jelly, the ultimate dissolution of self.

217

In 1970 when he embarked on this film, Hellman was a cult director who had staged the first West Coast production of Beckett's *Waiting for Godot* and directed two ultra-low-budget Westerns for Roger Corman (*The Shooting* and *Ride in the Whirlwind*) that had been hailed as masterpieces in Paris but never shown in America. *Two-Lane Blacktop* was going to transform his reputation, although the critical reception was mixed in the States and the public rejected the film as gloomy and obscure. In Britain the critics were ecstatic, but it was consigned to art houses. Hellman remained a cult director.

> **'What is this anyway, some kind of masculine power trip?'**

The great cult actor Warren Oates appeared in five Hellman pictures and his performance as GTO, the tough, vulnerable, optimistic loser, is one of his finest. His dynamism is set off by the convincingly passive performances of the professional musicians James Taylor and Dennis Wilson, the quintessence of cool, in their only important acting roles.

Two-Lane Blacktop uses only source music, the most significant number being Kris Kristofferson's 'Me And Bobby McGee' which The Girl selects from GTO's cassettes. 'Freedom's just another word for nothing left to lose' could serve as the movie's epigraph.

ODD/SALIENT FACTS Hellman never worked again for a major Hollywood picture, though he was brought in by Quentin Tarantino as an executive producer on *Reservoir Dogs*. Three of the film's leading players died in the 1980s – Oates had a heart attack at 54; Beach Boy Dennis Wilson drowned aged 38; Laurie Bird committed suicide in her early thirties, becoming something of a cult figure for her work in *Two-Lane Blacktop*, in Hellman's *Cockfighter* (a film banned in Britain) and in *Annie Hall* (playing Paul Simon's girlfriend). This is one of the few films in which the cars are listed among the cast in the final credits.

MEMORABLE MOMENTS GTO's first appearance, grinning as he passes the 55 Chevy.

The Girl's duffle bag containing all she owns abandoned in a roadside diner's car park.

The final scene from behind the driver's shoulder, from slow-motion to freeze frame, to the burning of the film.

KEY LINES

The Girl: 'What is this anyway, some kind of masculine power trip?'

The Mechanic: 'I don't believe I've ever seen you. Of course there's a lot of cars on the road like yours, they all get to look the same.'

GTO: 'Well, here we are on the road.'

The Mechanic, as GTO starts telling his life story: 'I don't want to hear about it, it's not my problem.'

UNDER THE RAINBOW
US, 1981, WARNER BROS, 95 MINS

D STEVE RASH; **PR** FRED BAUER; **SC** PAT MCCORMICK, HARRY HURWITZ, MARTIN BRADLEY SMITH, FRED BAUER, PAT BRADLEY; **PH** FRANK STANLEY; **M** JOE RENZETTI; **ED** DAVID BLEWITT **CAST** CHEVY CHASE (BRUCE THORPE), CARRIE FISHER (ANNIE CLARK), EVE ARDEN (THE DUCHESS), JOSEPH MAKER (THE DUKE), ROBERT DONNER (THE ASSASSIN), BILLY BARTY (OTTO KRIEGLING), MAKO (NAKAMURI), CORK HUBBERT (ROLLO SWEET), PAT MCCORMICK (TINY), ADAM ARKIN (HENRY HUDSON), RICHARD STAHL (LESTER HUDSON), FREEMAN KING (OTIS), PETER ISACKSEN (HOMER), JACK KAUSCHEN (LOUIS), BENNETT OHTA (AKIDO), GARY FRIEDKIN (WEDGIE)

THE STORY The year is 1939 and Rollo Sweet is a mid-Western dwarf who dreams of Hollywood stardom. Sure enough he travels west and finds himself cast as a Munchkin in *The Wizard of Oz*. He is one resident at an over-booked hotel filled not only with dwarfs and their chaperone Annie Clark, but also a bus-load of male Japanese tourists all dressed in white, a Duke who is paranoid about being assassinated, his wife and bodyguard Bruce Thorpe, a dwarf German spy, a Japanese spy dressed in a white suit, and a man bent on assassinating the Duke. As the dwarfs party riotously the various plots are foiled and Annie and Bruce fall in love. At the end, Rollo wakes up and finds it was all a dream, that all the characters in it were his friends from the Rainbow Mission, Culver City, Kansas, but he is in fact about to go off to appear as a Munchkin in *The Wizard of Oz*.

219

▲ *Under the Rainbow* Carrie Fisher and Chevy Chase amid the party-crazy Munchkins in the film that celebrates the cult of The Wizard of Oz.

THE FILM *Under the Rainbow* has a small, devoted following. It has some eccentric stars, was expensive but a box-office disaster, and was released in the UK directly on video. Its cult status has been aided by its use of the stories about the behaviour of the Munchkins around the period of the shooting of *The Wizard of Oz* (1939), which itself remains a cult while at the same time transcending that status to inspire something like a cinematic religion. The stories of the midgets are part of Hollywood legend and this film is jolly but not dark enough, not quite well enough made to do justice to the material. The spirit should have been more like that of *The Wild Party* (1975). Instead the plan of the film-makers was clearly to replicate the comedy thriller success of *Foul Play* (1978). But sadly the message got garbled somewhere from page to screen and instead of reuniting Chevy Chase with Goldie Hawn, the film-makers reunited Chase and Billy Barty which is not quite so sexy a partnership.

The basic idea of the film is that Rollo was inspired by Roosevelt and the New Deal to travel to Hollywood and become a star. The whole story is an alternative dream to that in *The Wizard of Oz*: with a Japanese spy and a German dwarf spy trying to rendezvous in a hotel packed with dwarfs and identically dressed Japanese men. *Under the Rainbow* is an artefact of the continuing cult of *The Wizard of Oz*.

ODD/SALIENT FACTS *The Wizard of Oz* is arguably the single most influential film in the history of the cinema and permeates American film culture. It has inspired countless gags, underpinned several films and even fuelled much of at least one career – that of Robin Williams. It is a continual reference point for Williams throughout his work, notably in *Good Morning Vietnam* (1987) which includes several skits along the lines of 'Follow the Ho Chi Minh Trail'. The extended Kung Fu sketch from *The Kentucky Fried Movie* (1977) concludes with the heroic fighter coming to, wearing Dorothy's dress, lying on a bed surrounded by characters from his dream. John Boorman's *Zardoz* (1974) is set in a strange, pretentious future and the film borrows its title and some of the plot from *The Wizard of Oz*.

David Lynch's *Wild at Heart* (1990) is essentially an updating of the Oz story with angelic visitations via floating red bubbles and Laura Dern's character stating: 'The whole world's wild at heart and weird on top. I wish I was somewhere over the rainbow.'

MEMORABLE MOMENTS In a climactic chase in which the good dwarfs chase the Nazi dwarf across the MGM lot, they run through the set of *Gone With the Wind*, the other iconic film (also directed by Victor Fleming) of 1939.

KEY LINE

The film's great inspired moment comes when Otto, the Nazi dwarf, arrives at the hotel to liaise with his Japanese counterpart. He has been briefed that the Japanese spy will introduce himself with the words: 'The pole is in the river.' Meanwhile in the hotel's restaurant, the duchess has misplaced her pearl brooch, which has fallen into her liver pâté. So, as Otto passes the table of one of the Japanese photographers, he hears him call to the duchess helpfully: 'The pearl is in the river.'

THE USUAL SUSPECTS

US, 1995, BLUE PARROT/GRAMERCY/POLYGRAM/BAD HAT HARRY/SPELLING FILMS INTERNATIONAL, 108 MINS

D BRYAN SINGER; **PR** BRYAN SINGER, MICHAEL MCDONNELL; **SC** CHRISTOPHER MCQUARRIE; **PH** NEWTON THOMAS SIGEL; **M** JOHN OTTMAN; **ED** JOHN OTTMAN

CAST STEPHEN BALDWIN (MCMANUS), GABRIEL BYRNE (KEATON), BENICIO DEL TORO (FENSTER), KEVIN POLLAK (HOCKNEY), KEVIN SPACEY (VERBAL), CHAZZ PALMINTERI (DAVE KUJAN), PETE POSTLETHWAITE (KOBAYASHI), SUZY AMIS (EDIE FINNERMAN), GIANCARLO ESPOSITO (JACK BAER), DAN HEDAYA (JEFF RABIN), PAUL BARTEL (SMUGGLER), CARL BRESSLER (SAUL BERG), PHILIP SIMON (FORTIER), JACK SHEARER (RENAULT), CHRISTINE ESTABROOK (DR PLUMMER), CLARK GREGG (DR WALTERS), MORGAN HUNTER (ARKASH KOVASH), KEN DALY (TRANSLATOR), CASTULLA GUERRA (ARTURRO MARQUEZ)

THE STORY Kujan is a cop investigating the case of a burnt-out boat on and around which 27 people were killed. He interrogates the limping Verbal who relates the story of the last six weeks. Five criminals — McManus, Hockney, Fenster, Keaton and himself — brought together for a police line-up, hatch a

▲ *THE USUAL SUSPECTS* Hockney (Kevin Pollak), McManus (Stephen Baldwin), Fenster (Benicio Del Toro), Keaton (Gabriel Byrne), and Verbal (Kevin Spacey) brought together for the fateful line-up.

plan. They steal a consignment of emeralds. Back in the present a badly burned Hungarian survivor from the boat says he confronted the devil, Keyser Söze. Verbal tells Kujan how the gang carried out another job, before meeting Kobayashi. He tells them that since each of them has unwittingly stolen from Söze, they must now do one final job for him — steal $91 million dollars of coke and/or the cash in a deal between Hungarian and Argentinian gangsters. Fenster is killed after trying to escape. Hockney, McManus and finally Keaton are killed in a job that turns out to be not about money or drugs, but a plot to silence a man planning to rat on Keyser Söze. Kujan convinces Verbal that Keaton was behind the affair, and Verbal walks free. Looking round the office, Kujan sees various names that have appeared in the story and realizes that the whole thing was invented on the spot by Verbal. Verbal whose limp suddenly vanishes is picked up in a car driven by Kobayashi and vanishes forever.

THE FILM Thiis brilliant film has an inbuilt narrative device that brings it an instant cult following. The audience ought to feel cheated by the belated revelation of an unreliable narrator but the twist comes so late and is so unexpected that the film is suddenly over and you immediately run back over an already labyrinthine plot to see what the implications are of this sudden change. Verbal uses the time before Kujan enters the office to build his story. He sizes up his opponent, sees him as a tough

220

guy and characterizes himself as a weakling who can't light his own cigarette, whose piss is like snot if he doesn't get enough to drink and who shits blood when beaten up.

The big cult question is if Verbal isn't Verbal, then is he Keyser Söze? Does Keyser Söze exist? Is/Was Keaton Söze? How about Redfoot? Did he exist at all? As he is not listed in the credits, is he perhaps Söze? Christopher McQuarrie has said: 'I know exactly who Keyser Söze is and Bryan Singer knows exactly who Keyser Söze is. Our opinions are completely different.'

ODD/SALIENT FACTS *The Usual Suspects* was a poster before it was a film. When encouraged to actually write the script McQuarrie reasoned: 'We got a poster, I guess we can have a movie.' Many details of the film were inspired, like Verbal's tale, by small things observed by the writer. The title comes from a magazine article (although it was also inspired by the repeated line from *Casablanca* (1942); the notion of the quartet in Skokie, Illinois, from the same label that appears in the film and the name of the devilish super-villain was adapted from that of a lawyer encountered by McQuarrie, by the name of Kayser Sume.

MEMORABLE MOMENTS Verbal tells the story of Söze's early life. In a dizzying, out-of-focus flashback, he talks of how the young man, then just a small-time Turkish dope dealer, returns to his home to find three men holding his family at gunpoint. They have already raped his wife and now demand his territory and all his business: 'Söze looks over the faces of his family, then he showed these men of will what will really was.' He shoots one man, then another, then his wife and children, before letting the last man go to tell the story.

KEY LINES

Verbal: 'It was all the cops' fault. You don't put guys like that into a room together. Who knows what can happen?'

Cop interrogating Hockney after initial heist: 'Do you know what happens if you do another term in the joint?'
Hockney: 'Fuck your father in the shower and then have a snack? Are you gonna charge me, dick-head?'

Kujan to Verbal: 'I'm smarter than you and I'm gonna find out what I wanna know and I'm gonna get it from you, whether you like it or not.'

Kobayashi outlining the job Keyser wants them to do: 'One job, one day's work, very dangerous. He does not expect all of you to live, but those of you who do will have $91 million to divide between you in any way you see fit.'

Verbal to Kujan: 'The greatest trick the devil ever pulled was convincing the world he didn't exist.'

VANISHING POINT

UK, 1971, 20TH CENTURY-FOX/CUPID PRODUCTIONS, 99 MINS

D RICHARD SARAFIAN; **PR** MICHAEL PEARSON; **SC** GUILLERMO CAIN (FROM A STORY OUTLINE BY MALCOLM HART; **PH** (DELUXECOLOR) JOHN A. ALONZO; **M SUP** JIMMY BROWN (USING ROCK, COUNTRY AND GOSPEL RECORDINGS); **ED** STEFAN ARNSTEN

CAST BARRY NEWMAN (KOWALSKI), CLEAVON LITTLE (SUPER SOUL), DEAN JAGGER (PROSPECTOR), VICTORIA MEDLIN (VERA), PAUL KOSLO (YOUNG COP), LEE WEAVER (JAKE), BOB DONNER (OLDER COP), TIMOTHY SCOTT (ANGEL, HIPPIE BIKER), GILDA TEXTER (NUDE RIDER), ANTHONY JAMES (FIRST MALE HITCH HIKER), ARTHUR MALET (SECOND MALE HITCH HIKER), KARL SWENSON (SANDY), SEVERN DARDEN (J. HOVAH), DELANEY & BONNIE & FRIENDS (J. HOVAH'S SINGERS)

THE STORY Two bulldozers block a Californian country road, police cars arrive, a CBS-TV news team prepare to report, a helicopter hovers. A suspect in a white 1970 Dodge Challenger approaches and then goes off into the grey desert to park among burnt-out auto bodies. The car goes back on to the road and as it passes another vehicle coming to the West, the frame freezes on the title CALIFORNIA SUNDAY 10.20 a.m. The next titles are TWO DAYS EARLIER and DENVER COLORADO FRIDAY 10.30 p.m. and the movie unfolds in flashback. Kowalski, a well-dressed, clean-shaven type, delivers a car he has driven non-stop from San Francisco to Sandy's Denver auto business. Refusing to rest, he picks up the white super-charged Challenger, and a fistful of benzedrine tablets from Jake, his black friend who bets him he can't make it to San Francisco by 3 p.m. the next afternoon. Crossing the deserts of Colorado, Utah and Nevada, he out-races cops and evades traps. An elderly man, Prospector, who lives by catching snakes, teaches him how to camouflage his car. A pair of vicious gays attempt to steal the car. Super Soul, a blind black DJ, publicizes the chase and sends him helpful messages. But a gang of rednecks break into the station, beat up Super Soul and his engineer, and put out dangerous disinformation. A hippie biker and his girlfriend living in a Death Valley shack help him make it to the Californian border. Meanwhile a series of flashbacks and police information bulletins have revealed that Kowalski served in Vietnam, was wounded and won the Medal of Honor. Subsequently he worked with distinction as a cop before being discharged for attacking a colleague who had attempted to rape a female suspect. In 1966 his countercultural girlfriend died while surfing. The movie ends with a smiling Kowalski driving at top speed at the road block and his white Challenger going up in flames.

THE FILM *Vanishing Point* is a time-capsule film of the 1960s ethos, all the purer for being a British-financed production shot entirely on location in the United States. The hero, Kowalski, is obviously named for that embodiment of the positive, aggressive American spirit, Stanley Kowalski, protagonist/antagonist of Tennessee Williams's *A Streetcar Named Desire*. Like Wyatt and Billy in *Easy Rider* and the Driver and Mechanic in *Two-Lane*

Blacktop, the countercultural road movies that preceded and followed it, *Vanishing Point* has a central character embarked on a death trip. On his side are a drug-dealer, a blind DJ who acts as a Greek chorus, an elderly desert dweller, a hippie biker and his girlfriend. Against them are arraigned the police of four states, Colorado, Utah, Nevada and California. In between, listening on the airwaves, waiting for something to happen, are the citizens of anonymous towns. The young protagonists of *Easy Rider* and *Two-Lane Blacktop* are outside the system. The middle-aged GTO in *Two-Lane Blacktop* remains an enigmatic chameleon. Kowalski is presented as someone who has paid his dues as a soldier and cop, joined the counterculture, been disillusioned, has only death to face and elects to die on his own terms in a mad assault against the bulldozers in his path.

ODD/SALIENT FACTS Guillermo Cain, the film's credited screenwriter, is a pseudonym for one of the most gifted writers of the second half of the twentieth century, the Cuban critic and novelist G. Cabrera Infante. Also, Iain Quarrier, credited as

▼ *VANISHING POINT* Two venomous gay hitchhikers fail to faze death-seeking Barry Newman.

'Creative Associate', was a British protégé of Roman Polanski and had minor roles in *Cul-de-Sac* and *The Fearless Vampire Killers*. Cleavon Little found permanent cult fame as the black sheriff in Mel Brooks's *Blazing Saddles*.

MEMORABLE MOMENTS Aerial shots of Kowalski making patterns in the sand of Death Valley.

Kowalski discovering his girl's surfboard washed up on the beach.

The Prospector arriving to capture the rattlesnake that threatens Kowalski.

The rednecks (maybe disguised policemen) smashing the radio station.

KEY LINES

DJ Super Soul: 'There goes the Challenger being chased by the blue, blue meanies on wheels. The vicious traffic squad cars are after an unknown driver, the last American hero, the electric sitar, the super driver of the Gold West [...]You can beat the road, you can even beat the clock, you can't beat the desert, nobody can.'

Prospector: The best way to get away is to root right where you are.'

Super Soul: 'Big Brother's not so much watching as listening in.'

THE WANDERERS

US/NETHERLANDS, 1979, ARROW FILMS, 117 MINS

D PHILIP KAUFMAN; **PR** MARTIN RANSOHOFF; **SC** PHILIP KAUFMAN AND ROSE KAUFMAN, BASED ON THE NOVEL BY RICHARD PRICE; **PH** (COL) MICHAEL CHAPMAN; **M** VARIOUS; **ED** RONALD ROOSE, STUART H. PAPPÉ

CAST KEN WAHL (RICHIE), JOHN FRIEDRICH (JOEY), KAREN ALLEN (NINA), TONI KALEM (DESPIE GALASSO), ALAN ROSENBERG (TURKEY), JIM YOUNGS (BUDDY), TONY GANIOS (PERRY), LINDA MANZ (PEEWEE), WILLIAM ANDREWS (EMILIO), ERLAND VAN LIDTH DE JEUDE (TERROR), VAL AVERY (MR SHARP), DOLPH SWEET (CHUBBY GALASSO)

THE STORY The Bronx, 1963. Turkey, Joey, Richie and Buddy, members of the Italian New York gang the Wanderers, are

▲ THE WANDERERS *The gang try out their unsubtle collective chat-up technique on another unsuspecting young New Yorker.*

saved from a beating at the hands of rival gang, the Baldies, by new kid Perry. Joey's brutal father is having an affair with Perry's alcoholic mother. Richie is dating Despie, the daughter of a local gangster, Chubby Galasso. Turkey has shaved his head in the hope of joining the Baldies. A liberal high-school teacher's lesson in racial harmony leads to racial conflict in the classroom between the Wanderers and various black gangs. Richie meets and instantly falls for the middle-class Nina, but tries to set her up with Joey. He, Buddy, Perry and Joey follow her in their car, but get lost and wander into the territory of the sinister Ducky Boys. They just manage to escape with their lives. During a party at Despie's house, Richie and Nina are caught making out in a car. Turkey, now a member of the Baldies, stumbles into the Ducky Boys and is killed. The following day President Kennedy is assassinated, and Richie and Despie make up. She is pregnant by him and Richie is forced to marry her. The arrival of the Ducky Boys at a football game unites the Wanderers with the black gangs and the Wongs who together drive them away. At Joey's bachelor party the different gang members join together in harmony. Nina passes the restaurant. Richie runs after her but only stops and watches as she goes into a folk club. Joey and Perry drive out west as Richie returns to his party where everyone joins in singing 'The Wanderer'.

THE FILM This is an episodic film, a series of adventures marking a specific time of change in American life. It is partly a light-hearted coming-of-age film with comic-book escapades, partly a serious look at the politicization of the country and its popular music, and how America was transformed by the death of Kennedy. The sequence in which the Baldies are coerced into joining the Marines is a comic sketch waiting for a punch line. Instead they just drive off, a bunch of no-hopers on their way to Vietnam. In the climactic sequence, Richie follows Nina but realizes that their paths only crossed briefly. He watches longingly as she takes her seat in the folk club where Bob Dylan, perhaps too emblematically, sings 'The times, they are a'changin'' and he realizes he isn't part of this world. It is the strangest and darkest of the Seventies coming-of-age films.

'Nobody fucks with the Baldies, man.'

ODD/SALIENT FACTS The film is the second, after *Bloodbrothers* (1978), to be adapted from a novel by Richard Price, who plays one of the bowling bankrollers. An authentic voice of New York street life, Price wrote the screenplay for *Sea of Love* (1989) and two for Scorsese, *The Color of Money* (1986) and the 'Life Lessons' segment from *New York Stories* (1989). *The Color of Money* is the belated sequel to *The Hustler* (1960), which is name-checked in the sequence in which Price appears. When Chubby Galasso gets his revenge on the bowling team that hustled Richie and his friends, he smashes the bowling hand of one of them in emulation of the famous scene in his favourite movie. When Walter Hill was accused of stealing from Kaufman in *The Long Riders* (1982), he quipped, referring to The Wanderers: 'If he can steal *The Warriors* from me then I can steal *The Great Northfield Minnesota* raid from him.'

MEMORABLE MOMENTS The Baldies, now including Turkey in their number, indulge in a game of 'cock 'n' roll' or 'cock and rock' with Richie and Joey. The two are taken to the park, and tied to a fence on a bridge over a stream. Each has one end of a length of twine tied around his penis, with the other tied around a hefty stone. Turkey throws the rock over the bridge, Joey and Richie scream until the rock, with plenty of twine to spare, hits the water.

The scene after Turkey's murder, where Joey wanders along the street. He sees a group of people, some weeping, staring into a shop window. As he gets closer he sees that it is a TV shop and they are watching the news of JFK's assassination.

KEY LINES
Turkey: 'Nobody fucks with the Baldies, man.'
Joey: 'Those guys look like pricks with ears.'

Galasso, on the racial divisions among high-school kids:
'It's a shame to see kids beating each other's brains out. Especially when there's no financial advantage.'

WHITE HEAT
US, 1949, WARNER BROS, 114 MINS
D RAOUL WALSH; **PR** LOUIS F. EDELMAN; **SC** IVAN GOFF, BEN ROBERTS; **PH** (BW) SID HICKOX; **M** MAX STEINER; **ED** OWEN MARKS
CAST JAMES CAGNEY (CODY JARRETT), VIRGINIA MAYO (VERNA JARRETT), EDMOND O'BRIEN (HANK FALLON/VIC PARDO), MARGARET WYCHERLEY (MA JARRETT), STEVE COCHRAN (BIG ED SOMMERS), JOHN ARCHER (PHILIP EVANS), WALLY CASSELL (COTTON VALETTI), FRED CLARK (TRADER), FORD RAINEY (ZUCKIE HOMMELL), FRED COBY (HAPPY TAYLOR), G. PAT COLLINS (READER), MICKEY KNOX (HET KOHLER), PAUL GUILFOYLE (ROY PARKER), ROBERT OSTERLOH (TOMMY RYLEY), IAN MACDONALD (BO CREEL), RAY MONTGOMERY (TRENT), MARSHALL BRADFORD (CHIEF OF POLICE)

THE STORY Cody Jarrett and his gang pull off a raid on a train in which four railway men are killed and one of his gang badly scalded. As the police are closing in, Jarrett gives himself up and confesses to a lesser crime committed at the same time as the train job. As Jarrett begins his two-year stretch, the Treasury Department send in their undercover specialist Hank Fallon to pose as Cody's cell mate, Vic Pardo, find out the truth about Jarrett's crimes and discover the identity of his money launderer. Pardo saves Jarrett's life and becomes a trusted friend. He helps comfort Jarrett when his beloved mother is killed for standing up to Big Ed, one of Jarrett's men taking advantage of his boss's absence. In fact Verna, Jarrett's wife, was having an affair with Ed and she shot Ma Jarrett in the back. Jarrett and Pardo escape from jail and Pardo becomes a gang member on Jarrett's next big job on a chemical plant. During the raid, Pardo is at last unmasked as a cop, but manages to escape. The police pick off the gang one by one until it is just Jarrett left. He makes his way to the top of a vast petrol tank. Fallon shoots Jarrett who in

▲ *WHITE HEAT* Cody Jarrett (James Cagney) goes out with a big bang and fulfils his promise: 'Made it, Ma. Top of the world.'

turn fires at the tank and disappears in a vast explosion.

THE FILM Cagney was on a bad box-office run during the late Forties when he chose this project to revive his fortunes. He reunited with Raoul Walsh, who had directed him in one of his best gangster films, *The Roaring Twenties* (1939). The project also marked his return to Warner Bros., the studio where he had had his early success and had become an icon (and had grown to loathe studio boss Jack). The writers based the action on the story of Ma Barker, and distilled all the brothers into one intense, violent, mother-fixated psychopath. It is at times a crude public information film showing off the cops' latest technology. We see their well-orchestrated, discreet pursuit of Ma Jarrett through the streets of a Californian town using three alternating

cars. They use spectrograph scans and fingerprints to establish a link between Jarrett and the train job. Later Fallon/Pardo improvises a radio which the cops use to track down the gang at the chemical plant.

At the same time it is a dark exploration of violent psychosis and betrayal. It is a study of an insane, unpredictable, vindictive cold-blooded killer. But the power of Cagney's personality makes him the magnetic force of the film. The audience roots for Jarrett and despises the anonymous, bland and deceitful cops. Jarrett is a brilliant crook, who is defeated not by his psychic flaws, but by the actions of others. On the first raid fellow gang members use his real name, tune in a radio, choose not to kill their badly wounded friend. His mother is spotted by the police while out buying strawberries for him. He is betrayed by Big Ed, Verna and finally by the only person he really trusted apart from his Ma, Pardo. As Jarrett, Cagney gives one of the great performances in the cinema. Orson Welles believed

Cagney to be the finest of all film actors, a 'displacer of air', saying: 'He played right at the top of his bent, but he was always true.'

ODD/SALIENT FACTS Cagney used his memories of his father's alcohol-induced seizures to produce his hysterical reaction to the news of Ma's death in the prison refectory. So as to get authentic reactions from the extras in the scene, they were not informed of what was going to happen. As one of them told John McCabe in his biography, *Cagney*: 'I was seated just two tables away from Cagney when they did the scene, and it scared the bejesus out of us sitting there. You'd swear to God he'd gone insane. I've looked at that scene lots of times, and you'll note that we all looked shocked. We were.'

MEMORABLE MOMENTS The most dramatic of all Cagney's memorable screen deaths as he goes up with the petrol tanks.

KEY LINES

Cody: 'You know something, Verna, if I turn my back for long enough for Big Ed to put a hole in it, there'd be a hole in it.'

Cody: 'A copper! A copper! How do you like that, boys. A copper and his name is Fallon and we went for it. I went for it, treated him like a kid brother and I was gonna split 50/50 with a copper. Maybe they're gonna pin a badge on him. Solid gold.'

THE WICKER MAN★

UK, 1973, BRITISH LION, 86 MINS (102 MINS IN RESTORED VERSION)

D *ROBIN HARDY;* **PR** *PETER SNELL;* **SC** *ANTHONY SHAFFER;* **PH** *(EASTMAN COLOUR) HARRY WAXMAN;* **ED** *ERIC BOYD-PERKINS;* **M** *PAUL GIOVANNI*

CAST *EDWARD WOODWARD (SGT. NEIL HOWIE), BRITT EKLAND (WILLOW MACGREGOR), DIANE CILENTO (MISS ROSE), INGRID PITT (LIBRARIAN), CHRISTOPHER LEE (LORD SUMMERISLE), LESLEY MACKIE (DAISY), AUBREY MORRIS (GARDENER/GRAVEDIGGER), IRENE SUNTERS (MRS MAY MORRISON), GERALDINE COWPER (ROWAN MORRISON), LINDSAY KEMP (ALDER MCGREGOR, PUBLICAN), RUSSELL WATERS (HARBOUR MASTER)*

> *'God had his chance, and in modern parlance, he blew it.'*

THE STORY Police Sergeant Neil Howie flies in to investigate the disappearance of a twelve-year-old girl, Rowan, on Summerisle, off the West coast of Scotland. Howie, a devout man, is shocked by the licentious conduct of the islanders. Eventually he's told Rowan is dead and buried, and seeks permission from the local laird, Lord Summerisle, to exhume the body. Summerisle tells him that when his grandfather brought prosperity to the island in the mid-nineteenth century, the newer religions were replaced by worship of pre-Christian gods. In Rowan's coffin Howie finds only a hare and becomes convinced that she's to be sacrificed at the May Day festivities to restore the island's fortunes. Dressed as a Fool, Howie joins the celebrations, finds Rowan and escapes with her but is trapped by Lord Summerisle and the villagers. Howie, an adult virgin and true believer, has been lured there and is to be the sacrificial victim. He's placed in a gigantic man-shaped wicker pyre, which is set on fire as Howie prays to his God and the celebrating islanders dance and sing.

THE FILM *The Wicker Man* is a subversive, double-edged fable about the attractions and terrors of the primitive and ritualistic. It simultaneously criticizes and endorses the hedonism of the 1960s in a gleefully ironic fashion. Howie, supposed hero and only representative of decent, conventional society, is a dim, guilt-ridden figure while the islanders, initially presented as suspicious, menacing rustics, led by the suave, charming Lord Summerisle, are a liberated, fun-loving community, determined to protect their way of life. The movie is blatant in the presentation of their obsession with procreation, rejection of traditional Western taboos about sexuality and worship of nature. Summerisle is a clean, brightly lit place, that combines edenic innocence with hidden threat, and, depending on your point of view, it is either devoid of evil or its evil is concealed under a seductive surface. The sense of a world ruled by ritual and in tune with nature is underlined by the constant use of folk music rather than the menacing scores associated with the horror flick.

The movie belongs to two traditions – films of witchcraft and paranoid thrillers about city folk who find themselves the victims of rural plotters and conspirators. It is imperfect, at times overplayed, and mildly risible. Some of its appeal came from its troubled history. It became an instant cult hit among a smallish group of horror fans when it was released with sixteen minutes cut by British Lion, a company undergoing a change of management and whose executives disliked the picture. It went into distribution as supporting feature to *Don't Look Now*, which made a sensational double-bill. There are thematic similarities and a close resemblance between Howie's pursuit of the fleeing morris dancer's red hobby horse with a dragon's head through the alleyways of Summerisle, and Donald Sutherland chasing the dwarf in the red coat around Venice. Because it wasn't given a press screening nor was much advertised, *The Wicker Man*'s reputation spread by word of mouth, as it did later when given a very limited distribution in the States.

ODD SALIENT FACTS The cinematographer Harry Waxman collaborated in 1946 on the Boultings Brothers' black-and-white political saga *Fame Is The Spur* with the great Günther Krampf, who worked on numerous key German expressionist movies of the 1920s including Murnau's *Nosferatu* (as assistant cameraman) and Pabst's *Pandora's Box*. Director Robin Hardy (born 1929) has only made one other film, *The Fantasist* (1986), a little-known thriller ripe for cultdom in which a serial killer stalks the streets of Dublin. Anthony Shaffer, a pasticheur of genius, scripted *Frenzy* (1972) for Hitchcock, and three Agatha Christie period pieces. *The Wicker Man* is his cinematic masterpiece.

MEMORABLE MOMENTS Howie landing by sea-plane and being brought ashore by a rowing boat with a sign against the evil eye (borrowed from Michael Powell's 1940 *Thief of Bagdad*) on its prow.

The succession of weird encounters as Howie searches the town for Rowan.

The Wicker Man afire and toppling over as the sun sinks into the sea.

KEY LINES:

The film's opening credit: 'The producers would like to thank Lord Summerisle and the people of his island off the west coast of Scotland for this privileged insight into their religious practices and for their generous co-operation in the making of this film.'

Miss Rose, the schoolteacher: 'The children find it far easier to picture the incarnation than the resurrection.'

Lord Summerisle: 'God had his chance, and in modern parlance, he blew it.'

WILD STRAWBERRIES (SMULTRONSTÄLLET)
SWEDEN, 1957, SVENSK FILMINDUSTRI, 91 MINS

D INGMAR BERGMAN; **PR** ALLAN EKELUND; **SC** INGMAR BERGMAN; **PH** (BW) GUNNAR FISCHER; **M** ERIK NORDGREN; **ED** OSCAR ROSANDER

CAST VICTOR SJÖSTRÖM (PROFESSOR ISAK BORG), NAIMA WIFSTRAND (BORG'S MOTHER), JULLAN KINDAHL (MISS AGDA, BORG'S HOUSEKEEPER), GUNNAR BJÖRNSTRAND (DR EVALD BORG), INGRID THULIN (MARIANNE BORG, EVALD'S WIFE), BIBI ANDERSSON (SARA, A HITCHHIKER/SARA, ISAK'S COUSIN), GUNNAR SJÖBERG (STEN ALMAN, AN ENGINEER), GUNNEL BROSTRÖM (BERIT, ALMAN'S WIFE), MAX VON SYDOW (HENRIK ÅKERMAN, GARAGE OWNER), GUNNEL LINDBLOM (CHARLOTTA, ISAK'S ELDER SISTER), GERTRUD FRIDH (KARIN, ISAK BORG'S WIFE), ÅKE FRIDELL (KARIN'S LOVER)

THE STORY The action takes place on one Saturday in June, 1957, when 78-year-old widower, Eberhard Isak Borg, Professor Emeritus of bacteriology in Stockholm, is to receive an honorary degree from his alma mater, Lund University, on the occasion of the fiftieth anniversary of his doctorate. At the last minute, after a disturbing nightmare in which he sees his own funeral, he decides to make the 600- kilometre journey by road rather than flying with his elderly housekeeper, and he sets out at 4 a.m. accompanied by Marianne, his daughter-in-law. Along the way he picks up three students hitchhiking to the continent, one of whom, Sara, reminds him of his cousin Sara, the great love of his adolescence. They also give a ride, briefly, to a bitterly quarrelling married couple, the Almans. Borg stops at the house where his family spent summers in his childhood, at the small town where he first practised as a young doctor, and at the home of his elderly mother. All these visits trigger off memories of his past which he experiences first through daydreams and reveries, then in a nightmare in which he is interrogated about his life and character and is shown his late wife with her lover in the woods. Marianne reveals to Borg that his son, a university lecturer at Lund, has become aloof, incapable of giving or receiving love, and cannot accept her pregnancy. Borg signals his new understanding of Marianne by telling her he has no objection to her smoking in the car, and he's touched by a naive tribute to him by Sara, the student hitchhiker. Arriving in Lund, he meets his son and

227

▲ *WILD STRAWBERRIES* Victor Sjöström and Naima Wifstrand, two of Scandinavia's greatest actors, embrace as son and mother.

housekeeper, attends the degree ceremony, is serenaded by the three students and retires to bed. As he falls asleep he conjures up a childhood memory of seeing his parents waving to him as they fish beside the lake at the summer house.

THE FILM Although initially thought obscure by some critics, *Wild Strawberries* is superbly lucid in its combination of reality, reverie and nightmare. It is one of the cinema's great studies of old age (though it's less successful in depicting the students) and brings together the outstanding director of the postwar Swedish cinema, Ingmar Bergman, with his revered mentor, Victor Sjöström, the greatest director of Swedish silent cinema, who here makes his final appearance. The way it combines a journey in time and space with an interior journey of self-discovery

prepared the way for what became a distinctive genre during the following decade – the road movie. Although immediately preceded by *The Seventh Seal*, Bergman's most recognisable and most potently iconic picture, *Wild Strawberries* is not only the film his fans most warm too, it is the one that is most frequently quoted, e.g. in Gilbert Cates's *Summer Wishes, Winter Dreams*, Woody Allen's *Another Woman*, André Téchiné's *Ma Saison Préférée*. In 1970, the readers of the *Sunday Times* were invited by an experimental psychologist to name the movies that came closest to reminding them of their own dreams; *Wild Strawberries* came fifth.

ODD/SALIENT FACTS *Smultronstället* actually means 'The wild strawberry place', referring literally to a strawberry patch and metaphorically to an epiphanous moment of peculiar happiness or contentment in the past, as in the first flashback when Borg sees his boyhood sweetheart Sara picking wild strawberries at the summer home. One of Bergman's favourite films is Sjöström's silent classic *The Phantom Carriage* (1921), in which a profligate man (played by Sjöström himself) is given the opportunity to review and reappraise his life in the manner that draws on *A Christmas Carol* and looks forward to *Wild Strawberries*. As Victor Seastrom, Sjöström had a successful career in Hollywood during the 1920s, directing several masterworks (*He Who Gets Slapped*, *The Scarlet Letter*, *The Wind*); Bergman visited Hollywood briefly but decided not to work there.

MEMORABLE MOMENTS Borg's surreal nightmare from which he wakes to make the journey south.

The elderly Borg seeing his face in the mirror held by Sara at the wild strawberry patch.

The smile on Borg's face as he falls asleep thinking of his parents.

KEY LINES

Isak: 'I really would like to tell you about a dream I had this morning'.
Marianne: 'I'm not very interested in dreams.'

Alman as examiner in Borg's nightmare: 'You are guilty of guilt ... Furthermore, Professor Borg, you are accused of some smaller, but nonetheless serious offences. Indifference, selfishness, lack of consideration.'

WINGS OF DESIRE
(DER HIMMEL ÜBER BERLIN)

WEST GERMANY/FRANCE, 1987, ROAD MOVIES
(BERLIN)/ARGOS FILMS (PARIS), 127 MINS

D WIM WENDERS; **PR** WIM WENDERS, ANATOLE DAUMAN;
SC WIM WENDERS, PETER HANDKE; **PH** (COL/BW) HENRI
ALEKAN; **ED** PETER PRZYGODDA; **M** JÜRGEN KNIEPER

CAST BRUNO GANZ (DAMIEL), SOLVEIG DOMMARTIN (MARION),
OTTO SANDER (CASSIEL), CURT BOIS (HOMER), PETER FALK
(HIMSELF)

THE STORY It is Berlin, 1986. Wearing dark overcoats and scarves, their hair done up in ponytails, Damiel and Cassiel are angels hovering over the divided city, listening to the unspoken thoughts of the citizens and consoling them, but unable to intervene in their lives. Only small children can see them. The American film star Peter Falk is in Berlin acting in a thriller set during the Third Reich, and seems to be aware of their presence. Cassiel becomes especially interested in Homer, an elderly man who carries in his memory the history of Berlin; Damiel falls in love with Marion, the French trapeze artist in a travelling circus whom he has heard declare she intends to change her life. After telling Cassiel that he intends to become human, Damiel wakes up beside the Wall a transformed person. He meets Falk, who reveals that 30 years ago he too was an angel, and then tracks down Marion at a rock concert and subsequently goes to work with her at the circus.

THE FILM *Wings of Desire* is a film of wit, charm and compassion, that uses black and white for the world as seen by the angels and colour for the world as experienced by human beings. It's less a story than a meditation on what it means to be human and a visual poem that uses the divided Berlin as a metaphor for modern men and women cut off from each other, from their own feelings, and from history. Some of the dialogue is extremely pretentious, the sequences involving Falk are rather whimsical (though Falk himself is a winning presence), and it is difficult to understand what the dull Dommartin has that would make Damiel turn in his wings for her. Yet it is a beguiling picture featuring in Bruno Ganz one of the art cinema's most charismatic stars, that avoids the sentimentality and sanctimoniousness afflicting most movies involving angels. Wenders is a cult director who reveres certain artists from earlier genera-

tions, and the film is 'dedicated to all the former angels, but especially Yasijiro, François and Andrej' (i.e. Ozu, Truffaut and Wajda).

ODD/SALIENT FACTS The film's German title translates as 'The Sky/Heaven above Berlin'. Curt Bois (1900–91), who plays the aged Homer, was one of the great German stage actors of the 1920s and '30s who worked with Erwin Piscator and Max Reinhardt before the coming of the Nazis, was in Hollywood during the 1940s (his films include *Casablanca*), and returned to Germany in 1950s, becoming a member of Brecht's Berliner Ensemble. The trapeze artist works for the Circus Alekan, named for the film's veteran French cameraman Henri Alekan, whose films include Cocteau's *Beauty and the Beast*. *Wings of Desire* preceded by some years Hollywood's latest cycle of angel films that began in the mid-1990s and was itself remade as *City of Angels* starring Nicolas Cage and Meg Ryan. In 1993, Wenders directed a less successful sequel, *Faraway So Near*, set in a re-united Germany.

MEMORABLE MOMENTS Damiel, Cassiel and other angels listening to people of different nationalities in a large public library.

Damiel surveying Berlin from the wings of the Victory statue atop its column in the Königsplatz.

Cassiel seeing that Damiel, after declaring his intention to join the material world, has left footsteps in the sand of the fenced-off area on the East German side of the wall.

▼ *WINGS OF DESIRE* Mortal acrobat Solveig Dommartin and immortal angel Bruno Ganz ponder their futures.

229

KEY LINES

Damiel (to Cassiel): 'It's great to exist as the spirit, to testify, day after day and forever on the spiritual in people's minds. But I do get tired of my physical existence, of forever hovering above. I wish I could grow a weight which would bind me to the earth. I wish I could say at each step, at each gust of wind, "Now". Say "Now" and "Now" and no longer "Forever" and "For eternity" … Every time we participated it was a pretence … It would be rather nice to come home after a long day and feed the cat like Philip Marlowe, to have a fever, black on my fingers from reading a newspaper. For once to find excitement not in the mind but in a meal.'

Homer (while flicking through a book of photographs by August Sandor): 'If I do give up, mankind will lose its storyteller, and once mankind has lost its storyteller it will have lost its childhood.'

Damiel (after becoming human and meeting Marion): 'To know now what no angel knows.'

WITCHFINDER GENERAL (US TITLE: THE CONQUEROR WORM)

UK, 1968, TIGON BRITISH, 87 MINS

D MICHAEL REEVES; **PR** TONY TENSER, ARNOLD L. MILLER, LOUIS N. HAYWARD; **SC** MICHAEL REEVES, TOM BAKER (FROM THE NOVEL BY RONALD BASSETT); **PH** (EASTMAN COLOR) JOHNNY COQUILLON; **M** PAUL FERRIS; **ED** HOWARD LANNING

CAST VINCENT PRICE (MATTHEW HOPKINS), IAN OGILVY (RICHARD MARSHALL), HILARY DWYER (SARA), RUPERT DAVIES (JOHN LOWES), ROBERT RUSSELL (JOHN STEARNE), MICHAEL BEINT (CAPTAIN GORDON), NICKY HENSON (TROOPER SWALLOW), PATRICK WYMARK (OLIVER CROMWELL), WILFRID BRAMBELL (MASTER LOACH)

THE STORY England, 1645. Matthew Hopkins is travelling through a country torn by civil war with his brutal assistant John Stearne, lining his pockets and identifying and executing

> 'Perhaps he had a motive. People have strange motives for the things they do.'

witches. He is invited to a small Suffolk town where peasants have denounced their priest, John Lowes. Sara, Lowes's niece, is betrothed to Richard Marshall, a farmer and officer in Cromwell's army. To save her uncle from torture she gives herself to the lecherous Hopkins. But after she has been raped by Stearne, the disgusted Hopkins proceeds to torture and hang Lowes. Marshall returns and vows vengeance on Hopkins and Stearne, who renew their alliance. Marshall hears that Hopkins is holding witchcraft trials in Lavenham, Suffolk. He is re-united with Sara only for them both to be arrested by Hopkins, charged with witchcraft and taken to the local castle. As Sara is being tortured, two of Marshall's comrades attack the castle. Marshall breaks free, blinds Stearne with his boot and is hacking Hopkins to death with an axe when Trooper Swallow breaks in to end the Witchfinder's life with a bullet. Sara lies on the torture table screaming, and the picture concludes with this freeze frame.

THE FILM This ferocious low-budget period horror movie, an exploitation version of Arthur Miller's *The Crucible*, is one of a small handful of pictures to touch on one of the major episodes of Western European history, the English Civil War and the Commonwealth. The film begins with a woman, protesting her innocence, being dragged to the gallows to be hanged as a witch. It ends with another woman, also accused of witchcraft, screaming on the block after her torturers have been killed. *Witchfinder General* is about a disturbed Puritan – part true believer, part opportunist – taking advantage of a divided, lawless nation to exercise his guilty licentiousness, greed and sadism under the guise of duty. His initially decent antagonist, Marshall, is corrupted by his instinct for revenge, his growing violence reflected in the increasingly demented way he gallops through the countryside. The film's exteriors are flat, open, more agoraphobic than idyllic; the interiors have the cold, precise tone of Van Dyck.

The great cult actor Vincent Price gives one of his most restrained performances as Matthew Hopkins, a historical figure who in reality lived to write his memoirs and died in his bed. The cult status of the film began with its original release when it was denounced for its sadism by most critics, and praised for its historical insight by a few. The most famous of the film's assailants was the playwright and former academic historian,

▲ *WITCHFINDER GENERAL Vincent Price and his sleazy accomplice Robert Russell go about their venal business.*

Alan Bennett (writing in *The Listener*); its foremost supporters were Tom Milne (*Monthly Film Bulletin*) and Robin Wood (*Movie*). Within weeks of the film's release, its 25-year-old director Michael Reeves died of a drug overdose, having directed three and a half movies, all in the exploitation horror genre, of which this is by some way his best.

ODD/SALIENT FACTS Michael Klinger and Tony Tenser, the owners of Tigon, the British exploitation company behind *Witchfinder General* and Reeves's *The Sorcercers*, had financed Polanski's first English-speaking films, the low-budget *Repulsion* (1965) and *Cul-de-Sac* (1966). Cinematographer John Coquillon went on to shoot four films for Sam Peckinpah, including *Straw Dogs* (1971) and *Pat Garrett and Billy the Kid* (1973). In the United States, *Witchfinder General* was released

as *The Conqueror Worm*, beginning with quotations from Edgar Allan Poe's macabre poem of that title, to give the impression that it was a continuation of Vincent Price's Poe series.

MEMORABLE MOMENTS Cutting from Marshall and Sara making love to Hopkins, dressed in black, riding through the countryside with his grim assistant.

The silhouette of Hopkins and his accomplices leading the captive Marshall and Sara up the hill to Lavenham Castle – a homage to Bergman's *The Seventh Seal*.

KEY LINES

The Revd. Lowes: 'It is not the King's armies which bring death this year. The lack of order in the land encourages strange ideas.'

Matthew Hopkins: 'Perhaps he had a motive. People have strange motives for the things they do.'

Matthew Hopkins: 'I intend to instigate a new method of execution, a fitting end to the foul ungodliness in womankind.'

Marshall to the soldier who shoots Hopkins to put him out of his misery: 'You took him from me! You took him from me!'

WITHNAIL AND I★

UK, 1986, HANDMADE FILMS, 107 MINS

D BRUCE ROBINSON; **PR** PAUL HELLIER; **SC** BRUCE ROBINSON;
PH PETER HANNAN; **M** DAVID DUNDAS, RICK WENTWORTH;
ED ALAN STRACHAN
CAST RICHARD E. GRANT (WITHNAIL), PAUL MCGANN (I),
RICHARD GRIFFITHS (MONTY), RALPH BROWN (DANNY), MICHAEL
ELPHICK (JAKE), DARAGH O'MALLEY (IRISHMAN), MICHAEL
WARDLE (ISACS PARKIN), UNA BRANDON-JONES (MRS PARKIN),
NOEL JOHNSON (GENERAL), IRENE SUTCLIFFE (WAITRESS),
LLEWELLYN REES (TEA SHOP PROPRIETOR), ROBERT OATES
(POLICEMAN ONE), ANTHONY WISE (POLICEMAN TWO), EDDIE
TAGOE (PRESUMING ED)

THE STORY Camden Town, London, 1969. It is nearly the end of 'the greatest decade in the history of mankind' and the two out-of-work actors are coming down off a 60-hour bender. Living in a seedy flat shared by rodents, resorting to embrocation for warmth, and lighter fluid for intoxication, they resolve to get out of the city for a few days to 'rejuvenate'. So they seek out Withnail's theatrical, camp Uncle Monty and persuade him to let them use his country retreat near Penrith. They travel there in a beaten-up Jaguar and have a boozy idyll, while struggling to stay warm and scavenge food. Petrified of Jake, the local poacher, they are joined by Monty, who has designs on I. Barely managing to resist Monty's amorous advances, I insists on returning to London having landed an acting role. There they face Danny, their drug dealer, squatting in their flat, an eviction notice and an acting job that will end their friendship.

THE FILM Withnail and I was relatively unsuccessful at the box office but grew, largely by word-of-mouth, into its current status as a modern cult classic. The casting is perfect, and in the film's central character, Withnail, the tragically failed actor, a neu-

'Warm up? We may as well sit around a cigarette.'

rotically deranged, hysterical, hilarious, doomed figure, it provides one of the great characters in British cinema. It was Grant's first screen role, and launched his career. Bruce Robinson, having written the screenplay for *The Killing Fields*, decided to have as his directorial debut a film loosely based on his own experiences as a drama student in the Sixties. He revealed in the introduction to the 10th Anniversary edition of his screenplay that Withnail was based on his friend Vivian who, like his fictional incarnation, was brilliant at being himself. He and Viv apparently used to visit the wolves in London Zoo often, and according to Robinson, a self-confessed liar, the chief model for the character of Withnail, died of cancer (at an unspecified date).

ODD/SALIENT FACTS 'While My Guitar Gently Weeps', which is playing on the soundtrack as Withnail & I return to their flat after Penrith, was written by George Harrison, the film's executive producer. Richard Starkey MBE is credited as special production consultant. The adoration of fans for the film has extended beyond the standard quotation of the film's many memorable lines into more dangerous territory. The *Withnail and I* drinking game apparently requires players to match the film's characters drink for drink. To be played correctly this would demand the consumption of: lighter fluid (presumably optional), two large gins and a pint of cider, several swigs of sherry and a rhesus-negative bloody Mary, a couple of shots of whisky, an assortment of red wines, a few large scotches, at least two pints and two quadruple whiskies, more wine and finally, and expensively, a 1953 Château Margaux. Richard E. Grant is a teetotaller, allergic to alcohol. In early drafts of the script the Paul McGann character was called Marwood.

MEMORABLE MOMENTS The confrontation with the aggressive Irishman in the Mother Black Cap, a Camden Town pub recreated in West London. Withnail reveals himself as an inventive coward, pleading with the man: 'I have a heart condition. I have a heart condition. If you hit me it will be murder. My wife is having a baby.'

The trip to uncle Monty's in which Monty reminisces about his acting career and reveals his love of vegetables.

The rolling and smoking of the Camberwell Carrot, about which Danny explains: 'I invented it in Camberwell and it looks like a carrot.'

KEY LINES

Withnail: 'I feel as sick as a pike.'

Withnail, having spat on the floor: 'Jesus, look at that. Apart from a raw potato, that's the only solid to have passed my lips in the last 60 hours.'

Withnail, desperately: 'I must have some booze, I demand to have some booze.'

Withnail on his hangover: 'I feel like a pig shat in my head.'

Withnail having arrived in the cottage: 'Warm up? We may as well sit around a cigarette.'

Withnail to the farmer: 'We've gone on holiday by mistake.'

Withnail in the tea rooms: 'We want the finest wines available to humanity.'

THE YELLOW SUBMARINE

UK, 1968, UNITED ARTISTS, 87 MINS

D GEORGE DUNNING; **PR** AL BRODAX; **SC** LEE MINOFF, AL BRODAX, JACK MENDELSOHN, ERICH SEGAL; **ST** LEE MINOFF; **PH** (COL DELUXE) JOHN WILLIAMS; **DES** HEINZ EDELMAN, JOHN CRAMER, GORDON HARRISON; **M** THE BEATLES, GEORGE MARTIN; **ED** BRIAN J. BISHOP

VOICES JOHN CLIVE (JOHN), GEOFFREY HUGHES (PAUL), PAUL ANGELUS (RINGO/CHIEF BLUE MEANIE), DICK EMERY (LORD MAYOR/BOOB)

THE STORY In Pepperland all is well until the Blue Meanies and their Chief freeze the people, turn everything grey and rid the country of music. Fred, the leader of Sergeant Pepper's Lonely Hearts Club Band escapes in his yellow submarine and travels to Liverpool. There he recruits The Beatles to help him and together they go back to Pepperland, travelling through the Sea of Time, the Sea of Science, the Sea of Monsters, the Sea of Green, the Sea of Holes, on the way picking up the verbose polymath Nowhere Man, Boob. In Pepperland, the band find instruments, and defeat the Blue Meanies bringing music and colour and love back to the land.

THE FILM By 1968, The Beatles had long since stopped playing live. The previous year they had dazzled the world with the ground-breaking Sgt Pepper's Lonely Hearts Club Band album, which, while representing their greatest achievement, also saw evidence of the band splintering, with individual creations now clearly audible and Paul having decisively taken the reins of the group. All four had been experimenting with acid for some time and John was well on the way to a drug dependence that would remain with him for much of the remainder of his life. Yet *Yellow Submarine*, as dated as it clearly is, remains a joyous expression of all that was most optimistic of the flower generation. The animation, under the overall design control of Heinz Edelman, is crazy but wonderfully positive and clever, offering a witty collage of modern art from Beardsley to Dalí. The film's cultural references range from *Ulysses* through *Frankenstein* and *King Kong* to The Goons and the Hamlet cigar ads. The story is filled out with The Beatles' bespoke cheeky scouse humour with relentless painful puns along the lines of John's comment, having evaded the 'dreaded vacuum flask': 'So long, sucker.' Essentially a collection of ingenious animated pop videos, with a sweet cameo coda from The Beatles themselves, this remains a superb record of its time, with the unashamedly hippie message of the indomitability of music and love.

ODD/SALIENT FACTS The American release version of the film lacks one song sequence, but, unlike the British version, has film

▼ *THE YELLOW SUBMARINE The animated Paul, John, Ringo and George bring music and colour back to Pepperland.*

of the conversion of the Blue Meanies to the joys of Peace and Love and Music. One of the acts of the Blue Meanies was to subvert the positive image of Pepperland, destroying the vast colourful YESes that decorated the landscape. The word 'Yes' played a crucial role in the life or, according to Albert Goldman, the mythology, of The Beatles. When John visited Yoko Ono's exhibition in Mason's Yard on 7 November 1966, one exhibit was a step-ladder leading to a magnifying glass suspended from the ceiling. In *The Lives of John Lennon*, Goldman writes: 'Lennon anticipated that he would read the sort of phrase that he would have put at the end of the climb, something like "Tee-hee!" or "Fuck you!" He was surprised and pleased to read "Yes".'

MEMORABLE MOMENTS Having regressed to childhood, the band suddenly ages, growing long beards and singing 'When I'm 64'. The dazzling images are interrupted by the slogan 'Sixty-four years is 33, 661, 440 minutes and one minute is a long time … let us demonstrate.' We then see the numbers marking the next 64 seconds rendered as illuminations of the art nouveau and psychedelic periods.

KEY LINES

Peering through one of the doors in Ringo's elaborate house,
George: 'Yes, dey do look very nice, don't dey?'
Ringo: 'Yes, dey do.'
John: 'Dey do, dough, don't dey?'
George: 'Yes, dey do.'
Ringo: 'Don't dey, dough?'
George: 'Doh.'

ZOO IN BUDAPEST

US, 1933, FOX, 85 MINS

D ROWLAND V. LEE; **PR** JESSE L. LASKY; **SC** DAN TOTHEROH, LOUISE LONG, ROWLAND V. LEE (FROM A STORY BY MELVILLE BAKER AND JOHN KIRKLAND); **PH** (BW) LEE GARMES; **ED** HAROLD SCHUSTER; **M** LOUIS DE FRANCESCO
CAST LORETTA YOUNG (EVE), GENE RAYMOND (ZANI), O. P. HEGGIE (DR GRUNBAUM), WALLY ALBRIGHT (PAUL VANDOR), PAUL FIX (HEINIE), MURRAY KINNELL (GARBOSH), RUTH WARREN (KATRINA), ROY STUART (KARL), FRANCES RICH (ELSIE), NILES WELSH (MR VANDOR), LUCILLE WARD (MISS MURST), RUSS POWELL (TOSKI), DOROTHY LIBAIRE (ROSITA)

THE STORY The handsome, fair-haired Zani, works as an assistant in the Budapest Zoo and has a close rapport with the animals. He has spent his whole life there. His mother died the day he was born; his father, a head keeper, was killed by a tiger three years later. The saintly zoo director, Dr Grunbaum, protects him from Herr Garbosh, the zoo's rigid bureaucratic manager, who wants to hand Zani over to the police for stealing (and destroying) furs from rich visitors. Zani loves 18-year-old Eve, who comes to the zoo every week in a party from her orphanage. She is about to be sent away to work at a tannery, and her friends help her escape just as the zoo closes. At the same time Paul, an upper-class child, gives his nanny the slip and hides in the zoo. Meanwhile Zani has stolen a fur and is being sought by the police. Zani finds a sanctuary for Eve in the cave of an unused bear garden, where they're joined by little Paul. Zani's enemy, the lazy, vindictive guard, Heinie spots them. Zani intervenes when Heinie attempts to rape Eve, and Paul accidentally makes all the animals run amok. As Dr Grunbaum tries to restore order, Zani rescues the trapped Paul with the help of Rajah, the elephant, and is badly mauled by a tiger. Paul's father adopts Eve, appoints Zani to care for the animals on his country estate, and the couple marry and settle down to rural bliss.

THE FILM This enchanting fairy tale takes place over a single day and night. Like *King Kong*, made at the same time, it juxtaposes the natural world with a repressive, unnatural society to produce a complex fable about freedom and imprisonment and the effects of unleashing primitive forces. The zoo is at once a prison and an Eden, its expressionist jumble of cages resembles something by Piranese, but the vast ponds where birds live freely suggest a primeval world. The orphans Zani and Eve are like the prelapsarian Adam and Eve with the Dr Grunbaum as a benevolent God. The world outside, the distant, exotic Budapest, parallels Depression America with its uncaring rich and bullied orphans. But it is not only the rich who oppress the animals by taking their furs; the zoo's employees act callously – the officious Garbosh, the vicious Heinie, encouraging animosity between Rajah the elephant and Sultan the tiger. Zani, the naif hero who understands and communicates with the animals, is a forerunner of today's animal rights activists as he steals furs and thus becomes an enemy of society. The movie turns into melodrama, and the role of Paul is more a plot device than a contribution to the film's moral structure.

The picture is held together largely by the magical images of Lee Garmes, one of Hollywood's great cinematographers, who had made several films with Josef von Sternberg and went on to collaborate with Wyler, Hitchcock, Ophuls and Hawks.

ODD/SALIENT FACTS *Zoo in Budapest* was the first production at the Fox studio by Jesse L. Lasky, who the previous year had been ousted from Paramount, the company he had co-founded. In her final film, *Hoopla* (1933), Clara Bow, 'The It Girl', played a tough girl with a travelling carnival and swam in the nude in the pool left over from *Zoo in Budapest*. In 1959 Rowland V. Lee (as writer-producer) worked once more with Lee Garmes on the widescreen biblical epic *The Big Fisherman*.

MEMORABLE MOMENTS Rajah the elephant being encouraged to spray water over Sultan, the caged tiger.

Eve half-concealed by bushes changing from her orphan's uniform into the special dress she and her friends have made.

Zani carrying Eve across the mist-shrouded lake to the sanctuary of the deserted bear-garden.

KEY LINES

Rich visitor to his wife: 'You are an animal, I am an animal, so imagine how we must smell to the other animals.'

Garbosh: 'People come to the zoo to see wild animals, and they see Zani petting them as if they were house-guests.'

Zani: 'In the zoo at night it's peaceful – no people to make the animals nervous.'

▼ *ZOO IN BUDAPEST* Blonde orphan Loretta Young kneels beside idealistic Gene Raymond who has given his all to quell chaos in the zoo.

235

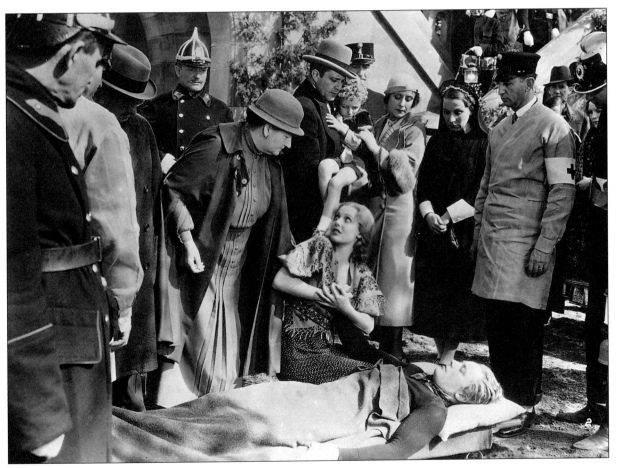

INDEX

237

239

240

PICTURE ACKNOWLEDGEMENTS

The publisher would like to thank the following for supplying images for this book. Every effort has been made to acknowledge all copyright holders. However, should any photographs not be correctly attributed, the publisher will undertake any appropriate changes in future editions of the book. The images listed below are protected by copyright.

Aquarius: 161, 197, 208.
Ronald Grant Archive: 29, 74, 167.
Kobal Collection: 98, 113, 137; 2, 23, 57, 72, 84, 138, 175, 225 Warner Bros; 42, 110, 129, 222 20th Century Fox; 21, 39, 45, 94, 97, 168 MGM; 17, 46-47, 115, 212, 216 Universal; 37, 89, 92, 106, 131, 155, 180 Columbia; 219 Orion; 24, 78, 122, 204, 206 Paramount; 27; Goskino; 34 Ladd Company/Warner Bros; 35 Allied Pictures; 44 SNC/Raymond Cauchetier; 48, 66, 101, 104, 109, 128, 136, 150, 200, 203 United Artists; 50, 120, 146, 149, 160, 188, 214 RKO; 51 New World; 53 Columbia/Persky-Bright/Reno; 55, 68 Rank; 58 Bunuel-Dali; 63 Allarts/Erato; 65 Compton-Tekli; 69 Producers' Releasing Corporation; 77 Riama-Pathe; 81 Concord/Warner Bros; 82 AFI/Libra; 88 RAO; 91 Herzog/Filmverlage Der Autoren/ZDF; 103 Columbia/Tri Star; 107 Warhol; 112 Memorial; 117 Wark Producing Company; 119, 194 Allied Artists; 124 Argos; 125 Films Du Carrosse/Sedif/Raymond Cauchetier; 133 Nero; 142 De Laurentiis Group; 143 AIP; 147 MTI/Orion; 152 Prana-Film GMBH, Berlin; 154 Two Cities; 158 Andre Paulve/Films DuPalais Royal; 162 Anglo Amalgamated; 165 British National/Anglo Amalgamated; 170 Embassy Pictures; 173 Republic; 174 Daiei Films; 178 Hammer/Columbia; 182, 184 Lux/Vides/Galatea; 186 Megalovision; 187 Associated British; 190 New Line Cinema; 191 Lion; 193 Metro; 196 MGM/UA; 201 Hal Roach/MGM; 205 Melvin Van Peebles; 211 Vortex-Henkel-Hooper/Bryanston,; 217 Universal/GTO; 223 PSO/POLYC International; 228 Svensk Filmindustri; 229 Road Movies/Argos Films/WDR; 231 Tigon; 235 Fox.
Pictorial Press Limited: 25, 32, 61, 171.
Subafilms 233.
Walt Disney Collection: 86.
Colour section: Kobal (in order): Warner Bros, Monty Python Films, Dreamland Productions, Live Entertainment, Zoetrope/UA, Warner Bros, Warner/Goodtime, Handmade Films, British Lion, 20th Century Fox, MGM, Universal, MGM, Columbia, Embassy, Orion, Universal, Warner Bros, 20th Century Fox, Paramount.